STEPS TO A NEW EDITION
OF THE HEBREW BIBLE

TEXT-CRITICAL STUDIES

Michael W. Holmes, General Editor

Number 10

STEPS TO A NEW EDITION
OF THE HEBREW BIBLE

Ronald Hendel

PRESS

Atlanta

Library of Congress Cataloging-in-Publication Data

Names: Hendel, Ronald S., author.
Title: Steps to a new edition of the Hebrew Bible / by Ronald Hendel.
Description: Atlanta : SBL Press, [2016] | Series: Text-critical studies ; number 10 | Includes bibliographical references and index.
Identifiers: LCCN 2016032650 (print) | LCCN 2016033404 (ebook) | ISBN 9781628371574 (pbk. : alk. paper) | ISBN 9780884141952 (hardcover : alk. paper) | ISBN 9780884141945 (ebook)
Subjects: LCSH: Bible. Old Testament—Criticism, Textual.
Classification: LCC BS1136 .H46 2016 (print) | LCC BS1136 (ebook) | DDC 221.4/46—dc23
LC record available at https://lccn.loc.gov/2016032650

Printed on acid-free paper.

The page that is destined for immortality can traverse the fire of textual errors, approximate translations, inattentive readings, and incomprehension.
— Jorge Luis Borges, "The Superstitious Ethics of the Reader"

Editors make, as well as mend.
— D. F. McKenzie, *Bibliography and the Sociology of Texts*

****

To the editors and advisors of the HBCE,
with gratitude.

CONTENTS

FOREWORD

Scholarship is an obsession and a labor of love. Two decades ago I formulated a plan to create a new critical edition of the Hebrew Bible. Much to my surprise, a number of excellent scholars agreed to take part, and the first volume of this series has appeared: Michael V. Fox's superb edition of Proverbs. Along the way the project gained a number of eminent critics, including Emanuel Tov and Hugh Williamson, names to conjure with in my profession. As a result of conversations among our editors and advisers and inspired by the precise arguments of our critics, the conceptual underpinnings and practices of the project have developed into a finely-grained structure.

The essays in this book are steps along the path of the new edition, detailing its theoretical and practical aims and exploring the wider conceptual and disciplinary horizons within which this project finds its conditions of possibility. Some of the essays are exploratory; all of them attempt to advance the status quo of the textual criticism of the Hebrew Bible. As a whole, they work—from various angles—to increase the analytical precision and the conceptual scope and self-awareness of the discipline. Textual criticism has a distinguished genealogy, and it is up to its current practitioners to keep it sharp, alive, and compelling. Otherwise, the barbarians win, and philology—the love of words—will die an unlamented death. But philology has life left, at least so I dream, and other old philologists, from Qimḥi to Cappel to Nietzsche, would surely agree.

Good scholarship is predicated on conversation among specialists. This is certainly true of the "steps" in this book. I owe a debt of gratitude to the editors and advisers of the HBCE project, particularly those who patiently commented on earlier versions of these chapters or otherwise helped my understanding of particular puzzles: Annelie Aejmelaeus, Sidnie White Crawford, Michael V. Fox, Leonard Greenspoon, Jan Joosten, Gary Knoppers, Michaël van der Meer, Andrés Piquer Otero, Bas ter haar Romeny, Julio Trebolle, Alexander Rofé, Ronald Troxel, Zipora Talshir, and Yair

Zakovitch. Outside of the charmed circle of HBCE, I wish to thank Hindy Najman, Armin Lange, Yosef Ofer, Annette Schellenberg, Konrad Schmid, Niek Veldhuis, and Molly Zahn for their guidance on various matters. There are many others whom I ought to thank for stimulating conversations about critical editions, including my friends Michael Segal, Eibert Tigchelaar, Emanuel Tov, and Hugh Williamson. Thanks also to John Kutsko and Bob Buller for taking on the HBCE project with energy and intelligence. I wish to thank the Norma and Sam Dabby Chair in Hebrew Bible and Jewish Studies for research support.

Finally, my thanks and love to Ann, Ed, and Nat, who don't have to read this book.

Earlier versions of some of these essays were presented at the Universiteit Leiden, the Universidad Complutense de Madrid, the University of Toronto, Eberhard Karls Universität Tübingen, and meetings of the Society of Biblical Literature and the International Organization for the Society of Old Testament Studies. I am grateful for these opportunities to engage in global conversation outside of my usual haunts.

Most of the chapters based on publications have been thoroughly revised, a few only lightly. The previous publications are:

Chapters 1 and 2: "The Oxford Hebrew Bible: Prologue to a New Critical Edition." *VT* 58 (2008): 324–51; and "The Oxford Hebrew Bible: Its Aims and a Response to Criticisms." *HBAI* 2 (2013): 63–99.

Chapter 3: "The Idea of a Critical Edition of the Hebrew Bible: A Genealogy." *HBAI* 3 (2014): 392–423.

Chapter 4: "What Is a Biblical Book?" Pages 283–302 in *From Author to Copyist: Essays on the Composition, Redaction, and Transmission of the Hebrew Bible in Honor of Zipi Talshir*. Edited by Cana Werman. Winona Lake, IN: Eisenbrauns, 2015.

Chapter 5: "The Epistemology of Textual Criticism." In *Reading the Bible in Ancient Traditions and Modern Editions: Studies in Textual and Reception History in Honor of Peter W. Flint*. Edited by Daniel K. Falk, Kyung S. Baek, and Andrew B. Perrin. Atlanta: SBL Press, forthcoming.

Chapter 7: "Assessing the Text-Critical Theories of the Hebrew Bible after Qumran." Pages 281–302 in *The Oxford Handbook of the Dead Sea Scrolls*.

Edited by Timothy H. Lim and John J. Collins. Oxford Handbooks. Oxford: Oxford University Press, 2010.

Chapters 8 and 9: "(Proto-)Masoretic Text and Ancient Texts Close to MT (Pentateuch)" and "Problems of Classification and Other Texts (Pentateuch)." Pages 59–84 in *The Hebrew Bible.* Vol. 1 of *In Textual History of the Bible.* Edited by Armin Lange and Emanuel Tov. Leiden: Brill, 2016.

Chapter 10: "The Contribution of Frank Moore Cross to Textual Criticism." *BASOR* 372 (2014): 175–82.

Chapter 11: "The Dream of a Perfect Text: Textual Criticism and Biblical Inerrancy in Early Modern Europe." Pages 542–66 in *Sybils, Scriptures, and Scrolls: John Collins at Seventy.* Edited by Joel Baden, Hindy Najman, and Eibert Tigchelaar. Leiden: Brill, 2016.

Chapter 12: "The Untimeliness of Biblical Philology." *Philology* 1 (2015): 9–28.

Chapter 13: "From Polyglot to Hypertext." Pages 19–33 in *The Hebrew Bible and Its Editions.* Edited by Andrés Piquer Otero and Pablo A. Torijano Morales. Leiden: Brill, 2016.

Appendix: "Comparing Critical Editions: BHQ Proverbs and HBCE Proverbs." *ZAW* 128 (2016).

Abbreviations

A	Aleppo codex
Ag. Ap.	Josephus, *Against Apion*
AGJU	Arbeiten zur Geschichte des antiken Judentums und des Urchristentums
AJSL	*American Journal of Semitic Languages and Literatures*
AmSci	*American Scientist*
AnBib	Analecta Biblica
ARevEnt	*Annual Review of Entomology*
Ant.	Josephus, *Jewish Antiquities*
ATANT	Abhandlungen zur Theologie des Alten und Neuen Testaments
B	London Pentateuch Codex (British Library Or. 4445)
b.	Babylonian Talmud
BASOR	*Bulletin of the American Schools of Oriental Research*
BCCT	Brill's Companions to the Christian Tradition
BCLSB	*Bulletin de la Classe des Lettres et des Sciences morales et politiques de l'Académie Royale de Belgique*
BDB	*A Hebrew and English Lexicon of the Old Testament: With an Appendix Containing the Biblical Aramaic.* Edited by Francis Brown, S. R. Driver, and Charles A. Briggs. Oxford: Clarendon, 1907
Ber.	Berakot
BETL	Bibliotheca Ephemeridum Theologicarum Lovaniensium
BHK	*Biblia Hebraica*, ed. R. Kittel
BHQ	Biblia Hebraica Quinta
BHRef	Bibliotheca Humanistica & Reformatorica
BHS	*Biblia Hebraica Stuttgartensia*
Bib	*Biblica*
BibInt	Biblical Interpretation Series
BICS	*Bulletin of the Institute of Classical Studies*

BJRL	*Bulletin of John Rylands University Library of Manchester*
BJSUCSD	Biblical and Judaic Studies from the University of California, San Diego
BRSS	Berkeley Religious Studies Series
BTT	Bible de Tous les Temps
ByzZ	*Byzantine Zeitschrift*
BZAW	Beihefte zur Zeitschrift für die alttestamentliche Wissenschaft
C	Cairo Codex of the Prophets
CBET	Contributions to Biblical Exegesis and Theology
CBH	Classical Biblical Hebrew
CD	Cairo Genizah copy of the Damascus Covenant
ConBOT	Coniectanea Biblica: Old Testament Series
CP	*Classical Philology*
CRAI	*Comptes-rendus des séances de l'Académie des Inscriptions et Belles-Lettres*
CRINT	Compendia Rerum Iudaicarum ad Novum Testamentum
CritInq	*Critical Inquiry*
CSSA	Cambridge Studies in Social Anthropology
CTHP	Cambridge Texts in the History of Philosophy
DCLS	Deuterocanonical and Cognate Literature Studies
Dial.	Justin Martyr, *Dialogue with Trypho*
DJD	Discoveries in the Judaean Desert
DSD	*Dead Sea Discoveries*
EDSS	*Encyclopedia of the Dead Sea Scrolls.* Edited by Lawrence H. Schiffman and James C. VanderKam. 2 vols. New York: Oxford University Press, 2000
EHMF	Early Hebrew Manuscripts in Facsimile
EJL	Early Judaism and Its Literature
ErIsr	*Eretz-Israel*
'Erub.	'Erubin
ETLC	Editorial Theory and Literary Criticism
f	feminine
FAT	Forschungen zum Alten Testament
FRLANT	Forschungen zur Religion und Literatur des Alten und Neuen Testaments
GBS	Guides to Biblical Scholarship
Gen. Rab.	Genesis Rabbah
GHand	Gorgias Handbooks

Giṭ.	Giṭṭin
harm(s).	harmonization(s)
HBAI	*Hebrew Bible and Ancient Israel*
HBCE	The Hebrew Bible: A Critical Edition
Hen	*Henoch*
HHS	Harvard Historical Studies
HSM	Harvard Semitic Monographs
HSS	Harvard Semitic Studies
HTR	*Harvard Theological Review*
HUBP	Hebrew University Bible Project
HUCA	*Hebrew Union College Annual*
HumLov	*Humanistica Lovaniensia*
Hypoth.	Philo, *Hypothetica*
ICC	International Critical Commentary
IJAL	*International Journal of American Linguistics*
IJCT	*International Journal of the Classical Tradition*
ILP	International Library of Philosophy
ISBL	Indiana Studies in Biblical Literature
J	Yahwist, a hypothetical source in the Pentateuch
JAJ	*Journal of Ancient Judaism*
JAJSup	Journal of Ancient Judaism Supplements
JBL	*Journal of Biblical Literature*
JCPS	Jewish and Christian Perspectives Series
JHI	*Journal of the History of Ideas*
JJS	*Journal of Jewish Studies*
JLC	Jewish Literature and Culture
JSJ	*Journal for the Study of Judaism*
JSJSup	Supplements to the Journal for the Study of Judaism.
JSOT	*Journal for the Study of the Old Testament*
JSOTSup	Journal for the Study of the Old Testament Supplement Series
JSS	*Journal of Semitic Studies*
JTS	*Journal of Theological Studies*
Jub.	Jubilees
Ketub.	Ketubbot
L	Leningrad (St. Petersburg) Codex
LAI	Library of Ancient Israel
LBH	Late Biblical Hebrew
LEC	Library of Early Christianity

LHBOTS	Library of Hebrew Bible/Old Testament Studies
LSTS	Library of Second Temple Studies
LXX	Septuagint
m	masculine
MasS	Masoretic Studies
MdB	Le Monde de la Bible
MedEnc	*Medieval Encounters: Jewish, Christian and Muslim Culture in Confluence and Dialogue*
Meg.	Megillah
Menaḥ.	Menaḥot
MG	*Materia Giudaica*
MMCH	Manuscrits médiévaux en caractères hébraïques
MS	Manuscript
MSU	Mitteilungen des Septuaginta-Unternehmens
MT	Masoretic Text
NTTSD	New Testament Tools, Studies, and Documents
OBO	Orbis Biblicus et Orientalis
OCM	Oxford Classical Monographs
OECS	Oxford Early Christian Studies
OG	Old Greek
OrT	*Oral Tradition*
OSHT	Oxford Studies in Historical Theology
OTL	Old Testament Library
OTS	Old Testament Studies
OtSt	*Oudtestamentische Studiën*
P	Priestly, a hypothetical source in the Pentateuch
PCA	*Proceedings of the Classical Association*
Ph&Lit	*Philosophy and Literature*
Philology	*Philology: An International Journal on the Evolution of Cultures, Languages and Texts*
QHenoch	Quaderni di Henoch
Questes	*Questes: Revue pluridisciplinaire d'études médiévales*
Rab	Second Rabbinic Bible, 1524–1525
RBL	*Review of Biblical Literature*
RBS	Resources for Biblical Study
RCHL	*Revue critique d'histoire et de littérature*
RevQ	*Revue de Qumran*
s	singular

S	Damascus Pentateuch Codex (Sassoon 507 = National Library of Israel MS Heb. 24°5702)
S&T	Studies and Texts (Philip W. Lown Institute of Advanced Judaic Studies)
Šabb.	Šabbat
SANER	Studies in Ancient Near Eastern Records
SBib	*Studies in Bibliography*
SBLDS	Society of Biblical Literature Dissertation Series
SBOT	Sacred Books of the Old Testament
SBPC	Studies in Book and Print Culture
SCL	Sather Classical Lectures
SCS	Septuagint and Cognate Studies
SDSS	Studies in the Dead Sea Scrolls and Related Literature
Sefarad	*Sefarad: revista de estudios hebraicos, sefardíes y de Oriente Próximo*
Šeq.	Sheqalim
SHCT	Studies in the History of Christian Thought
SJ	Studia Judaica
SJOT	*Scandinavian Journal of the Old Testament*
SLCTI	Scientific and Learned Cultures and Their Institutions
SP	Samaritan Pentateuch
SSD	Studies in Social Discontinuity
STDJ	Studies on the Texts of the Desert of Judah
TC	*TC: A Journal of Biblical Textual Criticism*
TCSt	Text-Critical Studies
TCT	Textual Criticism and the Translator
TECA	*Testimonianze Editoria, Cultura, Arte*
Text	*Textus*
TiLSM	Trends in Linguistics: Studies and Monographs
TISEJ	Tauber Institute for the Study of European Jewry
TJ	*Trinity Journal*
TSAJ	Texts and Studies in Ancient Judaism
V	Vatican Pentateuch Codex (ebr. 448)
var.	variant reading
VT	*Vetus Testamentum*
VTSup	Supplements to Vetus Testamentum
WF	Wolfenbütteler Forschungen
WUNT	Wissenschaftliche Untersuchungen zum Neuen Testament

Yad.	Yadayim
ZAW	*Zeitschrift für die alttestamentliche Wissenschaft*
ZWT	*Zeitschrift für wissenschaftliche Theologie*

Introduction

In the post-Qumran era, the textual criticism of the Hebrew Bible has become a sophisticated and conceptually rich field of inquiry. The biblical text is no longer seen as a unitary object but is irreducibly plural, dispersed in time and space. The study of textual history and textual change now includes the hermeneutics of ancient scribal traditions. The idea of a critical edition of the Hebrew Bible is, as we will see, a topic of intense debate. Issues of canonicity and textual authority intersect with analyses of biblical, parabiblical, and exegetical texts. The proliferation of variant readings in the Qumran texts raises difficult questions of filiation and innovation. There is little in the field that is uncontested, including its operational concepts such as "text," "edition," "author," and "error." For a book with the theological gravity of the Hebrew Bible, each of these terms has a history of contestation, which includes sectarian accusations of heresy and insanity. To the surprise of its practitioners, the field of textual criticism of the Hebrew Bible, as currently constituted, is far from dull.

Cesare Segre describes textual criticism as "a meeting place of logic and intuition, of rigor and flexibility."[1] It is a discourse that requires erudition and imagination, each yoked to the other and focused on particular cases. It is a unique conjunction of the empirical and the abstract, of friable parchment with curls of ink and the semiotics of prose, prophecy, and poetry. Moreover, the *realia* of ancient manuscripts is counterbalanced by the vast absence of lost texts. In its staunch insistence on the historicity of texts and language, even as their traces are dispersed and multiple, textual criticism entails a nexus of concepts that challenge the habitual assumptions of biblical scholarship, including its modern and postmodern varieties. As we will see, textual criticism has been a driver of innovative schol-

---

1. Cesare Segre, "Problemi teorici e pratici della critica testuale," in *Opera Critica*, ed. Alberto Conte and Andrea Mirabile (Milan: Mondadori, 2014), 356: "La critica testuale è un luogo d'incontro di logica e intuizione, di rigore e duttilità."

arship since the Renaissance, and in the post-Qumran era it is revitalizing the field of biblical studies once more.

Modern textual criticism studies the whole life of texts, including all their discernible transformations through time. Segre has formulated a concept of transmitted texts as diasystems (a term borrowed from the study of language contact).[2] At any given time, a text consists of several systems in contact: that of the first authorial or published edition and those of subsequent scribes. It is a superposition of writers and copyists in a potentially endless series. The object of textual criticism is to elucidate each system *and* the dialectic among them. In our case, this involves multiple editions, other exegetical, linguistic, and theological revisions, the reading tradition(s) transmitted in the systems of vocalization, accentuation, and annotation, and the interrelationships among these textual/semiotic systems. Synchrony and diachrony are interwoven in this pursuit, as they are in most historical inquiries.

In this book I advocate a new text-critical project that includes this range of inquiries, The Hebrew Bible: A Critical Edition (HBCE). This project will produce eclectic editions of each book of the Hebrew Bible, accompanied by extensive annotations, introductions, and text-critical commentary. The first volume has recently appeared: Michael V. Fox, *Proverbs: An Eclectic Edition with Introduction and Textual Commentary*, HBCE 1 (Atlanta: SBL Press, 2015). As this volume demonstrates, the theoretical and practical gain of this type of critical edition is substantial.

A project of this scope has many roots and precursors in the history of textual scholarship on the Hebrew Bible. Thinking through the issues involved in a new edition and responding to serious criticisms has led me to explore the intellectual genealogy of the discipline. There is much to learn from the textual critics of the pre-Qumran era, including both the well-known and the forgotten. In several of the following chapters I situate the HBCE project within the genealogy of the discipline by exploring the conceptual orientations and choices of past scholarship. In some respects, the HBCE project sheds a different light on the past, highlighting some forgotten moves as significant and some well-known moves as flawed or unnecessarily limiting. The HBCE project, in this sense, reconfigures the past textual criticism of the Hebrew Bible

---

2. Cesare Segre, "Critique textuelle, théorie des ensembles et diasystème," *BCLSB* 62 (1976): 279–92.

by its shift of concepts and procedures. Textual criticism, which strives, as Paolo Trovato states, "to preserve part of the memory of our past,"[3] changes its relationship to the past even as it seeks to restore it.

Before moving to the detailed discussions in the chapters, I wish to discuss two examples of textual complexity that will, I hope, position the HBCE project in the light of the *longue durée* of textual criticism of the Hebrew Bible. These examples—from Genesis and Joshua—illustrate the philological desire to restore or reconstitute lost readings based on close analysis of the textual witnesses. These examples show that, whether we acknowledge it or not, pondering the consequences of textual change is a core activity of biblical scholarship. The HBCE project is, in this respect, not a departure from past scholarship but a continuation of the large-scale trajectory of biblical philology.

Restoring Genesis 4:8: What Cain Said

Something is awry in the MT of Gen 4:8. The text in most editions reads:

וַיֹּאמֶר קַיִן אֶל־הֶבֶל אָחִיו וַיְהִי בִּהְיוֹתָם בַּשָּׂדֶה וַיָּקָם קַיִן אֶל־הֶבֶל אָחִיו
וַיַּהַרְגֵהוּ׃

Cain said to Abel, his brother, and when they were in the field, Cain rose up and slew Abel, his brother.[4]

The problem is that Cain does not say anything to Abel. This problem has perplexed scholars for millennia. When Jerome set about translating Genesis into Latin around 390 CE, he noted that the Samaritan Pentateuch and the Septuagint have a fuller reading here, נלכה השדה and Διέλθωμεν εἰς τὸ πεδίον (both: "Let us go out to the field"). Since Jerome held that the traditional Hebrew text (the consonantal MT of his time) was the unchanging *Hebraica veritas*, he initially dismissed the fuller reading. In his *Quaestiones Hebraicae in Genesim*, he writes: "What is found in our scroll [LXX], and in that of the Samaritans, namely, 'Let us go out into the

---

3. Paolo Trovato, *Everything You Always Wanted to Know about Lachmann's Method: A Non-standard Handbook of Genealogical Textual Criticism in the Age of Post-structuralism, Cladistics, and Copy-Text*, Storie e linguaggi 7 (Padova: Libreriauniversitaria, 2014), 13.

4. Unless otherwise stated, all translations are my own.

field,' is unnecessary."[5] However, when he made his translation of Genesis, he included a version of the fuller reading: *egrediamur foras* ("Let us go outside"). Evidently, Jerome changed his mind about the text of this verse, reaching around the *Hebraica veritas* to the LXX and SP.[6]

The medieval Masoretes were also divided about how to treat this verse. Although the oldest Masoretic codices with this section (L and C3, eleventh century CE) present it as a single unit, many later Masoretic codices insert a section division—a *pisqah be'emṣaʿ pasuq* ("section division in the middle of a verse")—after the first הבל אחיו ("Abel, his brother"), at the point where Cain should say something. As Emanuel Tov notes, this inner-verse division "signifies a break in content."[7] Here it signifies a textual-grammatical gap, which this Masoretic tradition indicates with blank text. The oldest dated codex known to me with this feature is Bibliothèque Nationale de France MS Hébreu 1, written in 1286 CE. (fig. 1).[8]

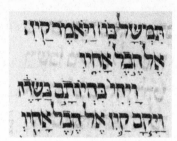

Many other codices and printed editions have this visual gap, including the Second Rabbinic Bible, edited by Jacob Ben Ḥayyim in 1524–1525. Ben Ḥayyim includes a Masoretic note (*Masora parva*) in the margin by this *pisqah*: כ"ח פסו' פסקי' במצו' פסוק ("28 verses with a *pisqah be'emṣaʿ pasuq*").[9] This note

Figure 1. MS Hébreu 1 (1286 CE) at Gen 4:8. Source: Bibliothèque Nationale de France.

5. *Jerome's Hebrew Questions on Genesis*, trans. C. T. R. Hayward, OECS (Oxford: Clarendon, 1995), 34; Jerome, *Quaestiones Hebraicae in Libro Geneseos*, ed. Paul de Lagarde (Leipzig: Teubner, 1868), 9: "superfluum ergo est quod in Samaritanorum et nostro volumine reperitur *transcamus in campum*." Origen also noted that this reading is not in MT, but according to the Jews it is ἐν τῷ ἀποκρύφῳ ("in the apocrypha"); Adam Kamesar, *Jerome, Greek Scholarship, and the Hebrew Bible: A Study of the Quaestiones hebraicae in Genesim*, OCM (Oxford: Clarendon, 1993), 100–101.

6. See Hayward, *Jerome*, 122.

7. Tov, *Textual Criticism of the Hebrew Bible*, 3rd ed. (Minneapolis: Fortress, 2012), 50.

8. Christian D. Ginsburg, *Introduction to the Massoretico-Critical Edition of the Hebrew Bible* (London: Trinitarian Biblical Society, 1897), 771; Bibliothèque Nationale de France, http://tinyurl.com/SBL7010k. The collations of Ginsburg, Kennicott, and de Rossi are not entirely reliable on this feature.

9. Moshe H. Goshen-Gottstein, *Biblia Rabbinica: A Reprint of the 1525 Venice Edition*, 2 vols. (Jerusalem: Makor, 1972), ad loc.

means that Masoretic scholars had counted and recorded this verse within this category of textual phenomena. In sum, the lacuna in the verse was explicitly marked in one Masoretic tradition and passed over silently in another. There was apparently dissent among the Masoretic scholars over how to respond to this textual problem.

The medieval Jewish commentators were also divided. David Qimḥi quoted here the Palestinian Targum (Targum Yerushalmi), which supplies a lengthy exchange between Cain and Abel, prefaced by Cain's invitation to Abel, קום ותא ניפוק לאפי ברא ("Come, let us go out to the open field").[10] This Aramaic reading is equivalent to LXX and SP and presumably relies on a Hebrew text with this reading. Qimḥi's quotation of the Palestinian Targum here arguably influenced Nachmanides's comment on this verse: אמר לו נצא השדה והרג אותו שם בסתר ("He said to him, 'Let us go out to the field,' and he killed him there in secret").[11] What Cain said to Abel—נצא השדה—may be Nachmanides's Hebrew retroversion of the reading in the Palestinian Targum. In any case, it approximates the reading in the Palestinian Targum, SP, LXX, and also the Syriac Peshiṭta.[12] Nachmanides is, in essence, doing textual criticism: he is seeking to solve the problem in the verse by recourse to the available textual evidence. He prefaces his restoration by saying על דעתי ("in my view"), making it clear that he is exercising his critical judgment in proposing this restoration of what Cain said. For Nachmanides, Qimḥi, the Masoretes, Jerome, and the others, the question of what Cain said to Abel is not purely a text-critical problem. It is also a historical problem, since they want to know what Cain actually said. Modern textual criticism differs by bracketing the historical question—and even the question of whether there is any history at stake—and focusing on the text as the object of inquiry. But

---

10. Cited from Bar Ilan Responsa Project, http://tinyurl.com/SBL7010l. Qimḥi's quotation is close to the wording of the Fragment Targums P and V, איתא ינפק תרינן לאפי ברא ("Come let us both go out to the open field"); Michael L. Klein, *The Fragment-Targums of the Pentateuch*, 2 vols., AnBib 76 (Rome: Biblical Institute Press, 1980), 1:47, 128.

11. Cited from Menachem Cohen, ed., *Mikra'ot Gedolot Ha-Keter: Genesis* (Ramat Gan: Bar Ilan University Press, 1997–1999), 1:62. My thanks to Itamar Kislev for alerting me to the literary relationship between Nachmanides and Qimḥi, which was established by Hillel Novetsky.

12. The Peshiṭta reading, ܢܙܠ ܠܦܩܥܬܐ ("Let us go to the valley"), reflects the tradition that Adam and Eve live on a mountain and Cain lures Abel to the valley below; see Sebastian Brock, "Jewish Traditions in Syriac Sources," *JJS* 30 (1979): 217.

the modern textualization of the Bible is not wholly discontinuous with the inquiries of premodern interpreters.[13] They too wanted to restore the lacuna in the text, and they made considerable efforts in annotation, collation, and analysis in order to gain a critical perspective on the problem and its most plausible solution. In the HBCE, we will restore this text, based on the SP, LXX, and the other textual evidence. The apparatus entry will read:[14]

ינפק תרינן) 4:8 SP G (Διέλθωμεν εἰς τὸ πεδίον) sim T^P נלכה השדה
(לאפי ברא) V (*egrediamur foras*) S (ܢܘܦܩ ܠܦܩܥܐ)] > M (parab,
prps triggered by repetition of ... קין אל הבל אחיו)

The diagnosis is that a proto-MT scribe committed a visual error (parablepsis = eye-skip), leaving out these two words, perhaps triggered by the repetition of a similar sequence:

... קין אל הבל אחיו (נלכה השדה) ויה ... קין אל הבל אחיו ויה
Cain to Abel, his brother, ("Let us go out to the field") ... Cain to Abel, his brother

The scribe's eye may have jumped from one cluster of words to another, accidentally leaving out what Cain said to Abel. This is not a certain solution, but it makes good sense of the textual evidence.[15] Moreover, this reading provides an elegant motive for Cain's crime and his punishment. As Nachmanides noted, this invitation enables Cain to kill Abel in secret. Biblical and ancient Near Eastern law presumes that in the field there is no one to hear a victim's cry (see the similar circumstance in the law of rape in Deut 22:27). Cain's plan fails when Yahweh hears Abel's blood crying

---

13. See Menachem Cohen, "The Idea of the Sanctity of the Biblical Text and the Science of Textual Criticism," in *The Bible and Us* [Hebrew], ed. Uriel Simon (Tel Aviv: Dvir, 1979), 42–69; trans. Ahava Cohen and Isaac B. Gottlieb at http://tinyurl.com/SBL7010c.

14. By convention, the minor versions and other secondary witnesses are listed only where they differ from MT. These include the Targums (T^O, T^P, T^J, etc.), Vulgate (V), Peshitta (S), Aquila (α'), Symmachus (σ'), Theodotion (θ'), the Hexapla Quinta (ε'), and rewritten Bible texts such as Jubilees, Pseudo-Philo, the Temple Scroll, etc. This rule varies by book, e.g., S is a more important witness in some books.

15. Hendel, *The Text of Genesis 1–11: Textual Studies and Critical Edition* (New York: Oxford University Press, 1998), 46–47.

out (Gen 4:10). There was no other witness to the crime, but Cain had not counted on a supernatural witness. Yahweh's report that the earth "opened its mouth to take your brother's blood from your hand" (4:11) even provides a metaphorical mouth to expand the resonance of the blood's cry, with its implicit message, "violence." In the field there is no one to hear a cry, but Cain's ruse fails because Yahweh hears the postmortem cry. The punishment then fits the crime. Because he spilled his brother's blood on the soil, Cain, the first tiller of the soil, is banished from the soil. Where he wanders, as he complains, anyone may kill him. Cain's terse invitation, נלכה השדה ("Let us go out to the field"), with its motive of secret murder, is punished by his wandering in a lawless place, far from the arable soil and hidden from God's face. As we see, the restoration suits the literary style and poetics of the story, and accords with the terse but resourceful diction of the J source. The literary analysis provides another level of support for the text-critical reasoning.

RESTORING JOSHUA 21:36–37: MISSING CITIES

The second example is another curious problem in MT—a lacuna at Josh 21:36 in the list of Levitical cities—which also raises the issue of how best to restore the text in a critical edition. According to the context, four cities are missing.[16] Some Masoretic codices have two verses at Josh 21:36–37 that supply the missing cities. But these verses are absent from the oldest codices, including the Aleppo Codex (A), the St. Petersburg (formerly Leningrad) Codex (L), and the Cairo Codex of the Prophets (C), all from the ninth–eleventh century CE. They are also absent from the Targum (Jonathan) of Joshua. A version of these two verses is in the LXX, but in Origen's Hexapla these LXX verses are marked with an obelus, indicating that they were lacking in MT. In sum, the evidence from roughly the third century CE to the thirteenth century (see below) indicates that these verses were missing in MT.

The two verses in the later MT codices are similar to the text of 1 Chr 6:63 and to LXX Josh 21:36–37. Here is a comparison of these texts, in translation, with the substantive variants italicized.

---

16. Two verses in this chapter—Josh 21:7, 38 (40)—report that the priestly clan of Merari was allotted twelve cities. The former verse specifies that they are from Reuben, Gad, and Zebulun. However, in the oldest MT codices, only eight cities are listed, all from Gad and Zebulun. The four cities from Reuben are lacking.

A, L, C, etc.

>

later MT codices
And from the tribe of Reuben, Bezer and its pasture lands, and
Jahaz and its pasture lands, Kedemoth and its pasture lands, and
Mephaath and its pasture lands: *four cities.*

MT and LXX 1 Chr 6:63
From the tribe of Reuben: Bezer, *in the wilderness,* and its pasture
lands, and Jahaz and its pasture lands, Kedemoth and its pasture
lands, and Mephaath and its pasture lands.

LXX Josh 21:36–37
From the tribe of Reuben, *the city of refuge for the manslayer,*
Bezer, *in the wilderness on the plain,* and its pasture lands, and
Jahaz and its pasture lands, Kedemoth and its pasture lands, and
Mephaath and its pasture lands: *four cities.*

On the basis of our current knowledge, the probable historical relationship
among these texts is as follows:[17]

1. Chronicles adapts a contemporary text of Joshua.[18]
2. Old Greek translation from a contemporary text of Joshua.[19]
3. Eye-skip in (proto-)MT Joshua, triggered by homoioteleuton (ואת
    ואת מגרשה ערים ארבע ⌢ מגרשה ערים ארבע) or homoiarkton
    (וממטה ⌢ וממטה).[20]

---

17. See the thorough analysis of Dominique Barthélemy, *Critique textuelle de l'Ancien Testament*, OBO 50 (Fribourg: Éditions Universitaires; Göttingen: Vandenhoeck & Ruprecht, 1982), 1:64–68.

18. Gary N. Knoppers, *I Chronicles 1–9*, AB 12A (New York: Doubleday, 2003), 443–48.

19. See Michaël van der Meer, "Joshua," in *The T&T Clark Companion to the Septuagint*, ed. James K. Aitken, T&T Clark Companions (London: Bloomsbury, 2015), 75–88; Emanuel Tov, "The Growth of the Book of Joshua in Light of the Evidence of the Septuagint," in *The Greek and Hebrew Bible: Collected Essays on the Septuagint*, VTSup 72 (Leiden: Brill, 1999; repr., Atlanta: Society of Biblical Literature, 2006), 385–96.

20. Tov, *Textual Criticism*, 223; Richard D. Nelson, *Joshua: A Commentary*, OTL (Louisville: Westminster John Knox, 1997), 236.

4. Medieval restoration based on MT Chronicles.

The last step is indicated by closeness of the text to Chronicles. As Richard Nelson cogently argues (building on the analysis of Dominique Barthé-lemy), "The loss was restored in some Hebrew witnesses by taking part of the corresponding text from Chronicles. This is evidenced by the absence of the tag line 'city of refuge for the killer,' the elimination of which is char-acteristic of the Chronicles parallel."[21] This tag line, את עיר מקלט הרצח, occurs consistently in this section of Josh 21 at verses 27 (Manasseh), 32 (Naphtali), and 36/38 (Gad). The MT plus in verses 36–37 appears to be a slightly reduced and systematized version of Chronicles (deleting במדבר, "in the wilderness," after Bezer), adapted to the context by supplying the expected count at the end, ערים ארבע ("four cities").

Once this MT plus appeared—arguably as an attempt to restore the missing text—there ensued some controversy in Masoretic circles about its authenticity.[22] Three Masoretic codices from the thirteenth century CE provide an entry into these disputes.

The earliest dated codex with these verses is the Madrid Codex (M1), written in 1280 CE, but it has a fuller text. The copyist wrote the plus quoted above with two additions: את עיר מקלט הרצח ("city of refuge for the killer") after ראובן (Reuben), and במדבר ("in the wilderness") after בצר (Bezer). These are arguably harmonizations with את עיר מקלט הרצח in Josh 21:27, 32, 36/38 and with במדבר in 1 Chr 6:63. A second hand, presumably the *naqdan*, erased את עיר מקלט הרצח and left במדבר unpointed, putting two small circles over it.[23] The resulting pointed text is the same as the plus quoted above. The erasure and pointing by the second hand indicates that the shorter plus was in the Masoretic codex that was his reference source. The plus seems to be slightly fluid, but there is already an authoritative Masoretic version of it.

A slightly later codex with this reading is the First Ibn Merwas Bible (British Library Or 2201), written in 1300 CE (fig. 2). The plus is fully

---

21. Nelson, *Joshua*, 236.

22. See Ginsburg, *Introduction*, 178–80.

23. Universidad Complutense Madrid Biblioteca Digital Dioscórides, http://tinyurl.com/SBL7010m. Yosef Ofer plausibly suggests that when the *naqdan* realized the error, he had already pointed the first phrase and therefore was compelled to erase it (rather than leave it unpointed). My thanks to Ofer for sharing with me his analysis of this text and guidance on related Masoretic matters.

pointed, but it is accompanied by a marginal note: "These two verses are not written in the codex called Hilleli."[24] This note refers to a lost authoritative Masoretic codex, known only from Masoretic notes. The author of this note was keenly aware of the absence of these verses in this master codex.

Another codex from around this period has a more assertive response from the Masoretic *naqdan*. In British Library Arundel Or 16, these verses were copied but not pointed (fig. 3). A long marginal note begins: "These verses are not written here in the Codex Sinai, the Codex of Rabbi Gershom, and the other old manuscripts. I regret this, but this is not their place, for their root is in Chronicles." [25] The *naqdan* refused to point these

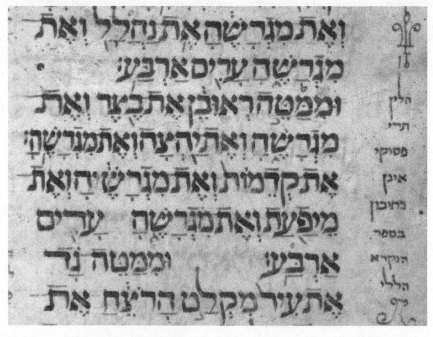

Figure 2. Or 2201 (First Ibn Merwas Bible) at Josh 21:36–37 with marginal note. Copyright: The British Library Board, Or 2201.

---

24. הלין תרי פסוקי אינן כתובין בספר הנקרא הללי, British Library, http://tinyurl.com/SBL7010o; quoted in Ginsburg, *Introduction*, 178 n. 1.

25. אין ב' פסוק' הללו כתוב' בספר סיני ובספר רבי' גרשם והעתקים מספרים אחרים. ואני מתחרט בכך. אך אין זה מקומן כי אם בד"ה עיקרם, British Library, http://tinyurl.com/SBL7010p; quoted in Ginsburg, *Introduction*, 179 n. 1. This codex dates to the thirteenth century according to George Margoliouth, *Catalogue of the Hebrew and Samaritan Manuscripts in the British Museum*, part 1 (London: British Museum, 1899), 85–86.

Figure 3. Arundel Or 16 at Josh 21:36–37 (unpointed) with marginal note.
Copyright: The British Library Board, Arundel Or 16.

words because he judged them to be inauthentic based on the textual evidence. The reasoning of this medieval Masoretic scholar is essentially the same as the modern textual critic.

In his Joshua commentary (early thirteenth century), David Qimḥi notes the textual diversity in the MT codices and states his preference for the shorter text based on the evidence of "old accurate manuscript[s]" (ספר ישן מדוייק): "There are corrected manuscripts that have in them, 'And from the tribe of Reuben, Bezer and its pasture lands, and Jahaz and its pasture lands, Kedemoth and its pasture lands, and Mephaath and its pasture lands: four cities,' but I have not seen these two verses in any old accurate manuscript, only in some corrected manuscripts."[26] Qimḥi is here

---

26. Qimḥi, commentary on Josh 21:7: יש ספרים מוגה בהם וממטה ראובן את
בצר ואת מגרשיה את יהצה ואת מגרשיה את קדמות ואת מגרשיה ואת מופעת ואת

expressing his text-critical judgment, based on his evaluation of the manuscript evidence.

The same textual judgment was expressed by Jacob Ben Ḥayyim in the Second Rabbinic Bible. The earlier printed editions included the plus at Josh 21:36–37, but on the basis of his collation of the Masorah and his "accurate Spanish manuscripts,"[27] Ben Ḥayyim omitted them. In his marginal note, he echoes Qimḥi: "There are corrected manuscripts that include in them, 'And from the tribe of Reuben, Bezer, etc.,' but this is not found in any of the old accurate manuscripts."[28]

Perhaps surprisingly, these two verses were included—in smaller print—in Rudolf Kittel's edition of Joshua in his *Biblia Hebraica*.[29] Kittel used the Second Rabbinic Bible as his base text, but he disagreed with Ben Ḥayyim's decision to omit this text. More surprisingly, Kittel retained this text—still in small print—when he switched over (at the urging of Paul Kahle) to the Leningrad Codex as his base text in the third edition.[30] In *BHS* these two verses remain, with the following explanation in the apparatus: v 36.37 > LC Mss 𝔅𝔗 (Syh c ob); exstat in mlt Mss Edd 𝔊𝔗ᴹˢˢ𝔅 cf 1 Ch 6,63 sq; 𝔖 tr post 34a.

All of this is surprising, because the *BHS* is a diplomatic edition featuring a single Masoretic manuscript, L. The editors state in the preface: "We have thought it best to reproduce the text of the latest hand of L with close fidelity. We have accordingly refrained from 'removing obvious scribal errors.'"[32]

If these verses are not in the text of the manuscript that *BHS* is transcribing "with close fidelity," why then are they included? The *BHS* editors seem to indicate that these verses *should* be in the text, even though they

---

מגרשיה ערים ארבע ולא ראיתי שני פסוקים אלו בשום ספר ישן מדוייק אלא מוגה במקצתם.

27. Jordan S. Penkower, "Rabbinic Bible," in *Dictionary of Biblical Interpretation*, ed. John. H. Hayes (Nashville: Abingdon, 1999), 2:362–63.

28. *Biblia Rabbinica*, at Josh 21:36:יש ספרי' מונה בהם וממטה ראובן את בצר וגו' ובכל הספ' המדוייקי' הישנים לא נמצא.

29. *BHK* (1st ed., 1905–1906), 1:324.

30. *BHK* (3rd ed., 1937), 356.

31. *BHS*, 391; translation: "vv. 36–37 lacking in L, C, other Masoretic manuscripts, the Second Rabbinic Bible, and the Targum; in the Syro-Hexapla marked with an obelisk; present in multiple manuscripts, printed editions, the LXX, Targum manuscripts, and the Vulgate; compare 1 Chr 6:63; the Peshiṭta translates these verses after v. 34a."

32. *BHS*, xii.

are lacking in L and the other early Masoretic codices. The editors of *BHS* have here reconstructed a critical eclectic text. The use of miniature type is a strategy for restoring the missing verses. The editors have departed from their stringent guidelines because, as textual critics, they felt a responsibility to include these verses in the text of a critical edition. Their text-critical judgment is arguably wrong, since this particular text is probably a medieval restoration based on Chronicles, as stated by the scholarly *naqdan* of Arundel Or 16 and implied by Qimḥi.[33] But the impulse of Kittel and the *BHS* editors is recognizable—one wants to restore a problematic text as best one can.[34] In this curious instance, the medieval scholars and the editors of *BHK* and *BHS* open the way for a more fully realized eclectic critical edition of the Hebrew Bible. In the HBCE Joshua, I expect that the restoration will be closer to the LXX reading than to the Chronicler's text.[35] There is no definitive solution, so I await the editors' judgments on how best to adjudicate the evidence and restore the four cities.

These cases of textual restoration illustrate some of the complexities of the text of the Hebrew Bible, the long history of textual inquiry, and the advantages—and risks—of a new kind of critical edition. The following chapters provide a more detailed justification of the HBCE project. They also provide other kinds of prolegomena—forays into the conceptual structure, procedures, and intellectual genealogy of textual criticism of the Hebrew Bible; new vistas on the history of the biblical text in the light of the Qumran biblical manuscripts; the mechanisms and motives of scribal change; the representational possibilities of the electronic HBCE; and even some theology, as in the early modern debate about church authority versus *sola Scriptura*, which curiously pivoted on text-critical issues. Finally, I argue that textual criticism has been and will continue to be untimely, disturbing our entrenched habits and assumptions, and opening our eyes to the multiplicity of the *Hebraica veritas*.

---

33. In his comment, Qimḥi credits Hai Gaon (eleventh century CE) for noting that the four cities missing in Joshua are to be found in Chronicles.

34. Kittel accepted that, in principle, an eclectic critical edition is the proper procedure, but he regarded it as impractical; see Ernst Würthwein, *The Text of the Old Testament: An Introduction to the Biblia Hebraica*, trans. Erroll F. Rhodes, 2nd ed. (Grand Rapids: Eerdmans, 1995), 42; and below, ch. 1.

35. So Barthélemy, *Critique*, 68; Nelson, *Joshua*, 236.

1

PROLOGUE TO
THE HEBREW BIBLE: A CRITICAL EDITION (HBCE)

The concept of the "definitive text" corresponds only to religion or exhaustion.
—Jorge Luis Borges, "The Homeric Versions"

Every edition is a theory.
—Bernard Cerquiglini, *In Praise of the Variant*

The discovery, analysis, and publication of the roughly two hundred biblical manuscripts (mostly fragmentary) from Qumran have ushered in a new era in the textual criticism of the Hebrew Bible.[1] Among the many issues now facing textual critics is how best to integrate the knowledge gained in the post-Qumran era with the aims and procedures for constructing new scholarly editions of the Hebrew Bible. Currently there are three new editions in process: the Hebrew University Bible Project (HUBP), the Biblia Hebraica Quinta (BHQ), and The Hebrew Bible: A Critical Edition (HBCE). These critical editions are motivated by different theories. HUBP and BHQ share a commitment to the model of a diplomatic edition, that

---

1. Moshe H. Goshen-Gottstein, "The Textual Criticism of the Old Testament: Rise, Decline, Rebirth," *JBL* 102 (1983): 365–99; Arie van der Kooij, "The Textual Criticism of the Hebrew Bible before and after the Qumran Discoveries," in *The Bible as Book: The Hebrew Bible and the Judaean Desert Discoveries*, ed. Edward D. Herbert and Emanuel Tov (London: British Library, 2002), 167–77; Emanuel Tov, "Textual Criticism of the Hebrew Bible 1947–1997," in *Perspectives in the Study of the Old Testament and Early Judaism: A Symposium on Honour of Adam S. van der Woude on the Occasion of His 70th Birthday*, ed. Florentino García Martínez and Ed Noort, VTSup 73 (Leiden: Brill, 1998), 61–81; see also the broad historical panorama of Bruno Chiesa, *Filologia storica della Bibbia ebraica*, 2 vols., Studi biblici 125, 135 (Brescia: Paideia, 2000).

is, a transcription of a single manuscript with textual variants and editorial judgments included in one or more critical apparatuses. Adrian Schenker, president of the editorial committee of BHQ, describes the relationship between these two editions as an *editio critica maior* (HUBP) and an *editio critica minor* (BHQ).[2]

The HBCE is another type of critical edition: an eclectic edition, that is, a critical text accompanied by an apparatus presenting the evidence and justifying the editorial decisions. The HBCE also includes an extensive text-critical commentary, which presents detailed arguments for the editorial decisions and other text-critical issues. An eclectic edition is both an alternative and a complement to the diplomatic editions. A comparable situation exists for Septuagint studies, for which there is a one-volume *editio critica minor* (the Rahlfs-Hanhart eclectic edition), a multivolume diplomatic *editio critica maior* (the Cambridge LXX), and a multivolume eclectic *editio critica maior* (the Göttingen LXX). The premise of the HBCE is that an eclectic *editio critica maior* offers substantive benefits to scholarship of the Hebrew Bible.

There are obstacles and advantages to an eclectic critical edition. To consider the latter first, one signal advantage (which some will doubtless consider a disadvantage) is that such a critical edition requires its editors to exercise their full critical judgment concerning the variant readings and textual problems of the Hebrew Bible. This contrasts with the existing diplomatic editions where the burden of making text-critical decisions often falls to the reader, who may be innocent of the discipline of textual criticism. Unfortunately, this creates a situation in which important text-critical judgments tend to be exercised by those least qualified to make them. It is arguable that textual critics ought to take up the burden of such decisions and not leave them to those uninitiated in the art. Such, at least, is the premise of the HBCE. The decisions and analyses will then be available for discussion, refinement, and refutation—the normal process of scholarship.

A second advantage will be the ability of such an edition to represent multiple early editions of biblical books in cases where such multiple edi-

---

2. Adrian Schenker, "Eine Neuausgabe der Biblia Hebraica," *ZAH* 9 (1996): 59; see also Schenker, "The Edition Biblia Hebraica Quinta (BHQ)," *HBAI* 2 (2013): 6–16; Richard D. Weis, "*Biblia Hebraica Quinta* and the Making of Critical Editions of the Hebrew Bible," *TC* 7 (2002), http://tinyurl.com/SBL7010i; and Michael Segal, "The Hebrew University Bible Project," *HBAI* 2 (2013): 38–62.

tions are recoverable. Analysis of the Qumran texts in relation to the other major versions—the MT, the SP, and the LXX—has made it clear that many books of the Hebrew Bible circulated in multiple editions during the Second Temple period.[3] The HBCE aims to produce critical texts of each ancient edition, which will generally be presented in parallel columns. The relationship among these editions will be discussed fully in the introductory chapter to each volume. In cases where one edition is not the textual ancestor of the other(s), a common ancestor to the extant editions will be reconstructed, to the extent possible.

Textual decisions regarding the nature and history of multiple editions are often difficult. There are no clear guidelines to pinpoint where a group of scribal revisions is sufficiently systematic to constitute a new edition; as Peter Shillingsburg asks, "when is a revised text a new work?"[4] Moreover, the stemmatic relationships among multiple editions are sometimes difficult to ascertain, so such decisions will always be provisional. Nonetheless, the ability to reproduce multiple editions will be a notable advantage of the HBCE concept and format. Diplomatic editions, since they are tied to a single manuscript, are not well suited to this task. In some biblical books multiple editions exist only in certain sections, so parallel columns will appear and disappear in the critical edition as needed. By producing critical texts of multiple editions, the HBCE will provide scholars with a

---

3. Important general and theoretical discussions include Emanuel Tov, *Textual Criticism of the Hebrew Bible*, 3rd ed. (Minneapolis: Fortress, 2012); Eugene Ulrich, *The Dead Sea Scrolls and the Origins of the Bible*, SDSS (Grand Rapids: Eerdmans, 1999); Eugene Ulrich, *The Dead Sea Scrolls and the Developmental Composition of the Bible*, VTSup 169 (Leiden: Brill, 2015); Zipora Talshir, "Texts, Text-Forms, Editions, New Composition and the Final Products of Biblical Literature," in *Congress Volume Munich 2013*, ed. Christl M. Maier, VTSup 163 (Leiden: Brill, 2014), 40–66; Reinhard Müller, Juha Pakkala, and Bas ter Haar Romeny, *Evidence of Editing: Growth and Change of Texts in the Hebrew Bible*, RBS 75 (Atlanta: Society of Biblical Literature, 2014); Adrian Schenker, ed., *The Earliest Text of the Hebrew Bible: The Relationship between the Masoretic Text and the Hebrew Base of the Septuagint Reconsidered*, SCS 52 (Atlanta: Society of Biblical Literature, 2003); and Julio Trebolle Barrera, "Qumran Evidence for a Biblical Standard Text and for Non-standard and Parabiblical Texts," in *The Dead Sea Scrolls in Their Historical Context*, ed. Timothy H. Lim (Edinburgh: T&T Clark, 2000), 89–106. See also below, ch. 9.

4. Peter L. Shillingsburg, *Resisting Texts: Authority and Submission in Constructions of Meaning*, ETLC (Ann Arbor: University of Michigan Press, 1997), 165–80. He sensibly argues that this question "has a variety of possible answers depending on one's theoretical position" (174). See further below.

valuable resource, since the Hebrew texts of the multiple editions are in most cases unavailable in the scholarly literature.

A third advantage will be the information on scribal hermeneutics contained in the apparatus and commentary. The apparatuses in the existing diplomatic editions are heterogenous, mixing primary readings (i.e., earlier and text-critically preferable) with secondary readings (scribal errors and revisions) and only selectively discriminating among them. The HBCE apparatus will systematically distinguish, to the best of the editor's ability, the primary from the secondary readings and will analyze the motivation or cause of the secondary readings. These analyses not only serve to justify the decisions made in the critical text, but will also enhance the value of the secondary readings for the study of the reception of the biblical text in scribal circles in the Second Temple period and beyond. Interpretive phenomena such as harmonization, explication, linguistic modernization, and exegetical revision open a window onto scribal interpretation in the period prior to the textual stabilization of the various biblical books.[5] These types of variants ought not to be seen as mere "corruptions"—as is the older text-critical nomenclature—but rather as evidence of the process of scripturalization, that is, the conceptual shifts by which texts became Scripture.[6] In this respect, the annotations of the apparatus will open new perspectives onto the early reception of the biblical text.

The practical obstacles to such an eclectic edition are many, chief among them the difficulty of using translation documents—above all, the LXX—for text-critical purposes. As Moshe Goshen-Gottstein cautioned, there is always a residue of uncertainty when retroverting the Greek

---

5. Important recent studies include Alexander Rofé, "The Historical Significance of Secondary Readings," in *The Quest for Context and Meaning: Studies in Biblical Intertextuality in Honor of James A. Sanders*, ed. Craig A. Evans and Shemaryahu Talmon, BibInt 28 (Leiden: Brill, 1997), 393–402; Alexander Rofé, "The Methods of Late Biblical Scribes as Evidenced by the Septuagint Compared with the Other Textual Witnesses," in *Tehillah le-Moshe: Biblical and Judaic Studies in Honor of Moshe Greenberg*, ed. Mordechai Cogan, Barry L. Eichler, and Jeffrey H. Tigay (Winona Lake, IN: Eisenbrauns, 1997), 259–70; and David Andrew Teeter, *Scribal Laws: Exegetical Variation in the Textual Transmission of Biblical Law in the Late Second Temple Period*, FAT 92 (Tübingen: Mohr Siebeck, 2014).

6. See James L. Kugel, "Early Interpretation: The Common Background of Late Forms of Biblical Exegesis," in *Early Biblical Interpretation*, ed. James L. Kugel and Rowan L. Greer, LEC 3 (Philadelphia: Westminster, 1986), 13–27.

translation into its Hebrew *Vorlage.*[7] Nonetheless, in most books of the Hebrew Bible the Greek translation technique is discernible and reliable, allowing a good measure of confidence in many retroversions. The degree of confidence varies depending on the literalness of the translation technique in each book. Most useful is where the LXX represents each Hebrew sense-unit by a Greek equivalent, yielding a creolized "translation Greek," which easily exposes the Hebrew words and syntax. Fortunately there exists a considerable body of scholarship on the important topic of translation technique in the LXX.[8] On the basis of such studies, the textual critic can proceed cautiously but profitably in the text-critical use of the LXX. In other words, the fact that much important textual evidence exists in translation documents does not render this evidence unusable for textual criticism. Because of the importance of the LXX, it may be relatively more difficult to produce a reliable critical text for the Hebrew Bible than it is for other texts, but this does not diminish the desirability or possibility of the task. The nature of the LXX translation technique will be addressed fully in the introduction to each volume in the HBCE.

The rationale for the HBCE rests on the presupposition that the goals and procedures for the textual criticism of the Hebrew Bible are not unique. As Bertil Albrektson has argued, "The textual criticism of the Hebrew Bible should not be regarded as a game of its own with special rules."[9] This means, among other things, that the production of scholarly editions with critical texts should be regarded as a viable activity, as it is in other fields.

---

7. Moshe H. Goshen-Gottstein, "Theory and Practice of Textual Criticism: The Text-Critical Use of the Septuagint," *Text* 3 (1963): 132.

8. On method and major issues, see James Barr, *The Typology of Literalism in Ancient Biblical Translations*, MSU 15 (Göttingen: Vandenhoeck & Ruprecht, 1979); Emanuel Tov, *The Text-Critical Use of the Septuagint in Biblical Research*, 3rd ed. (Winona Lake, IN: Eisenbrauns, 2015); Jan Joosten, *Collected Studies on the Septuagint: From Language to Interpretation and Beyond*, FAT 83 (Tübingen: Mohr Siebeck, 2012); and Anneli Aejmelaeus, *On the Trail of the Septuagint Translators: Collected Essays*, 2nd ed., CBET 50 (Leuven: Peeters, 2007).

9. Bertil Albrektson, "Translation and Emendation," in *Text, Translation, Theology: Selected Essays on the Hebrew Bible* (Farnham, UK: Ashgate, 2010), 99. See also Bruno Chiesa, "Textual History and Textual Criticism of the Hebrew Old Testament," in *The Madrid Qumran Congress: Proceedings of the International Congress on the Dead Sea Scrolls, Madrid, 18–21 March, 1991*, ed. Julio Trebolle Barrera and Luis Vegas Montaner, STDJ 11 (Leiden: Brill, 1992), 1:265: "it seems quite unnecessary to postulate an *ad hoc* status for the Biblical writings alone."

The HBCE does not aim to be a definitive text, which, as Borges observes, is a category that pertains only to religion or exhaustion. Rather the HBCE aims to be a reliable and circumspect critical eclectic edition and a worthy complement to the diplomatic editions. As is the case in the textual criticism of other works, the HBCE aims to stimulate further textual scholarship and expects to be superseded by future eclectic editions. It is not the dream of a final text, but a provisional work of scholarship, based on new evidence and the achievements of many textual critics.

Emanuel Tov has observed that while textual critics of the Hebrew Bible have generally been unfavorable to the production of critical texts,[10] many scholarly commentaries present critical texts in their translations and notes, and many modern translations construct their own implicit critical texts.[11] The HBCE, in this respect, is not a departure from standard scholarly practice but an attempt to do openly what scholars have been doing piecemeal or unsystematically all along. The format of a critical edition allows such scholarship to be undertaken fully and openly, inviting conversation and critique. There is obvious advantage in doing such work with full presentation of the data, problems, analyses, and arguments.

Having considered some of the advantages and obstacles in the production of an eclectic and plural edition of the Hebrew Bible, I turn to a detailed presentation of its procedures, terminology, and theoretical

---

10. Recent exceptions are Pier G. Borbone, *Il libro del profeta Osea: Edizione critica del testo ebraico*, QHenoch 2 (Turin: Zamorani, 1990); Anthony Gelston, "Isaiah 52:13–53:12: An Eclectic Text and a Supplementary Note on the Hebrew Manuscript Kennicott 96," *JSS* 35 (1990): 187–211; Giovanni Garbini, *Il Cantico dei Cantici: Testo, traduzione e commento* (Brescia: Paideia, 1992); Alessandro Catastini, *Storia di Giuseppe (Genesi 37–50)* (Venice: Marsilio, 1994); Ronald Hendel, *The Text of Genesis 1–11: Textual Studies and Critical Edition* (New York: Oxford University Press, 1998); and Kjell Hognesius, *The Text of 2 Chronicles 1–16: A Critical Edition with Textual Commentary*, ConBOT 64 (Stockholm: Almqvist & Wiksell, 2003). See further the considerations of Chiesa, "Textual History," 262–65.

11. Tov, *Textual Criticism*, 367–76; and Tov, "The Textual Basis of Modern Translations of the Hebrew Bible," in *Hebrew Bible, Greek Bible, and Qumran: Collected Essays*, TSAJ 121 (Tübingen: Mohr Siebeck, 2008), 92–106. Tov argues against eclecticism in translations for believing communities because of the lack of adequate scholarly resources to make textual decisions, the inherent subjectivity of the task, and the difficult (and usually unaddressed) theoretical issues. He does not contest the legitimacy of eclecticism in scholarly commentaries and other studies, which he grants is "accepted practice" (100).

orientation. In the next chapter I will address some of the criticisms of the project.

THE AIMS OF THE CRITICAL TEXT

A distinctive feature of the HBCE is its production of critical texts of the biblical books. This is the ordinary procedure for critical editions of other ancient books, such as the New Testament and the Greek and Latin classics, but is not the norm in textual criticism of the Hebrew Bible. The other ongoing editorial projects are diplomatic editions, which present a particular manuscript (L for BHQ; A for HUBP) with accompanying apparatus(es). In its apparatus, the BHQ offers judgments on the preferred reading, while the HUBP refrains from textual judgment. The HBCE, in contrast, presents a critical text that is constructed by the textual judgments of the editors. The method is eclectic, drawing together the best readings from many manuscripts and, where warranted, conjectural readings. In the diplomatic editions, the reader is implicitly invited to construct a "virtual" critical text. The HBCE constructs an actual critical text. As Paul Maas states in his guide to textual criticism, this is the classical aim of the discipline: "The business of textual criticism is to produce a text as close as possible to the original (*constitutio textus*)."[12]

As we will see, the business of textual criticism includes more than the constitution of a critical text, but this is an important feature of the discipline. Even if some editorial projects reject this goal, as do the BHQ and HUBP, they must explain why they do so, and the resulting arguments can be evaluated and contested by other textual critics. The idea of a critical text is at the center of textual criticism, even if this idea is held to be impossible or undesirable.

The HBCE takes a particular position on the concept of a critical text, which clarifies the nature of our project. Our critical texts aim to approximate the corrected archetype of each biblical book. The critical texts will also approximate the corrected hyparchetype(s) of each subsequent edition of that book. Instances of multiple editions will usually be presented in parallel columns. Where the archetype cannot be plausibly ascertained

---

12. Paul Maas, *Textual Criticism*, trans. Barbara Flower (Oxford: Clarendon, 1958), 1.

for a given book, the critical text will present one or more corrected hyp-archetypes of proto-M, proto-G, or other textual families.[13]

This aim requires a clear understanding of the text-critical categories *archetype*, *hyparchetype*, and *edition*, and their relationship to the *original* of a biblical book. The procedures of the HBCE are predicated on the details and implications of these concepts.[14]

The archetype of a book is, according to Sebastiano Timpanaro's lucid definition,

> a manuscript—even if it is later than the author by many centuries, even if it has been preserved by chance and is devoid of any "official" quality or authority, even if it is disfigured by errors or lacunas—from which all the others are derived.[15]

This manuscript is, as Michael Reeve states, the "latest common ancestor" of the extant manuscripts.[16] Occasionally this ancestral manuscript itself is extant, as is the case of Josephus, *Contra Apionem*, for which an eleventh-century Greek manuscript is the archetype of all the other Greek manuscripts.[17] However, it is usually the case for ancient books that the archetype has been lost.

The archetype of a book is not the original text but is, in E. J. Kenney's description, the "earliest inferable state of the text."[18] On the basis

---

13. E.g., Michael V. Fox, *Proverbs: An Eclectic Edition with Introduction and Textual Commentary*, HBCE 1 (Atlanta: SBL Press, 2015), presents in the critical text the corrected hyparchetype of proto-M, with the proto-G edition addressed in the text-critical commentary.

14. On these and other text-critical concepts, see Paolo Trovato, *Everything You Always Wanted to Know about Lachmann's Method: A Non-standard Handbook of Genealogical Textual Criticism in the Age of Post-structuralism, Cladistics, and Copy-Text*, Storie e linguaggi 7 (Padua: Libreriauniversitaria, 2014).

15. Sebastiano Timpanaro, *The Genesis of Lachmann's Method*, trans. Glenn W. Most (Chicago: University of Chicago Press, 2005), 50.

16. Michael D. Reeve, "Archetypes," in *Manuscripts and Methods: Essays on Editing and Transmission* (Rome: Edizioni di storia e letteratura, 2011), 118.

17. Heinz Schreckenberg, "Text, Überlieferung und Textkritik von *Contra Apionem*," in *Josephus' Contra Apionem: Studies in Its Character and Context with a Latin Concordance to the Portion Missing in Greek*, ed. Louis H. Feldman and John R. Levison, AGJU 34 (Leiden: Brill, 1996), 62. The archetype is MS Laurentianus 69,22. The later manuscripts have the same lacuna in 2.51–113 and other shared *Leitfehler*.

18. See further E. J. Kenney, "Textual Criticism," in *The New Encyclopædia Britan-*

of the variant manuscripts, one can infer a textual state (i.e., a manuscript) that is their latest common ancestor. It is important to note that the archetype may be many steps removed from the earliest ancestor, which we may, with some qualifications (see below), call the original. However, it *may* be identical with the original in many, most, or all details. In cases, such as the Hebrew Bible, where we lack the autographs of the books, we cannot know whether or to what degree the archetype is identical to the original.

The archetype and the original are distinguishable in terms of history and epistemology (i.e., what we can know about them). In historical terms, the original is the oldest common ancestor and the archetype is the latest common ancestor. There may have been some or many changes in a book's textual state during its transmission between these two points. There is also a crucial epistemological distinction. We cannot know the original because we lack access to it. But we can know the archetype, because it is inferable (by definition) through careful analysis of the existing manuscripts. Since our inferences are often fallible, in a practical sense we can only hope to *approximate* the archetype. We cannot plausibly claim to reconstruct all of its details perfectly. A careful distinction between the archetype and the original is a necessary prerequisite for a critical eclectic edition of the Hebrew Bible.

A further qualification is necessary to clarify the aim of our (or any) critical text. The archetype will contain scribal errors that can sometimes be detected and corrected. For instance, distinctive scribal errors that are in *all* the manuscripts derive from the archetype. If we can discern these errors, we are obliged as textual critics to correct them. In this respect the aim of a critical text is a *corrected* archetype. The correction of discernible errors in the archetype clarifies the aim of the HBCE, whose critical texts will approximate a *corrected* archetype of each biblical book and, where appropriate, *corrected* hyparchetypes.

A hyparchetype is the latest common ancestor of a particular textual family of a book. In some cases, this is equivalent to the hyparchetype of a particular edition. For example, for the books of the Pentateuch we can often establish three coherent textual families: proto-M, proto-SP, and proto-G. In theory we should be able to infer a hyparchetype for each of

---

nica, 15th ed. (Chicago: Encyclopædia Britannica, 1974), 18:192, http://tinyurl.com/SBL7010e.

the textual families. If one of these families uniquely preserves an edition of that book, as is sometimes the case, then that family's hyparchetype is also the hyparchetype of that edition.

The latest common ancestor of all the hyparchetypes is the archetype of the book. In the case of multiple editions, the archetype of the book is also the earliest inferable edition. We designate the edition represented by the archetype the first edition. There may have been earlier editions in the historical span from original to archetype, but we lack access to them.

A famous example of a hyparchetype is Paul de Lagarde's demonstration that all the medieval Masoretic manuscripts descend from a lost manuscript that contained the *puncta extraordinaria, nun suspensa,* and other unusual scribal marks.[19] Following the genealogical method of Karl Lachmann and others, Lagarde identified these scribal marks as *Leitfehler* (indicative errors, *errores significativi*) from which one can infer common ancestry. Since this distinctive cluster of errors cannot plausibly have originated independently in multiple manuscripts (i.e., by polygenesis), there must have been a manuscript with these odd features from which the medieval Masoretic manuscripts descend. (Ironically, the *puncta extraordinaria,* which Tov aptly calls "cancellation dots," originally designated "omit," but they were mistakenly transmitted rather than omitted.[20]) It is possible that this hyparchetype descends from several manuscripts that collectively had these features, which were then amalgamated in an effort at uniformity. Other variants may have been later incorporated "horizontally" from other manuscripts. Despite these uncertainties, we can infer a hyparchetype for the medieval manuscripts with this cluster of odd features. The medieval Masoretic manuscripts evince a clear genealogical affinity and are an identifiable sublineage within the larger proto-M textual family.[21]

There is a further analytical distinction between the archetype and the original. The archetype can change with the discovery of new manuscript evidence. With the discovery of the Qumran biblical texts, in some cases an earlier textual state of a biblical book is inferable than was previously possible. This means that the archetype is a different manuscript than it

---

19. Paul de Lagarde, *Anmerkungen zur griechischen Übersetzung der Proverbien* (Leipzig: Brockhaus, 1863), 1–2.

20. Emanuel Tov, *Scribal Practices and Approaches Reflected in the Texts Found in the Judean Desert,* STDJ 54 (Leiden: Brill, 2004), 187–98, 214–18.

21. See further below, ch. 8.

was previously. Hence, the practical goal of a critical text can change with the discovery of more evidence. In contrast, the original of the book does not change—but we cannot know it because it is outside of our epistemological horizon. The archetype can be, in this sense, a moving target, yet we can know it, if only approximately.

The concept of multiple editions of a biblical book also requires clarification. As a general rule, the HBCE regards a book or a portion of a book as having multiple editions if there is evidence of systematic revision, such as resequencing of text (verses, pericopes, or larger sections), new compositions, and systematic exegetical revisions (e.g., revisions of chronology). Local or ad hoc scribal changes, such as harmonizations, explications, linguistic modernizations, and small exegetical revisions do not, in our view, rise to the level of a new edition. There is no red line between a cluster of scribal changes and a new edition, hence the editor of each book will present the rationale for decisions regarding editions. New editions are, in loose terms, rewritten compositions within a given book.[22]

In cases of multiple editions, the critical text will generally present the corrected archetype of the first edition and the corrected hyparchetype(s) of subsequent editions in parallel columns. Where the genealogical relationship among the editions is not discernible, the corrected hyparchetype of each edition will be presented without notations of relative priority. The later changes (including scribal errors) in each edition will be presented and analyzed in the apparatus and commentary.[23]

In contrast to these historical textual states (archetypes, hyparchetypes, editions), the concept of the *original* of a biblical book is difficult

---

22. See the lucid treatment of this issue by Zipora Talshir, "Textual Criticism at the Service of Literary Criticism and the Question of an Eclectic Edition of the Hebrew Bible," in *After Qumran: Old and Modern Editions of the Biblical Texts; The Historical Books*, ed. Hans Ausloos, Bénédicte Lemmelijn, and Julio Trebolle Barrera, BETL 246 (Leuven, Peeters 2012), 33–60. Note that Chronicles is not a new edition of Samuel–Kings precisely because it is a different book. See further, below, ch. 5.

23. This formulation clarifies the HBCE presentation of multiple editions, which was queried by Eibert Tigchelaar, "Editing the Hebrew Bible: An Overview of Some Problems," in *Editing the Bible: Assessing the Task Past and Present*, ed. John S. Kloppenborg and Judith H. Newman, RBS 69 (Atlanta: Society of Biblical Literature, 2012), 51: "How the HBCE is going to distinguish between the original characteristics of variant editions—which should be attributed to an editor or author who consciously and consistently reworked a literary unit—and (subsequent) textual changes in the course of that edition's transmission."

to clarify. It is the earliest ancestor of all the textual families of a book, but since it is beyond our epistemological horizon, its precise form is unknowable. A useful starting point is Tov's definition, which attempts to combine the concept of an original with the concept of multiple editions, yielding a chronological series of textual states. The original, in Tov's formulation, is "the written text or edition (or a number of consecutive editions) that contained the finished literary product ... that stood at the beginning of the textual transmission process."[24]

The binary oppositions in this definition require qualification, particularly "finished" versus "beginning" and "literary" versus "textual." As Tov acknowledges, in practice these distinctions often overlap. Sometimes, as Shemaryahu Talmon famously argued, the copyist is "a minor partner in the creative literary process."[25] As such, "literary" and "textual" are not wholly separable concepts. Sometimes substantial compositional activity resumes, yielding a new edition of a biblical book, well after the process of textual transmission has begun. So there may be recursions and overlaps in the relationship between the "finished" literary work and the "beginning" of its transmission. In cases of "consecutive editions," Tov maintains that this entails a concept of multiple originals. He writes: "In these cases, the textual evidence does not point to a single 'original' text, but a series of authoritative texts produced by the same or different authors. Each of these stages may be considered a type of original text."[26]

In my view, Tov's definition has the right emphases, but it multiplies the concept of "original" unnecessarily and includes the questionable criterion of textual "authority." In cases where a book has consecutive editions, the first edition is best designated as the earliest inferable textual state (i.e., the archetype), and the later editions designated simply as later editions. There is no gain in calling the later edition of Jeremiah an original form of the book, except to emphasize that it is a finished literary product as much as is the earlier edition. By calling each edition an original, Tov introduces confusion into the distinction between his concept of an original form of a book and Talmon's concept of multiple "pristine original texts" (see below).

---

24. Tov, *Textual Criticism*, 165.

25. Shemaryahu Talmon, "The Textual Study of the Bible: A New Outlook," in *Qumran and the History of the Biblical Text*, ed. Frank Moore Cross and Shemaryahu Talmon (Cambridge: Harvard University Press, 1975), 381.

26. Tov, *Textual Criticism*, 167.

The idea that each original text (including editions) is authoritative brings a sociological/theological category into a book's textual history. While some form of positive reception of a book is implied by its transmission and preservation, it is unhelpful to conflate theological and text-critical categories.[27] We need not infer that each edition was authoritative to a particular community or that a nonauthoritative but systematic revision should not count as an edition. As Corrado Martone writes, "textual criticism (and text critics) ... should be ... interested also in texts that have never 'functioned as sacred scripture,' or in texts that could have done so."[28] The status (or lack thereof) of the rewritten Bible texts at Qumran is a salient example of texts that are arguably new editions, but some may have been regarded as *belles lettres*, or oddities, or were simply unknown.[29]

However one conceives the original form of a biblical book or even if one conceives it as an impenetrable blur, the important methodological point is that we have no direct access to it. We only have access to the manuscripts and to the historical textual states (archetypes, hyparchetypes, editions) that we can infer from the manuscripts. Therefore, formulating a definitive concept of the original of a biblical book is a purely theoretical enterprise. The pragmatic goal of a critical text involves the archetype and, for subsequent editions, hyparchetypes. An approximation of these textual states is the pragmatic goal, not a reconstitution (or, better, divination) of the original textual state.

It is important to note that the concept of a critical text concerns the transmitted book, not the book's constituent sources or earlier forms. These prior entities—such as J, P, the Ark Narrative, Second Isaiah, or the *ipsissima verba* of Jeremiah—belong to the literary prehistory of a book, at a time when there was no book of Jeremiah, Isaiah, Samuel, or Genesis. In other words, a critical edition tracks changes that occur during the textual

---

27. See similarly Michael W. Holmes, "From 'Original Text' to 'Initial Text': The Traditional Goal of New Testament Textual Criticism in Contemporary Discussion," in *The Text of the New Testament in Contemporary Research: Essays on the* Status Quaestionis, ed. Bart D. Ehrman and Michael W. Holmes, 2nd ed., NTTSD 46 (Leiden: Brill, 2013), 642–43.

28. Corrado Martone, "All the Bibles We Need: The Impact of the Qumran Evidence on Biblical Lower Criticism," in *The Scrolls and Biblical Traditions: Proceedings of the Seventh Meeting of the IOQS in Helsinki*, ed. George J. Brooke et al., STDJ 103 (Leiden: Brill, 2012), 53.

29. See further below, chs. 5 and 9.

transmission of books and not to literary states prior to the "finished literary product" (Tov's phrase) of a given book or edition.[30]

The original form of a biblical book is a theoretical limit or ideal concept for textual criticism, but it is in many ways an unreal goal. The actual—and achievable—goal of a critical text is the earliest inferable textual state, the corrected archetype, which we will supplement with the corrected hyparchetype(s) of variant editions. These are the best representations of accurate copies of the biblical books that we can achieve.[31] It is a work of historical restoration, which may not appeal to all biblical scholars, but which is warranted by the theory and practice of textual criticism.

THE DESIGN OF THE CRITICAL TEXT

Having sketched the aim of the critical text, I turn to the thorny issues involved in designing it. Rudolf Kittel granted that in theory a critical eclectic edition is superior to a diplomatic edition, but in practice it raises too many problems, including what to do about the details of spelling, vocalization, and accentuation.[32] He writes: "In principle one must therefore accept this arrangment [i.e., an eclectic edition] as the only proper one; the question can only be whether it is practical as well as easily accomplished, compared to the other, basically inferior alternative [i.e., a diplomatic edition]."[33] Previous eclectic editions, including Carl Heinrich Cornill's edition of Ezekiel and Paul Haupt's series, *The Sacred Books of the Old Testament*, produced purely consonantal Hebrew texts.[34] But this

---

30. This formulation responds to the query of Tov (*Textual Criticism*, 364) about whether the HBCE would choose to exclude some literary strata, such as the hymns of Hannah (1 Sam 2:1–10) and Jonah (Jonah 2), which were arguably added secondarily in the literary prehistory of the book. The concept of the archetype precludes the discrimination of such literary strata, since any composition attested in all the extant manuscripts is, by definition, in the archetype.

31. On the historical and ontological complexities in the idea of an "accurate copy" of a book, see below, ch. 4.

32. Rudolf Kittel, *Über die Notwendigkeit und Möglichkeit einer neuen Ausgabe der hebräischen Bibel: Studien und Erwägungen* (Leipzig: Deichert, 1902), 32–36, 77–78.

33. Ibid., 77–78: "Im Prinzip wird man also dieser Anordnung als der allein richtigen unbedingt zustimmen müssen, die Frage kann nur sein, ob sie praktisch ebenso leicht durch fürbar wäre, wie die andere grundsätzlich minderwertige."

34. Carl Heinrich Cornill, *Das Buch des Propheten Ezechiel* (Leipzig: Hinrichs,

strategy does not solve the problem of spelling, since it is impossible to formulate a consistent approach to the spelling of the archetype.

How does one move from the features of the existing Hebrew manuscripts—including the Dead Sea Scrolls, which have a plethora of spelling practices; the medieval manuscripts, most with slight variations of the Tiberian system(s) of vocalization and annotation, and some with other systems (e.g., Palestinian and Babylonian); and the SP, with its full spelling and distinctive vocalization tradition—to a coherent approach to the design of a critical text? One cannot produce a single verse without making speculative decisions about how to write the words, since spelling practices changed over time and were never systematized. The decisions necessary are dizzying, and some are philologically impossible.

A principled approach to these difficulties is provided by the concept of a copy-text, which was classically articulated by W. W. Greg in 1950.[35] Greg argued for a practical distinction between the "substantive readings" (i.e., the words or lexemes) of a critical text, which are the prime focus of the textual critic, and the "accidentals" of the text, which are everything else, including features of spelling, punctuation, and so on. He proposed that the editor should choose a good manuscript and follow it, within reason, for the accidentals. The editor should then use the normal procedures of textual criticism to determine the substantive readings of the critical text. The substantive readings are, as it were, instantiated and annotated on the page by means of the accidentals of the copy-text. He writes: "the copy-text should govern (generally) in the matter of accidentals, but ... the choice between substantive readings belongs to the general theory of textual criticism and lies altogether beyond the narrow principle of the copy-text."[36]

Greg proposes this strategy as a practical measure, not a philosophical theory, but he supports his distinction between substantive readings and accidentals with sound text-critical reasoning. He writes:

1886); the full title of Haupt's series is *The Sacred Books of the Old Testament: A Critical Edition of the Hebrew Text, Printed in Colors, with Notes, Prepared by Eminent Biblical Scholars of Europe and America under the Editorial Direction of Paul Haupt* (Baltimore: Johns Hopkins University Press, 1893–1904). Sixteen volumes were completed; for criticisms, see Tov, *Textual Criticism*, 362; and below, ch. 3.

35. W. W. Greg, "The Rationale of Copy-Text," *SBib* 3 (1950–1951): 19–36.

36. Ibid., 26.

> The distinction is not arbitrary or theoretical, but has an immediate bearing on textual criticism, for scribes (or compositors) may in general be expected to react, and experience shows that they generally do react, differently to the two categories. As regards substantive readings their aim may be assumed to be to reproduce exactly those of their copy, though they will doubtless sometimes depart from them accidentally and may even, for one reason or another, do so intentionally: as regards accidentals they will normally follow their own habits or inclination, though they may, for various reasons and to varying degrees, be influenced by their copy.[37]

The distinction between substantive readings and accidentals is amply attested in Hebrew manuscripts and scribal traditions. Scribes implicitly distinguished between the words—which they copied (or miscopied, or occasionally revised) diligently—and the accidentals, which were subject to a much greater degree of change and revision. Hence we see the plethora of spelling practices among the Qumran texts, even among scrolls where the substantives barely differ.

Similarly, among the medieval Masoretic manuscripts the spelling, vocalization, and accentuation differ in each manuscript, while the substantive readings are remarkably stable. Even in the best Masoretic manuscripts, such as A and L, some features of vocalization were never fixed. For example, regarding the fluidity of ḥateph vowels, the Masoretic treatise *Diqduqe ha-Ṭeʿamim* §19 states: "Some scribes, following a valid tradition read ḥateph qameṣ in many places … while others, also following a valid tradition, do not, but there is no (authoritative) source but the preference of the scribes."[38] One imagines the last generation of Masoretes—including Aharon ben Asher, Moshe ben Naphtali, and others—arguing over dinner about textual accidentals (such as the pointing of יששכר),[39] whereas the substantive readings were beyond cavil.

---

37. Ibid., 21.

38. Quoted in Israel Yeivin, *Introduction to the Tiberian Masorah*, trans. E. J. Revell, MasS 5 (Missoula, MT: Scholars Press, 1980), 283. On other variations in Tiberian Masoretic vocalization and notation, see 12–15, 256–63, 282–95.

39. According to the *Sefer ha-Ḥillufim* ("The Book of Variants"), Aharon Ben Asher, Moshe Ben Naphtali, and Moshe Moḥeh (otherwise unknown) vocalized this word differently: יִשָּׂשְׂכָר (implying a *qere perpetuum* יִשָּׂכָר), יִשַּׂשְׂכָר, and יִשְׁשָׂכָר, respectively; see Yeivin, *Introduction*, 138.

In scribal traditions from Qumran to the Tiberian Masoretes, including the Samaritan, Palestinian, and Babylonian scribal traditions, we can document a practical distinction between the treatment of substantive readings and accidentals. Since this distinction is cogent for the Hebrew Bible, we have adopted and adapted it for our design of the critical text.[40] I note that other scholars of Renaissance and modern literature have proposed revisions to Greg's model to accommodate the interplay between authors and compositors in the era of the printing press, but these revisions are not germane for the textual situation of the Hebrew Bible.[41]

In a previous discussion, I wrongly associated the distinction between substantive readings and accidentals with the difference between meaning and presentation. This is too simple.[42] Spelling does not directly affect the meaning of a word, but it does serve to disambiguate its meaning. Vocalization and accentuation also disambiguate meaning and syntax. Since these accidentals are either necessary (spelling) or useful (vocalization and accentuation), the HBCE critical text will use these features from the copy-text and will correct them where appropriate.

The copy-text will be L, our oldest complete manuscript of the Hebrew Bible. Since the accidentals of vocalization and accentuation in L are the product of medieval scribes, our critical text is open to the complaint of anachronism.[43] This complaint is technically correct. But our explicit use of the concept of copy-text requires that the reader be aware of the distinction between substantive readings and accidentals. The copy-text rule is a practical expedient that allows for the possibility of producing a critical

---

40. These clarifications about the copy-text and the substantive/accidental distinction were stimulated by the criticisms of Tigchelaar, "Editing," 53–60.

41. The revisions by Fredson Bowers and G. Thomas Tanselle to Greg's concept of copy-text, which focus on issues of authorial intention, have been aptly criticized by Jerome J. McGann, *A Critique of Modern Textual Criticism* (Charlottesville: University of Virginia Press, 1992), 24–36. In any case, Greg's model is better suited to the textual situation of the Hebrew Bible.

42. See Tigchelaar, "Editing," 55.

43. H. G. M. Williamson, "Do We Need a New Bible? Reflections on the Proposed Oxford Hebrew Bible," *Bib* 90 (2009): 164–67; similarly Adrian Schenker and Philippe Hugo, "Histoire de texte et critique textuelle de l'Ancien Testament dans la recherche récente," in *L'enfance de la Bible hébraïque: L'histoire du texte de l'Ancien Testament à la lumière de recherches récente*, ed. Adrian Schenker and Philippe Hugo, MdB 52 (Geneva: Labor et Fides, 2005), 22–23; and Tigchelaar, "Editing," 59.

text, but it does place a burden on the reader, since the substantives and accidentals must be weighed differently.

There are several ameliorating factors that lessen this dissonance. First, biblical scholars already know that the consonantal text is older than the medieval vocalization system. So a critical text with this overlay is not strange. Second, critical editions in other fields use anachronistic accidentals, including editions of Greek texts (including the New Testament, the LXX, and classical literature) that use rough breathings, accents, punctuation, and miniscule letters, all of which were scribal inventions of the Carolingian era (ninth century CE), roughly contemporary with the Tiberian Masoretes. Third, the phonology of the Tiberian vocalization system is not wholly or even mostly anachronistic.

Scholars have demonstrated that most of the phonetic features of this system accurately represent a reading tradition from the Second Temple period, and many of its features stem from the First Temple period.[44] For instance, many features of Classical Biblical Hebrew that became obsolete during the Second Temple period are accurately preserved, such as the distinction between the infinitive absolute and infinitive construct, the original (preterite) morphology of the converted imperfect in weak roots, the Qal passive verbal stem, and other grammatical forms and constructions. On the other hand, only a few features are arguably medieval, such as the change of the initial short vowel in the nominal pattern *maqtāl > miqtāl (e.g., *madbār > midbār), a feature that does not occur in Babylonian vocalization, earlier Greek and Latin transcriptions, or Samaritan Hebrew.[45] Some Tiberian vocalizations misinterpret biblical forms, such as the vocalization of some qal passives as niphals,[46] or the overabundance

---

44. See James Barr, *Comparative Philology and the Text of the Old Testament* (Oxford: Oxford University Press, 1968), 194–217; and recently Geoffrey Khan, *A Short Introduction to the Tiberian Masoretic Bible and Its Reading Tradition*, GHand (Piscataway, NJ: Gorgias, 2012), 43–62; Jan Joosten, "Textual Developments and Historical Linguistics," in Ausloos, *After Qumran*, 21–31; Jan Joosten, "The Tiberian Vocalization and the Edition of the Hebrew Bible," in *Making the Biblical Text: Textual Studies in the Hebrew and Greek Bible*, ed. Innocent Himbaza, OBO 275 (Fribourg: Academic Press; Göttingen: Vandenhoeck & Ruprecht, 2015), 19–32.

45. Thomas O. Lambdin, "Philippi's Law Reconsidered," in *Biblical and Related Studies Presented to Samuel Iwry*, ed. Ann Kort and Scott Morschauser (Winona Lake, IN: Eisenbrauns, 1985), 138–39.

46. H. L. Ginsberg, "Studies on the Biblical Hebrew Verb: Masoretically Misconstrued Internal Passives," *AJSL* 46 (1929): 53–56; and Jeremy Hughes, "Post-biblical

of definite articles in nouns prefixed by prepositions (*lə* and *bə* vocalized *lā* and *bā*).[47] But the majority of Tiberian vocalizations accurately preserve a very old reading tradition, which provides a useful and in many cases invaluable aid for understanding the words and grammar.

Having presented our rationale for the use of accidentals of the copy-text, I add an important qualification. As Greg advises, "the copy-text should govern (generally) in the matter of accidentals." But the parenthetical "generally" indicates an important caveat: "there is no reason for treating it as sacrosanct."[48] In cases where the accidentals are incorrect, due to scribal error or an incorrect reading tradition, the editor is free to make corrections. In our critical text we will correct the vocalization and accentuation in cases where the meaning of a word or sentence is affected. For instance, if a participle is misvocalized as a finite verb, or a noun misvocalized as a near-homonym, or a I-*yod* verb in the perfect misvocalized as an imperfect,[49] the editor will correct the vocalization in the critical text.[50] However, we will not restore the original morphology of substantive readings where the difference does not affect the meaning—*melek* will not be revocalized as *malk*, nor *Miryām* as *Maryām*. Such changes would be nearly infinite and of no semantic value. In this manner, we maximize the utility of the copy-text rule while allowing for appropriate—and finite—editorial corrections of the accidentals.

A further wrinkle applies to the use of accidentals in cases of multiple editions. If one column represents the hyparchetype of the proto-G edition and the other column the hyparchetype of the proto-M edition, only the proto-M column will have the overlay of the accidentals of vocalization and accentuation. The proto-G column will be a reconstructed consonantal

---

Features of Biblical Hebrew Vocalization," in *Language, Theology, and the Bible: Essays in Honour of James Barr*, ed. Samuel E. Balantine and John Barton (Oxford: Clarendon, 1994), 71–76.

47. James Barr, "'Determination' and the Definite Article in Biblical Hebrew," *JSS* 34 (1989): 325–33.

48. Greg, "Rationale," 30.

49. For examples of such verbal interchanges, see Joosten, "Textual Developments," 23–27.

50. The readings with corrected accidentals are marked with ceiling brackets. This treatment of accidentals revises my discussion in Ronald Hendel, "The Oxford Hebrew Bible: Prologue to a New Critical Edition," *VT* 58 (2008): 35, which limited such changes to the apparatus. Williamson's criticism ("Reflection," 165–66) was helpful in pointing out the logical inconsistency of that procedure.

Hebrew text. The only exception is where vocalization is useful to disambiguate a variant reading, such as where the same consonantal sequence in both columns has a different implicit vocalization in the proto-G edition. In such cases the proto-G form will be minimally vocalized. For instance, זרע may be minimally vocalized זֶרְע in the proto-G column to distinguish it from זְרֹעַ (e.g., 1 Sam 2:31), or יצא minimally vocalized יֹצֵא to clarify that it is a participle (e.g., 1 Sam 1:23). Since this ancient edition never had Masoretic vocalization, it seems strange to clothe it in this dress; but this occasional exception provides useful guidance for the reader.

Generally, where there is only one column of the critical text, all words will be vocalized in the style of the copy-text, including words that are lacking in L. Readings that differ from the copy-text, including differences of accidentals, will be marked by ceiling brackets: ⌈א⌉. This mark also serves to indicate a break in the accentual chain. Minuses in the critical text (vis à vis the copy-text) are marked with empty ceiling brackets: ⌈ ⌉.

In cases of *ketiv-qere*, we adopt the practical—and purely instrumental—rule that the *ketiv* is the copy-text, since it is "written" in the body of the text. The consequence for the design of the critical text is that the *qere* is marked with ceiling brackets when it is the preferred reading and so is the *ketiv* when it is the preferred reading but has a different vocalization than the copy-text (i.e., the *qere* vocalization). Other procedures could be imagined, but this one works passably well.

A final caveat concerns what we call the default rule. There are many cases where it is not possible to reach a compelling textual judgment about the history of the variant readings, that is, which one is most plausibly the archetype and which one is secondary (whether corrupted or revised). In cases where knowledge and evidence fails, the editor must make a decision without the support of a text-critical rationale. What should the editor do? Greg makes a sensible appeal to the copy-text as a default value:

> Suppose that the claims of two readings, one in the copy-text and one in some other authority, appear to be exactly balanced: what then should an editor do? In such a case, while there can be no logical reason for giving preference to the copy-text, in practice, if there is no reason for altering its reading, the obvious thing seems to be to let it stand.[51]

---

51. Greg, "Rationale," 31. This default rule, where the variants are described as "equally plausible as the archetypal reading," should not be confused with Talmon's

In some ways this default rule has a conservative bias, causing the critical text to err in favor of the copy-text rather than other witnesses. But it has the virtue of a consistent procedure and, as Greg adds, "at least saves the trouble of tossing a coin." [52]

In sum, the distinction between substantive readings and accidentals and the concept of a copy-text allow for a principled design of a critical text of the Hebrew Bible. It is not without some surprising features, but it solves many problems that earlier scholars thought to be insuperable.

THE APPARATUS AND TEXT-CRITICAL COMMENTARY

The heart of the edition is the apparatus and commentary. Here the editor presents the evidence and arguments that justify the decisions made in constituting the critical text. The apparatus and commentary accomplish two complementary purposes: (1) to explain these editorial decisions; and (2) to articulate the textual history of the variants, including the scribal motives—whether accidental or deliberate—that gave rise to them. In this sense the critical edition presents a panorama of the history and reception of the biblical text, from its earliest inferable state as a "finished" book through its small and large transformations as an interpreted text, including new editions, linguistic and theological updating, explication and harmonization, and scribal accidents. The random and the purposive are partners in the history of the biblical books. It is the burden of the apparatus and commentary to present and explore the book's reception history in its scribal transmission, from the earliest inferable state to the major manuscripts.

This is a historical, philological, and hermeneutical enterprise, which involves attention to every aspect of the text. It is an intensely detailed form of close reading, which runs along literary and historical axes. Some examples will help to display these layers of inquiry. The following examples are from Gen 1.

1:5 [1]יוֹם M SP G (ἡμέραν)] יומם 4QGen[g] T[OP] (יממא) S (ܐܝܡܡܐ) (explication)

---

theory of "pristine texts"; contra Tov, *Textual Criticism*, 164 n. 20. On Talmon's theory, see below, ch. 2.

52. Greg, "Rationale," 31 n. 18.

The secondary reading יומם is a LBH usage, meaning not "by day" (as it does in CBH) but "daytime." The LBH meaning derives from Aramaic יממא (Joosten 2008: 95–97). This revision disambiguates the meaning of יום ("day"), which can mean a (whole) day or daytime (as in English and other languages). "Daytime" clarifies the obvious contextual sense of [1]יום in 1:5, whereas [2]יום means "(whole) day." The Targums and Peshitta have the same reading in vv. 14, 16, and 18, suggesting a Hebrew parent text with יומם in these verses also (4QGen[g] lacks these portions).

As this entry illustrates, the apparatus line is followed by the commentary, which can be brief or expansive. This design keeps the data and analysis close, thereby demystifying the conventionally cryptic apparatus. The commentary details the relationship between the variants and the exegetical motivation of the revising scribe, who in this case chose to clarify the meaning of יום ("day") by adding a single letter (*mem*), yielding the LBH form יומם ("daytime").[53]

The commentary will also have entries that address other features of the textual history, including translation features (particularly in G) and vocalization. The following, from Gen 1:1, is an example of the latter.

1:1 בְּרֵאשִׁית M vocalizes this word as a construct form. Evidence from some Greek transliterations (βαρησηθ and βαρησειθ, which vary with βρασιθ and βρησιθ) and Samaritan reading tradition (*bārāšit*) may indicate that the determined (absolute) vocalization (בְּרֵאשִׁית) existed in some ancient reading traditions (but see the cautions of Rüterswörden and Warmuth 1993). The absolute form is explicable as a linguistic modernization of an archaic grammatical construction. Notably, the G translation, Ἐν ἀρχῇ, corresponds to the construct vocalization בְּרֵאשִׁית—it would have translated the absolute בְּרֵאשִׁית with the definite article, Ἐν τῇ ἀρχῇ (Wevers 1993: 1). The construct vocalization, which is anomalous in late and postbiblical Hebrew, is best understood as a preservation of the older form and syntax. The updated form—"In the beginning, (God created)"—gave rise to the exegetical inference that Gen 1:1 describes a creation *ex nihilo* (first attested in 2 Macc 7:28).

---

53. This variant is correctly analyzed in George J. Brooke, "The Qumran Scrolls and the Demise of the Distinction Between Higher and Lower Criticism," in *Reading the Dead Sea Scrolls: Essays in Method*, EJL 39 (Atlanta: Society of Biblical Literature, 2013), 4–5.

Entries such as this begin with the word or sequence addressed (in Hebrew, Greek, Aramaic, etc.). Since it is not a matter of variants, there is no prefixed apparatus. In this instance, the issue involves the vocalization and grammatical analysis of a word. The M vocalization here preserves a CBH construction—an asyndetic clause, with a noun phrase in construct with a verb—which was normalized to LBH grammar in some reading traditions, yielding an absolute noun phrase. This revision gave rise to a novel—and influential—interpretation of the verse.

The commentary will demonstrate that textual criticism is not just an esoteric discipline (though it is certainly that) but that it also entails a close reading of the text and its history of reception, which includes literary, linguistic, and theological dimensions. Of course, the registering of scribal errors—*reš/dalet* confusions, dittographies, eye-skips, and so on—is less hermeneutically complex, but it also elucidates the all-too-human history of the text in its inevitable scribal changes.

Notice that the form of the apparatus shows, *in nuce*, the direction of change. The lemma (from the critical text) is to the left of the bracket, and the secondary readings and their explanation(s) are to the right. All the substantive evidence is presented in the apparatus entry. By the convention of *eliminatio*, the testimonies of the minor versions— the Targums (T), the Syriac Peshiṭta (S), and the Latin Vulgate (V)—are explicitly listed only where they differ from M; where they are not listed, they are witnesses to M. By presenting all the substantive evidence and all the relevant arguments, the reader is in a position to evaluate them independently and to reach, where desired, different conclusions. This is a sine qua non for any scholarly apparatus—that it be clear, complete, and refutable.

Preliminary Conclusions

The relationship between the critical text and the apparatus and commentary articulates a theory of a critical edition that differs in many respects from the existing diplomatic editions. The arrow of change that is built into the structure of the apparatus mirrors the relationship between the critical text and the commentary that surrounds it on the page. The idea is to represent the historical changes in the text, from the corrected archetype to the major manuscripts, as a process of development, including the entropy of scribal error and the creative episodes of linguistic, literary, and theological revision.

In the latter, we detect the processes that made the books, as it were, "biblical," that is, sacred, intelligible, and relevant for its readers. This theory of a critical edition follows Eugene Ulrich's proposal that textual criticism should be concerned not only with establishing a better text, but also with the Hebrew Bible's pluriform history:

> The general project labeled "textual criticism of the Hebrew Bible" … must focus on the text of the ancient Hebrew Bible as it was, namely, diachronic and pluriform…. The purpose or function of textual criticism is to reconstruct the history of the texts that eventually became the biblical collection in both its literary growth and its scribal transmission; it is not just to judge individual variants in order to determine which were "superior" or "original."… Late layers or additions often have as much claim to being important tesserae in the biblical mosaic as do "original" or "early" elements of the developed text.[54]

The concept and design of the HBCE are responses to the dynamic textual condition of the biblical books, which expands wave-like from the first edition of a book to its plural textual receptions and elaborations.[55]

We will present the biblical text in a panoramic fashion, with the critical text surrounded by the apparatus and commentary on the scribal changes. Where there are multiple editions, we will present them in parallel columns, so that the emergence of textual plurality becomes available to the reader. The HBCE will not be a static text, but a dynamic representation of the textual history and details of scribal exegesis in each biblical book. The electronic version, the eHBCE, will further advance the representational possibilities.[56] This is our theory of what a critical edition should be. It will not be a perfect edition. But it will be a considerable advance and may stimulate the field of biblical scholarship in unexpected ways.

In his reflections on the (sometimes multiple) critical edition in the *Oxford Shakespeare*, Stephen Greenblatt observes that the "dream of the

---

54. Eugene Ulrich, "Multiple Literary Editions: Reflections toward a Theory of the History of the Biblical Text," in *The Dead Sea Scrolls and the Origins of the Bible*, SDSS (Grand Rapids: Eerdmans, 1999), 114–15.

55. This formulation supplies a theoretical rationale for presenting multiple editions of biblical books, responding in part to Tigchelaar's apt criticism: "this is perhaps the better part of wisdom, but the HBCE offers no theoretical foundation for this choice" ("Editing," 53).

56. See below, ch. 13.

master text," which was the initial stimulus for textual criticism and aimed at transparent access to the author's work, has led to a more chastened and realistic goal:

> Paradoxically, this feverishly renewed, demanding, and passionate editorial project has produced the very opposite of the transparency that was the dream of the master text. The careful weighing of alternative readings, the production of a textual apparatus, the writing of notes and glosses … all make inescapably apparent the fact that we do not have and never will have any direct, unmediated access to Shakespeare's imagination.[57]

In the case of the Hebrew Bible, we are not even dreaming of access to a single author, since the texts are multiauthored and editorially complex. But there is a similar realization of the nontransparency of a critical edition. We cannot have unmediated access to the master text; it is beyond our evidence and our capabilities. The dream of a perfect text is unreal, counterfactual. The best we can do is to make a critically responsible text, a useful and innovative edition, one that takes account of the evidence we have and the acumen we can muster. It will, however, open up a richer understanding of the grounds for its imperfection, which is to say, the complexities of the Hebrew Bible's textual condition. The HBCE does not presume to escape this limitation, but to engage it forthrightly, to make the best of it that we can, and to invite others to continue the work.

---

57. Stephen Greenblatt, "The Dream of the Master Text," in *The Norton Shakespeare, Based on the Oxford Edition: Essential Plays/The Sonnets*, ed. Stephen Greenblatt et al. (New York: Norton, 1997), 71.

2

A RESPONSE TO CRITICISMS

The difficulty is one which lies in the nature of the case, and is inevitable; and the only way to surmount it is just to be a critic.
  —A. E. Housman, "The Application of Thought to Textual Criticism"

As a critical edition project that departs from customary procedure in our field, the HBCE has attracted some detailed criticism. This is entirely proper, since serious debate about evidence, theories, and methods is the lifeblood of critical scholarship. Ideally, such debate is self-correcting, producing ever more precise analyses and yielding richer interpretive practices. We have had the benefit of thoughtful critiques by several scholars, including Emanuel Tov, Hugh Williamson, George Brooke, Eibert Tigchelaar, and Adrian Schenker.[1] Their criticisms have tested our ideas and procedures and in several instances have led our editorial committee to reconsider and improve them. In particular, the design of the critical text and our procedures regarding the copy-text have become more refined. Part of our project's goal is to raise the level of sophistication of text-critical discourse in our field, and such exchanges serve this end.

Some of the criticisms have been addressed in chapter 1, particularly concerning the practical and theoretical distinction between substantive readings and accidentals (including vocalization) and other aspects of the copy-text principle. The other major criticisms by these scholars may be subsumed under the following three headings: (1) the problem of the "original" of a biblical book; (2) the subjectivity of eclectic editions; (3) our limited knowledge of textual history. This division roughly corresponds to issues of theory, method, and evidence. I will address each in turn.

---

1. See ch. 1, notes 23, 30, 43, and 53. On briefer criticisms by biblical scholars who reject textual criticism *toto caelo* (such as David Carr and Brennan Breed, for different theoretical reasons), see below, chs. 6 and 12.

THE PROBLEM OF THE "ORIGINAL" OF A BIBLICAL BOOK

Brooke has argued that the new data from the Qumran biblical scrolls mandate changes in our approach to textual criticism, one of which is "give up the pursuit of the original text."[2] He rightly maintains that "the starting point of the modern discussion of the text should be the artifactual evidence itself," and "the best way to understandings of earlier forms of the text is through paying attention to how each generation of Jewish and Christian traditors of the text has understood and used the text."[3] Certainly we must start with the evidence, including evidence of scribal practices and hermeneutics, which the Qumran scrolls reveal in abundance. However, Brooke then draws an unusual conclusion. Because the Qumran evidence is so complex, he wrongly infers that there is no genealogical relationship among the texts and hence no need to posit an original text for each biblical book. He writes: "Faced with textual diversity in the earliest strata of the textual tell, the search for a pristine Ur-text has to be abandoned."[4] This is an unwarranted response to the textual diversity at Qumran. One might just as well say that faced with the diversity of bird species in the Galapagos Islands, the search for genealogical relationships and common ancestry among these species has to be abandoned. No ornithologist would accept this reasoning, and nor should any textual critic. Diversity of manuscripts and textual families is the normal situation for any scribally transmitted book. The hypothesis that these manuscripts and textual families are genealogically related is a plausible and perhaps necessary explanation for them, as it is for birds. The only other explanation is

---

2. George J. Brooke, "The Qumran Scrolls and the Demise of the Distinction between Higher and Lower Criticism," in *Reading the Dead Sea Scrolls: Essays in Method*, EJL 39 (Atlanta: Society of Biblical Literature, 2013), 7. See similarly Hans Debel, "Rewritten Bible, Variant Literary Editions and Original Text(s): Exploring the Implications of a Pluriform Outlook on the Scriptural Tradition," in *Changes in Scripture: Rewriting and Interpreting Authoritative Traditions in the Second Temple Period*, ed. Hanne von Weissenberg, Juha Pakkala, and Marko Marttila, BZAW 429 (Berlin: de Gruyter, 2011), 71–75; and, with appropriate nuance, James E. Bowley and John C. Reeves, "Rethinking the Concept of 'Bible': Some Theses and Proposals," *Hen* 25 (2003), 3–18; and Gary D. Martin, *Multiple Originals: New Approaches to Hebrew Bible Textual Criticism* (Atlanta: Society of Biblical Literature, 2010).

3. Brooke, "Qumran Scrolls," 8.

4. Ibid., 9.

polygenesis, that is, independent origins for different families of texts—and birds.

Brooke is here relying on Shemaryahu Talmon's theory of "pristine texts and traditions," in which different versions of biblical books or biblical verses derive from independent crystallizations of divergent oral traditions. In his latest presentation of this theory, Talmon argues that biblical literature was primarily oral until the late Persian period, at which time different oral versions of biblical books were committed to writing.[5] He writes: "the process culminating in the practically total substitution of written transmission for oral tradition [occurred] toward the end of the Persian age."[6] His evidence consists of the multiplicity of texts and textual families among the Qumran manuscripts and an erroneous theory about the absence of writing materials before the Persian period. He states: "For committing to writing long literary texts a scribe must have at his disposal large and easily transportable surfaces. There is no tangible evidence to show that such surfaces were in fact available in monarchic let alone the premonarchic era."[7] Based on these inferences and conjectures, he concludes that there cannot have been an original of any biblical book, since their written forms were always divergent: "a hypothesis which postulates the existence of a single Urtext is incompatible with the proposition which assumes the co-currency of 'various pristine texts.' These theories envision diametrically opposed transmission processes of the biblical text."[8] In Talmon's theory, the written texts stem from the multiform processes of oral tradition, hence the search for an original is misplaced.

---

5. Shemaryahu Talmon, "Textual Criticism: The Ancient Versions," in *Text and Canon of the Hebrew Bible: Collected Studies* (Winona Lake, IN: Eisenbrauns, 2010), 392–97. Talmon follows the model of oral tradition and literary history formulated by the Scandinavian school of pentateuchal criticism (Ivan Engnell et al.), which was criticized by Douglas A. Knight, *Rediscovering the Traditions of Israel*, SBLDS 9 (Missoula, MT: Scholars Press, 1975), 383–98, and references. A sophisticated revision of the Scandinavian theory has recently been proposed by David M. Carr, *Writing on the Tablet of the Heart: Origins of Scripture and Literature* (New York: Oxford University Press, 2005); but see the criticisms of his use of oral theory by Frank Polak, "Book, Scribe, and Bard: Oral Discourse and Written Text in Recent Biblical Scholarship," *Prooftexts* 31 (2011): 131–33; and my evaluation below, ch. 6.

6. Talmon, "Textual Criticism," 393.

7. Ibid., 398.

8. Ibid., 415.

Talmon's theory is logically possible, but the evidence weighs against it. Regarding the supposed lack of "large and easily transportable surfaces" (e.g., papyrus or parchment) for writing prior to the Persian period, Talmon misrepresents the material data. The oldest Hebrew inscription on papyrus is a seventh-century letter from Muraba'at, from the Judaean desert near the Dead Sea, where such perishable materials have a chance of surviving.[9] There is also a roughly contemporary papyrus legal document written in Moabite or Edomite, probably also discovered near the Dead Sea.[10] More decisively, we have hundreds of Hebrew seals and bullae from the monarchic period, which were used to sign and seal legal documents written on papyrus or parchment, also used on pottery vessels to indicate ownership. Many bullae (clay seal impressions) preserve impressions of papyrus fibers. The earliest is a collection of fragments of over 170 bullae from the Jerusalem dating to the late ninth and early eighth centuries BCE, probably from the dump of an administrative or commercial center.[11] A later example with a familiar royal name is a late eighth or early seventh century bulla with the inscription: "Belonging to Yehozerah, son of Hilqiyahu, servant of Hizqiyahu [Hezekiah]." The reverse bears the imprint of papyrus fibers and the string that bound the papyrus document.[12] There are many such bullae dating to the latter third of the monarchic period (ca. eighth–sixth centuries BCE).[13] This material evidence for the widespread use of papyrus writing materials is corroborated by the textual evidence in the Bible, which frequently mentions the use of scrolls for legal and literary purposes during this period (e.g., Isa 8:1; Jer 29:1; 32:10, 36; Ezek 2:9–10). Perhaps most intriguing is "the scroll of this law"

---

9. Shmuel Aḥituv, *Echoes from the Past: Hebrew and Cognate Inscriptions from the Biblical Period*, trans. Anson Rainey (Jerusalem: Carta, 2008), 213–15.

10. Ibid., 427–31.

11. Ronny Reich, Eli Shukron, and Omri Lernau, "Recent Discoveries in the City of David, Jerusalem," *IEJ* 57 (2007): 156–57, 161–63.

12. Ruth Hestrin and Michal Dayagi-Mendels, *Inscribed Seals: First Temple Period; Hebrew, Ammonite, Moabite, Phoenician and Aramaic* (Jerusalem: Israel Museum, 1979), 19 (no. 4).

13. See Yair Shoham, "Hebrew Bullae," in *Excavations at the City of David 1978–1985 Directed by Yigal Shiloh Volume 6: Inscriptions*, ed. Donald T. Ariel, Qedem 41 (Jerusalem: Hebrew University Institute of Archaeology, 2000), 29–57; Nahman Avigad, *Hebrew Bullae from the Time of Jeremiah: Remnants of a Burnt Archive* (Jerusalem: Israel Exploration Society, 1986).

(סֵפֶר הַתּוֹרָה הַזֹּאת), referring to a scroll that was arguably a source-text of Deuteronomy (Deut 28:61; similarly 29:20; 30:10; 31:26; and 2 Kgs 22:8).

A more telling criticism of Talmon's theory is that the kinds of variations that exist in the Qumran biblical texts are not indicative of oral traditions. For instance, he argues that "the existence of ancient different 'editions' of biblical books would seem to lend support to the contemporaneous currency of 'pristine' traditions."[14] He takes as an example the different versions of 1 Sam 11 in MT and 4QSam[a]. He argues for "the possibility that 4QSam[a] and MT preserve different primary accounts of Saul's wars against the Ammonites," in which case both are equally pristine crystallizations of oral tradition. He cites the variant at the juncture from chapter 10 to 11:

MT	וַיְהִי כְּמַחֲרִישׁ וַיַּעַל נָחָשׁ הָעַמּוֹנִי וַיִּחַן עַל־יָבֵשׁ גִּלְעָד
4QSam[a]	ויהי כמו חדש ויעל נחש העמוני ויחן על יבש
LXX[B]	ויהי כמו חדש ויעל נחש העמוני ויחן על יבש גלעד (Καὶ ἐγενήθη ὡς μετὰ μῆνα καὶ ἀνέβη Ναας ὁ Αμμανίτης καὶ παρεμβάλλει ἐπὶ Ιαβις Γαλααδ)

There are only two substantive variants here: כמחריש versus כמו חדש and the absence of גלעד in 4QSam[a]. The first variant is easily explicable as the result of a word misdivision and a *resh/dalet* confusion, secondarily filled out with *matres lectionis* (*waw* or *yod*). This kind of variation—which is entirely based on visual confusions—is characteristic of scribally transmitted texts, not oral traditions. The second variant, the absence of the second word in Jabesh-Gilead, is explicable because the scribe of 4QSam[a] accidentally omitted the whole sequence reproduced above and inserted it superlinearly. The omission of this sequence was triggered by a homoioteleuton from the previous "Jabesh-Gilead" to this one. When inserting the missing text, the scribe committed a smaller homoioteleuton by leaving out the word גלעד, which is the last word at the space where the insertion begins.[15]

---

14. Talmon, "Textual Criticism," 406.

15. Frank Moore Cross, Donald W. Parry, and Richard J. Saley, "4QSam[a]," in *Qumran Cave 4.XII: 1–2 Samuel*, ed. Frank Moore Cross, et al., DJD XVII (Oxford: Clarendon, 2005), 65–67. The large plus in 4QSam[a] before this reading is arguably an

We must conclude that both of these variants derive from the vicissitudes of the scribal copying of the book. In each case, a variant has been created by a scribal corruption (i.e., a visual misperception) of a previously existing text. (For our present purpose it does not matter which is the primary and which the secondary reading, though I would argue that the LXX[B] reading preserves the textual archetype.) To posit variant oral traditions that agree in every detail except for these visual miscues is not plausible. In oral prose traditions, the variations are generally more fluid and large-scale, such as those reflected in the many doublets in biblical narrative (e.g., the three wife-sister stories in Genesis; the two stories of the founding of Beersheba; the several type-scenes of meeting the future wife at the well; the two stories of David and Goliath, etc.). The concept of a virtually fixed text, such as evidenced in the example above, is foreign to the compositional techniques of oral traditional literature, particularly in prose narrative.[16] Hence we must regard Talmon's theory as unsupported or falsified by the evidence he cites.

Talmon advances an interesting methodological argument in support of his "pristine texts" model. He states: "We have no objective criteria for deciding which reading is original and which derivative. Therefore both have the same claim to be judged genuine pristine traditions."[17] I will address the issue of subjectivity and objectivity below. But it clearly does not follow that the lack of objective criteria for adjudicating among vari-

---

exegetical expansion, as argued by Alexander Rofé, "The Acts of Nahash according to 4QSam[a]," *IEJ* 32 (1982): 129–33. The telltale details are the unconverted *waw* + perfects (ונתן ... ונקר), which are characteristic of Late Biblical Hebrew; see Zipora Talshir, "Textual Criticism at the Service of Literary Criticism and the Question of an Eclectic Edition of the Hebrew Bible," in *After Qumran: Old and Modern Editions of the Biblical Texts; The Historical Books*, ed. Hans Ausloos, Bénédicte Lemmelijn, and Julio Trebolle Barrera, BETL 246 (Leuven, Peeters 2012), 46–50.

16. See Robert C. Culley, "Oral Tradition and Biblical Studies," *OrT* 1 (1986): 30–65; Ronald Hendel, *The Epic of the Patriarch: The Jacob Cycle and the Narrative Traditions of Canaan and Israel*, HSM 42 (Atlanta: Scholars, 1987); on the oral register of much biblical narrative, see Susan Niditch, *Oral World and the Written Word: Ancient Israelite Literature*, LAI (Louisville: Westminster John Knox, 1996); and Frank Polak, "Style Is More Than the Person: Sociolinguistics, Literary Culture and the Distinction between Written and Oral Narrative," in *Biblical Hebrew: Studies in Chronology and Typology*, ed. Ian Young, JSOTSup 369 (London: T&T Clark, 2003), 38–103; see also Robert S. Kawashima, *Biblical Narrative and the Death of the Rhapsode*, ISBL (Bloomington: Indiana University Press, 2004), 2–16.

17. Talmon, "Textual Criticism," 413.

ants entails that each reading is historically pristine. The impossibility of pure objectivity does not negate the value of textual criticism, which entails the exercise of critical judgment. Talmon, as I have previously observed, confuses the epistemological condition of textual criticism (i.e., the limits of what we can know) with the history and ontology of ancient texts.[18]

Tov has advanced other arguments against Talmon's theory of pristine texts and concludes: "the assumption of multiple pristine texts ... does not constitute a viable model that explains the development of the texts and the relation between the existing differences."[19] However, Tov offers a different argument against the idea of the original of a biblical book. As we have noted above, Tov argues each edition should be regarded as an original of that book. Hence, he maintains that the condition of multiple originals deprives a critical edition of a single original to aim for. He writes:

> There never was an "archetype" or "original text" of most Scripture books. For most biblical books, scholars assume editorial changes over the course of many generations or even several centuries. If this assumption is correct, this development implies that there never was a single text that may be considered *the* original text for textual criticism; rather, we have to assume compositional stages, each of which was meant to be authoritative when competed. Each stage constituted an entity that may be named an "original text."[20]

If each compositional stage is equally original, then, he writes, "we ought to ask ourselves which stage, if any, may be presented as original or archetypal in a modern edition."[21]

Tov's emphasis on the textual and literary autonomy of each edition is salutary,[22] but in my view it is unhelpful to characterize each edition as an "original text." As I stated above, it is sufficient to call each new edition a new edition, as we do for editions of modern books. Any edition may differ considerably from previous editions. (A striking example is Walt Whitman's *Leaves of Grass*, which was issued in roughly nine editions over

---

18. Ronald Hendel, "The Oxford Hebrew Bible: Prologue to a New Critical Edition," *VT* 58 (2008): 341–42.

19. Tov, *Textual Criticim*, 162.

20. Emanuel Tov, "Eclectic Text Editions of Hebrew Scripture," in *The Greek and Hebrew Bible: Collected Essays on the Septuagint*, VTSup 72 (Leiden: Brill, 1999), 125.

21. Ibid.

22. On the complicated issue of textual authority, see above, ch. 1.

the author's lifetime, with major differences among the editions.)[23] Yet there is a textual continuity and a genealogical relationship among a book's editions. The same kind of genealogical relationship arguably exists for the multiple editions of the biblical books. As Tov elsewhere emphasizes: "the great majority of the large-scale differences [i.e., different editions] … in our view were created in a linear way and not as parallel texts."[24] Hence, Tov's objection to the idea of an original text comes down to an issue of terminology that does not affect the genealogical model on which the idea of an original rests. As Tov rightly argues, the idea of an "original composition" that entered into scribal transmission "appear[s] to be correct on a theoretical level, and must therefore be adhered to."[25]

Tov also points to a more practical consequence of the divide between the theoretical models of "original text and editions" versus "multiple pristine texts." He writes:

> For the praxis of textual criticism, in our view one of the two positions should be accepted. Almost all scholars are involved with the evaluation of textual variants, but often they may not be aware that this procedure actually requires the acceptance of the idea of an original text in some form. For those who claim that a certain reading is preferable to another one are actually presupposing an original text, since they claim that the reading better reflects the original composition from the point of view of the language, vocabulary, ideas, or meaning. The very use of such an argument is based on the perception of an original text, since otherwise two or more different readings could have been "equally original" thus negating the need to make a decision.[26]

In other words, the very act of adjudicating among variants logically entails the genealogical model and not the pristine texts model. If one corrects a particular manuscript reading on the basis of another manuscript, or even one MT reading on the basis of another MT reading (e.g., a Samuel reading on the basis of Chronicles, or vice versa), one has already chosen the genealogical model of "original texts and editions" and not "multiple pristine texts."

---

23. See below, ch. 4.
24. Tov, *Textual Criticism*, 165.
25. Ibid., 169.
26. Ibid., 162–63.

Having argued for the theoretical validity of the genealogical model, with its reliance on the idea of an original (or first edition) of a biblical book, I emphasize (as I have done above) that the idea of the original of a biblical book is a problematic concept. It is necessary in theory, but it remains an abstract concept in the absence of the autographs. More important, it is not the goal of a critical edition. The archetype, that is, the manuscript that is latest common ancestor of the extant manuscripts, is the practical goal of textual criticism, not the original. The HBCE critical texts, as stated above, aim to approximate the corrected archetype of a biblical book or, if that is beyond reach, the corrected hyparchetype(s) of one or more textual families. The original is a chimera, a purely abstract goal, which can never be fully achieved. Moreover, we cannot know the extent to which we have achieved it. The original is both historically and epistemologically distinct from the actual goal of a critical text, which involves the archetype.

The distinction between original and archetype—which has long been essential to the genealogical method of textual criticism[27]—is important to acknowledge, because it defines the conditions of possibility of text-critical inquiry. One can "give up" the original text, as Brooke admonishes, but a textual critic cannot give up the archetype as an empirically warranted goal, at least insofar as one grants the actuality of the past. A critical edition is, after all, a genre of historical inquiry, and it derives its validity from the possibility of investigating and reconstituting details that are lost or fragmented in the present.

THE SUBJECTIVITY OF ECLECTIC EDITIONS

A consequence of Brooke's thesis that we should give up the pursuit of an original text is his exhortation: "Resist eclectic editions."[28] He correctly observes that "an eclectic edition is a scholarly invention" that "nowhere existed in any manuscript."[29] An eclectic edition is a genre of scholarly

---

27. See Michael D. Reeve, "Archetypes," 107–17 in *Manuscripts and Methods: Essays on Editing and Transmission* (Rome: Edizioni di storia e letteratura, 2011); Paolo Trovato, *Everything You Always Wanted to Know about Lachmann's Method: A Non-standard Handbook of Genealogical Textual Criticism in the Age of Post-structuralism, Cladistics, and Copy-Text*, Storie e linguaggi 7 (Padua: Libreriauniversitaria, 2014), 13–15, 63–67 and passim.

28. Brooke, "Qumran Scrolls," 13.

29. Ibid.

writing, and it is true that any particular eclectic edition never previously existed. (The same applies to diplomatic editions, which are also scholarly inventions, but which Brooke does not propose that we resist.) However, if an eclectic edition is done well, it approximates a particular manuscript, the archetype, though it also reaches behind the archetype when it detects and corrects its scribal errors. An eclectic edition aims at the earliest inferable textual state of a book, which is an empirical and justifiable goal.

Yet this goal will necessarily be imperfectly achieved. In this respect any critical text can be criticized as never having existed in all its details. But the point of this "scholarly invention" is to come closer to the original literary composition of a book than any of the extant manuscripts or printed editions. It is, in this sense, a work of restoration. It is a textual restoration of a book, comparable to the restoration of a painting by Rembrandt or Michelangelo. The difference is, of course, that a critical edition does not alter the old objects (the manuscripts), but rather provides another object, a restored and annotated text.

We may consider, for example, the value of correcting scribal errors, which is one of the main tasks of an eclectic edition. If there are good text-critical arguments for reading Rhodians (רֹדָנִים) rather than Dodians (דֹדָנִים) in Gen 10:4, then an eclectic edition should print the correct reading in the critical text.[30] In this case a proto-M scribe has committed a simple *resh-dalet* confusion, and there is no good reason to resist correcting this error. Even the methodologically conservative *Editionstechnik* school grants that the correction of scribal errors is a necessary part of text-editing. As Hans Zeller writes: "A textual fault obliges the editor to intervene in the text."[31] If one wants to read a printed edition of a text that is marred with typographical errors, then one does not want to read an eclectic edition. But then one has abandoned textual criticism, which, as A. E. Housman says, is "the science of discovering errors in texts and the art of removing it. That is its definition, that is what the name *denotes*."[32] I

---

30. MT Genesis reads דֹדָנִים, but SP and G read רדנים (Ρόδιοι), as does 1 Chr 1:7; see Ronald Hendel, *The Text of Genesis 1–11: Textual Studies and Critical Edition* (New York: Oxford University Press, 1998), 6–7.

31. Hans Zeller, "A New Approach to the Critical Constitution of Literary Texts," *SBib* 28 (1975): 263.

32. A E. Housman, "The Application of Thought to Textual Criticism," *PCA* 18 (1921): 68, http://tinyurl.com/SBL7010d (italics original).

would say that textual criticism consists of more than this, but it must do this at least.

But even if one grants the validity of correcting scribal errors, scholars have advanced other reasons to eschew eclectic editions. Tov writes: "The idea of producing eclectic (critical) editions is logical and has much to recommend it, but too many theoretical and practical problems stand in our way."[33] The main theoretical problem has to do with the concept of the original text, which I have considered above. This problem is ameliorated if one recognizes that the practical goal of an eclectic edition is the (corrected) archetype, not the original. The more basic problem, in Tov's view, is the subjectivity of eclectic method. He writes:

> [In] an eclectic edition ... the editor thus presents to the readers a personal view of the original text of the book of Genesis or Kings. Needless to say, the reconstruction of such an *Urtext* requires subjective decisions, and if textual scholars indulged their textual acumen, each scholar would create a different *Urtext*. If I were to follow this procedure myself, the *Urtext* I would create this year would differ from one five years hence.[34]

Although I would revise "Urtext" to "corrected archetype," his point is generally valid. There is subjectivity in the production of a critical text, and critical editions—even produced by the same editor—will change over time. What I question is whether this is a valid criticism or simply a response to the corrigibility of any work of historical scholarship.

I submit that Tov's criticism of subjectivity is overstated. The craft of textual criticism is not accurately characterized as "a personal view" or an "indulgence" of acumen. Textual criticism is, of course, not an objective procedure, but one that requires, by definition, critical judgment, κριτικός. To quote E. J. Kenney, "There is no escape from *ratio et res ipsa*, from the commitment of the critic to do what his name implies—to judge, to decide, to discriminate."[35] The absence of transcendental objectivity is the condition of all of our scholarly labors. As William James memorably writes,

---

33. Tov, "Eclectic Text," 131.

34. Emanuel Tov, "The Status of the Masoretic Text in Modern Text Editions of the Hebrew Bible: The Relevance of Canon," in *The Canon Debate*, ed. Lee M. McDonald and James A. Sanders (Peabody, MA: Hendrickson, 2002), 246.

35. E. J. Kenney, *The Classical Text: Aspects of Editing in the Age of the Printed Book*, SCL 44 (Berkeley: University of California Press, 1974), 136, quoting, in part, Richard Bentley.

"The trail of the human serpent is ... over everything."[36] But we can seek to critique our biases and faulty judgments, we can strive *toward* objectivity. This is what critical scholarship means—it entails being careful and self-reflective, and testing our judgments by the metal of cogent method and scholarly debate. This is how Friedrich Nietzsche—a classical philologist by training—defines objectivity:

> "Objectivity"—understood not as "contemplation without interest" (which is a nonsensical absurdity), but as the ability to have one's For and Against *under control*.... The *more* eyes, different eyes we can use to observe a thing, the more complete will our "concept" of this thing, our "objectivity," be.[37]

This is the way of philological scholarship.

Williamson responds similarly to the problem of subjectivity in eclectic editions. He notes that "there is an inevitable subjective element which means that scholars will almost always disagree with one another at this point or that."[38] Regarding the HBCE presentation of critical texts of multiple editions, including Hebrew retroversions from the Greek, he laments "the hazardously hypothetical nature of aspects of this programme."[39] He writes:

> This would be an extremely interesting scholarly exercise, but whether it would be appropriate for an edition calling itself the Bible is something on which opinions could well differ. However secure the retroversion (and the fact that so much is parallel to MT gives the exercise a greater degree of plausibility than might otherwise be the case) it seems questionable to present the results of what is inevitably scholarly acumen in this manner. It is material for commentaries, monographs and articles rather than a Bible text.[40]

---

36. William James, *Pragmatism and Other Writings*, ed. Giles Gunn (New York: Penguin, 2000), 33.

37. Friedrich Nietzsche, *Genealogy of Morals* 3.12; trans. Christoph Cox, *Nietzsche: Naturalism and Interpretation* (Berkeley: University of California Press, 1999), 111–12, emphasis original.

38. Williamson, "Reflections," 171.

39. Ibid., 169.

40. Ibid., 168.

Because of the inevitable subjectivity in such text-critical work, Williamson argues that it should not be presented in a critical edition but in other
scholarly genres where such subjectivity can be better contained. But I
would aver that if textual criticism is worth doing at all, there is no reason
not do it fully, with all the evidence and arguments exposed to critical
evaluation. Why should the eclectic method be practiced only covertly or
piecemeal, in translations, commentaries, articles, and monographs? If it
is legitimate at all, then it should be done with full disclosure. Even if it is
a mere "scholarly exercise" involving "scholarly acumen" (what else could
it be?), there is no reason to hide it away.

In my view, the debate over subjectivity versus objectivity in textual
criticism is misplaced, because it poses a false dichotomy. All of our judgments involve subjectivity. The question ought to be whether a particular
critical judgment is warranted, based on cogent analyses and arguments,
and alert to scribal practices and historical probabilities. As Kenney writes
(echoing Housman), textual criticism is "the art and science of balancing
historical probabilities."[41] The standard cannot be transcendental objectivity, but historical acuity, evidential scope, and explanatory adequacy. That
is the best we can do, until someone else does it better. Scholarship is a
dialogue and a process, a dialectic that involves elements of subjectivity
and objectivity, and that is forever corrigible.

The argument over subjectivity and objectivity in critical editions is
aptly addressed by Thomas Tanselle, a textual critic of English literature:

> In the continual give-and-take of arguments over subjectivity and objec-
> tivity, some scholars naturally take the position that editions presenting
> critical texts are less valuable (if granted any value at all) than editions
> containing facsimile or diplomatic (or computer "hypertext") reproduc-
> tions of texts as they appear in extant documents.... But any attempt to
> argue that they are necessarily superior to critical editions, or indeed
> that they constitute the only legitimate kind of edition, cannot possibly
> succeed. The two kinds must always coexist, for they represent two indis-
> pensable elements in approaching the past: the ordered presentation of
> artifactual evidence, and the creation, from that evidence, of versions
> of past moments that are intended to be more comprehensively faithful
> than the artifacts themselves—random (and perhaps damaged) survi-
> vors as they are.... Critical editions, however, are not merely inevitable;
> they are desirable. A text reconstructed by a person who is immersed in,

---

41. Kenney, *Classical Text*, 146.

> and has thought deeply about, the body of surviving evidence relevant to
> a work, its author, and its time may well teach the rest of us something
> we could not have discovered for ourselves, even if the reconstruction
> can never be definitive—and even if, indeed, it places us in a position to
> criticize its own constitution.... Some people may not be interested in
> reconstructing such events, but their lack of interest cannot render the
> effort invalid.[42]

By "critical editions," Tanselle refers to editions with critical texts, that is,
eclectic editions. There are clear justifications for eclectic editions, just
as there are for other kinds, including diplomatic editions. Each genre of
critical edition has its own distinctive virtues and limitations. An eclectic
edition may not appeal to the taste of some, for whom it involves "hazardously hypothetical" (Williamson's phrase) decisions. Tanselle's point is
that such lack of interest does not invalidate the task of producing eclectic
editions. It may well be that "the two kinds must always coexist, for they
represent two indispensable elements in approaching the past." An eclectic
edition attempts to restore all the recoverable phases of the past, while a
diplomatic edition may present the relevant evidence and invite the reader
to constitute a private "virtual" critical text. These different approaches are
not mutually exclusive, but operate along a range of possible responses to
the complicated condition of scribally transmitted texts.

The debate about eclectic editions is not a new development in biblical
scholarship. New Testament scholarship has its own lively history on this
topic, beginning with Erasmus's eclectic edition of 1516. For the Hebrew
Bible, this issue became prominent in the late nineteenth century, with
the work of Lagarde, Wellhausen, Cornill, and others.[43] A key turn in this
debate occurred in Theodor Nöldeke's review of Wellhausen's *Der Text der
Bücher Samuelis untersucht* (1871). Nöldeke, arguably the greatest Orien-
talist of his day, fulminated against the subjectivity of Wellhausen's eclectic method:

> It is unfortunate that even in this book the critic proceeds in an abso-
> lutely eclectic fashion, so that the decision between two readings often
> wholly depends on subjective judgment.... Wellhausen set his goal to
> reach virtually the original text. But I hope that no one will be tempted
> thereby to put his or anyone else's corrected readings into an edition of

---

42. G. Thomas Tanselle, "Editing without a Copy-Text," *SBib* 47 (1994): 3–5.
43. See below, ch. 3.

the Hebrew text.... A Hebrew edition of the Old Testament should never go beyond the Masoretic text. Because, after all, this is a text that once actually had to be reckoned with.[44]

Nöldeke's critique sets the table for Brooke, Tov, and Williamson: the subjectivity of eclectic method should preclude the production of eclectic editions. The very idea, he says, "provokes a gentle shudder in my philological sensibility" ("welche meinem philologischen Sinn einen gelinden Schauder erregt").[45]

Nöldeke's warning, that "a Hebrew edition of the Old Testament should never go beyond the Masoretic text," was quoted approvingly by Rudolf Kittel in his prolegomena to the *Biblia Hebraica* project. Kittel (like Tov) regarded an eclectic edition as a valid goal in theory but not in practice. Because of the subjectivity of the eclectic method, he argued (like Williamson) that such scholarship should be practiced only in scholarly commentaries and monographs:

> One should collect these pieces in commentaries and handbooks and use them for scholarly purposes, as well as one can depending on the degree of certainty of the respective suggestion: but one cannot produce a text edition of the Old Testament with them. On these points I can only agree with Nöldeke's warning.[46]

Nöldeke's warning continues to reverberate today in the criticisms of eclectic method and eclectic editions.

Adrian Schenker and Philippe Hugo update these arguments by emphasizing the degree of conjecture involved in producing an eclectic edition. They rightly emphasize the degree of uncertainty involved when retroverting Hebrew readings from the LXX, the difficulty of establishing the relationships among variant editions, and the hypothetical status of critical texts of the LXX. They argue, for instance, that reproducing the earlier edition of Jeremiah by retroverting the Hebrew *Vorlage* of the (reconstituted) Old Greek "contains too great a hypothetical proportion for it to be edited like the Hebrew text that is more original. This is the

---

44. Theodor Nöldeke, review of *Der Text der Bücher Samuelis untersucht*, by Julius Wellhausen, *ZWT* (1873): 118.

45. Ibid.

46. Rudolf Kittel, *Über die Notwendigkeit und Möglichkeit einer neuen Ausgabe der hebräischen Bibel: Studien und Erwägungen* (Leipzig: Deichert, 1902), 33.

reason that leads one to think that it is more reasonable to renounce it [i.e., an eclectic edition]."[47] Because of the degree of uncertainty, "it appears wiser to reproduce a concrete historical text—as does *BHK, BHS*, and HUB—rather than establish a critical text."[48] This is a reasonable position, but it relies on a choice of how much uncertainty is too much, not whether uncertainty is permissible in scholarship. I would aver that the degree of conjecture involved in establishing the substantive readings of the earlier edition of Jeremiah is relatively small. As Williamson observes (quoted above), "the fact that so much is parallel to MT gives the exercise a greater degree of plausibility than might otherwise be the case." There is no reason to renounce conjecture and judgment as such in textual criticism, just as there is no justification for disallowing conjectural emendations.[49]

The HBCE has its precursors in the tradition of Wellhausen and other critics. For such scholars an eclectic edition of the Hebrew Bible is a desirable goal, however difficult it may be to accomplish.[50] Wellhausen's diagnosis of the problematic state of textual criticism in his day is illuminating in ours, as is his concept of a richer and more methodologically self-conscious textual criticism:

> In this book I want to make a contribution to a future edition of the Old Testament. Directly, through a series of finished corrections that I submit; indirectly, through the method with which I obtain them. I am compelled to give the method as much weight as the results. It seems to me that textual criticism of the Old Testament is done too sporadically these days. One is content with individual emendations without engag-

---

47. Adrian Schenker and Philippe Hugo, "Histoire de texte et critique textuelle de l'Ancien Testament dans la recherche récente," in *L'enfance de la Bible hébraïque: L'histoire du texte de l'Ancien Testament à la lumière de recherches récente*, ed. Adrian Schenker and Philippe Hugo, MdB 52 (Geneva: Labor et Fides, 2005), 30.

48. Ibid., 27.

49. See further Jan Joosten, "Is There a Place for Conjectures in a Critical Edition of the Hebrew Bible? Reflections in Preparation of a Critical Text of 1 Kings," in *In the Footsteps of Sherlock Holmes: Studies in the Biblical Text in Honour of Anneli Aejmelaeus*, ed. Kristin De Troyer, Timothy M. Law, and Marketta Liljeström, BETL 72 (Leuven: Peeters, 2014), 365–75; and Alexander Rofé, "Emendation by Conjecture of the Masoretic Text" [Hebrew], *Tarbiz* (forthcoming).

50. Cf. the comment of James Barr, review of *Invitation to the Septuagint*, by Karen H. Jobes and Moisés Silva, *RBL* (2002), http://tinyurl.com/SBL7010a: "It may prove for a long time practically difficult to carry out Hendel's plan over the entire Bible, but the principle is an important one."

ing in a coherent assessment of the nature of the transmitted texts—one does not first attempt to learn about the constitution of the patient as a whole, but starts treating him immediately. Due to the nature of the variants, a more comprehensive approach seems worthwhile, especially in the case of the Old Testament, and it bears, especially here, the most rewarding fruit.[51]

The common practice of textual criticism, in his day and ours, consists of ad hoc and desultory emendations of the MT, without the necessary deep knowledge of the textual conditions and history of the biblical book in question. Wellhausen compares this common practice to a doctor who treats a patient's symptom immediately, without first assessing the health and history of the patient as a whole. Such a doctor is guilty of malpractice. One wants a trained and experienced doctor to conduct a full assessment of the patient's condition as a precondition for diagnosis and treatment. The same condition obtains in textual criticism—though, happily, with less dire consequences. Wellhausen advocates an eclectic method based on a detailed and comprehensive approach to a book's textual condition, which will produce more accurate diagnoses. This is the methodological ideal of our project. Each HBCE volume will present—in its introduction and commentary—a full investigation of the textual history and constitution of the book (including the translation techniques, multiple editions, etc.), on which basis judicious decisions can yield, as Wellhausen says, rewarding fruit.

I turn now to some less weighty arguments advanced by Brooke against eclectic editions. He states that such editions "might well lead to ignoring the authoritative text, which the majority of those using the text experience."[52] It is difficult to see how or why this should be so, since the MT is the only fully preserved Hebrew manuscript tradition of the Hebrew Bible and as such will obviously not be displaced by a scholarly edition. Most scholars will use the HBCE and the BHQ side by side, so there is no chance of the MT disappearing even in scholarly circles. Brooke also argues that "eclectic texts should be avoided for the very reason that they minimize the contribution of individual scribes and the specific creative

---

51. Julius Wellhausen, *Der Text der Bücher Samuelis untersucht* (Göttingen: Vandenhoeck & Ruprecht, 1871), iii.

52. Brooke, "Qumran Scrolls," 13.

traditions to which they may severally belong."[53] In my view the opposite is the case. The HBCE highlights the "contribution of individual scribes" and their "creative traditions" in the extensive commentary that surrounds the critical text. The genre of an eclectic edition is arguably an ideal instrument for observing the creative activities of scribes and their hermeneutics, since in this genre they are fully collected and discussed. An eclectic edition articulates the history of readings, such that one can observe the contributions of the scribes. Brooke further claims that "it is ... important to resist eclectic editions of the Hebrew Bible, because it is becoming increasingly evident that each scriptural book has its own complex story to tell."[54] As stated above, an eclectic edition is precisely the place to explore and explain the complex story of each biblical book. This is a reason to embrace such editions, where the complex textual history of the book is a primary focus.

Regarding other aspects of biblical studies, Brooke objects that "the production of eclectic editions ... encourages the continuation of the divorce of text criticism from other more literary approaches to the scriptural text."[55] In my view, once again, the reverse is the case. An eclectic edition highlights the textuality of a book in a way that opens up its plural discursive, interpretive, and historical features, including its earliest reception. As I have elsewhere shown (using the example of 1 Sam 17), the textual condition of biblical books is, when rightly viewed, a stimulus to literary criticism.[56] The increasing sophistication of our knowledge of the Bible's text should serve to break down artificial boundaries in biblical criticism, not reinforce them. In sum, Brooke's fears about the dangers of eclectic editions are unwarranted and may better be reformulated as notable advantages.

OUR LIMITED KNOWLEDGE OF TEXTUAL HISTORY

In the general introduction to BHQ, Schenker argues that the many lacunae in our knowledge of the textual history of the Hebrew Bible are sufficient reason to reject the production of an eclectic text: "not enough is known about the history of the development of the text of the Hebrew Bible and its

---

53. Ibid.

54. Ibid., 14.

55. Ibid.

56. Ronald Hendel, "Plural Texts and Literary Criticism: For Instance, 1 Samuel 17," *Textus* 23 (2007): 97–114.

various textual traditions to give a sound basis for constructing an eclectic text."[57] It is true that there is much we do not know about textual history. Nonetheless, I submit that if the goal is a corrected archetype and not a perfect *Urtext*, then we know enough about textual history to proceed. We are limited by the lacunae in our knowledge: our earliest manuscripts are from the third century BCE, whereas the originals (however one construes their form) of some biblical books are at least two centuries earlier. We can pursue the archetype of the surviving manuscripts, but we do not have the capacity to pursue the original. We can do only what our evidence and method allows us to do, and no more. As with any species of historical inquiry, we are limited by our understanding of the data and the efficacy of our scholarly procedures.

Granting the limits of our knowledge, we have sufficient evidence to correct obvious scribal errors, to adjudicate among variants, to propose responsible conjectures, and to ascertain the historical genealogy of the manuscripts to a reasonable but limited extent. That is to say, we can do textual criticism, even if our results are necessarily provisional and subject to debate. Because of the discovery and study of the Qumran scrolls, we know far more than our predecessors, but our knowledge is still finite. Nonetheless, this is a normal situation in textual criticism of other literatures. As Robert Browning observes regarding the limits of knowledge in classics: "our ignorance of the history of most Greek texts, in particular prose texts, is still abysmal."[58] Yet capable critical editions of Greek prose texts continue to be produced. The situation is not different for the Hebrew Bible. As Timpanaro wisely comments regarding other premodern books:

> The practical exigency remains that certain critical editions not be postponed forever for the sake of studying the history of the tradition in all its smallest details, that scholars not bury themselves so deeply in the study of medieval and Humanist culture that they forget to return to textual criticism.[59]

57. Adrian Schenker et al, *General Introduction and Megilloth*, BHQ 18 (Stuttgart: Deutsche Bibelgesellschaft, 2004), viii.

58. Robert Browning, "Recentiores non deteriores," *BICS* 7 (1960): 11; quoted in Kenney, *Classical Text*, 143.

59. Sebastiano Timpanaro, *The Genesis of Lachmann's Method*, trans. Glenn W. Most (Chicago: University of Chicago Press, 2005), 138.

By the same reasoning, textual critics of the Hebrew Bible should not bury themselves in the historical problems so deeply that they forget to do textual criticism. Specialized studies are necessary prolegomena to the production of critical editions, but there is no reason to postpone the latter until the former are complete. Specialized studies and critical eclectic editions should work in tandem, stimulating each other to greater sophistication.

A practical objection regarding our limited knowledge of textual history is advanced by Tov. He rightly states that an eclectic edition must make decisions on many topics that are not well understood. He writes:

> The creation of an eclectic edition involves the finding of solutions to all issues, including many which one would otherwise delegate to an apparatus. It requires solutions to small and large problems, many of which perhaps cannot be solved. Who can determine whether the text sequence of the Septuagint of Proverbs is preferable to that of the MT? Which chronology, that of the MT, the Samaritan Pentateuch, or the Septuagint, should one prefer in Genesis? In Kings, should one prefer the chronology of the Lucianic text to that of MT? Should we present as original the earlier Septuagint edition of Joshua–Judges, which combines these two books while omitting Judg 1:1–3:11?[60]

These are pertinent questions, which an eclectic edition must address. I would add that these are fascinating and complex issues, which require all the acumen that a textual critic can muster. These are the kinds of puzzles that make textual criticism intellectually challenging and (dare I say) fun, where academic inquiry takes on the color of a Sherlock Holmes mystery.[61]

The solutions adopted in the HBCE are as follows:

(1) Since the textual history of Proverbs is so complex that one cannot in many places restore a plausible archetype, the Proverbs volume (by Michael V. Fox) produces a corrected hyparchetype of the proto-M family in the critical text and fully comments on the hyparchetype of the proto-G

---

60. Tov, "Canon," 246.

61. The comparison with the evidential and inferential procedures of detectives is not idle; see Carlo Ginzburg, *Clues, Myths, and the Historical Method*, trans. John and Anne Tedeschi (Baltimore: Johns Hopkins University Press, 1989), 107–8; and below, ch. 5.

textual family in the commentary, including instances where this branch preserves Hebrew verses that are lacking in the proto-M family.[62]

(2) The Genesis volume (by Ronald Hendel) will reconstruct the archetype of the three editions of the chronology in Gen 5 and 11 in the critical text and will discuss the motives for the scribal revisions in the introduction and the commentary, with full details about the proto-M, Proto-SP, and proto-G editions. I have addressed this topic in previous publications.[63]

(3) In Kings, I have argued that the proto-M chronology should be preferred to the proto-G chronology, which is mostly preserved in the Lucianic text. The variants in the proto-G chronology, as Wellhausen, Gooding, and others have argued, are best construed as the result of a systematic revision, motivated by a local exegetical problem regarding the accession date of Omri.[64] The editors of 1 Kings (Jan Joosten) and 2 Kings (Andrés Piquer Otero) will present the earliest recoverable form of the chronology in the critical text, with the later edition presented in a parallel column and discussed in the commentary.

(4) The Joshua volume (by Leonard Greenspoon and Michaël van der Meer) will present the LXX plus in Josh 24:33*a–b* in a parallel column (in Hebrew retroversion). This plus clearly derives from a Hebrew Vorlage, but it is arguably a secondary expansion, motivated by the exegetical problem of the disappearance of the high priest Phineas in the subsequent narrative. A revising scribe supplied several details: a ceremony for the death of Phineas's father, Eliezer; a summary of Phineas's subsequent career and death; and a transition to the book of Judges in which Israel goes astray after Phineas's death (harmonized with Judg 2:11–13 and, oddly, 3:14). The editors will argue that this plus is not a remnant of an earlier edition

---

62. Michael V. Fox, *Proverbs: An Eclectic Edition with Introduction and Textual Commentary*, HBCE 1 (Atlanta: SBL Press, 2015).

63. Hendel, *Text of Genesis*, 61–80; Ronald Hendel, "A Hasmonean Edition of MT Genesis? The Implications of the Editions of the Chronology in Genesis 5," *HBAI* 1 (2012): 1–17; cf. Emanuel Tov, "The Genealogical Lists in Genesis 5 and 11 in Three Different Versions," in *Textual Criticism of the Hebrew Bible, Qumran, Septuagint: Collected Essays*, VTSup 167 (Leiden: Brill, 2015), 221–38.

64. Ronald Hendel, "The Two Editions of the Royal Chronology in Kings," in *Textual Criticism and Dead Sea Scrolls Studies in Honour of Julio Trebolle Barrera: Florilegium Complutense*, ed. Andrés Piquer Otero and Pablo A. Torijano Morales, JSJSup 157 (Leiden: Brill, 2012), 99–114.

(*pace* A. Rofé and Tov).[65] They will show that this plus is not isolated, but has parallels in G-Josh 6:26, 16:10, 19:47*a*–48*a*, and 21:42*a*–*d*, which are essential in assessing the plus in Josh 24:33*a*–*b*.

These specific answers to Tov's questions should emphasize the kind of work involved in producing the HBCE. We will certainly not solve every problem to everyone's satisfaction. We will rely on the guild of textual critics to point out the flaws in our arguments and to propose more compelling solutions. It will not be a perfect edition, which in any case is hardly thinkable. But it will involve serious efforts to expand our knowledge and to stimulate further work on the most interesting problems of our discipline.

Conclusions

The HBCE, as I have previously stated, will complement the other critical editions of the Hebrew Bible. The BHQ is a diplomatic *editio minor*, the HUB is a diplomatic *editio maior*, and the HBCE will be an eclectic *editio maior*. Each of these critical editions has its distinctive uses and virtues. An eclectic edition does not replace diplomatic editions, but rather sets its sights on a different aim. The HBCE aims to identify and restore the earliest inferable text and the subsequent editions of biblical books. The aim is to represent and discuss the full panorama of textual history, from a book's corrected archetype(s) to the latest scribal changes in the major manuscripts. This is an ambitious goal, which requires wide learning, keen judgment, and considerable effort.

Philology is not a one-way street. As Hindy Najman has recently observed:

> We are free to understand [texts] either backwards or forwards. We may take a retrospective approach, seeking to reconstruct an archetypal text or family of texts, and this is a very valuable pursuit. Or, we may take a prospective approach, studying the interpretive, religious and cultural developments that precede, succeed and intervene in the formation of texts.[66]

---

65. Cf. Alexander Rofé, "The End of the Book of Joshua according to the Septuagint," *Hen* 4 (1982): 17–36; Tov, *Textual Criticism*, 297–98; and Martin Rösel, "The Septuagint-Version of the Book of Joshua," *SJOT* 16 (2002): 17–18.

66. Hindy Najman, "Configuring the Text in Biblical Studies," in *A Teacher for All*

The HBCE aims to provide tools for understanding the Hebrew Bible in both directions—backward to the earliest inferable texts and editions and the imagined worlds of its authors and compilers, and forward to the textual changes, revisions, and interpretations in the early generations of Jewish and biblical culture. A critical edition need not be a prison house of variants; it can also be a productive source for new insights and scholarship, opening up the Bible and its textual life in plural dimensions.

Generations: Essays in Honor of James C. Vanderkam, ed. Eric F. Mason, JSJSup 153 (Leiden: Brill, 2012), 8.

3

THE IDEA OF A CRITICAL EDITION
OF THE HEBREW BIBLE: A GENEALOGY

The real text of the sacred writers does not now (since the originals have been so long lost) lie in any single MS. or edition, but is dispersed in them all.
　　—Richard Bentley, *Remarks upon a Late Discourse of Free-Thinking*

The aim of a critical edition of the Hebrew Bible has become a contested topic in recent years. The three major ongoing projects—BHQ, HUBP, and HBCE—have different aims and procedures, based on their different theories of a critical edition. I have addressed the distinctions among these theories, arguing that it is time to produce an eclectic edition, featuring a critical text and multiple editions, rather than relying solely on diplomatic editions featuring a particular Masoretic manuscript. This theory conforms to the traditional goals of textual criticism in most academic fields, but it is a relative novelty in the field of Hebrew Bible scholarship. The reasons for this situation are varied, including the complexity of the evidence and the intellectual history of our field.

The goals of any critical edition—including the HBCE—are shaped by the long history of scholarly discourse in this field. In the following I will address the key moments in the development of the idea of a critical edition of the Hebrew Bible, beginning in the Renaissance when modern textual criticism was born. The *longue durée* of our discipline will help to situate what is new and what is old in the HBCE project and will also shed light on the criticisms that some scholars have expressed about it, which are similarly a mixture of the new and the old. I will argue that an eclectic edition has long been a theoretical possibility, even if only now, in the post-Qumran era, is it a practical task.

The intellectual space within which this idea became thinkable is a result of historical permutations in the practices of *critica sacra* from the seventeenth through the nineteenth centuries, which have been refined by scholarly debate and research over the last century. With the impetus of the new manuscript discoveries from the Judean desert, it is arguably time to revisit and retheorize the received notions of what constitutes a critical edition of the Hebrew Bible. As Michel Foucault urges, a critical engagement with the genealogy of a practice entails rethinking the possibilities of the present.[1]

As with all such projects, the innovative features of the HBCE make possible a distinctive perspective on its precursors. As Jorge Luis Borges observes, each writer's work redefines its tradition in some measure:

> The word "precursor" is indispensable to the vocabulary of criticism, but one must try to purify it from any connotation of polemic or rivalry. The fact is that each writer *creates* his precursors. His work modifies our conception of the past, as it will modify the future.[2]

The conceptual structure of the HBCE creates a web of genealogical relationships to past work and similarly modifies the possible scope of future work. Hence my characterization of the history of the field will necessarily differ from earlier histories: some features will assume greater importance, some neglected figures will resurface, and the narrative will have its own distinctive plot. This is not to say that the following history will clash with the details in recent histories by Moshe Goshen-Gottstein, Dominique Barthélemy, or Bruno Chiesa (to list the most comprehensive),[3] but it is to say that each project deserves or entails its own intellectual genealogy.

---

1. Michel Foucault, "Nietzsche, Genealogy, History," in *The Foucault Reader*, ed. Paul Rabinow (New York: Pantheon, 1984), 81: "to follow the complex course of descent is to maintain passing events in their proper dispersion; it is to identify the accidents, the minute deviations—or conversely, the complete reversals—the errors, the false appraisals, and the faulty calculations that gave birth to those things that continue to exist and have value for us."

2. Jorge Luis Borges, "Kafka and His Precursors," in *Selected Non-fictions*, trans. Eliot Weinberger (New York: Penguin, 1999), 365, emphasis original.

3. I am particularly indebted to Chiesa, *Filologia storica della Bibbia ebraica*, Studi biblici 135 (Brescia: Paideia, 2000), vol. 2; see also Moshe H. Goshen-Gottstein, "The Textual Criticism of the Old Testament: Rise, Decline, Rebirth," *JBL* 102 (1983): 365–99; and below, nn. 4, 50; Dominique Barthélemy, *Studies in the Text of the Old*

My scope is limited to critical editions that incorporate all the known textual evidence. The history of modern editions of the MT is a different topic, which has been thoroughly treated by Goshen-Gottstein and others.[4]

THE GREAT POLYGLOTS: 1514–1657

The first modern critical editions of the Hebrew Bible were the great polyglots of Alcalá (1514–17), Antwerp (1569–72), Paris (1628–45), and London (1653–57).[5] These were the most ambitious—and costly—scholarly projects of their time. The aims and motivations of these projects were always complicated, involving the interplay of politics, theology, and scholarship. The motives included royal and ecclesiastical prestige, desires to reform the church and to refute heretics, irenic hopes to bridge differences among Christians, and, of course, the aim to return to the sources (the humanist motto, *ad fontes*) of God's word.

The concept of a critical edition changed noticeably from the first to the last of the great polyglots. In these changes we discern the development of the modern idea of the biblical text. They also illustrate the transition from the broad aspirations of the Renaissance humanists to the critical erudition of early modern scholars, what Anthony Grafton and Lisa Jardine call the transition from humanism to the humanities.[6] In this

---

Testament: An Introduction to the Hebrew Old Testament Text Project, trans. Stephen Pisano et al., TCT 3 (Winona Lake, IN: Eisenbrauns, 2012), 2–81; and Richard D. Weis, "'Lower Criticism': Studies in the Masoretic Text and the Ancient Versions of the Old Testament as Means of Textual Criticism," in *Hebrew Bible/Old Testament: The History of Its Interpretation*, ed. Magne Saebø (Göttingen: Vandenhoeck & Ruprecht, 2013), 3.1:346–92.

4. Moshe H. Goshen-Gottstein, "Editions of the Hebrew Bible: Past and Future," in *"Sha'arei Talmon": Studies in the Bible, Qumran, and the Ancient Near East Presented to Shemaryahu Talmon*, ed. Michael Fishbane and Emanuel Tov (Winona Lake, IN: Eisenbrauns, 1992), 221–42; Emanuel Tov, *Textual Criticism of the Hebrew Bible*, 3rd ed. (Minneapolis: Fortress Press, 2012), 70–74, and references; and, among earlier works, Christian D. Ginsburg, *Introduction to the Massoretico-Critical Edition of the Hebrew Bible* (London: Trinitarian Biblical Society, 1897).

5. Adrian Schenker, "The Polyglot Bible of Alcalá 1514–17," in Saebø, *Hebrew Bible/Old Testament*, 2:286–91; and Adrian Schenker, "The Polyglot Bibles of Antwerp, Paris and London: 1568–1658," in Saebo, *Hebrew Bible/Old Testament*, 2:774–84; and below, ch. 13.

6. Anthony Grafton and Lisa Jardine, *From Humanism to the Humanities: Educa-*

transition we see the cultural effects and the conceptual problems raised by textual criticism of the Hebrew Bible.

The first polyglot, the Complutensian Polyglot of Alcalá, was sponsored by Cardinal Francisco Jiménez de Cisneros, one of the most powerful men in Spain: archbishop of Toledo, chancellor of Castile, confessor to Queen Isabella, and head of the Inquisition, among other duties. He also founded the University of Alcalá. The university and the Polyglot were part of Cisneros's plan to purify Christianity in anticipation of the second coming. By disseminating Scripture in the original languages and by producing clergy with the skills to read and interpret them accurately, Cisneros was effectively the first reformer of the age.[7] Cisneros's intentions are expressed in the introduction to the Polyglot:

> Words have their own unique character, and no translation of them, however complete, can entirely express their full meaning. This is especially the case in that language through which the Lord Himself spoke.... And so that every student of Holy Scripture might have at hand the original texts themselves and be able to quench his thirst at the very fountainhead of the water that flows unto life everlasting and not have to content himself with the rivulets alone, we ordered the original languages of Holy Scripture with their translations adjoined ... so that the hitherto dormant study of Holy Scripture may now at last begin to revive.[8]

The goal is that of a Christian humanist, for whom the purification of the church entailed the study of Scripture in its original form. The multiplicity of sources in the Polyglot—MT, LXX, Vulgate, and (for the Pentateuch) Targum Onqelos—was designed to articulate the fuller meanings of Scripture. The Vulgate had pride of place, printed between the MT and the LXX. The differences among the texts could be ascribed to different nuances or emphases by the Holy Spirit, or, alternatively, to textual interference by

---

tion and the Liberal Arts in Fifteenth and Sixteenth-Century Europe (Cambridge: Harvard University Press, 1986).

7. See Richard H. Popkin, "Jewish Christians and Christian Jews in Spain, 1492 and After," Judaism 41 (1992): 255: "Ximines established just about all of the steps of the reformation before the Reformation, and died eight days after Luther posted up his theses."

8. Translated in John C. Olin, Catholic Reform: From Cardinal Ximenes to the Council of Trent, 1495–1563; An Essay with Illustrative Documents and a Brief Study of St. Ignatius Loyola (New York: Fordham University Press, 1990), 62–64.

Jewish and Greek scribes. In this respect, variations were a sign of plenitude or malice.

The Antwerp Polyglot was originally planned to reproduce the Complutensian Polyglot, which quickly became scarce (only six hundred were printed, and a large number were lost in a shipwreck). Its sponsor, King Philip II of Spain, sent his royal librarian, Arias Benito Montano, to lead the project. Montano was a philologist and an antiquarian, what we might call today a cultural historian.[9] He devoted the eighth volume of the Polyglot to a detailed ethnography of the ancient Hebrews, including chapters on geography, architecture, liturgy, weights and measures, body gestures, and chronology. In so doing, he provided a historical context for the biblical text, situating it in an alien place and time.

This act of historical and cultural distancing signals the beginning of a new perspective on the Bible, opening the sense of the biblical text as an ancient artifact that needs to be studied in its own context, not solely as an unmediated expression of the Holy Spirit. As Debora Shuger writes, "the discovery of Jewish antiquities transformed biblical scholarship from a philological to a historical discipline."[10] This is the first step toward historical-critical scholarship, in which modern textual criticism finds its conceptual space. Not surprisingly, this was a contentious move, and the Polyglot nearly failed to get papal approval. After the next papal succession, the Polyglot was placed on the *Index of Forbidden Books* (1607).

The Paris Polyglot includes no scholarly apparatus or appendices, but it is pivotal for the history of textual criticism as the *editiones principes* of the Samaritan Pentateuch and the Syriac Peshiṭta. The editor of the Samaritan text, Jean Morin, published an erudite and polemical book in which he argued that the SP was superior to the MT.[11] Morin correctly argued that the agreements between SP and LXX demonstrate that the latter translated a Hebrew parent text that in many cases diverges from the

---

9. See Zur Shalev, "The Antwerp Polyglot Bible: Maps, Scholarship, and Exegesis," in *Sacred Words and Worlds: Geography, Religion, and Scholarship, 1550–1700*, SLCTI 2 (Leiden: Brill, 2012), 23–72; Theodor W. Dunkelgrün, "The Multiplicity of Scripture: The Confluence of Textual Traditions in the Making of the Antwerp Polyglot Bible (1568–1573)" (PhD diss., University of Chicago, 2012), 262–363.

10. Debora K. Shuger, *The Renaissance Bible: Scholarship, Sacrifice, and Subjectivity*, New Historicism 29 (Berkeley: University of California Press, 1994), 34.

11. Jean Morin, *Exercitationes Ecclesiasticae in Utrumque Samaritanorum Pentateuchum* (Paris: Vitray, 1631).

MT. The argument for the superiority of SP and LXX over MT served an apologetic purpose, since it undermined the claims for the primacy of the MT, which had become an established position for Protestant theologians. Hence Father Morin was able to marshal textual criticism against the heretic Protestant sect.[12]

The ideological war between Protestant and Catholic theologians provided fuel for the claims and counterclaims of textual critics. Contested topics included the antiquity of Masoretic vocalization and the relative merits of the MT, SP, and LXX. In this polemically charged atmosphere, textual variations came increasingly to be construed as contradictions, not as signs of holy plenitude.[13] The drama was now between right and wrong texts, which exemplified and mobilized the ideological war between the right and wrong versions of Christianity. Modern textual criticism of the Hebrew Bible was born in the intellectual trenches of Catholic-Protestant polemics.[14]

The last and greatest of the polyglots was the London Polyglot. Its erudite *Prolegomena*, written by the editor-in-chief, Brian Walton, addressed the principles of textual criticism and the history of the textual witnesses. Walton's project shows subtle changes in the concept of a polyglot edition. The display of the versions side-by-side is both a vision of the word in its plenitude but is now also a means to repair scribal errors. The advertisement for subscriptions to the Polyglot combines these aims:

> The publishing of the Original Text, according the best Copies and Editions, with the most ancient Translations, which have been of greatest Authority in the Church ... are the truest Glasses, to represent the sense

---

12. On Morin's theological and political commitments, see Peter N. Miller, "Making the Paris Polyglot Bible: Humanism and Orientalism in the Early Seventeenth Century," in *Die europäische Gelehrtenrepublik im Zeitalter des Konfessionalismus*, ed. Herbert Jaumann, WF 9 (Wiesbaden: Harrassowitz, 2001), 71–84.

13. Peter N. Miller, "The 'Antiquarianization' of Biblical Scholarship and the London Polyglot Bible (1653–57)," *JHI* 62 (2001): 472: "Polyglot scholarship ... envisioned a Christianity able to accommodate differences of opinion in matters indifferent to faith and morals. Because the publication of the versions, especially side-by-side, made it easier to spot these differences, only those equipped with a suitable theology could remain unruffled by the prospect of such a Bible."

14. See below, ch. 11.

and reading which was then generally received in the Church of Christ, to whose Care the custody of the Scriptures is committed.[15]

Walton then adds the element of criticism: "The comparing of which together hath always been accounted one of the best means to attain the true sense in places doubtful, and to find out and restore the true reading of the Text where any variety appears."

Here is the incipient clash between textual plenitude and textual criticism. Walton writes elsewhere that the value of textual variants is to restore the text to its most correct form: "From comparing languages and exemplars ... one discerns the reading which is most acceptable."[16] Comparison is now preliminary to an act of textual restoration: "By this means we maintain the honour of the Text, and do what we can to prevent any mistakes for the future."[17] Walton maintained the Christian humanist ideal of returning to the sources, but now the sources are historicized: "They serve ... to declare the true sense and meaning of the Scripture, as it was understood *in those times, when they were made.*"[18] The true sense of Scripture is discerned by historical criticism, which at that time meant primarily textual criticism. This perspective unwittingly planted the seed for the obsolescence of the polyglots, since the goal is now to determine the "most acceptable reading," not the plenitude of all the versions.

Walton's project, including a lengthy appendix of variant readings, was vilified by conservative critics. The Puritan divine John Owen accused Walton (who was to become an Anglican Bishop) of villainy and atheism: "Of all the inventions of Satan to draw off the minds of men from the Word of God, this of decrying the authority of the originals seems to me the most pernicious."[19] Owen points to the danger of regarding Scripture as being marred by scribal errors: "If there be this liberty once given that they

---

15. Brian Walton, *A Brief Description of an Edition of the Bible, in the Original Hebr. Samar. and Greek, with the Most Ancient Translations of the Jewish and Christian Churches, viz. The Sept. Greek, Chaldee, Syriack, Aethiopick, Arabick, Persian, etc., and the Latine versions of them all* (London: Norton, 1653).

16. Brian Walton, *The Considerator Considered: Or, a Brief View of Certain Considerations upon the Biblia Polyglotta, the Prolegomena, and Appendix Thereof* (London: Roycroft, 1659), in *Memoirs of the Life and Writings of the Right Rev. Brian Walton*, ed. Henry John Todd (London: Rivington, 1821), 2:165.

17. Ibid., 100.

18. Ibid., 93, emphasis added.

19. John Owen, *Of the Divine Original, Authority, Self-Evidencing Light, and*

may be looked on as corruptions, and amended at the pleasure of men, how we shall be able to stay before we come to the bottom of questioning the whole Scripture, I know not."[20] This is the problem of the potentially corrosive force of historical and textual criticism, once it was unleashed on Sacred Writ. But Walton had no doubt that the erudite scholarship of the Polyglot confirmed the truths of Christian faith.

SACRED CRITICISM: 1650–1800

Walton's advocacy of textual criticism in the London Polyglot was a consequence of the achievement of Louis Cappel's *Critica Sacra*, published in 1650.[21] Cappel's work established the discipline of textual criticism of the Hebrew Bible by judiciously applying the methods of the philological scholarship of his day, as formulated by Joseph Scaliger, Isaac Casaubon, and others.[22] He brought criticism (which at the time referred primarily to textual criticism) into the domain of sacred texts.[23] The concept of *critica sacra* was innovative and controversial, but Cappel executed his task with controlled and abundant erudition. Lengthy chapters on topics such as *De variis lectionibus quae occurrunt circa litteram He* ("Of variant readings that occur around the letter *he*") are as difficult to contest as they are to read. In marshaling a vast array of variant readings, both within the MT and in its relation to other versions, Cappel established the viability and necessity of textual criticism of the Hebrew Bible. As Emanuel Tov writes, "The reader of Cappellus, *Critica Sacra* (1650) is amazed at the level of

---

Power of the Scriptures (Oxford: Hall, 1659), in *The Works of John Owen*, ed. Thomas Russell (London: Baynes, 1826), 4:383.

20. John Owen, *Of the Integrity and Purity of the Hebrew and Greek Text of the Scripture: With Considerations on the Prolegomena and Appendix to the Late Biblia Polyglotta* (Oxford: Hall, 1659), in *Works*, 4:536.

21. Louis Cappel, *Critica Sacra, sive de Variis quae in Sacris Veteris Testamenti Libris Occurrunt Lectionibus Libri Sex* (Paris: Cramoisy, 1650; repr., Halle: Hendel, 1775).

22. See Anthony Grafton, *Joseph Scaliger: A Study in the History of Classical Scholarship*. Vol. 1, *Textual Criticism and Exegesis* (Oxford: Clarendon, 1993); Anthony Grafton and Joanna Weinberg, *"I Have Always Loved the Holy Tongue": Isaac Casaubon, the Jews, and a Forgotten Chapter in Renaissance Scholarship* (Cambridge: Harvard University Press, 2011).

23. See François Laplanche, *L'Écriture, le sacré et l'histoire: Érudits et politiques protestants devant la Bible en France au XVIIe siècle* (Amsterdam: Holland University Press, 1986), 181–327.

knowledge, acumen, and critical insight displayed by this scholar, fore-shadowing all modern analyses."[24]

In the last chapter, Cappel drew together the implications of his analyses. First, the variant readings are attributable, for the most part, to ordinary scribal errors, such as known from other books:

> According to the universal fate and condition of all books, because of human frailty in the transcription of copies, one after another in the long succession of centuries, by men subject to error and fault, a multiplicity of variant readings came into the extant Sacred Codices.[25]

As a solution to the problems of variant readings and corrupted texts, Cappel proposed the production of a new critical edition of the Hebrew Bible:

> In our day, taking note of the variant readings, we could expect and prepare a new and refined edition of the Old Testament, in which are presented the best readings (annotated in the outer margin or at the end of the individual chapters).[26]

The variant readings would be refined, like gold, for the best readings, which would be placed in an apparatus alongside the MT. This is the first call for a diplomatic critical edition of the Hebrew Bible, encompassing data from all the textual witnesses.

Cappel made a further claim that is crucial for text-critical inquiry. He insisted that textual criticism not be subservient to the authority of a single manuscript or manuscript tradition, nor should it be guided by authoritative church doctrines. He insists: "we are not here contending with authority, but with reason."[27] That is to say, the textual critic exercises the task of criticism not by deferring to authority—whether textual

---

24. Tov, *Textual Criticism*, 20.

25. Cappel, *Critica Sacra*, 384: "Sed (quae fuit omnium omnino in universum librorum sors & conditio) humana fragilitate in transcriptione tot exemplariorum, quae alia ex aliis, tam longo tot saeculorum curriculo, descripta sunt ab hominibus errori & lapsui obnoxiis, irrespsisse in Sacros Codices, qui iam exstant."

26. Ibid., 434: "Ex eadem hac nostra de variis lectionibus observatione sperari & adornari posset nova & exquisita Vetus Testamenti editio arque Versio, in quam conferrentur optimae quaeque lectiones (ad marginem e regione, vel in singulorium Capitum calce, annotatae)."

27. Ibid., 396: "Non enim hic auctoritate sed ratione pugnamus."

or institutional—but by constructing reasonable arguments concerning which readings are the best and most suitable in their context, and therefore more likely to be original. The religious authority of the MT (Cappel was a Protestant) has no special purchase in textual criticism. He writes: "the reading that produces better and more sense is preferable, wherever it occurs,"[28] including all the textual sources.

Textual criticism traffics in critical analysis, not in claims of authority. Cappel made a distinction between the content of Scripture, which in his view was divinely inspired, and its textual transmission, which was a wholly human phenomenon. The accumulated errors in the texts are the product of human hands. The necessary remedy is textual criticism, a rational procedure whereby one can repair these accumulated errors and restore the text closer to its pristine state.

Cappel's book caused a scandal, and most of the copies were destroyed by the French Catholic authorities. Catholic and Protestant scholars alike denounced him. Johannes Buxtorf Jr., one of the best Hebraists of the day, wrote a heated rebuttal titled *Anticritica*.[29] He described Cappel's *Critica Sacra* as "the most pestilent poison," since it disturbed the authority of the MT.[30] Buxtorf argued that God cannot have permitted scribal errors to enter the MT. But Cappel's demonstration of the kinds and extent of scribal errors in the MT was too compelling to be refuted by appeal to textual miracles. Religious authority would have to be refashioned to acknowledge the human layer of textual transmission. As Anthony Collins recalled this scandal a generation later:

> What an uproar once there was, as if All were ruin'd and undone, when *Capellus* wrote One Book against the Antiquity of the *Hebrew Points*, and Another for *Various Lections* in the Hebrew Text it self? And yet Time and Experience has cur'd them of those imaginary Fears.... If Religion therefore was true before, though such Various Readings were in

---

28. Ibid., 747 (index): "*Lectio* quae meliorem et commodiorem fundit sensum, praeferenda est, ubicumque illa occurrat." On Cappel's concept of *lectio melior*, see Chiesa, *Filologia*, 362–63.

29. Johannes Buxtorf Jr., *Anticritica: Seu Vindiciae Veritatis Hebraicae* (Basel: Regis, 1653).

30. Ibid. [in *Dedicatio*]: "pestilentissimum Venenum"; quoted in John Sandys-Wunsch, *What Have They Done to the Bible? A History of Modern Biblical Interpretation* (Collegeville, MN: Liturgical Press, 2005), 92.

being; it will be as true and consequently as safe still, though every body sees them.[31]

Cappel established that the manuscripts, during the flux of history, had been subject to human inconstancy and error. He proposed to remove these errors, at least in part, by the production of a "new and refined" critical edition of the Hebrew Bible.

In Richard Simon's masterful *Histoire critique du Vieux Testament* (1678), he seconded Cappel's proposal. He advocated a diplomatic edition of the Hebrew Bible with variant readings in a marginal apparatus. He also proposed a new translation, which would incorporate the best readings in the body of the translation, yielding a translated critical text:

> Nobody can deny but that the Hebrew text is the original, although we have at present none but imperfect copies; and therefore it is necessary to join the ancient translations of the Bible with the Hebrew text, if we intend to restore as well as we can this first original.... Notwithstanding all these difficulties, we ought first of all to establish a Hebrew text, and observe the various readings according to the rules of criticism, as is customary for other books. In the translation these same variations may be translated and put in the margin, and the best reading may be kept for the body of the translation.[32]

Neither Cappel nor Simon attempted to produce such a critical edition. (There are rumors that Simon made a critical French translation of the Pentateuch, but it was never published.) Simon's book was banned, and he was expelled from his Catholic (Oratorian) order. Bishop Bossuet, who was responsible for the ban, declared the book "a mass of impieties and a rampart of freethinking."[33] Another bishop warned, criticism must not "enter the sanctuary of the Sacred Books."[34]

---

31. Anthony Collins, *A Discourse of Free-Thinking, Occasion'd by the Rise and Growth of a Sect call'd Free-Thinkers* (London, 1713), 63–64.

32. Richard Simon, *Histoire critique du Vieux Testament*, 2nd ed. (Rotterdam: Leers, 1685), 353–54; translation adapted from the English translation, *A Critical History of the Old Testament* (London: Davis, 1682), §III.2–3.

33. Quoted in P. J. Lambe, "Biblical Criticism and Censorship in *Ancien Régime* France: The Case of Richard Simon," *HTR* 78 (1985): 156.

34. Antoine Godeau, *Histoire ecclésiastique*, quoted in Benedetto Bravo, "*Critice* in the Sixteenth and Seventeenth Centuries and the Rise of the Notion of Historical Criticism," in *History of Scholarship: A Selection of Papers from the Seminar on the His-

The first scholar to carry out the program advocated by Cappel and Simon was Charles François Houbigant, who published his four-volume *Biblia Hebraica cum Notis Criticis* in 1743–1754.[35] It is an important work, although mostly forgotten today.[36] Many of Houbigant's text-critical analysis and conjectures are now commonplace in biblical scholarship. His diplomatic edition, with variants from the Samaritan Pentateuch in the margin and text-critical commentary following each chapter, was supplemented by a Latin translation that incorporated the results of his text-critical analyses. This was the first critical diplomatic edition of the Hebrew Bible. It had its virtues and faults—the latter include an impressionistic approach to conjectures and an idiosyncratic theory of Hebrew phonology—but it set a new standard for the field.

A critical edition with a critical Hebrew text that diverged from the MT was still unthinkable, but an eclectic translation based on the best readings from the critical edition was now a viable concept. In the following decades, Johann David Michaelis and Alexander Geddes produced multivolume eclectic translations of the Hebrew Bible in German and English, respectively.[37] Most modern translations have followed suit. Recently Tov has questioned the validity of this practice, arguing that it is unnecessarily

---

tory of Scholarship Held Annually at the Warburg Institute, ed. Christopher Ligota and Jean-Louis Quantin (Oxford: Oxford University Press, 2006), 191.

35. The prolegomena and textual notes to these volumes were later published separately: Charles François Houbigant, *Notae Criticae in Universos Veteris Testamenti Libros*, 2 vols. (Frankfurt am Main: Varrentrapp & Wenner, 1777).

36. See John Rogerson, "Charles-François Houbigant: His Background, Work and Importance for Lowth," in *Sacred Conjectures: The Context and Legacy of Robert Lowth and Jean Astruc*, ed. John Jarick, LHBOTS 457 (London: T&T Clark, 2007), 83–92; Mireille Hadas-Lebel, "Le P. Houbigant et la critique textuelle," in *Le siècle des Lumières et la Bible*, ed. Yvon Belavel and Dominique Bourel, BTT 7 (Paris: Beauchesne, 1986), 103–12.

37. Johann David Michaelis, *Deutsche Uebersetzung des Alten Testaments mit Anmerkungen für Ungelehrte*, 13 vols. (Göttingen: Dieterich, 1769–1785); Anthony Geddes, *The Holy Bible, or the Books Accounted Sacred by Jews and Christians; Otherwise Called the Books of the Old and New Covenants: Faithfully Translated from Corrected Texts of the Originals*, 2 vols. (London: Davis, 1792–1797). Geddes's translation comprises the Pentateuch and the Historical Books. On the cultural context of these projects, see Jonathan Sheehan, *The Enlightenment Bible: Translation, Scholarship, Culture* (Princeton: Princeton University Press, 2005), 182–217, 241–47.

subjective.[38] Bertil Albrektson has criticized Tov's argument, noting that it effectively denies the validity of textual criticism.[39]

THE HISTORICAL TURN: 1780–1900

The idea of a critical edition became more deeply rooted in historical issues in the late eighteenth and nineteenth centuries, as one would expect in the age of (mostly) German historicism. The key problem involved determining the historical relationships among the textual witnesses as a prerequisite for evaluating their variant readings. The work of Cappel, Walton, Simon, Houbigant, and others had been based primarily on *emendatio ope codicum* (emendation with the help of manuscripts) and *emendatio ope ingenii* (emendation with the help of ingenuity).[40] What was lacking was a way to elucidate the internal history of the textual evidence, which establishes the conditions for *selectio* and *emendatio*. For instance, if all medieval and early modern Hebrew manuscripts of the Bible derive from a single proto-MT text or textual family, then these variants have little independent value, except as testimony to the history of this textual family. If, on the other hand, the Samaritan Pentateuch belongs to a different textual family than the MT, its readings are of considerable value as potential testimony to the common archetype of MT and SP. The construction of a family tree (stemma) of manuscript relationships serves to determine the possible age and value of the variant readings from these textual witnesses. When it embraces this task, textual criticism becomes a fully historical discipline. As Karl Lachmann stated, "the establishment of a text according to its tradition is a strictly historical undertaking."[41]

---

38. Emanuel Tov, "The Textual Basis of Modern Translations of the Hebrew Bible," in *Hebrew Bible, Greek Bible, and Qumran: Collected Essays*, TSAJ 121 (Tübingen: Mohr Siebeck, 2008), 92–106.

39. Bertil Albrektson, "Masoretic or Mixed: On Choosing a Textual Basis for a Translation of the Hebrew Bible," in *Text, Translation, Theology: Selected Essays on the Hebrew Bible* (Farnham, UK: Ashgate, 2010), 121–34; e.g., 130: "Tov's argument against eclecticism is characterized by a marked reluctance to make textual judgements and choices."

40. See Sebastiano Timpanaro, *The Genesis of Lachmann's Method*, trans. Glenn W. Most (Chicago: University of Chicago Press, 2005), 46–47.

41. Karl Lachmann, *Kleinere Schriften: Zur classischen Philologie* (Berlin: Reimer, 1876), 2:252: "Die Feststellung eines Textes nach Ueberlieferung ist eine streng histo-

The historical turn in the late eighteenth century is exemplified in the text-critical researches of Johann Gottfried Eichhorn, particularly in his monumental *Einleitung in das Alte Testament* (1780–1783).[42] On the basis of Benjamin Kennicott's extensive—but ultimately disappointing—collation of Hebrew Bible manuscripts and editions, Eichhorn inferred that the extant Hebrew texts stem from a single recension. The variants in the medieval MT manuscripts collected by Kennicott were therefore of no value for reaching a pre-MT textual state: "From them alone no one can restore the correct original. The oldest are scarcely 800 years old, and all … follow the Masoretic recension, some with more and some with less accuracy."[43]

The historical relationships among the existing Hebrew texts could now be defined as a single recension or textual family, to be situated alongside the other textual families represented by the SP and the LXX (and its daughter versions). A clearer understanding of the history of these textual groupings would not be possible until the discovery of the biblical texts from Qumran. But in the meantime, Eichhorn had determined the internal affiliations of the existing Hebrew texts.

Eichhorn advocated a more historically and philologically informed critical text, beyond the incomplete efforts of Houbigant, Kennicott, and others:

> The next thing to be done would be to rectify the ancient Bible translators, and to identify with the utmost possible care their differences from our printed text … and after these preliminary labors to test the

---

rische Arbeit"; quoted in E. J. Kenney, *The Classical Text: Aspects of Editing in the Age of the Printed Book*, SCL 44 (Berkeley: University of California Press, 1974), 100.

42. Johann Gottfried *Eichhorn, Einleitung in das Alte Testament*, 1st ed., 3 vols. (Leipzig: Weidmanns, Erben & Reich, *1780–1783*); see the partial translation of the third edition: *Introduction to the Study of the Old Testament*, trans. G. T. Gollop (London: Spottiswoode, 1888). On Eichhorn's contributions, see Chiesa, *Filologia*, 410–15.

43. Eichhorn, *Einleitung*, 2:128–29 (§375): "Zwar wird aus ihnen allein niemand den hebräischen Text zu seiner ursprünglichen Richtigkeit wieder zurück bringen können. Denn die ältesten sollen kaum 800 Jahre haben, und alle … folgen der masorethischen Recension, nur bald mit mehrerer, bald mit wenigerer Genauigkeit." Eichhorn's views were subsequently elaborated by (and sometimes attributed to) E. F. K. Rosenmüller, *Handbuch für die Literatur der biblischen Kritik und Exegese* (Göttingen: Vandenhoeck & Ruprecht, 1797), 1:247.

entire critical apparatus for a decade with critical acumen, as it has been developed in the already established criticism of the New Testament and profane literature. Only after this and not sooner is an edition of the Old Testament to be hoped for, which returns the Hebrew text nearer to its original character.[44]

This was a massive task. The translations, particularly the LXX, needed rectification, that is, critical editions. Only then could a detailed comparison with the MT be undertaken. A few years earlier (1775) textual scholarship of the New Testament had reached a new watershed with the critical edition of J. J. Griesbach, who was Eichhorn's colleague at Jena. Bruce Metzger writes: "For the first time in Germany a scholar ventured to abandon the Textus Receptus at many places and to print the text of the New Testament in the form to which his investigations had brought him."[45] Eichhorn would not go so far, but his appeal to "the already established criticism of the New Testament and of profane literature" shows what the model should be for critical editions of the Hebrew Bible. Eichhorn insisted rightly: "Criticism must therefore exercise its office, if that original form, though not entirely, yet in part is to be restored."[46]

Eichhorn's text-critical plea for the Hebrew Bible went unheeded for decades. Kennicott's and Rossi's massive collations of Hebrew texts, and their disappointing yield, seemed to indicate an impasse. Scholars turned their efforts to other exegetical and historical issues—such as source criticism—for which Eichhorn's *Einleitung* also led the way.[47]

---

44. Ibid., 1:252 (§138): "Zunächst wären nun die alten Bibelübersetzer zu berichtigen, und dann ihre Abweichungen von unserm gedruckten Text mit möglichster Behutsamkeit aufzusuchen … und nach diesen Vorarbeiten der ganze kritische Apparat ein Jahrzehend lang mit kritischem Scharfsinn, der sich in der schon festern Kritik des N.T. und der Profanlitteratur gebildet hätten, zu prüfen.—Hierauf erst, und früher nicht, lässt sich eine Ausgabe des A. T. hoffen, die den Hebräischen Text seiner ursprünglichen Beschaffenheit wieder näher bringt."

45. Bruce M. Metzger and Bart D. Ehrman, *The Text of the New Testament: Its Transmission, Corruption, and Restoration*, 4th ed. (New York: Oxford University Press, 2005), 167.

46. Eichhorn, *Einleitung*, 1:253 (§139): "Die Kritik muss also auch an ihnen ihr Amt verwalten, wenn sie zu derselben, wo nicht gänzlich, doch zum Theil wieder zurückgebracht werden sollen."

47. A minor exception is Johann Jahn, *Biblia Hebraica Digessit, et Graviores Lectionum Varietates Adjecit* (Vienna: Wappler & Beck, 1806). Jahn's edition includes

The historical turn in textual criticism was extended and consolidated by the work of Lachmann and other classical and New Testament scholars in the mid-nineteenth century. The "Lachmann method" emphasized the necessity of establishing the stemmatic relationships among the texts by tracing the history of shared innovations or "indicative errors" (*Leitfehler*). Sebastiano Timpanaro summarizes this methodological insight: "only coincidence in error can indicate the kinship between two manuscripts; coincidence in the correct reading proves *nothing*, since it is a fact of conservation that can also occur in manuscripts unrelated to one another."[48] It is important to add that not all errors qualify as *Leitfehler*. As Paolo Trovato states:

> The only ones that really count are those that do not have an intrinsically high probability of occurring independently of the exemplar—that is, errors that are not polygenetic.... Only monogenetic errors should be used as indicative errors ... to reconstruct a genealogy of the copies known to us.[49]

The power of this genealogical method was illustrated by Paul de Lagarde in his *Anmerkungen zur griechischen Übersetzung der Proverbien* (1863). By approaching the *puncta extraordinaria* and *literae suspensae*—which are shared by all MT manuscripts—as indicative errors (he calls them *Schreibfehler*), he deduced that all these manuscripts descend from a single archetype that contained these scribal marks.[50] (The superlinear dots

---

variants from Kennicott-Rossi and the versions, but does not represent a departure from the procedures of Houbigant, Michaelis, et al.

48. Timpanaro, *Genesis*, 89 n. 18 (italics original).

49. Paolo Trovato, *Everything You Always Wanted to Know about Lachmann's Method: A Non-standard Handbook of Genealogical Textual Criticism in the Age of Post-structuralism, Cladistics, and Copy-Text*, Storie e linguaggi 7 (Padua: Libreriauniversitaria, 2014), 55–56.

50. Lagarde, *Anmerkungen*, 1–2. In his thorough review of the evidence, Moshe H. Goshen-Gottstein concludes that Lagarde was essentially correct, with the proviso that one must allow for the theoretical possibility of an extra-Masoretic "trickle" of variants persisting in the manuscripts: "Hebrew Biblical Manuscripts: Their History and Their Place in the HUBP Edition," in *Qumran and the History of the Biblical Text*, ed. Frank Moore Cross and Shemaryahu Talmon (Cambridge: Harvard University Press, 1975), 82 n. 3: "According to the criteria applied here, the study of the variants—far from overthrowing the Lagardian thesis—comes almost near upholding it.... It is

originally meant "delete," but, ironically, were never deleted.[51]) Lagarde dated this "single exemplar" (*einem einzigen Exemplar*) to the aftermath of the Second Jewish Revolt.[52] In order to go farther back than the MT archetype, it would be necessary to restore the original form of the LXX. To this end, he proposed an eclectic edition of the LXX,[53] on which he toiled for much of his professional career but did not complete.

Lagarde's translation of the Lachmann method into Hebrew Bible/Old Testament studies set a new standard. As Moshe Goshen-Gottstein writes: "he did more than anyone else to lay the foundations of textual criticism of the Bible as a philological discipline."[54] In his *Anmerkungen* Lagarde asserted: "All studies of the Old Testament hover in the wind if they are not based on the most authentic text possible. Scholarship requires more than haphazard and casual remarks: its essence is method."[55] That method, he insisted, is historical, critical, and—not least important—eclectic. He articulated a fundamental thesis: "The manuscripts of the Greek translation of the Old Testament are all either indirectly or directly the result of eclectic activities; therefore whoever is to restore the correct text must likewise be eclectic."[56]

Although he did not explicitly draw out the implication, Lagarde's call for eclectic method applies equally to the Hebrew text. The manuscripts

---

rather for theoretical considerations that one is bound to limit Lagarde's formulation to being only 'almost right.' "

51. On these marks, which are also found in the Qumran scrolls, see Emanuel Tov, *Scribal Practices and Approaches Reflected in the Texts Found in the Judean Desert*, STDJ 54 (Leiden: Brill, 2004), 214–18.

52. Paul de Lagarde, *Materialen zur Kritik und Geschichte des Pentateuchs* (Leipzig: Teubner, 1867), xii. However, Lagarde's arguments for this date are very dubious, including an Arabic legend and an allegation of Jewish falsification of the antediluvian chronology in Genesis 5; see Goshen-Gottstein, "Biblical Manuscripts," 57–58.

53. Lagarde, *Anmerkungen*, 2.

54. Goshen-Gottstein, "Biblical Manuscripts," 55. On Lagarde's repugnant legacy in other works, see Ulrich Sieg, *Germany's Prophet: Paul de Lagarde and the Origins of Modern Antisemitism*, TISEJ (Hanover, NH: Brandeis University Press, 2012).

55. Lagarde, *Anmerkungen*, 3: "Alle untersuchungen aber über das alte testament schweben in der luft, wenn sie nicht auf den möglichst beglaubigten text zurückgehn. die wissenschaft verlangt mehr als einfälle und beiläufige bemerkungen: ihr wesen ist die methode."

56. Ibid.: "Die manuscripte der griechischen übersetzung des alten testaments sind alle entweder unmittelbar oder mittelbar das resultat eines eklektischen verfahrens; darum muss, wer den echten text wiederfinden will, ebenfalls eklektiker sein."

are all directly or indirectly the result of eclectic activities, yielding the expected accretion of scribal errors, explications, and revisions. Whoever attempts to restore the text must likewise adopt eclectic procedures in order to reverse the eclecticism of the manuscripts. Lagarde's argument implies that a Hebrew archetype is inferable from the hyparchetypes of LXX and MT. (Note that his Lachmannian method implies the technical use of "archetype" as the manuscript that is the latest common ancestor of the extant texts.[57])

Julius Wellhausen took up this challenge in *Der Text der Bücher Samuelis untersucht* (1871). He stated his aim to contribute to a new critical eclectic edition of the books of Samuel. His contribution concerned method as well as his particular results. His comments on text-critical method are worth quoting, since they remain pertinent:

> In this book I want to make a contribution to a future edition of the Old Testament. Directly, through a series of finished corrections that I submit; indirectly, through the method with which I obtain them. I am compelled to give the method as much weight as the results. It seems to me that textual criticism of the Old Testament is done too sporadically these days. One is content with individual emendations without engaging in a coherent assessment of the nature of the transmitted texts—one does not first attempt to learn about the constitution of the patient as a whole, but starts treating him immediately. Due to the nature of the variants, a more comprehensive approach seems worthwhile, especially in the case of the Old Testament, and it bears, especially here, the most rewarding fruit. It modifies in specific ways the usual notions of what is an actual change and what is not, what is possible and what is impossible, what is prudent and what is risky, and allows in many cases to conjecture with a certainty—I hope I am not mistaken—that allows the conjecture scarcely to appear as such.[58]

---

57. In his critical edition of Lucretius, Lachmann famously reconstructed the physical characteristics and format of the archetype (e.g., twenty-six lines per page), which explains the properties of the extant manuscripts, but which are not properties of the original. On the distinction between archetype and original, see above, ch. 1.

58. Julius Wellhausen, *Der Text der Bücher Samuelis untersucht* (Göttingen: Vandenhoeck & Ruprecht, 1871), iii: "In dem vorliegenden Buche möchte ich zu einer dereinstigen Ausgabe des Alten Testaments einen Beitrag liefern. Direct, durch eine Reihe fertiger Verbesserungen, die ich vorlege—indirect, durch die Weise wie ich sie gewinne. Ich sehe mich veranlasst, auf die Methode beinah eben so viel Gewicht zu legen als auf die Resultate. Mir scheint, dass man gegenwärtig in der Textkritik des

Wellhausen is here committed to the kind of critical edition that prevails in other fields and, more importantly, to the comprehensive study of the text-critical particulars of a book rather than the customary ad hoc "cure" of individual problems. Wellhausen emphasizes that textual criticism is a discipline with its own methods and procedures and that it requires immersion in all the textual characteristics of a book before one begins to propose solutions.

This model of text-critical method remains cogent today. Moreover, not only the method but also Wellhausen's results have stood the test of time. Kyle McCarter writes: "Wellhausen established the outline of an eclectic text of Samuel which better than any other reconstruction has withstood the influx of new data brought about by subsequent research and discovery"[59]—most consequentially, the fragmentary scrolls of 4QSam[a,b,c], and the reevaluation of the LXX in the light of the scrolls.

The next step was taken by Carl Heinrich Cornill in his critical eclectic edition, *Das Buch des Propheten Ezechiel* (1886). It is a work of immense erudition. Cornill describes his aim:

> I wanted to edit the book of Ezekiel as a trained classical philologist would edit a Greek or Latin writer, and thus make a contribution to the unduly neglected field of *philologia sacra*. The treatment of Old Testament writings has in recent times shifted exclusively to writing commentaries; I wished to show what preparatory work must be undertaken before one may produce a commentary.[60]

A.T. zu sporadisch verfahre. Man begnügt sich mit einzelnen Emendationen, ohne auf eine zusammenhängende Würdigung der Natur des überlieferten Texts einzugehen, man kommt nicht dazu, die Constitution des Patienten erst im Ganzen kennen zu lernen, sondern heilt gleich ungeduldig auf ihn ein. Eine umfassendere Betrachtungsweise ist aber grade im Alten Testament durch die Natur der Varianten nahe gelegt und trägt grade hier die lohnendsten Früchte. Sie modificiert in sehr eigenthümlicher Weise die gewöhnliche Begriffe davon, was überhaupt Aenderung sei und was nicht, was mögliche und was unmögliche, was vorsichtige und was gewagte, und erlaubt in vielen Fällen mit einer Sicherheit—ich hoffe mich nicht zu täuschen—zu conjiciren, welche die Conjectur kaum noch als solche erscheinen lässt."

59. P. K. McCarter Jr., *1 Samuel: A New Translation with Introduction, Notes, and Commentary*, AB 8 (Garden City, NY: Doubleday, 1980), 5.

60. Carl Heinrich Cornill, *Das Buch des Propheten Ezechiel* (Leipzig: Hinrich, 1886), v: "Ich wollte das Buch Ezechiels so bearbeiten, wie ein geschulter klassischer Philologe einen griechischen oder lateinischen Autor edieren würde, und damit einen Beitrag zu der vielfach ungebührlich vernachlässigten Philologia Sacra lief-

There are, however, flaws in Cornill's concept of a critical edition. He reconstructs a text that fluctuates between the finished book (as it entered into textual transmission) and the *ipsissima verba* of the prophet. His extensive reordering and deletion of verses suggests a conflation of the tasks of textual criticism and redaction criticism. Nonetheless, Cornill's edition set a new standard, even if the goal was not fully achieved.

Moshe Goshen-Gottstein's evaluation of Cornill's edition—the first eclectic edition of a book of the Hebrew Bible—captures a sense of the difficulties of his task:

> Not only did Lagarde's *Proverbs* and Wellhausen's *Samuel* stand out as landmarks of a period, but Cornill's commentary on Ezekiel stands out as an almost unique case of a valiant attempt to [produce an edition] ... according to the new Lagardian ideal that full-fledged textual stemmatic analysis—i.e., a full-scale textual evaluation of each source and its manuscript evidence—is the prerequisite for the critical treatment of a biblical book.... The fact that he simply did not have all the tools to carry out what he had undertaken and that no exegete after him ever dared to attempt a similar tour de force—strikes me, in hindsight, as a big question mark at the very start of the new period of exegetical and text-critical sophistication. The triumph of the Wellhausen-Lagarde refinement of procedure contained the seeds of failure."[61]

I differ from Goshen-Gottstein's final diagnosis. The Wellhausen-Lagarde refinement of method and procedure is a major accomplishment, which in the post-Qumran era we have the opportunity to resume and extend further.

Alongside the refinements of the Wellhausen-Lagarde school, another important step in the historical turn of textual criticism was taken by Abraham Geiger in his *Urschrift und Uebersetzungen der Bibel in ihrer Abhangigkeit von der inner Entwickelung des Judenthums* (1857). Geiger cogently argued that many scribal revisions in early biblical texts— "expansions, clarifications ... [and] explanatory schemes"—illustrate the "inner development" of Judaism in the Second Temple period and are

---

ern. Die Behandlungsweise der alttestamentlichen Schriften hat sich in der letzten Zeit zu ausschliesslich auf das Commentarschreiben verlegt: ich wünschte zu zeigen, welche Vorarbeiten vorausgegangen sein müssen, ehe man sich ans Commentieren machen darf."

61. Goshen-Gottstein, "Rise, Decline, Rebirth," 382.

important subjects for historical study.[62] He established that many of the variants in the MT, SP, and LXX are instances of what we now call inner-biblical exegesis. Geiger observes: "What in a later time took place on the basis of exegesis must take place in an earlier time through revision, because the Bible had not yet been firmly closed and sealed."[63] Hence the study of scribal emendations discloses the inner life of the Bible. He wrote in a letter to his son: "Only as a mirror to the entire centuries-long development of a people does it [i.e., the biblical text] become clear, comprehensible."[64]

This is an important step in a fully historicized textual criticism. Variants that are due to scribal exegesis should not be viewed as corruptions to be erased or discarded, but are rather part of the inner history of the biblical text, which a critical edition should savor and elucidate. As Bernard Cerquiglini admonishes, such variants should not be relegated to a "prisonlike" margin.[65] A fully historicized critical edition should highlight the many instances of scribal exegesis and present each book in its multiple early forms.

Many of Geiger's specific arguments about sectarian motivations for scribal variants have been revised or contested.[66] But the cogency of his general position has been confirmed by recent scholarship. As Alexander Rofé restates Geiger's contribution: "the principle aim of biblical text-criticism … is not the recovery of a presumed original text, but rather the pursuit, step by step, of the history of the text."[67] I would add an exegetical

---

62. Abraham Geiger, *Urschrift und Uebersetzungen der Bibel in ihrer Abhangigkeit von der inner Entwickelung des Judenthums* (Breslau: Hainauer, 1857), 72. On Geiger's contribution, see Weis, "Lower Criticism," 351–58; and Chiesa, *Filologia*, 417–19.

63. Geiger, *Urschrift*, 72: "Was jedoch in späterer Zeit auf dem Boden der Exegese geschah, das musste in früherer Zeit, als die Bibel noch nicht fest abgeschlossen war, durch Ueberarbeitung geschehen." Translation adapted from Ken Koltun-Fromm, *Abraham Geiger's Liberal Judaism: Personal Meaning and Religious Authority*, JLC (Bloomington: Indiana University Press, 2006), 47.

64. Quoted in Kolton-Fromm, *Geiger*, 63.

65. Bernard Cerquiglini, *In Praise of the Variant: A Critical History of Philology*, trans. Betsy Wing, Parallax (Baltimore: Johns Hopkins University Press, 1999), 73.

66. See Alexander Rofé, "The Historical Significance of Secondary Readings," in *The Quest for Context and Meaning: Studies in Biblical Intertextuality in Honor of James A. Sanders*, ed. Craig A. Evans and Shemaryahu Talmon, BibInt 28 (Leiden: Brill, 1997), 393–402.

67. Ibid., 402.

note: in order to recover the history of the text, one must have as a touch-stone the earliest recoverable state (i.e., the archetype). Textual criticism aims for a history of readings, extending from the archetype to the extant manuscripts. A historically sophisticated critical edition must present each step of a book's textual history, to the extent that it is recoverable, and not rest on one step alone.

CRITICISMS AND REACTIONS: 1873–1970s

In 1873 Theodor Nöldeke wrote an influential review of Wellhausen's *Text der Bücher Samuelis*, which set the tone for critical editions of the next century. As against Wellhausen's advocacy of a new edition that would incorporate the best readings into the body of the text, Nöldeke rejects the validity of this goal. His argument recapitulates, in some respects, Bux-torf's criticism of Cappel, but with a secularized and historicized twist. At issue is the historicity of the MT, not its theological authority. Nöldeke states: "A Hebrew edition of the Old Testament should never go beyond the Masoretic text. Because, after all, this is a text that once actually had to be reckoned with."[68] The MT manuscripts have a historical facticity that a critical edition cannot claim. An eclectic text would lack the historical authority of lived experience (of having been "reckoned with"), irrespec-tive of its improved textual state. This is an important claim, which is worth examining in detail.

Nöldeke's argument is as follows:

> It is unfortunate that even in this book the critic proceeds in an abso-lutely eclectic fashion, so that the decision between two readings often wholly depends on subjective judgment.... Wellhausen set his goal to reach virtually the original text. But I hope that no one will be tempted thereby to put his or anyone else's corrected readings into an edition of the Hebrew text. I don't share the contempt for the "fashion" that edi-tions first aim at producing a text of a certain time, and I even think that *a Hebrew edition of the Old Testament should never go beyond the Masoretic text. Because, after all, this is a text that once actually had to be reckoned with*; many sure corrections might be applied in details, there is

---

68. Theodor Nöldeke, review of *Der Text der Bücher Samuelis untersucht*, by Julius Wellhausen, *ZWT* (1873): 118: "Eine Ausgabe des hebräischen AT soll nie über den massoretischen Text hinausgehen. Denn das ist doch ein Text, der einmal wirklich gegolten hat."

still much—including much that seems in part totally harmless—which was previously different than now, without us being able to reconstruct the original: the introduction of individual more or less secure corrections into a connected text of a later recension might result in a motley form, which has never even approximately existed, and which provokes a gentle shudder in my philological sensibility. Add to that the uncertainty of much of the original orthography. What exists now as actual studies of such interconnected text recensions are not really suited to invalidate my view that such things cannot be done.[69] (italics added)

Nöldeke's objection concerns Wellhausen's method ("thoroughly eclectic"), the inherent subjectivity of the method ("depends on subjective judgment"), and the resulting critical text, which might combine different recensions and orthographies and therefore yield an unhistorical text ("which has never even approximately existed.") Each of these observations is accurate to some degree. But I submit that they do not preclude the viability of a carefully constructed critical text. The gentle shudder of Nöldeke's philological sensibility is an overreaction to problems that can be solved or contained by the normal procedures of textual criticism.

Let us consider the problem of subjective judgment, which is intrinsic to the eclectic method and to textual criticism generally. Nöldeke's position constitutes a qualified rejection of the *bona fides* of textual criticism,

---

69. Ibid.: "Misslich ist es nun freilich auch bei unserem Buche, dass der Kritiker durchaus eklektisch verfahren muss, so dass die Entscheidung zwischen zwei Lesarten oft ganz dem subjectiven Ermessen anheimfällt.… Wellhausen stellt sich das Ziel, geradezu den ursprünglichsten Text zu erreichen. Doch will ich hoffen, dass sich dadurch noch Niemand verleiten lässt, seine oder ähnliche verbesserte Lesarten in eine Ausgabe des hebräischen Textes zu setzen. Ich theile durchaus nicht die Verachtung für die 'Mode,' bei Ausgaben zunächst Herstellung des Textes einer bestimmen Zeit zur erstreben, und bin sogar der Ansicht, eine Ausgabe des hebräischen A. T. soll nie über den masorethischen Text hinausgehn. Denn das ist doch ein Text, der einmal wirklich gegolten hat; so viel sichre Verbesserungen sich auch im Einzelnen anbringen lassen, sehr Vieles und darunter wohl Manches, was zum Theil ganz unverfänglich aussieht, war früher anders als jetzt, ohne dass wir das Ursprüngliche erschliessen könnten: die Einführung einzelner mehr oder weniger sicherer Verbesserungen in einen zusammenhängenden Text späterer Rezension ergiebt unter allen Umständen eine buntscheckige Gestalt, welche so nie auch nur annähernd existiert hat und welche meinem philologischen Sinn einen gelinden Schauder erregt. Dazu kommt noch die Ungewissheit über Manches in der ursprünglichen Orthographie. Was bis jetzt an wirklichen Versuchen solcher zusammenhängender Textesrecensionen vorliegt, ist auch nicht grade geeignet meine Ansicht von der Unthunlichkeit solcher zu entkräften."

including its procedures, aims, and epistemology. With his exacting standard, Nöldeke would be compelled to object to any critical eclectic edition of any text, including the standard scholarly editions of his time, such as the New Testament, LXX, and all of classical literature.[70] However, it is unlikely that Nöldeke would have gone so far. Yet somehow the Hebrew Bible does not belong to the category of ancient books amenable to textual criticism. Why should it not be treated like the other literatures of antiquity, including the other books of the Christian Bible?

The problem derives, I submit, from an unrealistic standard for the historical objectivity of critical editions of the Hebrew Bible. Here is historicism biting its own tail, establishing a standard of objectivity that no historical endeavor can achieve. Is a perfect reconstitution of the biblical text possible? I agree with Nöldeke that it is not, for more reasons than he adduces. Does this mean that a judicious critical edition, featuring a critical text, is a historical abomination? No more so than any other critical edition of an ancient book. A critical text is a scholarly approximation of the archetype (i.e., the latest common ancestor), which may also approximate the original text of the book. But, by the very condition of textual scholarship, it is not a perfect reconstitution of the original. To expect the latter is unwarranted—it is to confuse scholarship with divination. The textual critic is not in the same position as the legendary translators of the LXX (according to the accounts of Pseudo-Aristeas and Philo), whose every word was perfect.

The procedures of textual criticism, and the standards to which it should be held, are those of historical scholarship. As Lachmann, Lagarde, and others clarified, textual criticism is a historical discipline. As such, its epistemological scope is limited to probabilities, not certainties. Marc Bloch clearly describes this condition of historical inquiry:

> To what extent, however, are we justified in mouthing this glorious word "certainty"? Mabillon, long ago, admitted that the criticism of charters could not attain "metaphysical" certainty. He was quite right. It is only for the sake of simplification that we sometimes speak of evidence rather than of probabilities.... So far as it finds certainty only by estimating the

---

70. Note that the first volume of Lagarde's eclectic edition of the Septuagint had already been issued—*Genesis Graece* (Leipzig: Teubner, 1868)—as had eclectic editions of the New Testament by Lachmann (1831) and Tischendorf (1869–1872).

probable and the improbable, historical criticism is like most other sciences of reality.[71]

Such is also the condition of textual criticism. As E. J. Kenney states: "Textual criticism, then, must be approached and viewed as the art and science of balancing historical probabilities."[72] This can be done well or poorly, but even when done exceedingly well—as Wellhausen on Samuel—it is necessarily fallible and incomplete. This is why the procedures of textual scholarship include review, criticism, debate—the normal discursive practices of scholarship, which (ideally) produce a self-correcting body of knowledge about how best to interpret the data. Informed judgment is, by definition and necessity, the task of the critic. If one's standard is higher than historical scholarship can yield—or beyond what human labor can achieve—then one must choose to settle for a particular manuscript or printed edition, and one must eschew textual criticism. Paul Maas extends this caveat further: "Anyone who is afraid of ... an uncertain text had best confine himself to dealing with autograph manuscripts."[73]

The Italian critic Gianfranco Contini aptly describes the provisional status of a critical edition: "a critical edition is, like any other scientific act, a mere working hypothesis, the most satisfactory, namely, the most economic one, and one which proves apt to connect a system of data."[74] A critical edition differs from a scientific model in that it is difficult to test or falsify, short of new manuscript discoveries (such as the Dead Sea Scrolls, which have allowed some of Wellhausen's proposals about Samuel to be tested).

Nöldeke's aversion to "subjective judgment" may therefore be countered by a more adequate understanding of the theoretical and practical conditions of textual criticism. His fear of the mixing of different recensions is a different matter. This fear is wholly justified, as in cases where a scholar will "correct" an early edition of a text by substituting a later editorial expansion. This does indeed constitute a text-critical abomination,

---

71. Marc Bloch, *The Historian's Craft*, trans. Peter Putnam (New York: Vintage, 1953), 133.

72. Kenney, *Classical Text*, 146.

73. Paul Maas, *Textual Criticism*, trans. Barbara Flower (Oxford: Clarendon, 1958), 17.

74. Translated in Paola Pugliatti, "Textual Perspectives in Italy: From Pasquali's Historicism to the Challenge of 'Variantistica' (and Beyond)," *Text* 11 (1998): 163.

a *sha'atnez*. But this problem does not preclude the production of viable critical texts. We must distinguish between textual editions and between good and bad scholarship. The existence of error does not constitute an argument against the possibility and advantages of textual scholarship, including well-conceived critical texts.

Despite these flaws, what Chiesa calls the "*diktat* of Nöldeke" has held sway for over a century.[75] Rudolf Kittel relied on Nöldeke's rejection of the validity of a critical eclectic edition in his prolegomena to a new edition, *Über die Notwendigkeit und Möglichkeit einer neuen Ausgabe der hebräischen Bibel* (1902). Kittel had previously participated in Paul Haupt's project, *The Sacred Books of the Old Testament*—more popularly known as *The Polychrome Bible*—which was planned as a new English translation with indications of the original sources, but which secondarily also produced critical Hebrew texts.[76] Kittel produced the volume on Chronicles in 1895.[77] He repudiated this project in his later study, quoting and expanding Nöldeke's critique. Building on Nöldeke's rhetoric of the "motley form" (*buntscheckige Gestalt*) of an eclectic edition, Kittel conjures the metaphor of a garment sewn of old rags:

> It is not possible to produce a consistent form of the text from individual, but basically not very numerous cases, in which the conjecture gives us an idea of greater or lesser probability of the author's opinion. A number of old rags, which might be original but with varying probabilities, do not constitute the genuine old garment, even if they are artfully sewn on a new garment which looks similar to the old one. One should collect these pieces in commentaries and handbooks and use them for scholarly purposes, as well as one can depending on the degree of certainty of the respective suggestion: but one cannot produce a text edition of the Old Testament with them. On these points I can only agree with Nöldeke's warning.[78]

---

75. Chiesa, *Filologia*, 426.

76. See Carl Heinrich Cornill, "The Polychrome Bible," *The Monist* 10 (October, 1899): 3: "Originally the work was intended to be only a new translation with brief commentary on the matter; the publication of the Hebrew text, which has appeared first, is due to an American gentleman who placed the necessary means at Professor Haupt's disposal."

77. Rudolf Kittel, *The Books of Chronicles: Critical Edition of the Hebrew Text Printed in Colors Exhibiting the Composite Structure of the Book*, SBOT 20 (Baltimore: Johns Hopkins University Press, 1895).

78. Rudolf Kittel, *Über die Notwendigkeit und Möglichkeit einer neuen Ausgabe*

Although Kittel grants that an eclectic critical text is the ideal goal of textual criticism, he argues that the only practical and achievable goal is to reprint the *textus receptus* and list variants and emendations in the margin or footnotes. This approach is conservative in several senses: it conserves the MT in all its important details, it stays with an old model of critical editions, and it resists the innovations of the Lagarde-Wellhausen method. Kittel writes:

> The frequently subjective character of any new production of the text makes it appear very advisable to refer all changes to the margin, for example in the form of footnotes, and in the text itself to present the Masoretic *textus receptus*. Obviously, in this way the objective and lasting value of this text as a historically transmitted entity most clearly comes into its own.[79]

Kittel argued, following Nöldeke, that a critical edition should attend only to the MT edition of biblical books. He states: "the tradition of the synagogue was completely right when it preferred the text-form from which the MT grew over all the other previous peripheral recensions of the Hebrew Bible, including that of the Alexandrian translator."[80] While

---

der hebräischen Bibel: Studien und Erwägungen (Leipzig: Deichert, 1902), 33: "Aber aus einzelnen, im Grunde nicht sehr zahlreichen, Fällen, in denen die Konjektur uns des Verfassers Meinung mit grösserer oder geringer Wahrscheinlichkeit erraten lässt, Lässt sich keine einheitliche Textgestalt herstellen. Eine Anzahl alter, vielleicht und mit abgestufter Wahrscheinlichkeit dem ursprünglichen Kleide angehöriger Lappen, auch wenn sie Kunstgerecht auf ein neues, dem alten ähnlich sehendes, Gewand genäht sind, stellen noch nicht das ächte alte Kleid dar. Man sammle diese Stücke in Kommentaren und Handbüchern und verwerte sie zu wissenschaftlichen Zwecken, so gut man es nach dem Grade der Sicherheit vermag, den die betreffende Vermutung ansprechen kann; aber eine Textausgabe des Alten Testamentes ist mit ihnen nicht zu gewinnen. In diese Punkte kann ich der Warnung Nöldekes nur beistimmen."

79. Ibid., 77: "Der vielfach subjective Character jeder Neugestaltung des Texts wird es Vielen empfehlenswert erscheinen lassen, alle Änderungen an den Rand, etwa in der Form von Fussnoten, zu verweisen und im Texts selbst den massoretischen textus receptus darzubieten. Auf diese Weise käme selbstverständlich der objective und bleibende Wert dieses Textes als seiner historisch überlieferten Grösse am deutlichsten zur Geltung."

80. Ibid., 46: "Die Tradition der Synagoge vollkommen im Rechte war, wenn sie jene Textgestalt, aus der MT herausgewachsen ist, allen anderen ehedem umlaufenden Rezensionen der hebräischen Bibel, so auch derjenigen der alexandrinischen Übersetzer, vorzog."

this position may be "completely right" for synagogues, it is difficult to defend as a coherent decision for textual criticism. One can argue, as has Dominique Barthélemy, that the goal of textual criticism is to establish a canonical text, but this is at best a partial—and perhaps eccentric—goal for textual criticism (see below). Kittel's decisions—to exclude other editions, to banish textual judgment to the margins, and to propose that such judgment properly belongs in scholarly monographs or handbooks, not in critical editions—had the effect of consigning textual criticism to the margins of biblical scholarship.

Kittel's concept of a critical edition also raises an obvious question: Why juxtapose an eclectic apparatus with the *textus receptus*? Is this not an inconsistent halfway measure? When Johann Bengel printed the New Testament *textus receptus* with a critical apparatus in 1734, it was an important step, but his contemporary, Johann Wettstein, complained that this decision was aimed "to evade all scandal and satisfy infirm consciences."[81] As Jonathan Sheehan observes:

> The division between text and apparatus provides a space for a contained textual criticism. Bengel's work was a prime example here, where the apparatus held revolutionary implications for the text, but where the division between the two was rigorously maintained.[82]

James Barr made a similar criticism of Kittel's *Biblical Hebraica* series:

> [The] editing of the text of the Hebrew Bible has had something of the schizophrenic about it. In printing the text the aim has been the faithful reproduction of the Massoretic original taken as model; in the apparatus (or apparatuses, since the kinds of evidence may have to be separated out) the editor betrays his awareness that the text he has printed may be very remote from that which was written by the biblical writer.... Might it not therefore be better to seek to print the text that the editor thinks is the farthest back that the evidence can reach?[83]

---

81. Quoted in Sheehan, *Enlightenment*, 109.
82. Ibid., 108.
83. James Barr, "The Nature of Linguistic Evidence in the Text of the Bible," in *Language and Texts: The Nature of Linguistic Evidence*, ed. H. H. Paper (Ann Arbor: Center for the Coordination of Ancient and Modern Studies, 1975), 54.

Barr extended this criticism in a later review of the *Bibla Hebraica Stuttgartensia*:

> The effect of *BHS* is above all to reveal the deep contradictions underlying the purposes served by current critical editions of the Hebrew Bible.... It is not clear that we can continue for ever with a procedure where important ancient witnesses are displayed only as marginal annotations to the MT.[84]

As Barr's comments indicate, the critical mood was shifting, largely due the renewal of textual criticism in the wake of the manuscript discoveries from the Dead Sea.

AFTER QUMRAN: 1970s–PRESENT

I will be briefer about this period, since there are several excellent surveys and retrospectives.[85] By the late 1970s and early 1980s a new era of textual criticism of the Hebrew Bible was at hand. Biblical manuscripts more than a millennium older than our oldest MT manuscripts were published, enabling a reassessment of the history of the biblical text and an analysis of the genealogical relationships among the previously existing texts (i.e., MT, LXX, SP, etc.). Moreover, there were now important new tools for textual criticism, including new volumes of the Göttingen LXX—a critical eclectic edition, following Lagarde's prescription—and other critical editions existing or in progress for the Peshitta, Vulgate, and other versions. Tov's monograph, *The Text-Critical Use of the Septuagint* appeared in 1981, which taught a new generation how to use the LXX critically and responsibly.

---

84. James Barr, review of *Biblia Hebraica Stuttgartensia*, ed. Karl Elliger and Wilhelm Rudolph, *JSS* 25 (1980): 104–5.

85. See Arie van der Kooij, "The Textual Criticism of the Hebrew Bible before and after the Qumran Discoveries," in *The Bible as Book: The Hebrew Bible and the Judaean Desert Discoveries*, ed. Edward D. Herbert and Emanuel Tov (London: British Library, 2002); Emanuel Tov, "Textual Criticism of the Hebrew Bible 1947–1997," in *Perspectives in the Study of the Old Testament and Early Judaism: A Symposium on Honour of Adam S. van der Woude on the Occasion of His 70th Birthday*, ed. Florentino García Martínez and Ed Noort, VTSup 73 (Leiden: Brill, 1998); Chiesa, *Filologia*, 429–41.

In 1979 Frank Cross, one of the scrolls editors, called for a change in critical practices based on the new state of affairs. He called for a return to the eclectic critical method of the Lagarde-Wellhausen school, as had already been adumbrated by Barr:

> The existence of identifiable textual families makes possible genuine progress in establishing an eclectic text, progress on the way to establishing a text of biblical works closer to their archetypes.... The sole way to improve a text, to ferret out error, is to trace the history of readings, to determine an archetype which explains or makes transparent the introduction of error or corruption. There is and will be resistance to "eclectic" methods. The prestige of the *textus receptus* is formidable. Probably a greater obstacle is the inertia which slows scholars from changing methods and perspectives in which they were trained and which have grown habitual in their scholarly practice. The potentialities for progress in the new discoveries will be fully realized only in a new generation of textual critics. Even in major text-critical projects of relatively recent date [i.e., the HUBP], we note the persistence of an older perspective.... Many barriers hindering the practice of a genuine eclectic criticism have fallen in our day, and new opportunities may be seized.[86]

As post-Qumran textual scholarship expanded, more scholars would question the status quo and call for a return to the genealogical method, entailing the production of fully critical eclectic editions. The Italian school of biblical scholars began to produce such editions: Giorgio Borbone on Hosea, Alessandro Catastini on Gen 37–50; Giorgio Garbini on Song of Songs. Other eclectic critical editions appeared: Anthony Gelston's edition of Isa 52–53; my edition of Gen 1–11; Kjell Hognesius's edition of 2 Chr 1–16. [87] The concept of a fully critical edition, featuring a critical biblical text, was making inroads. It was now a concept that was thinkable

---

86. Frank Moore Cross, "Problems of Method in the Textual Criticism of the Hebrew Bible," in *The Critical Study of Sacred Texts*, ed. Wendy Doniger O'Flaherty, BRSS 2 (Berkeley: Graduate Theological Union, 1979), 50, 54.

87. Pier G. Borbone, *Il libro del profeta Osea: Edizione critica del testo ebraico*, QHenoch 2 (Turin: Zamorani, 1990); Alessandro Catastini, *Storia di Giuseppe (Genesi 37–50)* (Venice: Marsilio, 1994); Giovanni Garbini, *Il Cantico dei Cantici: Testo, traduzione note e commento* (Brescia: Paideia, 1992); Anthony Gelston, "Isaiah 52:13–53:12: An Eclectic Text and a Supplementary Note on the Hebrew Manuscript Kennicott 96," *JSS* 35 (1990): 187–211; Ronald Hendel, *The Text of Genesis 1–11: Textual Studies and Critical Edition* (New York: Oxford University Press, 1998); Kjell Hognesius, *The Text*

by textual critics and was beginning to become a real, if to some unsettling, practice.

In the 1980s, Dominique Barthélemy injected a new twist to the concept of a critical edition—the criterion of canon.[88] This is comparable to some exegetical moves by Brevard Childs and others at the time but has some unique features. In the course of deliberations on a new edition in the *Biblia Hebraica* series, Barthélemy argued that a critical edition should aim to produce not the final literary form of a book but a later text-form, the oldest canonical form. The task of a critical edition, he writes, should be "to determine the text of the Holy Bible; that is, to produce the oldest literary form which can be proved to have functioned as a sacred book within a community."[89] The production of such an edition would diverge from the customary practices of textual criticism. In cases where a corrupt text can be shown to have been canonical, the edition would not correct those corruptions: "The [Hebrew Old Testament Project] committee ... preferred to retain that corrupt form which attests to the earliest age in which the writing can be shown to have been read as sacred Scripture."[90] On the basis of these canonical considerations, Barthélemy argued later that textual criticism should aim primarily to reconstitute "the canonical state fixed between the two revolts against Rome,"[91] in other words, the hyparchetype of MT as it existed in the late first and early second century CE. Barthélemy's project essentially aimed to restore the biblical text-type known from the Judean desert sites of Masada, Murabba'at, Naḥal Ḥever, and elsewhere.

---

of 2 Chronicles 1–16: A Critical Edition with Textual Commentary, ConBOT 64 (Stockholm: Almqvist & Wiksell, 2003).

88. Barthélemy, *Studies*, which collects the prefaces to *Critique textuelle de l'Ancien Testament*, 4 vols., OBO 50 (Fribourg: Éditions Universitaires; Göttingen: Vandenhoeck & Ruprecht, 1982–2005); see also James A. Sanders, "Stability and Fluidity in Text and Canon," in *Tradition of the Text: Studies Offered to Dominique Barthélemy in Celebration of His 70th Birthday*, ed. Gerard J. Norton and Stephen Pisano, OBO 109 (Fribourg: Éditions Universitaires; Göttingen: Vandenhoeck & Ruprecht, 1991), 202–17; and Sanders, "The Task of Text Criticism," in *Problems in Biblical Theology: Essays in Honor of Rolf Knierim*, ed. H. T. C. Sun and K. L. Eades (Grand Rapids: Eerdmans, 1997), 315–27.

89. Barthélemy, *Studies*, 96.

90. Ibid., 97.

91. Ibid., 236.

Bertil Albrektson cogently criticized Barthélemy's proposals on several grounds, including the oddity of a critical edition that prefers obviously corrupt readings to convincing conjectures. He also pointed out that "canonical" is a standard that applies to books, not to individual readings:

> Canonicity seems to be a property which is first and foremost attributed to books.... Canonical authority may be ascribed to the Book of Jeremiah, but it seems absurd to credit a single letter that is in all probability a simple scribal error with this mysterious quality.[92]

Moreover, Albrektson observes, "authenticity is a concept hard to define and above all irrelevant to a strictly scholarly textual criticism," in which religious evaluations of the stages in a book's textual history are immaterial. As Eugene Ulrich has more recently argued, in textual criticism "canonical text is a term usually used improperly ... and should be avoided," for the simple reason that "in Judaism and in Christianity it is books, not the textual form of books, that are canonical."[93] In other words, Barthélemy's use of canon as a criterion in textual criticism involves a category error.

Others advanced similar criticisms of Barthélemy's concept of a critical edition. According to Barr, it "gives the impression of an odd and isolated position, ill related to what is generally thought in textual criticism."[94] Chiesa describes Barthélemy's proposal as a "surprising and singular eccentricity," which derives from the contradictory desires of a faith-oriented textual criticism.[95] It is another permutation of the inner tensions of *critica sacra*.

The editorial committee of the BHQ did not adopt Barthélemy's concept of a canonical critical edition. However, Barthélemy's views are reflected in the contradictory presentation of its editorial aims. The project's *General Introduction* states: "The aim of this edition ... is to indicate the earliest attainable form(s) of the text based on the available

---

92. Bertil Albrektson, "Translation and Emendation," in *Text, Translation, Theology: Selected Essays on the Hebrew Bible* (Farnham, UK: Ashgate, 2010), 101–2.

93. Eugene Ulrich, "The Canonical Process, Textual Criticism, and the Latter Stages in the Composition of the Bible," in *The Dead Sea Scrolls and the Origins of the Bible*, SDSS (Grand Rapids: Eerdmans, 1999), 59.

94. James Barr, review of *Critique textuelle de l'Ancien Testament: Tome 1*, ed. Dominique Barthélemy, *JTS* 37 (1986): 450.

95. Chiesa, *Filologia*, 429.

evidence."[96] This is the classical aim of textual editions. However, Adrian Schenker has recently qualified this position, adverting to Barthélemy's view that the textual history of the Hebrew Bible begins no earlier than its extant manuscripts:

> There is a first stage of development of the biblical writings that lies beyond—or more precisely, before—textual history and textual criticism. This period lies between the origins of the biblical writings and the first appearance of physical textual witnesses in the form of manuscripts and, in the case of the Hebrew Bible, of early translations. This first period lies outside textual history, involving instead the realm of literary criticism.[97]

"Thus," Schenker writes, "the *BHQ* never introduces data stemming from literary criticism dealing with the first stage." It is concerned with evidence from the second stage, when there are extant textual witnesses, beginning in "the 4th century B.C.E. in exceptional cases … but in most cases dating to the 3rd and 2nd centuries B.C.E."[98] Hence the BHQ edition aims for the period *after* the textual branching evidenced by many of the variants in the extant witnesses, including the cases of multiple editions. It therefore excludes the use of conjecture to ascertain the preferred readings behind many such variants.

But this exclusion conflicts with the project's stated aim of indicating "the earliest attainable form(s) of the text based on the available evidence" (quoted above). The *General Introduction* explicitly allows for the conjecture of a preferred reading that "is not directly attested by any of the extant witnesses, but is only implied by their evidence."[99] This is as it should be, but it conflicts with the view that such scholarship is "literary" and lies outside of the domain of textual criticism. In sum, the BHQ concept of a critical edition is incompletely theorized. It is marred by internal contradictions that reflect Barthélemy's unusual view of textual criticism.

---

96. Adrian Schenker et al., *General Introduction and Megilloth*, BHQ 18 (Stuttgart: Deutsche Bibelgesellschaft, 2004), xv.

97. Adrian Schenker, "The Edition Biblia Hebraica Quinta (BHQ)," *HBAI* 2 (2013): 9–10.

98. Ibid., 10.

99. Schenker, *General Introduction*," xvii.

I have elsewhere described and commented on the concept of a critical edition in the HUBP.[100] This new critical edition was initiated by Goshen-Gottstein in 1955, and its volumes began to appear in 1995. It is, in some ways, the natural outcome of Nöldeke's *diktat*. Goshen-Gottstein stated his goal clearly: "to present nothing but the facts,"[101] thereby eschewing the goals and methods of classical textual criticism. The current editor, Michael Segal, presents this goal more neutrally: "The HUBP edition aims to present the reader with all the material related to the textual history of the Hebrew text, without any prejudicial assumptions or preconceived notions regarding their development."[102]

The HUBP is a critical edition shaped by monumental erudition. In the Pentateuch, it reconstructs the missing text of the Aleppo Codex, but it prescinds from reconstructing a preferred or prior text. Rather, it presents a mass of textual data, mingling ancient and medieval Hebrew variants, and translations that may or may not differ from the MT, accompanied by compressed "hints" (as Goshen-Gottstein called them) about the editor's text-critical judgment of selected readings.

I have maintained that

> It is arguable ... that it is a category mistake to think that textual criticism should strive to be objective and eschew as far as possible the exercise of text-critical judgment. The HUBP, in this respect, is not only a reaction against the unsystematic practices of earlier textual critics, but is also clearly colored by the positivism and "scientism" of the early post-WWII era.[103]

In the longer historical view, the HUBP represents a post-Qumran manifestation of Nöldeke's philological shudder, shaking off the impossible burden of Wellhausen's project. However, in its latest volume the editors slightly revise their position, granting that "the full description of the process of digesting the evidence and a comprehensive philological and

---

100. Ronald Hendel, "The Oxford Hebrew Bible: Prologue to a New Critical Edition," *VT* 58 (2008): 338–42.

101. Moshe H. Goshen-Gottstein, *The Book of Isaiah: Sample Edition with Introduction* (Jerusalem: Magnes, 1965), 7.

102. Michael Segal, "The Hebrew University Bible Project," *HBAI* 2 (2013): 39.

103. Hendel, "Prologue," 338–39.

textual commentary remain a *desideratum*."[104] The HBCE is dedicated precisely to this task.

Conclusions

Five years after his critical edition of Ezekiel, Cornill reflected on the difficulty of the task:

> This is indeed a field whose cultivation demands a great deal of expertise and unusual circumspection: for many preliminary questions must first be settled and much preliminary work done.... But these tasks are as rich in reward as they are difficult of execution, and are the indispensable preliminary to a reasonable textual criticism of the Old Testament.[105]

This is an apt coda for such an enterprise. From Cappel to Cornill, from Buxtorf to Barthélemy, from Geiger to Goshen-Gottstein, many preliminary questions have been examined and debated. There has been progress and regress. An examination of the history of the idea of a critical edition in our field (including diplomatic and eclectic editions) is a necessary preliminary, for it allows us to see the options explored and the paths not taken. It is important for scholars to be aware of how past configurations of knowledge and practice have shaped the present situation. The *status quo* is not inevitable or necessary; it is the result of a thousand decisions, habits, accidents, and hesitations. A new critical edition provides an opportunity to reassess past contributions and to redefine the genealogy of the present.

The idea of a critical diplomatic edition of the Hebrew Bible was first conceived by Cappel and first implemented (imperfectly) by Houbigant. The BHQ and HUBP are their modern heirs. The idea of a critical eclectic edition was first conceived by Eichhorn, revived by Wellhausen, and

---

104. Moshe H. Goshen-Gottstein, Shemaryahu Talmon, and Galen Marquis, *The Book of Ezekiel*, HUBP (Jerusalem: Magnes, 2004), xv.

105. Carl Heinrich Cornill, *Einleitung in das Alte Testament mit einschluss der Apokryphen und Pseudepigraphen* (Freiburg: Mohr, 1891), 295–96: "Freilich ist dies Feld ein derartiges, dass sein Anbau grosse Sachkenntnis und äusserste Vorsicht erheischt: denn es müssen erst viele Vorfragen erledigt und viele Vorarbeiten gethan sein.... Aber diese Aufgaben sind auch eben so lohnend, als sie schwierig sind und die unentbehrlichen Vorbedingungen für eine rationelle Textkritik des AT." Translation adapted from Cornill, *Introduction to the Canonical Books of the Old Testament*, trans. G. H. Box (New York: Putnam's, 1907), 510–11.

implemented (imperfectly) by Cornill. The HBCE is their modern heir. These projects have a shared genealogy, which bifurcate into distinctive paths. The most distinguished ancestors of these forking paths are two great scholars, Nöldeke and Wellhausen. While Nöldeke's legacy is well-established, the proliferation of textual knowledge as a consequence of the Qumran scrolls arguably enables us to resume Wellhausen's goal on a new level.

It is important to emphasize that a critical edition is a particular genre of scholarly literature, with its own past and its own conditions of possibility. An edition is in dialogue with all other past and present editions. In this respect the HBCE is complementary to BHQ and HUBP (and to the great polyglots), even as its theory of a critical edition differs. No edition can accomplish all things; there are always multiple aims, potentials, and limitations.

I concur with Jerome McGann's description of this genre:

> A critical edition is a kind of text which does not seek to reproduce a particular past text, but rather to reconstitute for the reader, in a single text, the entire history of the work.... As such, the critical edition embodies a practical goal which can be (within limits) accomplished, but it equally embodies an illusion about its own historicity.[106]

The HBCE seeks to represent the text in all of its early historical dimensions, from the archetype to the early editions to the details of scribal exegesis. It will draw out the multiple temporalities of the text and will explore the different phases in its textual life. Our edition does not pretend to offer a "final" text, but is rather a scholarly recovery and exploration of a plural text. It does not hide its own historicity, but situates itself within the genealogy of critical editions. In its several aims, the HBCE expands the potential of its peculiar genre.

---

106. Jerome J. McGann, *A Critique of Modern Textual Criticism* (Charlottesville: University of Virginia Press, 1992), 93–94.

4
WHAT IS A BIBLICAL BOOK?

A theory of the work does not exist, and the empirical task of those who naively undertake the editing of works often suffers in the absence of such a theory.

—Michel Foucault, "What Is an Author?"

When Foucault wrote these words in 1969, it is fair to say that textual critics had yet to think through many of the theoretical entailments of their editorial practices. Since then much intellectual ferment has occurred around the topic of textual criticism, primarily in the fields of medieval and modern literature. Theoretical reflection about textual criticism of the Hebrew Bible is still in its early stages, despite important advances stimulated by the biblical texts from Qumran.[1] In the following I will attempt to construct the outlines of what a theory of critical editions of the biblical books ought to look like, drawing on pertinent literature from the philosophy of language and art. In order to make these theories more suitable to the task at hand, I will historicize the (mostly) unhistorical character of these theories, thereby adding complexity to their formulations. I will begin with the general question "What is a book?" and then move to the particular question "What is a biblical book?"—with an eye to how these issues clarify the concept and task of a critical edition.

---

1. See Emanuel Tov, *Textual Criticism of the Hebrew Bible*, 3rd ed. (Minneapolis: Fortress, 2012), 155–90; Eugene Ulrich, *The Dead Sea Scrolls and the Developmental Composition of the Bible*, VTSup 169 (Leiden: Brill, 2015), 15–27; Zipora Talshir, "Texts, Text-Forms, Editions, New Composition and the Final Products of Biblical Literature," in *Congress Volume Munich 2013*, ed. Christl M. Maier, VTSup 163 (Leiden: Brill, 2014); Michael V. Fox, "Is Text Criticism Possible?" in *Proverbs: An Eclectic Edition with Introduction and Textual Commentary*, HBCE 1 (Atlanta: SBL Press, 2015), 1–15; Ronald L. Troxel, "What Is the 'Text' in Textual Criticism?" *VT* 66 (2016): 603–26.

WHAT IS A BOOK?

In the course of a discussion of intellectual property rights and book piracy, Immanuel Kant asked the question, "What is a book?"[2] His answer lays the groundwork for our inquiry:

> A book is a writing (it does not matter, here, whether it is written in hand or set in type, whether it has few or many pages), which represents a discourse that someone delivers to the public by visible linguistic signs.[3]

Kant refers to a book as, in the first instance, a physical object, that is, a "writing" ("Schrift"), which can be a manuscript or a printed text. He then specifies its semiotic function: it "represents a discourse" ("eine Rede vorstellt"). A book accomplishes this function by means of semiotic symbols: "visible linguistic signs" ("sichtbare Sprachzeichen"). There is also a process of dissemination: someone must deliver it to the public ("an das Publicum hält"). In sum, a book is a physical object that conveys a discourse to the reading (or listening) public.

Kant emphasizes the duality of the material and the abstract in the constituency of a book: "On the one hand a book is a corporeal *artifact* (*opus mechanicum*) that can be reproduced.... On the other hand a book is also a mere *discourse* of the publisher to the public."[4] It is this double nature of a book—as a reproducible material artifact and as the semiotic representation of a discourse—that requires further examination in order to formulate a coherent concept of a book. Kant's deceptively simple question, "What is a book?," opens up a labyrinth of complicated ideas.

---

2. Kant's reflections were aimed at the problem of copyright law; see Roger Chartier and Peter Stallybrass, "What Is a Book?" in *The Cambridge Companion to Textual Scholarship*, ed. Neil Fraistat and Julia Flanders (Cambridge: Cambridge University Press, 2013), 188–90.

3. Immanuel Kant, *The Metaphysics of Morals*, ed. and trans. Mary Gregor, CTHP (Cambridge: Cambridge University Press, 1996), 71–72; Kant, *Die Metaphysik der Sitten*, 2nd ed. (Königsberg: Nicolovius, 1803), 1:127: "Ein Buch ist eine Schrift, (ob mit der Feder oder durch Typen, auf wenig oder viel Blättern verzeichnet, ist hier gleichgültig) welche eine Rede vorstellt, die jemand durch sichtbare Sprachzeichen an das Publicum hält."

4. Kant, *The Metaphysics of Morals*, 72, emphasis added; Kant, *Metaphysik*, 129: "das Buch einerseits ein körperliches Kunstproduct (*opus mechanicum*) ist ... andrerseits aber ist das Buch auch bloße Rede des Verlegers ans Publicum."

Two further sets of distinctions will help us to unpack these complexities. The philosopher Nelson Goodman has formulated an important distinction between *autographic* and *allographic* arts. This will help us to understand how a book differs from other kinds of representational art. A second distinction, formulated by Charles Peirce and developed by Richard Wollheim and others, is between *types* and *tokens*. This clarifies the duality of a book as a physical and abstract object.[5] I submit that a selective linking of these theories is feasible, despite the fact that these philosophers often disagree on some (in my view, secondary) features. These sets of distinctions attend to complementary aspects of the constituency of a book and, by extension, a biblical book.

AUTOGRAPHIC AND ALLOGRAPHIC ARTWORKS

Goodman's distinction draws attention to the difference between arts where only the autograph is the artwork (hence *autographic* artworks) and those where the artwork exists in multiple authentic copies (hence *allographic* artworks), none of which need be the autograph.[6] Arts such as painting or sculpture are *autographic*, since the artwork is a single object, locatable in space and time. Only the original is the work of art; copies are fakes or facsimiles. Arts such as literature and music are *allographic*, since the artwork exists in multiple and dispersed copies, and any accurate copy is an authentic instantiation of the artwork.

An example of a famous autographic artwork is the Mona Lisa. It is a particular object made by Leonardo da Vinci. It once hung in the bathroom of Louis XIV and is now on display in the Louvre. It is possible to steal the Mona Lisa—indeed it was stolen in 1911 and recovered two years later. A copy of the Mona Lisa is either a (usually cheap) reproduction or a (very expensive) forgery. Even an identical physical copy—perhaps made by a 3D printer—would still be a forgery, since it does not share the same

---

5. The relevance of these contributions by Wollheim, Peirce, and Goodman for textual criticism was pointed out by James McLaverty, "The Mode of Existence of Literary Works of Art: The Case of the *Dunciad Variorum*," *SBib* 37 (1984): 83–91; see also (with different theoretical parameters) Peter L. Shillingsburg, "Text as Matter, Concept, and Action," *SBib* 44 (1991): 31–82; Adrian Wilson, "What Is a Text?" *Studies in History and Philosophy of Science* 43 (2012): 341–58.

6. Nelson Goodman, *Languages of Art: An Approach to a Theory of Symbols* (Indianapolis: Bobbs-Merrill, 1968), 99–123.

history of production as the actual Mona Lisa. This is why the detection of forgeries is essential for museums and collectors of autographic arts. Authenticity is a property of the original, not of copies.

A comparable example of an allographic artwork is James Joyce's *Ulysses*. Unlike the Mona Lisa, any copy of *Ulysses* is the artwork, whether it is a printed edition, a photocopy, an e-book, or any other transcription (say, a tattoo version). The concept of forgery does not apply to allographic artworks. The distinguishing feature that makes this condition possible is its semiotic notation. As Goodman states, "an art seems to be allographic just insofar as it is amenable to notation."[7] That is, the objects exist as artworks by means of what Kant calls "visible signs," whether these signs are linguistic, musical, or some other kind (e.g., computer code). Hence the artwork can be reproduced without limit. One can produce a forgery of a particular *instance* of a work, such as a rare printing or manuscript, but one cannot forge the artwork itself.

The medium of notation makes allographic arts plural, with no single instance counting as the artwork itself to the exclusion of the others. Even the autograph is not *the* artwork itself, since the autograph can be lost and, as long as other copies survive, the artwork still exists. Only if the autograph and all copies are lost does the artwork cease to exist. It then becomes a lost artwork, like Aristotle's treatise on comedy or the *Sefer ha-Yashar* (cited in Josh 10:13 and 2 Sam 1:18).

Goodman emphasizes the *correctness* of notation in a valid copy of an allographic artwork. This is an important and complicated issue. As Goodman observes, the criterion of correctness does not include features of presentation that are inessential to the notation system. These secondary or contingent features can vary without affecting the validity of the copy:

> Let us suppose that there are handwritten copies and many editions of a given literary work. Differences between them in style and size of script or type, in color of ink, in kind of paper, in number and layout of pages, in condition, etc., do not matter. All that matters is what may be called *sameness of spelling*: exact correspondence of sequences of letters, spaces, and punctuation marks. Any sequence—even a forgery of the author's manuscript or of a given edition—that so corresponds to a correct copy is itself correct, and nothing is more the original work than is such a correct copy.[8]

---

7. Ibid., 121.
8. Ibid., 115, emphasis original.

The criterion of correct copy consists solely of the notation itself, not differences in the features of presentation or physical material. This roughly corresponds to Greg's distinction between the substantives and accidentals in the texts of literary works.[9] Goodman maintains that a work of allographic art consists of the sequences of "character[s] in a notational scheme … in a vocabulary of syntactically disjoint and differentiated symbols." He concludes: "A literary work, then, is … the text or script itself,"[10] or what we might call the substantive readings, represented in visual symbols.

This conclusion has obvious implications for the production of critical editions. If a book is the text's notational scheme, then accuracy of notation is the primary value. The constitution of the best attainable copy of a sequence of "character[s] in a notation scheme" is an apt definition of the task of textual criticism.

However, aspects of Goodman's model require qualification. Goodman posits absolute notational fidelity in order for a copy to count as a correct copy of an artwork. He argues that "even replacement of a character in a text by another synonymous character … yields a different work."[11] Other philosophers of art have taken issue with this exacting standard, since it does not correspond to the use of these concepts in ordinary language. Susan Wilsmore cites a salient example:

> Virginia Woolf published *To the Lighthouse* in both England and America at the same time with small but important differences of text. Some say that the American version is the better version.… [But r]eaders on both sides of the Atlantic believe they have read the very same work by Virginia Woolf. Are they wrong? The way in which we discuss such cases, as different versions of the same work, makes clear that they need not be.[12]

In sum, if we want the theory to accommodate ordinary usage,[13] we will need to modify Goodman's criterion of "sameness of spelling" as a condition of the validity of a copy of a work. Variants in spelling, words, and

---

9. See W. W. Greg, "The Rationale of Copy-Text," *SBib* 3 (1950–1951): 19–36, and above, ch. 1.

10. Goodman, *Languages of Art*, 209.

11. Ibid.

12. Susan Wilsmore, "The Literary Work Is Not Its Text," *Ph&Lit* 11 (1987): 312; similar criticisms are advanced by Nicholas Wolterstorff, *Works and Worlds of Art* (Oxford: Clarendon, 1980), 101–5.

13. This is not among Goodman's aims, but it is among mine.

word sequences are a commonplace in copies of literary works. Textual critics know that it could hardly be otherwise.

Furthermore, for many books, including the Hebrew Bible and other pre- and early modern books, "sameness of spelling" is not a felicitous condition, since spelling was not a fixed system. We can redefine this criterion as "sameness of words and word-sequences" or "sameness of substantive readings." But it remains the case that there are differences in words and word-sequences (i.e., substantive readings) among copies that in ordinary usage count as authentic copies of the artwork. What we are accustomed to regard as "correct copies" may have considerable variants, as the example of Woolf's *To the Lighthouse* illustrates, and as does the condition of biblical books.

A degree of variation among its copies must be included within a coherent concept of a book. I would modify Goodman's model by noting that books are *doubly* allographic, in the etymological sense of "different writing." As Goodman maintains, they are allographic such that correct copies count as instantiations of the artwork, but they are also allographic in the sense that variants exist among the copies that count as valid instantiations of a book.

In consequence we should ask, since copies vary, in what does the correctness of a copy consist? Can we specify a limit to the range of allowable variation? In ordinary practice, there are no obvious rules or limits that are generally applicable. But local traditions and cultural authorities will, on occasion, assign and enforce limits. A publisher may withdraw a garbled printing of a book. A scribal tradition—such as the medieval *Soferim*—may have internal practices of quality control. The extent of allowable variation depends on local practices and mechanisms of enforcement, which involve the historical relationships *around* the book, including the implicit rules of the reading community and the interests of the bibliographical authorities.

In some cases, a single variant may suffice to invalidate a copy of a book. A striking example is the infamous "Wicked Bible," a 1631 printing of the King James translation. This printing omits the second "not" from Exod 20:13, yielding "Thou shalt commit adultery." (This may have been an act of industrial sabotage by a disgruntled typesetter.)[14] The local bibliographical

---

14. David Norton, *A Textual History of the King James Bible* (Cambridge: Cambridge University Press, 2005), 81.

authority, King Charles I, supported by his bishops, required that all copies be destroyed. This extreme case illustrates the possible kinds and extent of variation that are permissible for a copy to count as a correct—and licit— instantiation of the book.

This example also shows how the history of production enters into the constituency of a book. Copies of books vary, sometimes a little, and sometimes too much. How, then, can we map the relationship between a book and its copies? In Goodman's terms, an authentic copy is one that correctly represents the notation of the autograph. The relationship between a copy and the autograph is a historical one. But there are other features of the relationship between a book and its local instantiations that Goodman's model does not cover, including the variations among valid copies of a book. How can copies differ but still instantiate the same book? Another way to put this is to ask, why do we distinguish between particular copies—which can differ in their notation—from the work that they are copies of? This brings us to another distinction, that of *type* and *token*.

TYPE AND TOKEN

Charles Peirce, founder of semiotics and pragmatism, introduced the terms *type* and *token* to clarify the curious duality of physical and abstract objects in our systems of communication. This is the duality pointed to by Kant in his definition of a book. Peirce uses the curious example of the word "the," which, in different senses of its usage, is a visible sign and an abstract object:

> There will ordinarily be about twenty *the*'s on a page [of a MS or a printed book], and of course they count as twenty words. In another sense of the word "word," however, there is but one word "the" in the English language; and it is impossible that this word should lie visibly on a page or be heard in any voice, for the reason that it is not a Single thing or Single event. It does not exist; it only determines things that do exist. Such a definitely significant Form, I propose to term a Type.... In order that a Type may be used, it has to be embodied in a Token.[15]

---

15. Charles Sanders Peirce, "Prolegomena to an Apology for Pragmaticism" (1906), in *Collected Papers of Charles Sanders Peirce*, ed. Charles Hartshorne, Paul Weiss, and Arthur W. Burks (Cambridge: Harvard University Press, 1933), 4:537.

The word *the*, which is a single abstract object or *type*, has multiple, dispersed instantiations, which are its sensible *tokens*. In Peirce's example, this type—the word *the*—has around twenty tokens on a page. The type exists as an abstract object within the system of language. Its physical instantiations exist as blots of ink or, if one reads the page aloud, as audible noises.

This duality of abstract and concrete objects corresponds to Kant's description of a book as a "mere *discourse*" and a corporeal object. A book as a discourse is a type (an abstract semiotic object), and the physical object with its visible symbols is its token (a concrete semiotic object). The type-token relationship has been successfully extended to other semiotic domains, such as mathematics, physics, and biology. In these domains, as W. V. Quine observes, "type and token nicely span the abstract and concrete."[16]

Richard Wollheim has influentially applied this distinction to literary works:

> In philosophical language, a literary work of art is a *type*, of which your copy or my copy or the set of words read out in a particular hall on a particular evening are the various *tokens*; it is a type like the Union Jack or the Queen of Diamonds, of which the flags that fly at different mastheads and have the same design, or the cards in different packs with the same face, are the tokens.[17]

A literary work is, in this sense, a type, an abstract object. The physical instantiations of a literary work are its tokens. The situation is analogous to the semiotics of playing cards—there is only one Queen of Diamonds, but there are as many copies of her as there are decks of cards. As Wollheim says, "*Ulysses* and *Der Rosenkavalier* are types, my copy of *Ulysses* and tonight's performance of *Rosenkavalier* are tokens of those types."[18]

The type-token relationship is pertinent to the concept of a book, which, as we have seen, entails a relationship between multiple physical copies and the book of which they are copies. Can we specify more clearly how a book exists as an abstract object? It is not equivalent to any one of

---

16. W. V. Quine, *Quiddities: An Intermittently Philosophical Dictionary* (Cambridge: Harvard University Press, 1987), 218.

17. Richard Wollheim, *On Art and the Mind* (Cambridge: Harvard University Press, 1974), 104.

18. Richard Wollheim, *Art and Its Objects: An Introduction to Aesthetics* (New York: Harper & Row, 1971), 65.

its copies, but it somehow, as Peirce says, "determines" those copies as its embodiments. What does this mean? The situation of books may be analogous to words or playing cards but seems to have additional complexities, for example, the problem of variant copies of a book.

Some of these complexities derive from the history of the production and transmission of books. Wollheim touches on some of these historical conditions: "In the case of any work of art that it is plausible to think of as a type, there is ... a piece of human invention."[19] The individual tokens each descend from that "piece of human invention," and the invention is the occasion that creates the type. So there is history behind the type-token relationship. But how then should we think of the book as a type? Does it have particular qualities? Is it a Platonic ideal of the written notation, or is it simply a name for a once-existing historical object, perhaps the original of which the tokens are copies?

Wollheim argues that it is incorrect to regard a type as historical object or as a class of historical objects. One might think that "a novel, of which there are copies, is not my or your copy but is the class of all its copies."[20] This formulation, he argues, fails at several points. If the copies are not perfect matches, then this raises the problem of how we know that these particular copies belong to a given class. To say that they "resemble each other in all relevant respects" does not suffice, since we cannot specify what those relevant respects are. More to the point, this is precisely the question that we are trying to answer:

> To say that certain copies or performances are of *Ulysses* or *Rosenkavalier* because they resemble one another seems precisely to reverse the natural order of thought: the resemblance, we would think, follows from, or is to be understood in terms of, the fact that they are of the same novel or opera.[21]

The problem that we cannot specify precisely how the copies resemble each other is the reason that Goodman restricts his theory to perfect copies of the autograph's notation. Inexact copies raise the problem of how it is we group the copies together and distinguish them from copies of another work. Hence Wollheim argues that the type is something more or other

---

19. Ibid., 69.
20. Ibid., 7.
21. Ibid, 9.

than a class of similar objects—the criterion of similarity is simply too malleable (a point on which Goodman agrees).

I suggest that history and culture supply some necessary conditions for construing the type-token relationship of a book and its copies. A given book type (such as *Ulysses* or *To the Lighthouse*) is a historical *and* a regulative or normative concept that operates within our semiotic discourses. A book has pragmatic, semiotic, and historical features that makes it different from a word (*the*) or a card (the Queen of Diamonds). A book is a type—an abstract object—that seems overtly to relate an instance of invention to its variant physical manifestations. This distinguishes books from other types (such as *the* or the Queen of Diamonds) for which the instance of invention seems irrelevant to their semiotic work. Whereas a word is a relational type, a book has relational features *and* an implicit history of production and transmission.

This implicit history is linked to the seeming paradox that we, as physical creatures, can know about abstract objects (i.e., types). As Linda Wetzel observes, "*Being a token* is a relational property,"[22] and that relation is, in part, historical and social. Outside of the historical context of its reading community, a book—let's say, the Mayan *Popul Vuh*—is just a combination of wood pulp and ink. The type-token relationship is a linguistic and social fact, which relies on a historical community of readers (even if that history is discontinuous, as in the case of books in long-forgotten languages).

A further historical twist on this semiotic relationship requires attention. Prior to the historical event when a book is published (when, in Kant's terms, a writing is delivered to the public), there is arguably a type-token relationship in the private act of writing. Joyce had a general concept of *Ulysses* that he was trying to instantiate by writing it. We may regard this as a phase in the *prehistory* of the book, since, in Kantian and ordinary language, the writing is not yet a book. The transition from private writing to publication (making public) is arguably the occasion when a book begins to exist. This historical event constitutes the birth of the public type-token relationship. In this respect, as Wetzel comments, "types can have spatio-temporal *properties*," such that they are occasioned by tangible events.[23] A type is an abstract object that we produce when we make a book. It has

---

22. Linda Wetzel, *Types and Tokens: On Abstract Objects* (Cambridge: MIT Press, 2009), 123, emphasis original; see also Linda Wetzel, "Types and Tokens," in *The Stanford Encyclopedia of Philosophy*, http://tinyurl.com/SBL7010j.

23. Wetzel, *Types and Tokens*, 151, emphasis original.

historical properties but is not a concrete object. But with it we collectively sort out and render meaningful things that are. *Ulysses* is a type—an abstract semiotic object—with which we render meaningful all the copies of the book.

ABSTRACTION AND CHANGE

The two theories of a book that I have explored—the book as an allographic artwork and the book as constituted by a type-token relationship—are generally compatible (including a revision of Goodman's theory to include variant copies), but they diverge on an important point. The type-token model posits the existence of abstract objects (types), whereas the model of allographic artworks only refers to particular objects: the autograph and its copies.

In this respect, Goodman's is a nominalist theory, which only grants the existence of individual physical objects, whereas the type-token theory is a realist theory, which also grants the reality of abstract objects and classes. Nominalist theories are appealing to the empirically-minded, for whom the idea of abstract objects smacks of supernaturalism or Platonism. However, as W. V. Quine somewhat ruefully observes (since he is a nominalist by inclination), nominalism is an "ill-starred project," since "to the nominalists' sorrow science is saddled with abstract objects."[24] It seems we are compelled to grant the reality of abstract objects, even if their existence seems contrary to common sense. But, at least they are *our* abstract objects; as Wetzel says, "they are the abstract objects we specify them to be."[25]

If we grant the existence of types as abstract objects, then by necessity they do not change. *Ulysses* as a type cannot morph into *To the Lighthouse*. But, as we have seen, we must construe the concept of types in a way that accommodates change among their tokens. In order to clarify this requirement, let us consider two extreme examples of the relationships between a type and its variant tokens: Joyce's *Ulysses* and Whitman's *Leaves of Grass*. These "discourse[s] that someone delivers to the public by visible linguistic signs" were historically complicated events, opening up further complications in the concept of a book.[26]

---

24. Quine, *Quiddities*, 228–29.
25. Wetzel, *Types and Tokens*, 123.
26. See also Fox's discussion (*Proverbs*, 10–14) of the complicated cases of Shakespeare and Jane Austin.

There have been (depending on how one counts them) eighteen editions of *Ulysses*, from the first edition published in Paris in 1922 to the critical edition issued in 1984.[27] The problem that occasioned these multiple editions is the uncertain text of the first edition. The transition from manuscript to book was cluttered by copyists' errors, incorrect corrections by copyists and printers, and Joyce's authorial corrections and revisions. The manuscripts, typescripts, and printer's proofs are a mess.

As a consequence, the first edition of *Ulysses* contains many scribal errors and passages of dubious authenticity. Subsequent editions attempted to correct the errors, but also introduced new ones. Hans Gabler's critical edition of 1984 may be the best representation of what we may call (with a measure of ambiguity) Joyce's final text, but aspects of Gabler's method and many of his editorial decisions have been criticized by Joyce scholars. The point that is relevant to us, however, is the unity of the type despite the variability of its tokens. Gabler's edition differs considerably from previous copies and editions, but it is nonetheless a token of *Ulysses*. Each of the variant tokens of *Ulysses* instantiate a single abstract type. The type therefore accommodates historical and editorial change, on the condition that all the copies have a historical relationship to a particular piece of human invention. All the copies are members of a (messy) family tree. The type encompasses a family of tokens, whose internal relationships may be complicated or irrecoverable.

Walt Whitman's *Leaves of Grass* was also issued in multiple editions but for a different reason.[28] The first edition of 1855 consisted of twelve poems. Whitman continued to revise, supplement, and occasionally delete poems until the so-called deathbed edition of 1891–1892, which consisted of nearly four hundred poems. After preparing the latter edition, he wrote to a friend, "I now consider it *finished* as I propose and laid out." Many poems in the later editions differ considerably from their earlier versions. For instance, the elder Whitman deleted some of the homoerotic lines in "Song of Myself," creating a less controversial poem. In sum, the editions differ. Nowadays Whitman scholars tend to use the 1980 *Variorum Edition*, which reproduces each of the multiple editions. In the case of *Leaves of Grass*, the tokens vary considerably, yet by common con-

---

27. On the following, see Paul Eggert, *Securing the Past: Conservation in Art, Architecture and Literature* (Cambridge: Cambridge University Press, 2009), 164–78.

28. Walt Whitman, *Leaves of Grass: A Textual Variorum of the Printed Poems*, ed. Sculley Bradley et al. (New York: New York University Press, 1980), 1:xv–xxviii.

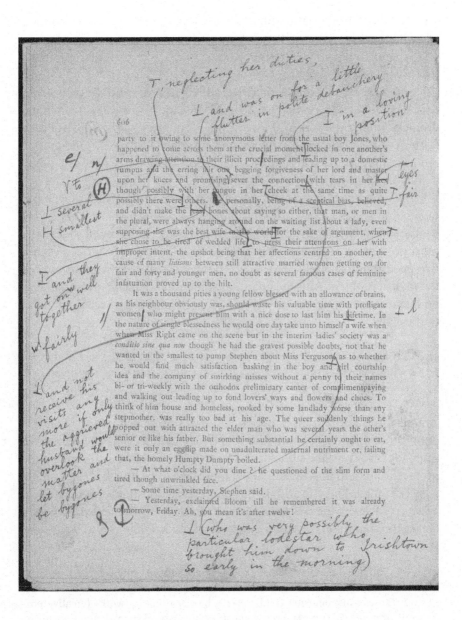

Printer's proof of *Ulysses* with author's corrections and revisions
(Harry Ransom Center, The University of Texas at Austin)

sent each is an instantiation of *Leaves of Grass*. The book accommodates all of its tokens, including those that are considerably different editions. The type of *Leaves of Grass* is an abstract entity that includes among its tokens vast textual change.

Both of these theoretical models—allographic arts and the type-token relationship—can be revised to accommodate the historical fact of textual diversity among the tokens. Moreover, both models can be construed, in some respects, as both descriptive and normative, since the allographic model highlights the criterion of correct copies, and the type-token model highlights the regulative function of types.

The normative features of these models raises the question of whether one should prefer a particular copy or token of a book over another. Many people choose to read any available copy of a book. Some prefer to read the most prestigious copy, irrespective of its relationship to other copies and irrespective of its notational defects. Thomas Tanselle aptly points out the theoretical problem with the common situation in which a person makes no distinction among copies or prefers a particular copy because of habit or prestige:

> They should realize that what they are doing is equating the text of the document before them with the text of a work—just as if the object before them were a painting.[29]

Tanselle does not present a theory of the work/text distinction,[30] but his criticism of treating a book as if it were a painting has a Goodmanian resonance. To consider a book as a single physical object is to conflate the properties of autographic and allographic artworks. To privilege a single copy (i.e., token) is to overlook the complex relationship between a token and its type. It also ignores the changes that inevitably characterize a book's copies through time. It is to misconstrue a book's ontology and its history.

---

29. G. Thomas Tanselle, *A Rationale of Textual Criticism* (Philadelphia: University of Pennsylvania Press, 1989), 70.

30. Tanselle distinguishes (ibid., 18–19) between literary works (creative productions from the past), texts (arrangements of linguistic elements), and documents (manuscripts or printed books). See further Fox, *Proverbs*, 4–9, who concurs with Tanselle's emphasis on authorial intention in the concepts of the work and text. I prefer to emphasize the work's intention (*intentio operis*), which may differ from (but interacts with) authorial intention (*intentio auctoris*); see Umberto Eco, *Interpretation and Overinterpretation* (Cambridge: Cambridge University Press, 1992), 25, 67–88.

What Is a Biblical Book?

The complex nature of a book is clearly relevant to the concept of a biblical book. Although some scholars have suggested that the concept of a book was radically different in antiquity,[31] I submit that the key features of allographic artworks and the type-token relationship are entailed in the concept of a book in ancient Israel, including the period when the biblical books were produced and circulated. (The word *biblical* is anachronistic in this context, but I use it as shorthand for "books that came to be included in the Hebrew Bible.")[32] In his reflections on how these books came to be canonical, Eugene Ulrich comments on the ancient conceptual distinction between a biblical book and its copies, given that the copies circulated in diverse text-forms and editions. He notes that the concept of "canon" pertains to books in the abstract (in our vocabulary, as types) irrespective of the book's diverse textual instantiations:

> Canon concerns biblical books, not the specific textual form of the books. One must distinguish two senses of the word "text": a literary opus and the particular wording of that opus. It is the literary opus, and not the particular wording of that opus, with which canon is concerned.

---

31. See John Barton, "What Is a Book? Modern Exegesis and the Literary Conventions of Ancient Israel," in *Intertextuality in Ugarit and Israel: Papers Read at the Tenth Joint Meeting of The Society for Old Testament Study and Het Oudtestamentisch Werkgezelschap in Nederland en België, held at Oxford, 1997*, ed. Johannes C. de Moor, OTS 40 (Leiden: Brill, 1998), 2: "no-one had yet combined two ideas which form parts of our concept of a book, one physical, the other metaphysical." I submit that the dual concept of a book is native to biblical discourse; see below. For the (non-)concept of book in postbiblical Jewish hermeneutics (where the boundaries are mostly the individual verse or the whole Hebrew Bible), see Benjamin D. Sommer, "The Scroll of Isaiah as Jewish Scripture, or, Why Jews Don't Read Books," *Society of Biblical Literature 1996 Seminar Papers* (Atlanta: Scholars Press, 1996), 225–42.

32. The term *Scripture*, which some scholars prefer, has its own confusions, since many more books were regarded as scriptural (e.g., at Qumran) than were included in the Hebrew or Greek Bibles. For the terminological issue, see Molly M. Zahn, "The Problem of Characterizing the 4QReworked Pentateuch Manuscripts: Bible, Rewritten Bible, or None of the Above?" *DSD* 15 (2008): 317–19; and Molly M. Zahn, "Talking about Rewritten Texts: Some Reflections on Terminology," in *Changes in Scripture: Rewriting and Interpreting Authoritative Traditions in the Second Temple Period*, ed. Hanne von Weissenberg, Juha Pakkala, and Marko Marttila, BZAW 419 (Berlin: de Gruyter, 2011), 95–102.

> Both in Judaism and in Christianity it is books, not the textual form of books, that are canonical.... [A book] is an abstraction, not a text that one can pick up and read.[33]

The dual nature of a book—as an abstract object and its physical instantiations—is implicit in the discourses and practices involving books in ancient Israel. The concept of canonical or sacred books entails this distinction. A canonical book is a type, which is instantiated by each of its valid tokens in circulation.

At Qumran, for instance, a particular book-scroll could be written in the notation of any of several textual families—proto-MT, proto-SP, a proto-LXX—or anything in between.[34] When a Qumran document cites ספר משה, "the book of Moses" (i.e., the Pentateuch),[35] the book referred to is a type, an abstract semiotic object, which is instantiated in all of its variant manuscript copies, as long as the copies survive the scrutiny of the bibliographical authorities. 4QpaleoExod[m], a proto-SP text written in paleo-Hebrew script, was as much a copy of Exodus as 4QExod[b], which is an older manuscript with (probably) a proto-LXX text, written in the square script. In ancient Israel, a biblical book was an abstract type, with many variant tokens in circulation.

The Hebrew word ספר ("book, document") can apply to the type and its tokens, just as the English word *book*. A scroll as a physical object, with or without writing, is a מגלה. A written scroll can be referred to as a ספר ("book") or as a מגלת ספר ("book-scroll").[36] The relationship between a biblical book and any particular book-scroll of that book is an instance of the relationship between a type and its tokens. In order to clarify this

---

33. Eugene Ulrich, "The Canonical Process, Textual Criticism, and the Latter Stages in the Composition of the Bible," in *The Dead Sea Scrolls and the Origins of the Bible*, SDSS (Grand Rapids: Eerdmans, 1999), 57–58; see also Ulrich, "The Notion and Definition of Canon," in *Developmental Composition*, 275–76.

34. See below, chs. 8 and 9.

35. On this terminology at Qumran and its implications, see Michael Segal, "Biblical Interpretation: Yes and No," in *What Is Bible?*, ed. Karin Finsterbusch and Armin Lange, CBET 67 (Leuven: Peeters, 2012), 63–80.

36. On the lexical issues, see Avi Hurvitz, "The Origins and Development of the Expression מגלת ספר: A Study in the History of Writing-Related Terminology in Biblical Times," in *Texts, Temples, and Traditions: A Tribute to Menahem Haran* [Hebrew], ed. Michael V. Fox et al. (Winona Lake, IN: Eisenbrauns, 1996), 37*–46*.

relationship, I will use the term *book-scroll* (following Menahem Haran) to refer to these tokens.[37]

To illustrate the type-token relationship, let us consider the case of 4QGen[h-title] (= 4Q8c), a fragment of a title page of Genesis. This sheet would have been wrapped around a book-scroll to protect and identify it, like a dust jacket on a modern book. This fragment displays the word ברשית, which is a colloquial and informal spelling (absent the medial א) of the first word of the book of Genesis. (It was customary in antiquity to use the first word or phrase—the *incipit*—as the name of a literary work.) As Emanuel Tov observes, this sheet "may have been attached to any Genesis scroll, preserved or not."[38] That is, the designation ברשית is relational, identifying a book-scroll with the book of which it is a copy. The designation refers to any copy, any book-scroll, that counts as an instantiation of Genesis. We have fragments of approximately nineteen manuscripts of Genesis from Qumran. Each of them differs in some details of notation from the others, yet each of them is an authentic copy of the literary work that we call Genesis. The book's title performs the semiotic function of linking the tokens to their type.

The history of the book's title illustrates some further features of the type/token relationship, which pertains not only to books but also to individual readings and words (see the duality of the word "the," discussed above). I have been using the word *Genesis* as the name of a Hebrew book. The oldest Hebrew designation is בראשית (or, as above, the colloquial ברשית), which means roughly "in the beginning (of)." The English name of the book derives from Gen 2:4 in the LXX: Αὕτη ἡ βίβλος γενέσεως (= זה ספר תולדות), "This is the book of the generations/origins [*geneseos*]." In Greek, the book came to be called Genesis, since this seems to be a self-identification of the book in the LXX of 2:4: "*This* is the book of Genesis."

The word *this* (αὕτη = זה) does not refer to a particular book-scroll of Genesis. It designates a book (ספר) in the sense of a type, an abstract object. This deictic particle ("this") points to the book as such and relates it to the book-scroll at hand. It says, "this is the book of Genesis," which identifies the type of this particular token.

---

37. Menahem Haran, "Book-Scrolls in Israel in Pre-exilic Times," *JJS* 33 (1982): 161–73; Haran, "Book-Scrolls at the Beginning of the Second Temple Period: The Transition from Papyrus to Skins," *HUCA* 54 (1983): 111–22.

38. Emanuel Tov, *Scribal Practices and Approaches Reflected in the Texts Found in the Judean Desert*, STDJ 54 (Leiden: Brill, 2004), 121.

Interestingly, this Greek name derives from a textual variant of Gen 2:4. MT and SP read אלה תולדות ("These are the generations") rather than זה ספר תולדות ("This is the book of generations"), which is the reading reflected in LXX. The longer reading in the LXX of Gen 2:4 is arguably the result of a scribal harmonization with Gen 5:1, which reads זה ספר תולדת ("This is the book of generations") in all the textual versions. The two verses are related as introductory tags to the "generations" of something ("heaven and earth" in 2:4; "Adam" in 5:1), and as a consequence a scribe in the proto-G tradition has harmonized the wording of these two introductory tags.[39] The longer and the shorter variant readings (אלה תולדות versus זה ספר תולדות) are tokens of the same type: the text of Gen 2:4. Note that the book of Genesis is an abstract type and so also is its text. That is, when we refer to the text of Gen 2:4, we are referring to a type, which encompasses all of its variant tokens. But there is also, as I have emphasized, a historical relationship between these variants.

The type/token relationship at the level of text and variants clarifies Tov's comment that "the 'biblical text' is an abstract unit that is not found in any one single source."[40] Like Ulrich's observation about the biblical books, Tov observes that the biblical text has a dual nature, consisting of an abstract object and its physical manifestations. In other words, the biblical text is a type, and the extant manuscripts and printed editions are its tokens. The concept of the biblical text is constituted by a type-token relationship. This terminology lends analytical precision to the apt observations of Tov and Ulrich.

If Genesis (or Exodus, etc.) is a biblical book that has variant instantiations and its text likewise has variant instantiations, can we specify any criteria by which a particular book counts as a valid token of Genesis and its text? Are there any limits to variation, such that a particular book-scroll becomes an invalid token? In medieval Jewish book-scroll manufacture, biblical books were subjected to stringent quality controls. For instance, the Babylonian Talmud (Menaḥot 29b) recounts a disagreement over the number of permitted corrections in a column of a Torah scroll (Rab says two, another sage says three, and a third says that these may be mitigated if there is one column with no mistakes). In some scribal circles, too many corrections invalidated a Torah scroll. Among the Qumran scrolls, we find

---

39. Ronald Hendel, *The Text of Genesis 1–11: Textual Studies and Critical Edition* (New York: Oxford University Press, 1998), 34.

40. Tov, *Textual Criticism*, 341.

evidence of scribal conventions regarding corrections in a book-scroll, but nothing that indicates criteria for an invalid copy.[41]

By the time of the Mishnah (ca. 200 CE), there were also sectarian textual boundaries. According to m. Yad. 4.5, biblical scrolls written in paleo-Hebrew script (כתב עברי, "Hebrew script") do not defile the hands, that is, they do not count as holy Scripture. Only biblical scrolls written in the square script (כתב אשורית, "Assyrian script") defile the hands. Most scholars attribute this rule to the sectarian boundary between the early rabbis and the Samaritans. As Tov writes, "the rabbis [or their precursors, RH] rejected the writing in the paleo-Hebrew script ... due to party politics, since some of their opponents used biblical scrolls written in that script."[42] In addition to this rule excluding paleo-Hebrew scrolls, there was also a gradual exclusion (or extinction) of biblical scrolls in the square script that did not conform to the inner circle of the proto-M family. The biblical scrolls from the Bar Kokhba caves are all written in square script, and nearly all are from the inner circle of the proto-M family.[43] These developments (ca. late first and early second centuries CE) are the first clear indications of the narrowing of valid tokens of biblical books.

For the earlier period, I propose a thought experiment. If a book-scroll of Leviticus lacked one or more of the ritual laws (i.e., God's commandments), would this lacuna suffice to make it an invalid book-scroll of Leviticus in a Jewish community (whether Judean or Samaritan)? I think so. If the missing law was particularly cherished in that community, then the likelihood of invalidation would be even greater.

This hypothetical situation is pertinent to a group of manuscripts called 4QReworked Pentateuch (4Q158 + 4Q364–367) that has occasioned a lively debate over whether they should be regarded as books of the Pentateuch (and hence renamed 4QPentateuch) or whether they are a kind of commentary in the form of "rewritten" biblical books.[44] These man-

---

41. On corrections in the Qumran manuscripts, see Tov, *Scribal Practices*, 222–30.

42. Ibid., 247.

43. See below, ch. 8.

44. See Michael Segal, "4QReworked Pentateuch or 4QPentateuch?" in *The Dead Sea Scrolls: Fifty Years after their Discovery*, ed. Lawrence H. Schiffman, Emanuel Tov, and James C. VanderKam (Jerusalem: Israel Exploration Society, 2000), 391–99; Sidnie White Crawford, *Rewriting Scripture in Second Temple Times*, SDSS (Grand Rapids: Eerdmans, 2008), 39–59; Molly M. Zahn, *Rethinking Rewritten Scripture: Composition and Exegesis in the 4QReworked Pentateuch Manuscripts*, STDJ 95 (Leiden: Brill, 2011), 1–12 (and 245–58 for her transcription and reconstruction of 4Q158); Eugene

uscripts, as Tov characterizes them, "contain long stretches of unaltered Scripture text as well as small and large exegetical additions and changes."[45] Since these types of variation are typical in copies of other biblical books, Tov concludes: "the manuscripts of this group should therefore be considered Scripture."[46] That is, they are copies of the Pentateuch in the same way as the other book-scrolls that are tokens of pentateuchal books.

However, as Moshe Bernstein has cautioned, among the variants in these manuscripts are omissions of laws.[47] 4Q365 (frag. 28) jumps from Num 4 to Num 7, skipping all the ritual laws in between, including laws concerning purity, sacrifice, and adultery. Unless these laws were reinserted elsewhere in the book-scroll (which is not ascertainable because of the fragmentary condition of the manuscript), this poses the problem raised above. Similarly, 4Q367 (frag. 2) jumps from Lev 15:15 to 19:1, omitting the laws in the intervening chapters, including the purity laws for menstruation and sexual intercourse, the instructions for the Day of Atonement, and the laws of incest. According to the Qumran sectarian documents, the laws omitted in 4Q365 and 4Q367 were very important, constituting some of the boundary conditions for the community.[48] Bernstein's question—"Can we imagine and explain a text of the Pentateuch which did not contain all of its legal material?"[49]—takes on particular salience when we consider the importance of these laws for the community.

I suggest that these omissions would signal to its readers at Qumran and elsewhere that these book-scrolls were not tokens of the Pentateuch but tokens of another kind of book, perhaps of the kind that one Qumran

---

Ulrich, " 'Nonbiblical' Scrolls Now Recognized as Scriptural," in *Developmental Composition*, 187–94; Emanuel Tov, "From 4QReworked Pentateuch to 4QPentateuch (?)," in *Textual Criticism of the Hebrew Bible, Qumran, Septuagint: Collected Essays*, VTSup 167 (Leiden: Brill, 2015), 45–59. For 4Q364–367, see Emanuel Tov and Sidnie White (Crawford), "Reworked Pentateuch," in *Qumran Cave 4. VIII: Parabiblical Texts, Part I*, DJD XIII (Oxford: Clarendon, 1994), 187–351.

45. Emanuel Tov, "Reflections on the Many Forms of Scripture in Light of the LXX and 4QReworked Pentateuch," in *Collected Essays*, 3.

46. Ibid., 19; similarly, Ulrich, Crawford, and, with some qualifications, Zahn and Segal (above, n. 44).

47. Moshe Bernstein, "What Has Happened to the Laws? The Treatment of Legal Material in 4QReworked Pentateuch," *DSD* 15 (2008): 24–49.

48. E.g., CD 3:13–15 and 6:18–19 on the festivals, including the Day of Atonement; and CD 5:7–11 on the incest laws, citing Lev 18:13.

49. Bernstein, "What Has Happened," 48.

text calls a "book of the Second Torah" (ספר התורה שנית).[50] That is, the omission of ritual laws, along with some striking new laws (e.g., for the festivals of wood and new oil)[51] would signal that the book-scroll is not a token of the "First Torah" but is a token of the "Second Torah,"[52] a secondary work or metadiscourse on the Torah. A particular reading community, perhaps at Qumran, could have regarded both as authoritative.

As Sidnie White Crawford observes, 4QRP "ceased to be copied after the Hasmonean period and was lost in the tradition."[53] These manuscripts raise the issue of boundary conditions for what counts as a valid copy of a biblical book in the late Second Temple period. There were such boundaries, as the different designations for Genesis and Jubilees indicate.[54] Our discussion of Genesis and 4QRP illustrates the complex relationships of books and their book-scrolls, of types and their tokens, in the era of Qumran, during the time when books of the Bible came to be regarded as such.

CONCLUSION: EDITING BIBLICAL BOOKS

Biblical scholars have long acknowledged a distinction between the biblical books and their physical witnesses in scrolls, codices, and printed editions. The concept of the biblical text has the same duality. The scholar who inaugurated modern textual criticism of the Hebrew Bible, Louis Cappel, wrote in the seventeenth century:

---

50. Timothy H. Lim, "Authoritative Scriptures and the Dead Sea Scrolls," in *The Oxford Handbook of the Dead Sea Scrolls*, ed. John J. Collins and Timothy H. Lim (Oxford: Oxford University Press, 2010), 317, quoting 4Q177.

51. Added at Lev 24:2 in 4Q365 frag. 23; these festivals are found in the Temple Scroll and other texts; see Emanuel Tov and Sidnie White (Crawford), "Reworked Pentateuch," 290–96; Crawford, *Rewriting Scripture*, 49–51; Zahn, *Rethinking*, 102–8.

52. This is the locution of Jub. 6:22, which seems to self-consciously situate itself as a Second Torah; see Lim, "Authoritative Scripture," 316; Hindy Najman, *Seconding Sinai: The Development of Mosaic Discourse in Second Temple Judaism*, JSJSup 77 (Leiden: Brill, 2003), 48.

53. Sidnie White Crawford, "The 'Rewritten Bible' at Qumran: A Look at Three Texts," *ErIsr* 26 (1999): 5.

54. CD 16:3–4 refers to Jubilees as "the book (ספר) of the divisions of the periods according to their jubilees and their weeks"; this designation echoes the first verse of Jubilees as an *incipit*. Cf. the references in CD 7:15 and many other Qumran texts to the Pentateuch as ספר מושה ("the book of Moses") or ספר התורה ("the book of the Law"); see Segal, "Biblical Interpretation," 67–69.

> Truly, the authentic Hebrew text, considered as such, is one thing, and the actual Jewish codex is another, in which the text as such is contained (as in other codices).[55]

Tov reiterates this distinction in his comment, quoted above, that "the 'biblical text' is an abstract unit that is not found in any one single source." He adds elsewhere: "these sources shed light on and witness to the biblical text, hence their name: 'textual witnesses'…. No textual source contains what could be called *the* biblical text."[56] This distinction between the biblical text and its variant physical instantiations is clarified by the theoretical work of Kant, Goodman, Peirce, and Wollheim, with the historicizing qualifications that I have proposed.

By asking "What is a book?" and its corollary "What is a biblical book?," I have attempted to elucidate the relationship between the abstract and physical qualities of a book, which affects our understanding of the textual variations among its copies. I have argued that two distinctions—between allographic and autographic arts, and between a type and its tokens—allow us to think more precisely about the biblical books as works with multiple and dispersed instantiations. As the observations of Ulrich, Tov, and Cappel demonstrate, this condition is pertinent to the biblical books, both in our thinking and in the conceptual world of ancient Israel. A careful exploration of these concepts has multiple implications for the theory and practice of editing biblical books.

First, it enables us to understand more clearly the distinction between the biblical text and its physical instantiations. It provides the intellectual apparatus to comprehend clearly that, as Tov stresses, "MT and the biblical text are *not* identical concepts."[57] The biblical text as such is a type, which is instantiated in its many variant tokens. The MT is also a type, which is

---

55. Louis Cappel, *Critica Sacra, sive de Variis quae in Sacris Veteris Testamenti Libris Occurrunt Lectionibus Libri Sex* (Paris: Cramoisy, 1650; repr., Halle: Hendel, 1775), 603; quoted in Laplanche, *L'Écriture, le sacré et l'histoire: Érudits et politiques protestants devant la Bible en France au XVIIe siècle*, (Amsterdam: Holland University Press, 1986), 242, 878: "Verum aliud est ipse authenticus textus hebraeus in se consideratus, aliud hodiernus codex judaïcus, in quo textus ipse (ut in aliis codicibus) continetur."

56. Tov, *Textual Criticism*, 3, emphasis original.

57. Tov, *Textual Criticism of the Hebrew Bible* (Minneapolis: Fortress, 1992), xxxviii, emphasis original. In subsequent editions the author omitted this sentence, perhaps, like the elder Whitman, preferring a less controversial tone.

instantiated in its variant tokens. Those who regard a particular token as if it were *the* biblical text—whether for reasons of habit, religious conservatism, or naïve empiricism—are committing the mistake of confusing an allographic artwork with an autographic one. They are treating a book as if it were a painting. Scholars know that any particular copy of MT (such as L, A, or *BHS*) is not the original "piece of invention"; hence it is unwarranted to treat it as if it were. Any medieval manuscript or printed edition is an object that tokens its type. To read a particular physical copy as if it were the only authentic copy of Genesis (or Exodus, etc.) is a category mistake. Of course, one can choose to read any available copy of a book, but scholars should be aware that it is not intellectually defensible to invest a particular copy of a book with the authority of an autographic artwork.

Second, the criterion of accurate notation clarifies the distinction between the substantive readings of an edition (= the notation as such) and the "accidental" features of presentation, which are secondary to the notation as such. The accidental features include spelling (which can change without affecting the semantics of the notation) and other para-textual elements such as vocalization, accentuation, verse division, and so on (which disambiguate the semantics of the notation). A critical edition should focus on accuracy of notation (in its allographic sense) and can adopt any reasonable strategy for presentational features.

Third, variant editions of a book count as instantiations of that book. The case of Whitman's *Leaves of Grass* is exemplary, since its editions vary considerably. In the case of the books of the Hebrew Bible, the variant editions that circulated in antiquity were not produced by a single author (although in some cases we cannot exclude this possibility), so the situation is more complicated than Whitman's editions. But variant editions of biblical books circulated during the Second Temple period, and they seem to have been generally regarded as valid copies (see the existence of variant editions of Jeremiah, Samuel, Judges, Exodus, etc., at Qumran). In a critical edition, it is valid to reproduce any or all of these editions, as is the case for Whitman's book. Each edition is a valid token of the book and therefore can or should be represented in a critical edition.

Fourth, the concept of a book clarifies that one of the chief goals of a critical edition is to recover, to the extent feasible, the notation of the book at the point when it became a book, that is (in Kant's phrase) when "someone delivers [it] to the public." The goal of a critical edition is not the reconstitution of earlier compositional phases, such as a book's constituent sources or editorial layers, since these are literary features that predate the book as such. The goal is to approximate the notation of the book in its state when it entered into public circulation, as well as the notation of subsequent editions of the book when they entered into public circulation. It may be impossible to specify the relevant historical events of "publication" with precision, but it is a coherent goal, even if it remains, for the biblical books, an ideal goal or limit condition.[58] A critical edition should attend to each of the phases in the book's punctuated history as a book, including substantially different editions (as with Whitman's book).

Finally, tying together some of these points, a critical eclectic edition of a biblical book is a valid token of that book. This responds to a criticism by Hugh Williamson that an eclectic edition does not, in his view, count as a Bible.[59] According to ordinary usage, critical editions—of *Ulysses*, *Leaves of Grass*, the Gospel of Mark, and so on—are tokens of that type, unless one has a situation where the local bibliographical authorities declare it invalid. It is certainly the case that critical editions of the Bible, such as *BHS*, are invalid in some communities that adhere to a particular authoritative edition (such as the Hebrew *textus receptus*, which derives from the Second Rabbinic Bible of 1524–1525, an eclectic edition of MT!). The HBCE editions of biblical books will count as tokens of those books in this ordinary sense. We are not creating editions that will omit the laws of Yom Kippur and incest (cf. 4QRP) or mandate adultery (the Wicked Bible), so the ordinary criteria for valid tokens will apply.

The concept of biblical books includes critical editions as valid tokens, within the limits established and policed by local bibliographical authorities. This concept has a descriptive and normative sense, since there is a

---

58. In the case of the Pentateuch, we may point to the account of Ezra's reading the ספר תורת משה ("Book of the Torah of Moses") in Neh 8, which, if it actually occurred, may possibly be dated to October 2, 458 BCE; see Hendel, *Text of Genesis*, 114. In any case, it is the Bible's representation of the "publication" (i.e., making public) of the Pentateuch. Scholars sometimes regard the publication of a biblical book as the occasion when it was deposited in the temple archive; see, Tov, *Textual Criticism*, 30 n. 15 and references; but cf. Stefan Schorch, "The Libraries in 2 Macc 2:13–15, and the Torah as a Public Document in Second Century BC Judaism," in *The Books of the Maccabees: History, Theology, Ideology; Papers of the Second International Conference on the Deuteronomical Books, Pápa, Hungary, 9–11 June, 2005*, ed. Géza G Xeravits and József Zsengellér, JSJSup 118 (Leiden: Brill, 2007), 169–80, who questions whether the temple archive housed a collection of sacred books.

59. H. G. M. Williamson, "Do We Need a New Bible? Reflections on the Proposed Oxford Hebrew Bible," *Bib* 90 (2009): 175.

tacit preference for copies with accurate notation. This is what a critical eclectic edition aims to accomplish. The criticism that a particular critical text never previously existed, that is, it does not replicate a past copy in all details, is correct but misses the point of what a critical edition is and does. Even if a critical edition is (necessarily) imperfect, it aims to provide a better copy of the notation of the book than the other extant copies. It therefore ought to be preferred by informed readers.

In sum, to echo Foucault, the practical task of editing the biblical books suffers in the absence of a cogent theory of a biblical book. I have attempted to outline such a theory and to draw out its implications for the production of a fully critical edition, that is, an edition with a critical text, apparatus, and commentary. A biblical book is constituted by the relationship between an abstract object and its (varying) corporeal manifestations. When it is unread, a copy of a book is, as Borges says, "literally, geometrically, a volume, a thing among things."[60] Only when it is opened does the tangible thing entail a semiotic event, a type-token relationship, a discourse made public by visible signs. Our scholarly editions should respond to the complex nature of biblical books.

---

60. Jorge Luis Borges, *Seven Nights*, trans. Eliot Weinberger (New York: New Directions, 1984), 76.

5

THE EPISTEMOLOGY OF TEXTUAL CRITICISM

The point is that *this* is how we play the game.
—Ludwig Wittgenstein, *Philosophical Investigations*

Observe the small facts upon which large inferences may depend.
—Arthur Conan Doyle, *The Sign of Four*

The rebirth of textual criticism of the Hebrew Bible in the wake of the discovery of the Dead Sea Scrolls has occasioned serious attention to issues of methodology. The most explicit and sustained engagement with such issues is found in the works of Emanuel Tov, particularly in his successive editions of *Textual Criticism of the Hebrew Bible* and in his recent essay, "The Relevance of Textual Theories for the Praxis of Textual Criticism."[1] While Tov's formulations are characteristically thoughtful and erudite, they are hampered by a commitment to a version of empiricism and scientism, common among philologists, that shies away from vigorous pursuit of the theoretical underpinnings of our disciplinary practices. I propose to explore the epistemology of textual criticism in dialogue with Tov's formulations. My goal is to bring into focus the implicit rules of our discipline along with their conceptual entailments. Only when we understand these tacit practices can we properly evaluate them in ways that both conserve and expand their potential.

---

1. Emanuel Tov, *Textual Criticism of the Hebrew Bible*, 3rd ed. (Minneapolis: Fortress, 2012), 270–81; and Tov, "The Relevance of Textual Theories for the Praxis of Textual Criticism," in *A Teacher for All Generations: Essays in Honor of James C. Vanderkam*, ed. Eric F. Mason, JSJSup 153 (Leiden: Brill, 2012), 23–35; an earlier formulation is Tov, "Criteria for Evaluating Textual Readings: The Limitation of Textual Rules," *HTR* 75 (1982): 429–48.

I am guided by the idea that text-critical reason has its reasons, even if they are difficult to elucidate fully. In other words, the implicit rules of our discipline—including our patterns of discovery and justification—are more than just habits or intuition. These rules are worth thinking about and, where necessary, criticized and revised. But it is difficult to see beneath our entrenched procedures, which often seem to the specialist to be self-evident. As the philosopher Peter Lipton aptly observes, "It is amazingly difficult to give a principled description of the way we weigh evidence. We may be very good at doing it, but we are miserable at describing how it is done."[2] My attempt to do so for textual criticism is therefore provisional and exploratory.

Tov has consistently maintained that textual criticism is a subjective art and a form of common sense. These terms imply a contrast with more objective inquiries, such as science. As he emphasizes in the third edition of *Textual Criticism of the Hebrew Bible*, text-critical analysis "is an *art* in the full sense of the word.... This procedure is as subjective as can be. *Common sense*, rather than textual theories, is the main guide, although abstract rules are sometimes helpful."[3] His emphasis on the subjective nature of the discipline is expanded in a new introductory section called "Subjectivity of This Book," wherein he emphasizes that "almost every paragraph in this book attests to subjectivity."[4] I maintain that the contrasts of subjective versus objective and art versus science do not accurately characterize the implicit rules and technique of textual criticism. In order to gain some clarity on the rules of this particular game, we must eschew simple oppositions and cast our analytical net more widely.

Housman's Fleas

As Tov observes, his position on the epistemology of textual criticism essentially restates the arguments of A. E. Housman in his classic essay, "The Application of Thought to Textual Criticism."[5] With biting wit, Hous-

---

2. Peter Lipton, *Inference to the Best Explanation*, 2nd ed., ILP (London: Routledge, 2004), xi.

3. Tov, *Textual Criticism*, 280–81, emphasis original; this section is a revision of Tov, "Criteria," 445–46.

4. Tov, *Textual Criticism*, 22.

5. Tov, "Criteria," 430; Tov, *Textual Criticism*, 1.

man maintained that textual criticism consists of a rigorous application of common sense:

> [Textual criticism] is not a sacred mystery. It is purely a matter of reason and of common sense. We exercise textual criticism whenever we notice and correct a misprint. A man who possesses common sense and the use of reason must not expect to learn from treatises or lectures on textual criticism anything that he could not, with leisure and industry, find out for himself. What the lectures and treatises can do for him is to save him time and trouble by presenting to him immediately considerations which would in any case occur to him sooner or later.[6]

To illustrate his argument, Housman adduces the metaphor of a dog hunting for fleas:

> A textual critic engaged upon his business is not at all like Newton investigating the motions of the planets: he is much more like a dog hunting for fleas. If a dog hunted for fleas on mathematical principles, basing his researches on statistics of area and population, he would never catch a flea except by accident. They require to be treated as individuals; and every problem which presents itself to the textual critic must be regarded as possibly unique.[7]

Housman contrasts the dog's (and textual critic's) subjective common sense with the Newtonian scientist's objective principles. While I endorse Housman's emphasis on the necessity of applying thought to textual criticism, I contest his—and Tov's—insistence that textual criticism is an application of common sense to texts. It is true that, as Housman says, "we exercise textual criticism whenever we notice and correct a misprint." But textual criticism involves more than common sense and ingenuity. It is a historical discipline that engages with complicated physical evidence and abstract objects and that requires erudition and methodological tact. Like any complex cultural practice, our discipline depends on all sorts of theoretical and empirical underpinnings. The question is whether we are—or want to be—aware of these implicit rules, theories, and practices.

---

6. A. E. Housman, "The Application of Thought to Textual Criticism," *PCA* 18 (1921): 68; http://tinyurl.com/SBL7010d.

7. Ibid., 68–69.

Although Housman aims to demystify the practice of textual criticism, his position arguably evades what Christopher Lloyd calls a discipline's "hidden epistemologies":

> The problem of hidden epistemologies is that they can mislead practitioners into believing that "common sense" (for which we should read "the currently prevailing idea of naïve empiricism") or personal empathic insight or rhetorical persuasiveness are the only possible arbiters of interpretation and explanation.[8]

In this respect, Housman's and Tov's appeal to common sense is misleading. It masks the implicit rules of the inquiry and creates an aura of self-evident authority for its practitioners. It is a strategy of justification, not explanation. Appeals to "common sense" or "art" serve to ward off detailed inquiry into the foundations of the discipline. To be sure, this is not Tov's or Housman's intention—they simply hold that the procedures of textual criticism are self-evident. However, I submit that mystification and institutional justification are consequences of this position.

To claim that textual criticism is a subjective art not only mystifies the technique but also romanticizes it. Aviezer Tucker aptly criticizes this form of esotericism in historical disciplines:

> *Historiographical esotericism* holds that historians do possess knowledge of history, but it is impossible to explicitly explain how or why. Therefore historians cannot teach how to obtain knowledge of history any more than statesmen of great virtue can teach it to their children and pupils according to Plato. Historiographical wisdom would resemble Socratic virtue, gourmet baking and beer brewing, an art that cannot be reduced to any "recipe," sets of theories and methods that can be described, replicated, and explained abstractly, or explicitly taught to novices.[9]

The metaphor of Housman's fleas argues that textual criticism is a matter of native talent. He emphasizes that textual critics are born, not made, that its art is "not communicable to all men, nor to most men."[10] A natural practice or art cannot be explicitly criticized. As Tucker observes, this

---

8. Christopher Lloyd, *The Structures of History*, SSD (Oxford: Blackwell, 1993), 4.

9. Aviezer Tucker, *Our Knowledge of the Past: A Philosophy of Historiography* (Cambridge: Cambridge University Press, 2004), 19, emphasis original.

10. Housman, "Application of Thought," 84.

is a flawed explanation, which deflects inquiry into a complex scholarly practice. I suggest that Housman's fleas is the wrong metaphor. The textual critic is more like a detective or a diagnostician than a dog hunting fleas.

THE EVIDENTIAL PARADIGM

In a celebrated essay, "Clues: Roots of an Evidential Paradigm," Carlo Ginzburg argues that the historian at work is akin to a detective who analyzes clues to solve a case, or a doctor who examines symptoms to cure a patient, or a psychoanalyst who uncovers a patient's past traumas.[11] These tasks rely on what Ginzburg calls a semiotic and evidential paradigm, which infers past causes from present traces and effects.[12] Like these other disciplines, textual criticism infers past textual states from the clues in the surviving manuscripts. Like its congeners, textual criticism deals with individual cases, which may be puzzling or opaque. Based on a meticulous analysis of the clues, it infers the probable causes and history of textual change. It is an inferential and historical enterprise, relying on the epistemic procedures of diagnosis and conjecture. As Ginzburg observes, "As with the physician's, historical knowledge is indirect, presumptive, conjectural."[13]

Notably, the core disciplines of the evidential paradigm—including history, textual criticism, medicine, and forensics—became mature during the latter half of the nineteenth century. Ginzburg writes, "Towards the end of the nineteenth century—more precisely in the decade 1870–80—a presumptive paradigm began to assert itself in the humane sciences that was based specifically on semiotics."[14] Disciplines that elucidate individual, nonreproducible past phenomena "could not avoid turning to the conjectural [paradigm] ... When causes cannot be reproduced, there is nothing to do but to deduce them from their effects."[15]

---

11. Carlo Ginzburg, "Clues: Roots of an Evidential Paradigm," in *Clues, Myths, and the Historical Method*, trans. John and Anne Tedeschi (Baltimore: Johns Hopkins University Press, 1989), 96–125; first published as "Spie: Radici di un paradigma indiziario," in *Crisi della ragione*, ed. Aldo Gargani (Turin: Einaudi, 1979), 59–106.

12. Ginzburg notes ("Clues," 189 n. 49) that he is building on "some memorable pages on the 'probable' character of historical knowledge" in Marc Bloch, *The Historian's Craft*, trans. Peter Putnam (New York: Vintage, 1953), 124–33.

13. Ibid., 106.

14. Ibid., 102.

15. Ibid., 117.

At the beginning of this crucial decade, Julius Wellhausen published his text-critical monograph, *Der Text der Bücher Samuelis untersucht* (1871), which laid the foundation for all subsequent textual criticism of the Hebrew Bible. Notably, he begins the book with an analogy between the procedures of textual criticism and medicine. Both disciplines, he implies, share—or *ought* to share—certain exemplary epistemic practices. In contrast to the ad hoc corrections made by contemporary textual critics, he urges that, like an expert diagnostician, the critic must examine the whole patient, including a full history, before treating a particular condition:

> It seems to me that textual criticism of the Old Testament is done too sporadically these days. One is content with individual emendations without engaging in a coherent assessment of the nature of the transmitted texts—one does not first attempt to learn about the constitution of the patient as a whole, but starts treating him immediately.... A more comprehensive approach seems worthwhile.[16]

Wellhausen's prescriptive analogy with the "more comprehensive approach" of medical diagnostics highlights the epistemic practices of the evidential paradigm. Just as the doctor infers the causes from a comprehensive examination of the patient's symptoms and history, so the textual critic should undertake a "coherent assessment of the nature of the transmitted texts" before inferring the causes of textual change and making judgments about the best available (or earliest inferable) reading. In this semiotic paradigm, one must examine, collate, and question, based on detailed knowledge, before moving on to the diagnosis and—with luck—a cure. Not surprisingly, the fictional medical doctor, John Watson, describes Sherlock Holmes's forensic task in a way that also corresponds to his medical practice: "to frame some scheme into which all these strange and apparently disconnected episodes could be fitted."[17] With some slight modifications, this description applies well to the work of the textual critic.

Ginzburg emphasizes that the focus on individual cases distinguishes the evidential paradigm from Newtonian science. The latter focuses on general phenomena or laws, of which individual cases are messy instantiations.

---

16. Julius Wellhausen, *Der Text der Bücher Samuelis untersucht* (Göttingen: Vandenhoeck & Ruprecht, 1871), iii.

17. Arthur Conan Doyle, *The Hound of the Baskervilles: Another Adventure of Sherlock Holmes* (New York: Grosset & Dunlap, 1902), 69.

In Newtonian science, the matrix of cause and effect is reproducible, but in the evidential disciplines, the cases are singular and the causes unreproducible. (In this respect, historically based sciences, such as evolutionary biology and paleontology, qualify as evidential disciplines, since they deal for the most part with individual cases, not general laws. The rise of genetics, however, blurs these boundaries.[18])

The difference between the general law and the individual case entails different epistemic rules. In the evidential disciplines, Ginzburg writes:

> The object is the study of individual cases, situations, and documents, precisely *because they are individual*, and for this reason get results that have an unsuppressible speculative margin: just think of the importance of conjecture (the term itself originates in divination) in medicine or in philology.[19]

Textual criticism involves conjecture precisely because, like medicine and history, it deals with individual cases. As an evidential and semiotic discipline, it is neither art nor science.

From these considerations, we can refine Tov's characterization of textual criticism as a subjective art. Its subjectivity is constrained by its epistemic goal, to infer past states from present textual details. Like a good detective or diagnostician, the textual critic must be able to assess the situation, assemble relevant evidence, imagine possible causes, and distinguish degrees of probability. The critic reconstitutes the most plausible past. It is an indirect, inferential process, and may end in success or failure. But it is a rational and analytic procedure, not mere art or intuition.

Against Housman, the practices of textual criticism are not simply reducible to the application of common sense. If this were so, it would be difficult to explain why its practices have changed over the years. This situation also holds true for other evidential disciplines. In the medieval and early modern period, doctors—or, more often, barbers—bled their patients and attributed the etiology of symptoms to witchcraft, macrocosmic analogy, or other fabulous causes. During the same period, biblical scholars and theologians often regarded textual variants in the Hebrew Bible as deliberate falsifications caused by Jews or the devil. Modern text-

---

18. See Stephen J. Gould, "Evolution and the Triumph of Homology, or Why History Matters," *AmSci* 74 (1986): 60–69.

19. Ginzburg, "Clues," 106, emphasis original.

critical diagnoses are based on different background assumptions than our medieval forebears.

In sum, textual criticism has a historically contingent genealogy, which yields the theories and rules that determine our selection of relevant data and constrain our explanations of causes. The epistemic procedures of the modern evidential paradigm inform our analyses and judgments. Dogs (and their wolf ancestors) have always hunted for fleas in roughly the same way. Textual criticism emerged at specific times and places, and responded to local causes and quarrels. Its procedures have changed for the better and will, one hopes, continue to do so.

THE LOGIC OF ERROR AND INNOVATION

The practice of textual criticism consists of two complimentary phases: studying the history of the texts (*historia textus*) and restoring the earliest inferable state of the text (*constitutio textus*). The practical goal is the production of critical editions that combines the fruits of both of these inquiries. Let us turn to the first phase, *historia textus*, for which the most important evidence is errors and innovations.

By error and innovation I mean transcriptional mistakes and deliberate revisions, respectively. These are the two main kinds of secondary readings (physical damage is a third). In older textual criticism, all textual change is usually subsumed under the category of "error," and more recently textual change is often subsumed under the category of "innovation."[20] The important point here is that only certain kinds of errors and innovations serve as reliable clues for textual history. The best clues are (in the traditional terminology) "indicative errors" (*Leitfehler, errores significativi*).[21] This category consists of errors or innovations that are shared between manuscripts and are monogenetic, that is, derived from a single text. Changes that are likely to have been created independently (polygenetic errors) have no implications for textual affiliation. Innovations or errors that exist only in one manuscript (*errores*

---

20. Paolo Trovato, *Everything You Always Wanted to Know about Lachmann's Method: A Non-standard Handbook of Genealogical Textual Criticism in the Age of Post-structuralism, Cladistics, and Copy-Text*, Storie e linguaggi 7 (Padua: Libreriauniversitaria, 2014), 54.

21. Ibid., 54–57, 109–17.

singulares) also have no implications for textual affiliation. Only shared derived innovations are reliable clues for textual history.

Michael Reeve aptly elucidates the general principle of inferring historical relationships by means of indicative errors:

> The main principle ... [is] that when copies share an innovation absent from the rest they are related (more closely, that is, than by being copies of the same work); if none of those that share the innovation can plausibly be regarded as the one where it originated, it must have originated in a lost ancestor common to them all. With luck, the extant copies and their postulated ancestors can be arranged in a family tree.[22]

The logic of shared derived innovation and error is key not only for textual history, but also for historical inquiry in other evidential disciplines, including linguistics and biology.[23] As Ginzburg observes, the "use of gaps and mistakes as clues" to reconstitute forgotten histories is characteristic of the epistemology of the evidential disciplines.[24]

As Sebastiano Timpanaro has shown, this concept has long been tacitly used by textual critics, including Karl Lachmann in his 1850 edition of Lucretius.[25] The common-error principle was first elucidated explicitly by classicist Paul Lejay in 1903:[26]

> A family of manuscripts is constituted by their common errors, or, if one prefers the more exact term, by their common innovations. Thus, the existence of a series of correct and authentic readings in several manuscripts cannot prove that these manuscripts derive from a common source. Only errors are probative.[27]

---

22. Michael D. Reeve, foreword to Trovato, *Everything*, 10.

23. Michael D. Reeve, "Shared Innovations, Dichotomies, and Evolution," in *Manuscripts and Methods: Essays on Editing and Transmission* (Rome: Edizioni di storia e letteratura, 2012), 55–103; see further Henry M. Hoenigswald and Linda F. Wiener, eds., *Biological Metaphor and Cladistic Classification: An Interdisciplinary Perspective* (Philadelphia: University of Pennsylvania Press, 1987).

24. Carlo Ginzburg, "Family Resemblances and Family Trees: Two Cognitive Metaphors," *CritInq* 30 (2004): 555.

25. Sebastiano Timpanaro, *The Genesis of Lachmann's Method*, trans. Glenn W. Most (Chicago: University of Chicago Press, 2005), 102–14.

26. Jean-Baptiste Camps, "Copie, authenticité, originalité dans la philologie et son histoire," *Questes* 29 (2015): 42; cf. Reeve, "Shared Innovations," 57–58.

27. Paul Lejay, Review of *Aeli Donati quod fertur Commentum Terenti*, ed. Paul

In 1937 Paul Maas coined the term *Leitfehler* (translated in 1958 as "indicative error") to denote this category of common errors and innovations.[28] This principle was transferred from textual criticism to historical linguistics during the spread of the evidential paradigm in the nineteenth century. As Henry Hoenigswald observes, "[August] Schleicher transferred the principle of the exclusively shared copying error from manuscript work to linguistics" in his *Stammbaumtheorie* (family-tree theory) of the Indo-European languages.[29] The linguistic principle of shared innovation was first explicitly articulated by Berthold Delbrück in 1880: "we have as conclusive evidence [for subgrouping] only those *innovations which are developed in common*."[30] This principle has become a touchstone in linguistic method.[31] As Hoenigswald comments, "while shared retentions are compatible with a subgrouping, innovations are indicative of one."[32]

In his 1966 work *Phylogenetic Systematics*, Willi Hennig made this concept central to biology.[33] He coined the term *synapomorphy* for

---

Wessner, *RCHL* 56 (1903): 171: "Une famille de manuscrits est constituée par leurs fautes communes, ou, si l'on préfère ce terme plus exact, par leurs innovations communes. Ainsi, l'existence d'une série de leçons correctes et authentiques dans plusieurs manuscrits ne peut prouver que ces manuscrits dérivent d'une source commune. Les fautes seules sont probantes."

28. Paul Maas, "Leitfehler und stemmatische Typen," *ByzZ* 37 (1937): 289–94.

29. Henry M. Hoenigswald, "Language Families and Subgroupings, Tree Model and Wave Theory, and Reconstruction of Protolanguages," in *Research Guide on Language Change*, ed. Edgar C. Polomé, TiLSM 48 (Berlin: de Gruyter, 1990), 442.

30. Trans. adapted from Berthold Delbrück, *Introduction to the Study of Language: A Critical Survey of the History and Methods of Comparative Philology of the Indo-European Languages*, trans. E. Channing (Leipzig: Breitkopf & Härtel, 1882), 137; Berthold Delbrück, *Einleitung in das Sprachstudium: Ein Beitrag zur Geschichte und Methodik der vergleichenden Sprachforschung* (Leipzig: Breitkopf & Härtel, 1880), 135: "Es bleiben streng genommen nur *gemeinsam vollzogene Neuerungen* als beweiskräftig übrig" (emphasis original). Quoted by C. Douglas Chrétien, "Shared Innovations and Subgrouping," *IJAL* 29 (1963): 67.

31. See Lyle Campbell, *Historical Linguistics: An Introduction*, 2nd ed. (Cambridge: MIT Press, 2004), 190–201. For this principle in Semitic linguistics, see Robert Hetzron, "Two Principles of Genetic Reconstruction," *Lingua* 38 (1976): 89–108, esp. 96–99.

32. Hoenigswald, "Language Families," 443.

33. Willi Hennig, *Phylogenetic Systematics*, trans. D. Dwight Davis and Ranier Zangerl (Urbana: University of Illinois, 1966).

derived traits shared by two or more taxonomic units, and emphasized that synapomorphies are the only reliable basis for establishing genealogical affiliation:

> The supposition that two or more species are more closely related to one another than to any other species, and that, together they form a monophyletic group, can only be confirmed by demonstrating their common possession of derived characteristics ("synapomorphy")…. Only the latter category of resemblance can be used to establish states of relationship.[34]

From texts to languages to species, shared derived errors are the chief clues for genealogical relationships and descent.

Some textual critics maintain that the overall profile of agreements and disagreements is sufficient to establish textual affinities among manuscripts. Its advantage over the genealogical (or common-error) method is that tabulation of all agreements and disagreements does not involve text-critical judgment. It can be done by mechanical comparison and thereby avoids the subjectivity of identifying shared derived innovations. However, this method does not withstand scrutiny. As Michael Weitzman states, "without the notion of error, one cannot even draw a stemma for two manuscripts AB, showing whether A derives from B or B from A or both from a lost source…. The notion of error cannot be sidestepped."[35] Agreement in correct readings has no probative value for genealogical inferences, nor do changes that are likely to be polygenetic. Only monogenetic innovations are indicative.

A necessary qualification is that, as Trovato states, "once a preliminary stemma has been sketched on the basis of indicative errors, lists of [other] … readings matching the distribution of indicative errors can provide a valuable control in complicated traditions."[36] Trovato calls these "characteristic readings" or "confirmatory readings." Hence a pattern of characteristic readings can supplement or confirm the analysis based on indicative errors.

---

34. Willi Hennig, "Phylogenetic Systematics," *ARevEnt* 10 (1965): 104.

35. Michael P. Weitzman, "The Analysis of Open Traditions," *SBib* 38 (1985): 95, 97; see further Michael P. Weitzman, *The Syriac Version of the Old Testament: An Introduction* (Cambridge: Cambridge University Press, 1999), 263–69.

36. Trovato, *Everything*, 116.

A recurring problem in elucidating the historical relationships among texts is what Giorgio Pasquali called "horizontal" or "transversal" transmission, which yields an "open tradition." As Gianfranco Contini elucidates:

> In the simplest case … [textual] transmission is "vertical" (Pasquali's term), that is, from copy to copy without deviations, and it is univocal, that is, it concerns a text that is fixed, with no alternatives. Pasquali calls "horizontal" or "transversal" a tradition in which more than one exemplar intervenes, by collation or contamination.[37]

In cases where horizontal transmission has taken place, the stemmatic relationships become equivocal or indeterminate. As Weitzman observes, "the same *apparatus criticus* admits more than one genealogy in an open tradition."[38] Relationships can still often be discerned, but there is a significant degree of uncertainty about which is the most probable of the possible stemmata. For a manuscript B that has been affected by horizontal transmission from A or C, Weitzman presents the following alternative stemmata as analytically equivalent:[39]

Since there is arguably some degree of horizontal transmission at some point (or several points) in the proto-SP genealogy, these alternative stemmata can represent the relationships between MT (=A), SP (=B) and LXX (=C) in the Pentateuch. The SP shares many small and medium-sized harmonizations with LXX (against MT) throughout the Pentateuch, but it also shares the expanded edition of the tabernacle text in Exod 35–40 with MT (against LXX). Horizontal transmission seems necessary to posit here.[40]

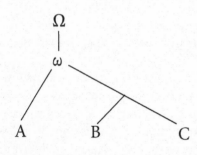

---

37. Quoted in Trovato, *Everything*, 128.

38. Weitzman, "Open Traditions," 88.

39. Ibid., 92.

40. For the stratum of shared harmonizations in SP and LXX, see Kyungrae Kim, "Studies in the Relationship Between the Samaritan Pentateuch and the Septuagint" (PhD diss., Hebrew University, 1994). Kim counts roughly 230 (mostly short) harmonizing pluses shared by SP and LXX. For additional long harmonizing/exegetical pluses shared by SP and LXX (at Exod 22:4; Lev 15:3; and Lev 17:4), see David Andrew

In the domain of horizontal transmission, the logic of error and innovation encounters its own uncertainty principle. Inferences based on the best clues—indicative errors, synapomorphies—yield an equivocal history. Despite its blurred lines, even an equivocal history provides an evidential basis for inferences concerning the opposite of error—the identification of the earliest inferable readings in the textual tradition.

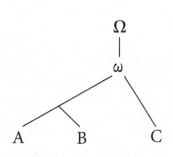

Inference to the Best Explanation

The second phase of text-critical inquiry is textual evaluation and restoration (*constitutio textus*). This phase relies on the inferences drawn from textual history. However, it is at the same time a prerequisite for textual history, since only by evaluating readings can we identify the *Leitfehler* that are the primary clues for ascertaining textual affiliation. This is a circular procedure, as is the case in all historical and conjectural disciplines. As Housman rightly observed, "the task of the critic is just this, to tread that circle deftly and warily."[41] Once again, this is not pure subjectivity or art, but a condition of the epistemic paradigm of textual criticism.

The procedure of textual evaluation and restoration is briefly described by Tov:

> It is the art of defining the problems and finding arguments for and against the originality of readings. The formulation and weighing of these arguments are very central to textual criticism.... Therefore, it is the choice of the most contextually appropriate reading that is the main task of the textual critic.[42]

Teeter, *Scribal Laws: Exegetical Variation in the Textual Transmission of Biblical Law in the Late Second Temple Period*, FAT 92 (Tübingen: Mohr Siebeck, 2014), 35–58, 76–99. See below, ch. 9.

41. Housman, "Application of Thought," 80.

42. Tov, *Textual Criticism*, 281.

Tov qualifies this statement by adding, "This procedure is as subjective as can be." Tov's description is accurate as far as it goes, but it is hampered by the pejorative weight of "art" and "subjective." The oppositions of art/science and subjective/objective are blunt and inadequate instruments. Textual evaluation and restoration are inferential procedures, which should not be equated with pure subjectivity. These overly simple oppositions mask the actual procedures of textual evaluation.

Charles Sanders Peirce coined the word *abduction* to describe the kind of inferential process that we are describing. The term refers to a two-step process of generating hypotheses and selecting among them. He writes:

> The first starting of a hypothesis and the entertaining of it, whether as a simple interrogation or with any degree of confidence, is an inferential step which I propose to call *abduction*.... This will include a preference for any one hypothesis over others which would equally explain the facts, so long as this preference is not based upon any previous knowledge bearing upon the truth of the hypotheses, nor on any testing of any of the hypotheses, after having admitted them on probation. I call all such inference by the peculiar name, *abduction*, because its legitimacy depends upon altogether different principles from those of other kinds of inference.[43]

In recent philosophy, this species of inference is usually called "inference to the best explanation." Lipton aptly describes the roots of this process in our desire to explain unknown phenomena:

> We infer the explanations precisely because they would, if true, explain the phenomena. Of course, there is always more than one possible explanation for any phenomenon—the tracks might have instead been caused by a trained monkey on snowshoes, or by the elaborate etchings of an environmental artist—so we cannot infer something simply because it is a possible explanation. It must somehow be the best of competing explanations.[44]

The two-step process of hypothesis generation and selection—abduction, or inference to the best explanation—accurately describes the procedures of

---

43. Charles Sanders Peirce, "Abduction and Induction," in *Philosophical Writings of Peirce*, ed. Justus Buchler (New York: Dover, 1955), 151.

44. Lipton, *Inference*, 56.

textual evaluation. It is also generally characteristic of the evidential paradigm. As Lipton observes, this is the inferential procedure of detectives, doctors, textual critics, and—with some additional qualifications—scientists:

> The sleuth infers that the butler did it, since this is the best explanation of the evidence before him. The doctor infers that his patient has measles, since this is the best explanation of the symptoms. The astronomer infers the existence and motion of Neptune, since that is the best explanation of the observed perturbations of Uranus.[45]

The chief difference for the scientist is the possibility of empirically testing the best explanation. The "Neptune hypothesis" was confirmed when the planet Neptune was actually sighted through a telescope. Historical disciplines usually lack this possibility of empirical confirmation (or falsification), with the occasional exception of archaeological discoveries that confirm an explanation that was previously hypothetical. Notably, the discovery of the biblical manuscripts from Qumran have confirmed a number of previously hypothetical text-critical inferences.[46]

The two-step process of inference to the best explanation involves different criteria and kinds of judgment in each step. The first step, the generation of hypotheses, requires a combination of imagination and background knowledge, in which one considers a range of plausible causes. Lipton comments: "We must use some sort of short list mechanism, where our background beliefs help us to generate a very limited list of plausible hypotheses."[47] In textual evaluation, we leave out a multiplicity of implausible hypothesis, such as the "monkeys in a room" scenario, or alien thought-control, or (usually) divine intervention.

The generation of hypotheses in textual evaluation (*constitutio textus*) will include scenarios like the following:

1. A is the earliest inferable reading and B is historically secondary (e.g., an error or a revision based on A).

---

45. Ibid.

46. Tov, *Textual Criticism*, 329; Emanuel Tov, "The Contribution of the Qumran Scrolls to the Understanding of the Septuagint," in *The Greek and Hebrew Bible: Collected Essays on the Septuagint*, VTSup 72 (Leiden: Brill, 1999; repr., Atlanta: Society of Biblical Literature, 2006), 289–90.

47. Lipton, *Inference*, 149.

2.   B is the earliest inferable reading and A is historically secondary.
3.   A conjectural reading (C*) is the earliest inferable reading, from which the extant readings are historically derived.
4.   A textual problem is identifiable, but there are no plausible hypotheses to explain it.

This kind of short list of hypotheses is easily generated. The most complicated and, indeed, subjective, is number (3), the plausible conjecture. As E. J. Kenney observes, "the making of conjectures, as distinct from testing them, is intelligent guesswork."[48]

The second step, testing the hypotheses and selecting among them, is a more rigorous process. Here is where, as Tov says, one formulates and weighs the arguments for and against each of the hypotheses. Background knowledge is crucial in this step as well, since one must be familiar with the general tendencies of scribal transmission and the history of the textual evidence (derived from the prior inquiries into *historia textus*) in order to adjudicate among the different hypotheses.

It is in testing the hypotheses that the so-called rules or guidelines of textual criticism come into play, such as *lectio difficilior* (the difficult reading is to be preferred) or *lectio brevior* (the shorter reading is to be preferred). As Tov characteristically observes, these are not "objective criteria."[49] But they are an important part of the textual critic's background knowledge. Timpanaro aptly describes the relationship between the text-critic's knowledge of general textual phenomena and the evaluation of a particular case: "[the] task ... demands an effort to understand how various general tendencies contribute on any given occasion to the production of a single and particular error."[50] As with the other conjectural disciplines, the diagnosis of the cause of a particular clue or symptom depends on the background knowledge and acuity of the sleuth, doctor, or textual critic, including knowledge of how scribes, criminals, or diseases characteristically behave, alongside a detailed understanding of the particular case.

---

48. J. Kenney, "Textual Criticism," in vol. 18 of *The New Encyclopædia Britannica*, 15th ed. (Chicago: Encyclopædia Britannica, 1974), 192; http://tinyurl.com/SBL7010e.

49. Tov, *Textual Criticism*, 270.

50. Sebastiano Timpanaro, *The Freudian Slip: Psychoanalysis and Textual Criticism*, trans. Kate Soper (London: NLB, 1976), 84.

One of the rules of textual criticism has particular salience in the critical selection of the best explanation. As Kyle McCarter observes:

> There is really only one principle, a fundamental maxim to which all others can be reduced. This basic principle can be expressed ... most precisely with the question, *Utrum in alterum abiturum erat?* "Which would have changed into the other?"—that is, "Which is more likely to have given rise to the other?" This is the question the critic asks when he is ready to choose between alternative readings. When answered thoughtfully, it will provide the solution to most text-critical problems.[51]

This principle, which was formulated by eighteenth century New Testament critics, is described by Bruce Metzger and Bart Ehrman as "the most basic criterion for the evaluation of variant readings."[52]

The reason that this principle is so basic is that it presents with clarity the epistemic situation of textual criticism as an evidential discipline. As Kenny states, the textual critic weighs historical probabilities. The existing texts and variants are clues to the history of readings. Our selection of the historically earlier reading recapitulates, on the level of the individual case, the general task of *historia textus*. The analysis of error and innovation, in this phase, allows us to infer the direction of historical change that reveals the earlier and later reading. We infer the causes of the innovations by abduction, and so infer the history of readings. In so doing we attempt to explain the relationships among the available clues, which consist of errors, innovations, and older readings.

Notably, in the phase of testing hypotheses, emendations are subject to the same evaluative procedures as extant readings. As Kenney emphasizes, "the emendation itself, can and must be controlled and tested by precisely the same criteria as are used in deciding between variants."[53] A hypothesis that derives the extant reading(s) from a conjecture faces the same selective criteria: the careful formulation of arguments for and against each hypothesis, the testing and weighing of historical probabilities.

---

51. P. Kyle McCarter Jr., *Textual Criticism: Recovering the Text of the Hebrew Bible*, GBS (Philadelphia: Fortress Press, 1986), 72.

52. Bruce M. Metzger and Bart D. Ehrman, *The Text of the New Testament: Its Transmission, Corruption, and Restoration*, 4th ed. (New York: Oxford University Press, 2005), 300.

53. Kenney, "Textual Criticism," 192.

I emphasize that the critic's capacity for judgment is involved in each step of this inductive process. In the first step, one must use judgment to exclude implausible hypotheses and to formulate plausible ones. In the second step—the formulating and weighing of arguments for and against each hypothesis—the necessity of critical judgment is most acute. In this stage, the cogency of analysis and argumentation is what counts, and distinguishes the good from the bad critic. When done properly, the selection of the best explanation is an exacting intellectual process, combining extensive background knowledge with critical tact. It is not an art, but a complex weave of analysis and inference, which requires technical mastery.

However, we must make a further caveat. The best explanation is not necessarily the true explanation. In theory even Sherlock Holmes can be wrong. This is the epistemic condition of the conjectural and evidential paradigm. As Lipton observes, "Inference to the Best Explanation requires that we work with a notion of potential explanation that does not carry a truth requirement."[54] The best explanation might be true, but we cannot know this to be the case. This is a limit condition of evidential disciplines. As Tucker writes about historical inquiry generally:

> Historiography ... attempt[s] to provide a hypothetical description and analysis of some past events as the best explanation of present evidence. This knowledge is probably true, but it is not true in an absolute sense. The most that historiography can aspire for is increasing plausibility.[55]

A complementary observation concerns the limits of our text-critical imagination. If none of the entries on the short list of hypothesis is true, then selecting among them cannot yield a true explanation. Increasing plausibility is the relevant standard, not absolute truth.

Our explanatory ability is limited by the incompleteness of our textual evidence and by the imperfection of our powers of inference. A perfect text-critical procedure is not at hand. Like all historical inquiry, we see the past indirectly through our (always fallible) evaluation of its present traces. As Ginzburg writes, "direct knowledge of such a connection is

---

54. Lipton, *Inference*, 69.
55. Tucker, *Knowledge of the Past*, 258.

not possible. Though reality may seem to be opaque, there are privileged zones—signs, clues—which allow us to penetrate it."[56]

CONCLUSION: THE LIFE OF TEXTS

As Housman observes, "the things which the textual critic has to talk about are not things which present themselves clearly and sharply to the mind."[57] Housman is right, which complicates his view that the procedures of textual criticism are merely applied common sense. The epistemic underpinnings of textual criticism are hard to trace, but it is an enterprise that affords us a critical perspective on our practices, exposing their possibilities and limitations, and perhaps even allowing us to improve them. We should not avoid such hard thinking about the implicit rules and procedures of our discipline.

As Ginzburg observes, textual criticism partakes of the epistemic practices of the evidential paradigm. In its roots, this paradigm derives from instinctive and ancient skills, as when a hunter-gatherer analyzes animal tracks. In the mid- to late nineteenth century, a congeries of disciplines refined these procedures, including philology, forensics, medicine, and history. These disciplines infer causes from their present effects, from particular clues, signs, or symptoms. They are semiotic disciplines that, through conjecture and inference, conjure portions of the past from existing traces. But the reconstituted past always has a measure of uncertainty. The knowledge constructed through these disciplines always has blurred margins.

The inferential process at the heart of these disciplines is abduction or inference to the best explanation. This is a two-step process that requires imagination and judgment. In the first step the critic generates hypotheses, and in the second step the critic tests them. The tests consist of arguments for and against each hypothesis and a comparison of their relative merits. Where no positive solution avails, the critic must admit that the problem cannot be plausibly solved, and should have a way to accommodate the analytical impasse. Admitting defeat is a necessary part of the game.

A crucial part of the epistemology of these disciplines is the logic of error and innovation. Indicative errors, shared derived innovations,

---

56. Ginzburg, "Clues," 123.
57. Housman, "Application of Thought," 72.

synapomorphies, are central clues to the history of the phenomena. A recognition of this principle constituted a turning point in each discipline. The logic of innovation enables the critic to construct a logically sound (and plausibly accurate) stemma as a map to the past history of a particular reading, text, language, or organism. The procedure for elucidating the earliest (or archetypal) reading involves the same practice as the genealogy of a text, but in reverse, where the preferred reading is the earliest inferable node of the historical sequence. The two phases of text-critical inquiry, *historia textus* and *constitutio textus*, thus partake of similar rules and spiral around each other in a nexus of interconnected inferences. The more the critic plays the game, the more the rules seem a diverse unity, a syntax and semantics of a single diffuse language.

The critical testing of hypotheses involves knowledge of scribal practices, such as the scribal tendency to simplify complex forms, to modernize, to explicate. These tendencies are summarized in the term *lectio difficilior preferendum est* ("the difficult reading is to be preferred"). But this rule is just a reminder of general tendencies; it is not an invariable law. The rule, as Housman and Tov emphasize, is not a substitute for thought. The rules one finds in the handbooks are mnemonic aids, nothing more. A difficult reading that is impossible or that is unsuitable in the context should not be preferred. As Marc Bloch cautions, "The reagents for the testing of evidence should not be roughly handled. Nearly all the rational principles, nearly all the experiences which guide the tests, if pushed far enough, reach their limits in contrary principles or experiences."[58] The game requires that the textbook rules be handled with care, lest they become obstacles to the intelligent testing of hypotheses and evidence.

The Italian textual critic, Paolo Chiesa, writes, "Textual criticism is the discipline that … [studies a work's] transformations in the course of time" and that aims to "publish a 'reliable' text of a given work."[59] It cannot produce a perfect text of a given work. Perfection is not available in the evidential disciplines. Well-warranted, reliable, increasingly plausible explanations of the extant evidence—these are the standards for our inquiries. We are dealing with historical probabilities and warranted inferences, not mathematical proofs. If Ginzburg is correct, this is because

---

58. Bloch, *Historian's Craft*, 120.
59. Quoted in Trovato, *Everything*, 165.

the evidential paradigm deals with particular cases, not with general laws, and therefore is hedged with an inevitable margin of uncertainty.

These are the rules of the game that we play. It is not an art or a science but something in between: a diagnostic technique, a way of reading the tracks of the past, a pursuit of the text in all its historical transformations.

6

A Typology of Scribal Error

I saw some scribes err and miss the author's intention.
　—Yosef ben Moshe Al-Ashkar, *Sefer Ṣafenat Paʿaneaḥ* (1529)

The frailties and aberrations of the human mind, and of its insubordinate servants, the human fingers.
　—A. E. Housman, "The Application of Thought to Textual Criticism"

Lists and typologies of errors in the Hebrew Bible have been compiled intermittently since late antiquity. In the Babylonian Talmud, Rab Ḥisda warns against common graphic and aural errors:

In order that it be a perfect text, one must not write א as ע; ע as א; ב as כ; כ as ב; ג as צ; צ as ג; ד as ר; ר as ד; ה as ח; ח as ה; ו as י; י as ו; ז as ג; נ as ז; ט as פ; פ as ט; curved letters as straight [i.e., final letters]; straight letters as curved; מ as ס; ס as מ. (b. Šabb. 103b)

The minor tractate Masseket Soferim (or Ḥilqot Soferim, "Laws of Scribes," ca. ninth century CE) includes extensive instructions about the correction of scribal errors and lists variants from parallel biblical texts (Ps 28 // 2 Sam 22; Isa 36–39 // 2 Kgs 18–20). The Masorah written into the margins of medieval codices is aptly described as an "error-correcting code" by Yosef Ofer and Alexander Lubotzky, using the language of information theory.[1] Additional lists of variants and oddities were compiled by Masoretic scholars, including *Sefer ʾOklah we-ʾOklah* (named after the first pair

---

1. Yosef Ofer and Alexander Lubotzky, "The *Masorah* as an Error Correcting Code" [Hebrew], *Tarbiz* 82 (2013): 89–114.

of variants in the list) and *Sefer ha-Ḥillufim* ("The Book of Variants"). both ninth–tenth century CE.[2]

Despite these instructions and lists, medieval and early modern copyists of the Hebrew Bible continued to produce scribal errors. Moshe Goshen-Gottstein aptly described this as a consequence of "the ever-active and repeated force of the law of scribes," referring to the typical independently generated small errors and changes "formally common to medieval Hebrew MSS and premedieval sources."[3] The scribal production of error and change in biblical manuscripts, it seems, has never ceased.

Beginning in the seventeenth century, modern textual critics of the Hebrew Bible have compiled analytical typologies of scribal error and innovation.[4] The categories tend to be agglutinative, as in Friedrich Delitzsch's monumental collection of over three thousand (real and imagined) errors, *Die Lese- und Schreibfehler im Alten Testament*.[5] In more recent handbooks, the organizing categories of scribal change tend to turn on quantity (pluses, minuses, and interchanges)[6] or agency (unintentional versus intentional change).[7] Both of these axes of change are relevant, but

---

2. Fernando Díaz-Esteban, *Sefer Oklah we-Oklah* (Madrid: Consejo Superior de Investigaciones Científicas, 1975); Lazar Lipshütz, *Kitāb al-Khilaf: Mishael Ben Uzziel's Treatise on the Differences between Ben Asher and Ben Naphtali*, HUBP (Jerusalem: Magnes, 1965); see Israel Yeivin, *Introduction to the Tiberian Masorah*, ed. and trans. E. J. Revell, MasS 5 (Missoula, MT: Scholars Press, 1980), 128–31, 141–44; Emanuel Tov, *Textual Criticism of the Hebrew Bible*, 3rd ed. (Minneapolis: Fortress, 2012), 44; Geoffrey Khan, *A Short Introduction to the Tiberian Masoretic Bible and Its Reading Tradition*, GHand (Piscataway, NJ: Gorgias, 2012), 67.

3. Moshe H. Goshen-Gottstein, "Hebrew Biblical Manuscripts: Their History and Their Place in the HUBP Edition," in *Qumran and the History of the Biblical Text*, ed. Frank Moore Cross and Shemaryahu Talmon (Cambridge: Harvard University Press, 1975) 74.

4. Notable examples are Louis Cappel, *Critica Sacra, sive de Variis quae in Sacris Veteris Testamenti Libris Occurrunt Lectionibus Libri Sex*, (Paris: Cramoisy, 1650; repr., Halle: Hendel, 1775), books 3–5; and Johann Gottfried Eichhorn, *Einleitung in das Alte Testament*, 3rd ed., 3 vols. (Leipzig: Weidmann, 1803), 1:210–43 = *Introduction to the Study of the Old Testament*, partial trans. of 3rd ed. by G. T. Gollop (London: Spottiswoode, 1888), 169–95.

5. Friedrich Delitzsch, *Die Lese-und Schreibfehler im Alten Testament, nebst den dem Schrifttexte einverleibten Randnoten, klassifiziert* (Berlin: de Gruyter, 1920).

6. Tov, *Textual Criticism*, 219–62; P. Kyle McCarter Jr., *Textual Criticism: Recovering the Text of the Hebrew Bible*, GBS (Philadelphia: Fortress Press, 1986), 26–61.

7. Paul D. Wegner, *A Student's Guide to Textual Criticism of the Bible: Its History,*

there are some inconcinnities—some types of change can occur intentionally or unintentionally (e.g., synonymous variants; see below), and
some changes of different quantity (plus or minus) are caused by the same
scribal mechanism (eye-skip).

It is difficult to construct a typology that is analytically useful, one that
illuminates the mechanisms and motivations of scribal error.[8] One com-
plication is that many scribal errors have multiple causes. A graphic error,
for instance, can be motivated by the semantic context or by anticipation
or reminiscence of graphically similar sequences. Like other kinds of cognitive slips, a slip of the pen is often overdetermined. As Sebastiano Timpanaro observes in his reflections on textual criticism and psychoanalysis,
"the explanation of errors of transcription ... nearly always refers us to a
conjuncture of several causes (palaeographic, psychological-cultural, and
so on) ... virtually all errors are multidetermined."[9]

We should acknowledge the multiple and intersecting causes of
scribal error. Nonetheless, if we can construct a plausible typology that
addresses how scribal errors happen, it would constitute an advance in our
understanding of textual change in the Hebrew Bible. In the following, I
attempt to construct such a typology, building on a contribution of Eugène
Vinaver, a textual critic of medieval English and French literature. I will
adapt Vinavers's typology to scribal errors in the Hebrew Bible, which I
will supplement with some discussion of scribal revision. I will also pro-

---

Methods, and Results (Downers Grove, IL: IVP Academic, 2006), 44–55; Ernst Würthwein and Alexander A. Fischer, The Text of the Old Testament: An Introduction to the
Biblia Hebraica, trans. Erroll R. Rhodes, 3rd ed. (Grand Rapids: Eerdmans, 2014),
172–82; similarly, Bruce Metzger and Bart D. Ehrman. The Text of the New Testament:
Its Transmission, Corruption, and Restoration, 4th ed. (New York: Oxford University Press, 2005), 250–71; and Adrian Schenker, General Introduction and Megilloth,
BHQ 18 (Stuttgart: Deutsche Bibelgesellschaft, 2004), lxxxv–lxxxviii, with some further subdivisions (e.g., "change arising through ignorance") and an agnostic category
("change ... but not commenting on the motivation of the change").

8. Note Emanuel Tov's criticism of the typology in the BHQ General Introduction:
"The details in this particular categorization are problematical. It is hard to know for
whom this abstract system of subdividing the descriptions into different categories is
helpful" ("The Biblia Hebraica Quinta: An Important Step Forward," in Hebrew Bible,
Greek Bible, and Qumran: Collected Essays, TSAJ 121 [Tübingen: Mohr Siebeck, 2008],
196–97).

9. Sebastiano Timpanaro, The Freudian Slip: Psychoanalysis and Textual Criticism,
trans. Kate Soper (London: NLB, 1976), 84 n. 3.

vide a critique of David Carr's recently proposed category of "memory variants," which, if correct, would falsify my (and Vinaver's) analysis of the mechanisms of scribal error.

MECHANISMS OF TRANSCRIPTION

In 1939, Vinaver published a typology of scribal error that incorporates an analysis of the "mechanism of transcription," that is, the scribe's visual, cognitive, and motor processes in the movement between text and copy.[10] It is an elegant contribution, illustrated with examples from Arthurian and other medieval romances, including *Merlin* and *Quest of the Holy Grail*. Vinaver describes with precision the eye movements and focalization of memory involved in scribal copying:

> [The copyist's] object is to transfer the text from the original to the copy, and his eye must travel at regular intervals from one to the other. While looking at the original he will endeavour to retain as much as possible of what he sees. The visual or mental impression thus received must then be transferred to the copy, and while the scribe's eye goes from one to the other this impression must remain intact. Once it has been placed on the copy, the scribe must look again at the original. This time he has to bear in mind the last letter, word, or words he has written down, so as to find in the original the point at which he left it a moment ago. Thus the process of transcription requires a constant shifting of the line of vision from one plane to another, and with each movement of his eyes the copyist has to carry mental or visual impressions which help him, first to reproduce part of his text, and then to find his way back to it. This may be shown by the following chart:—

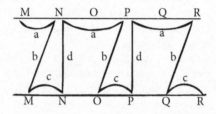

---

10. Eugène Vinaver, "Principles of Textual Emendation," in *Studies in French Language and Mediaeval Literature Presented to Professor Mildred K. Pope* (Manchester: Manchester University Press, 1939), 351–69. This essay is oft-cited; e.g., Metzger and Ehrman, *Text of the New Testament*, 250 n. 1.

Our chart shows that the scribe's eye must perform four distinct movements: (a) the reading of the text; (b) the passage of the eye from the text to the copy; (c) the writing of the copy; and (d) the passage of the eye from the copy back to the text. Any accident that may legitimately be called a "scribal error" must, therefore, occur in the course of one of these movements.[11]

Vinaver astutely observes that different kinds of scribal error occur in each of these four distinct movements—a, b, c, and d—based on the different kinds of scribal attention that are active in each. The kinds of attention in the various phases involve the interactions of eye, mind, and hand. The following are the causes of error in each phase: (a) misreading; (b) misremembering; (c) miswriting; and (d) mistaken return. Let us turn to these four movements to elucidate the kinds of scribal error that naturally occur in the transmission of the biblical text.

For my evidential base, I will use examples from the book of Proverbs, drawing on Fox's extensive discussions of scribal error and innovation in his HBCE edition.[12] For the individual cases, I refer the reader to his commentary, which I summarize in my remarks. My analysis is, in a sense, a second order of research, based on the resources provided by his exemplary edition.

(A) The Reading of the Text

As the scribe's eye goes from M to N in the source text, the scribe is liable occasionally to misunderstand the sequence of graphemes, yielding what are often called paleographical errors, including graphic confusions, metatheses, transpositions, haplographies, dittographies, word misdivision, and so on. The basic principle for these types of error is that the act of reading is synthetic, with the brain interpreting the sequence of graphemes as intelligible words and phrases. As Timpanaro describes this process:

> Our reading, and to a greater or lesser extent that of classical and medieval copyists also, is nearly always synthetic: we do not look at all the letters of a word one after the other, but when we have recognized some

---

11. Ibid., 353.

12. Michael V. Fox, *Proverbs: An Eclectic Edition with Introduction and Textual Commentary*, HBCE 1 (Atlanta: SBL Press, 2015).

letters and glanced at the word as a whole we mentally "integrate" the rest of the letters.[13]

The problem is that we can mentally integrate the letters wrongly and therefore "see" a different word. Wittgenstein calls this process "seeing-as," for example, when one sees a drawing of a duck as a rabbit or vice versa.[14] It involves a perceptual switch between one form (*Gestalt*) and another. These are visual and cognitive slips that change the reading in the mind's eye.

The conditions for such cognitive slips include the semantic context and the scribe's mentality, for example, linguistic skills and habits, and powers of concentration. Timpanaro aptly describes the psychological dimensions of this kind of scribal error:

> The palaeographic error, it is true, has its origin in a misunderstanding of a written sign. However, a psychological (or psycho-cultural) mistake is very often grafted onto this, so that what is produced is an erroneous word which resembles the correct word in its written aspect, but also is determined by the influence either of its context or of words sounding like it which are more familiar to the copyist, closer to his everyday experience.[15]

The habits and experience of the copyist are, in this respect, a second semiotic system, through which the semiotic system of the text is filtered. Cesare Segre calls this two-layered structure a "diasystem" (by analogy with the hybridity of language contact) and argues that the critic is obliged to analyze both systems to the extent feasible.[16] Attention to the textual diasystem—the interaction between the semiotic systems of text and copyist—is part of the task of the textual critic.

Paleographical errors that occur in movement (a) are easily illustrated for the Hebrew Bible. An ample source for such errors is the *ketiv-qere*. In Proverbs, as in other books, most of the *ketiv-qere* variations consist of graphic interchange, metathesis, aural interchange, grammatical variants,

---

13. Timpanaro, *Freudian Slip*, 22.

14. Ludwig Wittgenstein, *Philosophical Investigations*, trans. G. E. M. Anscombe, 3rd ed. (New York: Macmillan, 1968), 193–205.

15. Timpanaro, *Freudian Slip*, 21.

16. Cesare Segre, "Critique textuelle, théorie des ensembles et diasystème," *BCLSB* 62 (1976): 279–92.

and synonymous words or word-forms.[17] (Another frequent kind of *ketiv-qere* is the disambiguation of grammatical number, which is a deliberate revision, not a paleographical slip.)

The following examples illustrate the kinds of perceptual errors that occur in this first movement, reading the text. In each case, the earlier reading is listed first. The second reading is a slip of cognitive processing, usually a visual error (seeing-as) and occasionally an auditory error (hearing-as).

Graphic Confusion

14:34 חסד M "disgrace"] חסר* G (ἐλασσονοῦσι) S (ܡܚܣܪ) and perhaps 4QProv[b] (חס֯ר) "diminishes" (ד → ר)

This is an instance of *dalet/reš* confusion. The uncommon meaning of "disgrace" for חסד (an Aramaism) facilitated a scribe's (or perhaps a translator's) perception of the word as a masculine singular verb, חסר ("diminishes"). This meaning suits the context but is the wrong gender—the subject חטאת ("sin") is feminine, which makes a masculine verb ungrammatical.

Metathesis

14:32 בתומו* G (τῇ ἑαυτοῦ ὁσιότητι) S (ܗܠܝܢ ܕܠܐ ܢܟܠܐ) "on his innocence"] במותו M 4QProv[b] "on his death" (תמ → מת)

A metathesis of ת and מ switched the word from תומו ("his innocence") to מותו ("his death"). The proverbial saying, "the wise man relies on his innocence," changes to an odd claim in M, "the wise man relies on his death." In later exegetical traditions, this striking scribal error became a prooftext for the afterlife.

Dittography with Graphic Confusion (= Near Dittography)

3:24 תשב* G (κάθῃ) SyrH (ܬܬܒ) "you sit"] תשכב M "you lie down" (כב → ב)

---

17. Fox, *Proverbs*, 24–29.

A near-dittography of ב → כב turned תשב ("you sit") into תשכב ("you lie down"). This misperception is also motivated by the scribe's anticipation of the verb in the second half of the verse, ושכבת ("you lie down"). This scribal error simplifies the verse and yields the banal parallelism: "When you lie down … and when you lie down."

Word Misdivision

> 14:13 אחרית ‹ה›שׂמחה conjecture, "the end of pleasure"] אחריתה שׂמחה M "its end, pleasure" (תה# → ת #ה)

Incorrect division of words is a relatively common visual error, even though all the extant biblical manuscripts have spaces or word separators (the latter in paleo-Hebrew manuscripts).[18] In this case, the misperception is motivated by the scribe's reminiscence of אחריתה ("its end") in the previous verse. The correct word division (supplied by conjecture) restores the proverb: "Even in merriment a heart may hurt // And the end of pleasure is sadness."

Aural Error

> 26:2 לא M^K G (οὐδενί) ≈ S (ܠܡܢ) T (לא) "not"] לו M^Q ≈ V (in quempiam) "to him" (לא → לו)

A relatively frequent kind of misperception is aural error, where similarity of sound, not similarity of graphic sign, is the cause. This kind of transcriptional error requires that the scribe "hear" the word as another word, whether the dictation be an actual voice or what textual critics call "internal dictation" (dictation interne, coined by Alphonse Dain): "the habit of reading words and saying them silently to oneself before copying them out."[19]

Notably, Malachi Beit-Arié adduces evidence that medieval biblical scribes dictated aloud to themselves. According to Sefer Ḥasidim, a medieval work by Judah ben Samuel of Regensburg: "one who used to copy the Bible and the commentaries would read aloud and write, and everything

---

18. Tov, Scribal Practices, 131–35.
19. Reeve, foreword to Trovato, Everything, 11.

that he would write he would first read aloud."[20] We do not know whether scribes in the Second Temple period read aloud or dictated internally, but these are equivalent mechanisms for aural errors. In this verse, לֹא ("not") is the better reading ("a gratuitous curse will *not* come"), but there is sufficient contextual ambiguity to allow a scribe to "hear" לוֹ, yielding: "a gratuitous curse will come *to him*."[21]

Synonym with Graphic or Aural Trigger

5:3 זרה M S (ﬡﬣﬣﬡ) "strange woman"] זנה* G (γυναικὸς πόρνης) (cf. Midrash Proverbs) "harlot" (נ → ר)

23:27 זרה* G (ἀλλότριος) "strange woman"] זונה M S (ﬡﬤﬡ) "harlot" (נ → ר)

In both of these cases, a scribe "saw" or "heard" זרה ("strange woman") as ז(ו)נה ("harlot"). These are thematic synonyms in the diction of Proverbs. The interchange is motivated by either visual or aural cues or a combination of both. A graphic confusion of ר → נ is possible, as is an aural confusion. (Both are "liquid" phonemes; cf. the textual interchange of ויתן [Ps

---

20. Malachi Beit-Arié, "Transmission of Texts by Scribes and Copyists: Unconscious and Critical Inferences," *BJRL* 75 (1993): 41, quoting J. Wistenetzki, ed., *Das Buch der Frommen* (Berlin: Nirdamim,1891), par. 733 = par. 1363: אחד היה מעתיק מן הספרים ומן הפירושים והיה קורא בפיו וכותב וכל מה שהיה כותב היה קורא בפיו תחילה.

21. There are many such aural errors in biblical books; see Tov, *Textual Criticism*, 233–34; Menahem Kister, "Textual and Lexical Implications of Phonetic and Orthographic Phenomena" [Hebrew], *Leshonenu* 78 (2016): 7–20. An example from Genesis is the *bet/pe* interchange (פ → ב) in a recently published fragment from Qumran or the Bar Kokhba caves, which reads בפנות ("in the corners"?) for בבנות ("among the daughters") in Gen 34:1; see Esther Eshel and Hanan Eshel, "New Fragments from Qumran: 4QGenᶠ, 4QIsaᵇ, 4Q226, 8QGen, and XQpapEnoch," *DSD* 12 (2005): 135–37 and fig. 1. On the paleographical differences between this fragment and 4QGenᶠ, see Eibert Tigchelaar, "Notes on Three Qumran-Type Yadin Fragments Leading to a Discussion of Identification, Attribution, Provenance, and Names," *DSD* 19 (2012): 212–13 n. 48, who notes that the uneven writing and spacing of the fragment indicates that it was "written by an inexperienced scribe." The aural error is consistent with this attribution.

18:33] and ויתר [2 Sam 22:33].) Contextually, זרה is the better reading in these verses (note the alliteration with צרה ["narrow"] in 23:27b).

Shemaryahu Talmon has argued that many synonymous variants may be "pristine" variants, that is, equally original and rooted in independent crystallizations of oral traditions.[22] In these instances, however, it is easy to see how one synonym could be misperceived in place of the other. It is not necessary to infer the existence of independent pristine variants or traditions from this common kind of scribal change.[23]

(B) The Passage of the Eye from the Text to the Copy

In the second movement, the scribe's eye travels from the source-text to the copy, landing where the blank space in the copy begins. There is little chance of spatial error here (in contrast to the return movement in [d]). There is, however, a possibility of misremembering. Since slips of memory only show up in slips of the pen, the errors of memory that occur in this movement are only instantiated in the writing of the copy, to which we now turn.

(C) The Writing of the Copy

In this movement—involving motion of hand, not eye—errors of misremembering are mingled with errors of miswriting, as in the following:

Forgetting

5:3 *אל תקשיב לאשת אולת G (μὴ πρόσεχε φαύλῃ γυναικί) "do not hearken to the worthless woman" (cf. Midrash Proverbs)] > M

---

22. Shemaryahu Talmon, "Synonymous Readings in the Masoretic Text," and "Double Readings in the Masoretic Text," in *Text and Canon of the Hebrew Bible: Collected Studies* (Winona Lake, IN: Eisenbrauns, 2010), 171–216 and 217–66, esp. 219: "synonymous readings have no direct bearing on the criticism and emendation of the text, since by definition it is impossible to decide which one is intrinsically preferable to another." See similarly Raymond F. Person, "The Ancient Israelite Scribe as Performer," *JBL* 117 (1998): 601–9.

23. See the critique in Tov, *Textual Criticism*, 163–65, and above, ch. 2.

In this *lapsus calami*, a scribe forgot a line. Midrash Proverbs seems to allude to this verse, so it may have been present in some medieval MT manuscripts.

Dittography

30:16 מים M S (ܡܝܐ) "water"] מים מים* G (ὕδατος καὶ ὕδωρ) "water water" (מים מים → מים)

Dittographies and haplographies in movement (a) produce relatively meaningful variants, since they are produced by perceiving one word as another. But dittographies and haplographies also happen as miswritings in phase (c). In this phase, such slips characteristically produce garbled or meaningless text. This is the case here, where one מים ("water") is miswritten as two, yielding a garbled text: "the earth, which is not sated with water, water and fire, which does not say, 'Enough.'" The additional "water" yields five subjects, contradicting the topic statement, "four that do not say, 'Enough.'" (30:15). Furthermore, the singular verb אמרה ("says") in the last clause excludes the plural subject, "water and fire." The verse should read, as in M, "the earth, which is not sated with water, // and fire, which does not say 'Enough.'"

Distorted Dittography

25:20 מעדה בגד ביום קרה M ≈ S (ܘܥܒܪ ܟܢ ܡܛܠ ܚܘܒܬܐ ܘܗܐ ܘܪܫܥܐ ܟܡܐܟܐ ܘܗܟܢ) "One who removes a garment on a cold day" (cf. 25:19 מועדת מבטח בוגד ביום צרה)] > G

A scribe here mistakenly wrote the second half of 25:19 twice but garbled it the second time. 25:19b reads, "A broken tooth and a shaky foot, a treacherous refuge in a day of trouble." The participle מועדת ("shaky," from מעד) becomes מעדה ("one who removes," an Aramaism from עדה) in the dittography, and the sequence בוגד ביום צרה ("treacherous in a day of trouble") morphs into בגד ביום קרה ("garment on a cold day"). These are all simple visual or aural errors, with ת → ה (graphic similarity) and צ → ק (both are emphatic phonemes), and omission of medial ו. But it makes no sense in context and seems an odd excrescence.

Haplography

> 3:35 ‹מרימ‹ים› conjecture, "gain (pl.)"] מרים M "gain (sg.)" (ימים
> → ימ)

A scribe miswrote ימים as ימ. The plural subject כסילים ("fools") requires a plural predicate, which is suppled here by conjecture. It is easy to see how a scribe could omit the third *ym* in the sequence כשילים מרימים, "fools gain contempt."

Synonym

> 3:1 מצותי M S (ﻣﻬﻤﺒﺪﺗﻨ) S "my commands"] *אמרי G (τὰ δὲ ῥήματά μου) "my words" (אמרי → מצותי)

> 5:1 תבונתי M "my understanding"] *אמרי G (ἐμοῖς δὲ λόγοις) S (ﻟﻤﻼﺣﺘﻤﻴ) "my words" (cf. 4:20 אמרי) (אמרי → תבונתי)

Synonymous variants can be created by misreading or misremembering. Those produced by misreading are more likely to be motivated by paleographical triggers, as above in movement (a). The variants in these verses, involving the synonyms מצותי ("my commands"), תבונתי ("my understanding"), and אמרי ("my words"), have no graphic trigger and are therefore more likely to be caused by misremembering. In both of these cases, the secondary reading is arguably the commonplace אמרי ("my words"), which in the second case is motivated by reminiscence of אמרי in a parallel proverb (5:1 // 4:20).

(D) The Passage of the Eye from the Copy Back to the Text

Errors of transcription in movement (d) are caused by a mistaken return of the scribe's eye from N in the copy to a wrong N in the source text, as illustrated in Vinaver's diagram to the right. Because of this eye-skip (or parablepsis, lit. "looking aside"), the scribe literally overlooks the word sequence O–P, which lies between N_1 and N_2.

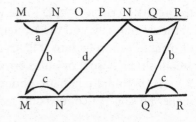

This error is due to homoioteleuton (similar endings), homoiarkton (similar beginnings), homoiomeson (similar middles), or a combination. An eye-skip can also go backward, to a previous N, and repeat the already transcribed text. The mechanism of eye-skip can therefore shorten the text or expand it.

Eye-Skip

21:10 נפש רשע אותה רע M "The soul of the wicked man desires what is bad"] נפש רשע* G (ψυχὴ ἀσεβοῦς) S (ܢܦܫܗ ܕܪܫܝܥܐ) "The soul of the wicked man" (רע ⌢ רשע)

After writing רשע ("wicked man") in the copy, a scribe's eye mistakenly returned to the end of the graphically similar word רע ("bad") in the source text, thereby overlooking the intervening phrase אותה רע ("desires what is bad"). This eye-skip is triggered by a combination of homoiarkton and homoioteleuton in the two similar words, רשע and רע.

Eye-skip

11:8–10a > 6QpapProv (באבד ⌢ אבדה)

A large eye-skip seems to exist in a Qumran fragment of Proverbs, 6Qpap-Prov (6Q30). As reconstructed by Esther Eshel, the fragment contains Prov 11:5–10 but has a noticeable gap between verses 7 and 10b.[24] Eshel proposes that "the omission of Prov 11:8–10a … may be the result of a variant text or a scribal error due to the similarity between אבדה (v. 7) and באבד (v. 10)."[25] A scribe's eye-skip between these two words would leave out all of 11:8–10a:

> The righteous man is extricated from trouble, // and the wicked comes into his place. // By (his) mouth the impious man harms his fellow, // but the righteous are extricated by knowledge. // When it goes well with the righteous, // the city rejoices.

---

24. Esther Eshel, "6Q30, a Cursive Šin, and Proverbs 11," *JBL* 122 (2003): 544–46.
25. Ibid., 545; so also Fox, *Proverbs*, 187.

Despite the fragmentary nature of 6QpapProv, this is a relatively clear case of eye-skip, with the scribe's eye wrongly returning from אבדה (11:7) in the copy to באבד (11:10) in the source text. This eye-skip is motivated by a common sequence, אבד, in the two words.

SCRIBAL REVISION

Transcriptional error is a major category of scribal change in biblical books. The other major category, scribal revision, has its own motivations, which can be broadly described as exegetical and modernizing. Until the end of the Second Temple period, some scribal traditions had freedom, within limits, to revise the text. Small harmonizations and explications are relatively common, and less common but still abundant are large harmonizations and new literary production, including new editions. In addition to these exegetical changes (which usually expanded the text), Second Temple period scribes often modernized the text in spelling, morphology, syntax, and lexicon. The kinds and degrees of allowed revision varied among scribal schools and traditions.[26]

Many instances of scribal revision occur in Proverbs, generally with the goal of modernizing, enhancing, or clarifying the text's meaning. Because of the agglutinative nature of the book, scribes also occasionally added new proverbs. The following is a sample of these scribal innovations.

Explication

5:22 ילכדנו "will catch him"] + את הרשע M S (ܠܥܘܠܐ) "the wicked (man)"

The line, "(his iniquities) will catch him," has been expanded by an explicating plus, clarifying that the object suffix, "him," refers to "the wicked (man)." This explication is unnecessary and grammatically awkward. But it illustrates a style of hyperclose reading, meticulous in its attention to detail, characteristic of some groups of ancient scribes and interpreters.

14:1 חכמות "wisdom"] + נשים M G (γυναῖκες) S (ܢܫܐ) "women"

---

26. See Sidnie White Crawford, "Scribal Traditions in the Pentateuch and the History of the Early Second Temple Period," in *Congress Volume Helsinki 2010*, ed. Martti Nissinen, VTSup 148 (Leiden: Brill, 2012), 167–84; and below, ch. 9.

Another case of (over)explication, this plus is in all the texts and versions. The unusual form חכמות ("wisdom") is singular and takes a singular verb (בנתה, "has built"). But it looks plural. A scribe tried to clarify this term by adding נשים ("women"), yielding "the wisest of women," perhaps based on a similar construction in Judg 5:29. The singular verb excludes this plus, which in any case banalizes the semi-mythical status of Wisdom in this verse.

18:22 אשה "woman, wife"] + טובה* G (ἀγαθήν) SyrH (ἀγαθήν) S (ܛܒܬܐ) T (טבתא) similarly rabbinic (e.g., b. Ber.18a) "good"

The proverb, "He who has found a woman (or 'wife') has found something good," can be seen as missing something, since there are some very wicked women in Proverbs, including some who are already married (e.g., Prov 7:19; 21:9, 19; 30:20). A Hebrew scribe added טובה ("good") to clarify that only some women qualify: an אשה טובה ("a good woman"). As Fox notes, the existence of this variant in the Syro-Hexapla and rabbinic quotations indicates that it was in their Hebrew sources.

Elaboration

16:30 fin] + כר הרעה הוא* G (οὗτος κάμινός ἐστιν κακίας) "he is a furnace of evil"

The line, "he winces his lips, while he plans evil," is supplemented in G by another metaphor, כר הרעה הוא ("he is a furnace of evil"). This sequence is adapted from 16:27, where the worthless man is a כרה רעה ("digger of evil"). As Fox observes, when "transferred to the present verse, the phrase was misdivided as כר הרעה…. This division error shows that the transfer took place in Hebrew."[27] The plus is a deliberate literary elaboration, whose technique is near-literal transfer of text.

New Proverb

23:23 אמת קנה ואל תמכר // חכמה ומוסר ובינה M "Buy truth and do not sell it, // wisdom and discipline and understanding"] > G

---

27. Fox, *Proverbs*, 253.

A short proverb appears at M 23:23 that is missing in G. It is simple and formulaic. There is no transcriptional or exegetical motive for a proto-G scribe to omit it, so we infer that it is a late plus in the proto-M tradition of Proverbs, after the branching apart of the proto-M and proto-G textual families of Proverbs.

New Proverb

9:12a-b ‏כי עזב‎ // ‏וירדף עוף מעופף‎ // ‏תומך שקר ירעה רוח‎*
‏ומעגלי שדהו טעה‎ // ‏דרכי כרמו‎ G (ὃς ἐρείδεται ἐπὶ ψεύδεσιν,
οὗτος ποιμανεῖ ἀνέμους, // ὁ δ' αὐτὸς διώξεται ὄρνεα πετόμενα· //
ἔλιπεν γὰρ ὁδοὺς τοῦ ἑαυτοῦ ἀμπελῶνος, // τοὺς δὲ ἄξονας τοῦ ἰδίου
γεωργίου πεπλάνηται·) "He who grasps deceit, he will shepherd the winds, // and he will pursue a flying bird. // For he has abandoned the roads of his own vineyard, // and has wandered from the paths of his own field."] > M

This proverb in G 9:12 is absent in M, but there is no transcriptional or exegetical motive to omit it. It appears to be a new proverb in the proto-G tradition of Proverbs, after the separation of the proto-G and proto-M textual families of Proverbs. Fox elucidates several clues in the Greek that indicate the presence of a Hebrew *Vorlage*.[28] Most notable is Greek ἐρείδεται ("support oneself on"), which is a postclassical meaning of Hebrew ‏תומך‎ ("grasp"). The Greek formulation, "He who supports himself on deceits," makes little sense, but is intelligible as a mistranslation of the underlying Hebrew. The Syriac also has this new proverb. An additional expansion (12c, not included here) is arguably an inner-Greek expansion of 9:12b. These new proverbs illustrate the late textual growth of the book in both Hebrew and Greek scribal traditions.

Excursus: "Memory Variants"

In two recent books, Carr has argued for the existence of what he calls "memory variants" in biblical texts.[29] He holds that these variants are evidence that "many [manuscripts] may have been produced from memory

---

28. Ibid., 166–68.
29. David M. Carr, *Writing on the Tablet of the Heart: Origins of Scripture and Literature* (New York: Oxford University Press, 2005), esp. 228–34; David M. Carr, *The*

rather than from visual copying."[30] I address his position here for two reasons: (1) he regards the book of Proverbs as a particularly rich source for such variants, presumably because proverbs are an oral genre; and (2) if he is correct, it undermines my typology of scribal error. Moreover, he maintains that his model for the transmission of biblical books renders problematic the HBCE project and the general practices of textual criticism of the Hebrew Bible.

Carr defines memory variants as "the sorts of variants that happen when a tradent modifies elements of text in the process of citing or otherwise reproducing it from memory."[31] These kinds of changes include "exchange of synonymous words, word order variation, presence and absence of conjunctions and minor modifiers."[32] He also regards textual harmonization as a type of memory variant. Such changes, he argues, "manifest a different sort of variation from traditions transmitted in a purely literary context."[33]

However, his examples from Proverbs and other biblical books do not support this claim. As Fox comments, "These [types of variants] are not exclusive to oral transmission or even predominant in it. As far as I can tell, there are no diagnostic criteria distinguishing memory variants from visual ones.... Aural variants too can occur in written transmission."[34] I agree with Fox and will extend his critique. The features that Carr attributes to "memory variants" are more cogently explained by the mechanisms of transcription addressed above. Furthermore, the varieties of transcriptional error do not support his theory of the transmission of biblical books by memory.

I advert to Goshen-Gottstein's "law of scribes,"[35] which includes most or all the changes that Carr attributes to memory variants, including (in Goshen-Gottstein's list) "syntactic assimilation, dittography and homoioteluton, omission and addition of particles (especially ו), substitution of synonymous words, changes on the basis of parallel passages, addition and

---

Formation of the Hebrew Bible: A New Reconstruction (New York: Oxford University Press, 2011), esp. 25–36, 58–65.

30. Carr, *Tablet*, 230.

31. Carr, *Formation*, 17.

32. Ibid., 33.

33. Ibid., 13.

34. Fox, *Proverbs*, 81.

35. See above, n. 3.

omission of suffixes and change of their number."[36] The operation of the law of scribes in medieval and early modern codices demonstrates that such changes are common in a "purely literary context" (Carr's phrase). As Goshen-Gottstein observes, "what sets medieval MSS apart is the fact that they contain practically exclusively variations of the types which can arise again and again through scribal activity."[37] In this period, there is no question that the texts were copied literarily, since memorized transmission was strictly prohibited.[38]

The examples that Carr cites from Proverbs and other biblical books are all easily explained as errors of transcription. For instance, he regards many of the *ketiv-qere* variations as memory variants. He writes: "In the case of Proverbs, the written (ketib) form of several sayings diverges in ways characteristic of memorized texts, while the orally read (qere) form of the tradition often appears to harmonize one saying to another."[39] His examples are harmonizations of parallel proverbs, for example, between נכרים ("foreigners") and נכריה ("foreign woman") in 20:16 // 27:13.[40] The details are as follows:

Prov 20:16 נכרים M[K] "foreigners"] נכריה M[Q] "foreign woman"
Prov 27:13 נכריה M "foreign woman"

Carr holds that the *ketiv* (נכרים and נכריה) reflects the original variation of oral-written composition in these parallel proverbs and that the *qere* of 20:16 (נכריה) is a harmonization with the *ketiv* of 27:13, indicating the memorized transmission of the texts. However, as Fox comments, the variation between נכרים and נכריה is most easily explained as a graphic confusion of ם/ה.[41] The better reading in both proverbs is arguably נכרים ("foreigners"), which is parallel in both instances to זר ("stranger"). The

---

36. Moshe H. Goshen-Gottstein, "Die Jesaiah-Rolle und das Problem der hebräischen Bibelhandschriften," *Bib* 35 (1954): 433.

37. Goshen-Gottstein, "Biblical Manuscripts," 274–75.

38. b. Meg. 18b: כך אמרו חכמים אסור לכתוב אות אחת שלא מן הכתב ("Thus said the Sages, 'It is forbidden to write a single letter except from a copy'"); cited in Emanuel Tov, *Scribal Practices Practices and Approaches Reflected in the Texts Found in the Judean Desert*, STDJ 54 (Leiden: Brill, 2004), 11.

39. Carr, *Formation*, 29.

40. Ibid., 29–30.

41. Fox, *Proverbs*, 284. This graphic confusion is amply attested, e.g., the variation in the king's name, אבים (Abiyam) versus אביה (Abiyah) in 1 Kgs 14–15 and 2 Chr 13.

variant נכריה ("foreign woman") in a proverb about providing collateral for loans is unintelligible. Fox writes, "נכריה is problematic … by implying that it is a woman—an alien or stranger, no less—who is taking a loan and needs a guarantor."[42] The proverb is odd and terse, which provides an opportunity for a scribe to commit this simple transcriptional error.

It is possible that the *qere* of 20:16 (נכריה) is a secondary harmonization to 27:13, but this is also a normal transcriptional error. Such small harmonizations do not entail a context of memorization in contrast to literary transcription. It is worth noting that the *ketiv* of 20:16 (נכרים) is also an ancient variant in 27:13; it is attested in the LXX and Vulgate. So there may be more harmonizing and/or graphic confusions than Carr's account admits. This cascade of variants is typical in the transmission of parallel passages. This situation of textual entropy is a product of the law of scribes.

Another of Carr's examples directly contradicts the claim that memory variants are a "different sort of variation from traditions transmitted in a purely literary context."[43] Carr includes synonymous variants in this class, adopting Talmon's argument that such synonyms are often "pristine variants" rooted in independent crystallizations of oral traditions. Carr's example is a variation between MT and LXX in a parallel proverb in 4:20 // 5:1:[44]

Prov 4:20 אמרי M G (ἐμοῖς λόγοις) "my words"
Prov 5:1 תבונתי M "my understanding"] *אמרי G (ἐμοῖς δὲ λόγοις) "my words"

Carr rightly infers that אמרי ("my words") in G Prov 5:1 is a harmonization with the parallel term in 4:20. But, as I have observed above (regarding this instance and others), the substitution of synonyms is a normal phenomenon in literary copying. To be sure, synonymous variants are memory variants, because their generation relies on a lapse or misprision in the scribe's act of reading or in his short-term memory. But such memory slips are wholly at home in the setting of literary transcription.

In this instance, Carr produces a memory variant of his own. He writes, "the MT of Prov 5:1b tells him to incline his ears to his father's

---

42. Ibid.
43. See above, n. 33.
44. Carr, *Formation*, 31.

'wisdom' (חכמה)."[45] This is an error of transcription: the MT of Prov 5:1b reads תבונתי ("my understanding"). (N.B. I have corrected Carr's transcriptional error in my citation of the variants above.) Carr has produced a synonymous variant by misreading or misremembering the text of Prov 5:1, where חכמתי ("my wisdom," 5:1a) and תבונתי ("my understanding," 5:1b) are in parallel. By transcribing one synonym instead of the other, Carr illustrates the mechanisms of transcriptional error. Instead of serving as an example of a memory variant in his sense, it serves as an example of transcriptional error in a literary context. The scribe's eye—or his mind's eye—jumped from one synonym to another.

Slips of the pen are often slips of memory. Carr's examples are evidence for what we already knew: the scribal eye and hand are fallible, as are the mechanisms of memory and cognition. Carr's examples provide no warrant for a separate category of memory variants that entails oral memorization and/or the absence of written manuscripts. Biblical scribes in the Hebrew and Greek traditions did sometimes create new proverbs, perhaps drawing from oral tradition. But the normal context of scribal transcription *includes* the effects of memory, as one can see from the examples above. Some errors—such as those of anticipation or reminiscence—are obviously memory variants. The inference that Carr draws from such errors—that slips of memory entail the absence of written source-texts—is unwarranted, and in the instance above, is contradicted by his own transcription.

Carr concludes from his discussion that the ordinary procedures of textual criticism of the Hebrew Bible are incorrect. He writes, "in so far as the sayings in Proverbs were reproduced—in whole or in part—through memory, the search for an Ur-text and clear lines of dependence and revision often will be fruitless."[46] This conclusion, if correct, would negate my discussion above and erase the value of Fox's HBCE edition of Proverbs. More generally, Carr urges "skepticism about text-critical attempts to reconstruct an eclectic [text] of biblical books for times preceding the identification of authoritative reference copies," that is, the period prior to the textual primacy of MT.[47] In particular, "this phenomenon renders problematic the Oxford [now HBCE] project of reconstruction of a broader eclectic text of the Hebrew Bible preceding the proto-Massoretic

---

45. Ibid.
46. Ibid., 33.
47. Carr, *Tablet*, 292.

tradition."[48] Carr's model for the transmission of biblical texts would indeed render problematic the HBCE project. However, Carr's model is not supported by the evidence or the analysis.[49] Many scribal errors and innovations are memory variants to one degree or another. But for the Hebrew Bible, a typological contrast between memory variants and transcriptional variants does not hold.[50]

Conclusions

The object of a typology of scribal error is to clarify the motives and mechanisms of textual change. This is useful knowledge for the textual

---

48. Ibid., 292 n. 4.

49. I hasten to add that his analysis might well obtain in other cases, such as biblical quotations in Qumran texts and rabbinic literature; see Edward L. Greenstein, "Misquotation of Scripture in the Dead Sea Scrolls," in *The Frank Talmage Memorial Volume*, ed. Barry Walfish (Haifa: Haifa University Press, 1993), 1:76: "The fact that the Qumran sectarians were fluent in Scripture makes it eminently plausible that their minds were vulnerable to contamination by some other biblical passage than the one they might be trying to recall or copy." As Tov observes (*Texual Criticism*, 112), short texts such as *tefillin* and *mezuzot* may often have been written by memory.

50. A different flaw in Carr's argument is his representation of this contrast in other fields—classics, medieval literature, and Assyriology—which he adduces as a strong analogy for biblical studies (*Formation*, 13–25). Recent scholarship in these fields focuses on scribal revision as the main mechanism of major textual change, rather than independent crystallizations of oral performance or memorization. Important discussions in these fields that complicate Carr's picture include Margalit Finkelberg, "The *Cypria*, the *Iliad*, and the Problem of Multiformity in Oral and Written Tradition," *CP* 95 (2000): 1–11; Keith Busby, *Codex and Context: Reading Old French Verse Narrative in Manuscript* (Amsterdam: Rodopi, 2002), who aptly distinguishes between "mirror copying" and "the willful scribe"; and John D. Niles, "Orality," in *The Cambridge Companion to Textual Scholarship*, ed. Neil Fraistat and Julia Flanders (Cambridge: Cambridge University Press, 2013), 213: "vernacular literature [in contrast to higher status Latin texts] tended to be refashioned in the act of its copying." On the similar phenomenon of "open" books in medieval Hebrew literature, see Israel M. Ta-Shma, "The 'Open' Book in Medieval Hebrew Literature: The Problem of Authorized Editions," *BJRL* 75 (1993): 17–24; and Beit-Arié, "Transmission." On the dominance of "reproduction from a master copy" in Akkadian scribal traditions of the first millennium BCE, see Karel van der Toorn, *Scribal Culture and the Making of the Hebrew Bible* (Cambridge: Harvard University Press, 2007), 125–41 (quote from 125); and Martin Worthington, *Principles of Akkadian Textual Criticism*, SANER 1 (Berlin: de Gruyter, 2012), 5–32.

critic, whose responsibility is to diagnose and map the transformations of
the text, from its earliest inferable state to the early manuscripts. It is also
useful for biblical scholars generally, so that they can be cognizant of the
vicissitudes of the text that they read and comment on. The biblical text is
not a procrustean object but has internal eddies and pools that differ from
manuscript to manuscript. Textual change is a constant, a condition that
exegetes ignore to their peril. But it is not a pure flux. There are regularities
in scribal error, just as there are in other kinds of cognitive slips. Awareness of the kinds and circumstances of change will make the interpreter
more agile and alert.

When we attend to mechanisms of scribal error, it is clear that the
central cause is human frailty. Scribes—like the rest of us—are imperfect.
As Timpanaro observes, "the majority of mistakes in transcription [are] ...
errors due to distraction ... to which anyone transcribing or citing a text
may be subject—whether scholar or lay man, mediaeval monk or modern
typist or student."[51] It is laborious, meticulous work to copy a book of the
Hebrew Bible. It combines powers of concentration, anxiety, and boredom.

The high stakes and potential consequences of scribal error in biblical
texts are dramatically presented in a story in the Babylonian Talmud about
Rabbi Meir, a second century CE sage and biblical scribe. The story illustrates the importance and, less directly, the inevitability of scribal error:

> When I was studying under Rabbi Akiba I used to put calcanthum
> [קנקנתום] into the ink and he said nothing about it, but when I came to
> Rabbi Ishmael, he said to me, "My son, what is your occupation?" I said
> to him, "I am a scribe," and he said to me, "My son, be meticulous in your
> work, for your work is heaven's work; should you omit a single letter or
> add a single letter, you would destroy the whole universe." I replied to
> him, "I have a certain ingredient called calcanthum, which I put into the
> ink." He said to me, "Can one put calcanthum into the ink? Does not the
> Torah say 'He shall write' (Num 5:23) and 'He shall wipe it out' (Num
> 5:23)? Writing should be able to be wiped away."—What is the relation
> between the question of the one and the reply of the other? Does he not
> mean to say, "There is no question about omissions or additions, for they
> are my duty, but (I have even taken precautions) against the possibility of
> a fly coming to sit on the crown of a *dalet*, and by wiping it, turn it into
> a *resh*." (b. 'Erub. 13a)[52]

---

51. Timpanaro, *Freudian Slip*, 20.
52. כשהייתי לומד אצל ר' עקיבא הייתי מטיל קנקנתום לתוך הדיו ולא אמר לי

In this dialogue, a question about the permissibility of using calcanthum (an ingredient in iron-gall ink)[53] becomes a warning about making a single error in a Torah scroll—"should you omit a single letter or add a single letter, you would destroy the whole universe." According to the anonymous comment after the dialogue, Rabbi Meir means to say that he uses calcanthum in the ink so that he cannot accidentally turn a *dalet* into a *resh* by swatting a fly. By using indelible ink, he preserves the integrity of the universe.

Scribal errors must be prevented, lest disaster ensue. Yet there is a hidden irony in this exchange, which frames the issue of scribal errors differently. Rabbi Meir is a חכם וסופר ("sage and scribe," b. Giṭ. 67a.) who is also famous for writing a Torah scroll with some peculiar variant readings.[54] According to Gen. Rab. 9:5, Rabbi Meir's Torah scroll read at Gen 1:31 טוב מות, ("death is good") rather than טוב מאד ("very good"). This is an aural variant, in which מאד was "heard" (presumably by internal diction) as מות due to the quiescence of 'aleph and the aural similarity of *dalet*

דבר וכשבאתי אצל ר' ישמעאל אמר לי בני מה מלאכתך אמרתי לו לבלר אני אמר לי
בני הוי זהיר במלאכתך שמלאכתך מלאכת שמים היא שמא אתה מחסר אות אחת או
מייתר אות אחת נמצאת מחריב את כל העולם כולו אמרתי לו דבר אחד יש לי וקנקנתום
שמו שאני מטיל לתוך הדיו אמר לי וכי מטילין קנקנתום לתוך הדיו והלא אמרה תורה
(במדבר ה) וכתב (במדבר ה) ומחה כתב שיכול למחות מאי קא"ל ומאי קא מהדר ליה
הכי קא"ל לא מיבעיא בחסירות וביתירות דבכי אנא אלא אפילו מיחש לזבוב נמי דילמא
אתי ויתיב אתגיה דדל"ת ומחיק ליה ומשוי ליה רי"ש.

53. There were two main types of ink in antiquity, carbon ink and iron-gall ink. The older type, carbon ink, can be wiped away when wet, while iron-gall ink etches into parchment and must be scraped away; see David Diringer, *The Book Before Printing: Ancient, Medieval and Oriental* (New York: Dover, 1982), 548–52. In the Qumran scrolls analyzed by Yoram Nir-El and Magen Broshi ("The Black Ink of the Qumran Scrolls," *DSD* 3 [1996]: 157–67), only carbon ink was found. However, on some biblical scrolls (4Qpaleo-Exod[m], 4QExod-Lev[f], 4QLev[d], 4QDan[d]) the ink has eaten through the leather, indicating corroded metal in the ink, either from iron-gall ink or leaching from metal inkwells; see Tov, *Scribal Practices*, 53. According to our passage, the use of iron-gall ink for Torah scrolls became a matter of debate among rabbinic schools. See Masseket Soferim 1, אין נותנין קנקנתום בדיו ("One may not put calcanthum in ink").

54. Tov, *Textual Criticism*, 112–13; Jonathan P. Siegel, *The Severus Scroll and 1QIsa[a]*, MasS 2 (Missoula, MT: Scholars Press, 1975), 43–48; Nathan R. Jastram, "The Severus Scroll and Rabbi Meir's Torah," in *The Text of the Hebrew Bible: From the Rabbis to the Masoretes*, ed. Elvira Martín-Contreras and Lorena Miralles-Maciá, JAJSup 13 (Göttingen: Vandenhoeck & Ruprecht, 2014), 137–46.

and *taw*. In this case the transcriptional error—or perhaps the rumor of this reading—has a strange existential consequence. In another reported variant in Rabbi Meir's scroll, God clothes Adam and Eve with כתנות אור ("garments of light") rather than כתנות עור ("garments of leather," Gen 3:21) (Gen. Rab. 20:12). This is another aural variant, in which עור was "heard" as אור, with an unusual, apparently mystical or esoteric, consequence.[55]

This eminent rabbi-scribe of the second century wrote a Torah scroll with famous variants, yet the universe was not destroyed. There is irony in these rabbinic narratives.[56] Scribal errors must not happen, but they do happen, even at the hands of an expert scribe. The sanctity of the Torah depends on its perfection, but scribal errors incessantly change it. Illumination (which is the lexical root of "Meir" and is manifested in the garments of "light") is the consequence of the Torah, but its light varies in different manuscripts. The ideal and the real are in tension in these stories. Similarly, the ideal and the real—the impossibility and inevitability of scribal errors—are in tension throughout the history of the biblical text.

---

55. See Galit Hasan-Rokem, "Rabbi Meir, the Illuminated and the Illuminating: Interpreting Experience," in *Current Trends in the Study of Midrash*, ed. Carol Bakhos, JSJSup 106 (Leiden: Brill, 2006), 240–41.

56. Daniel Boyarin, "Patron Saint of the Incongruous: Rabbi Me'ir, the Talmud, and Menippean Satire," *CritInq* 35 (2009): 539: "in the farrago that is the Talmud the most important intellectual practices of the rabbinic community are being advanced sincerely and queried at the same time with the effect, not of their undermining, but of their ironization."

7

ASSESSING THE TEXT-CRITICAL THEORIES
OF THE HEBREW BIBLE AFTER QUMRAN

A history of the vicissitudes of all the biblical books.
— Baruch Spinoza, *Tractatus Theologico-Politicus*

With the discovery of the (mostly fragmentary) manuscripts of biblical books from Qumran and nearby sites, our understanding of the history of the biblical text has been transformed. Previously, our evidence for the early history of the biblical text consisted of three major versions—the Masoretic Text (MT), the Septuagint (LXX), and the Samaritan Pentateuch (SP)—each with an unbroken chain of transmission to the present day. Each of these versions stems from the Second Temple period, and each is related to the others by a web of identical and divergent readings. One of the most important results of the discovery of the Qumran texts is an enhanced understanding of the history and relationships of these major versions. Hence, the discovery of the Qumran biblical texts entails not only the existence of new evidence, but a rediscovery of the importance of the textual evidence that we already had.

In the following, I will assess the major text-critical theories of the Hebrew Bible after Qumran by a twofold strategy. First I will survey the textual situation at Qumran and the relationships among the Qumran texts and the major versions (MT, LXX, and SP), using as a perspicuous example the book of Exodus. Then I will address the adequacy of the text-critical theories, testing their strengths and weaknesses against this evidence. The major protagonists in the theoretical discussion are Frank Cross, Shemaryahu Talmon, Emanuel Tov, and Eugene Ulrich.[1]

---

1. On the postmodern critique of textual criticism as such, see ch. 12 below.

I will build on Ulrich's argument that each of the theories has validity in explaining specific configurations of the data and that it may be possible to construct the outlines of a multilayered theory that accommodates the most powerful insights of each. I will also address the epistemological commitments of each theory, which will help distinguish between conflicts among the theories and conflicts of a more philosophical nature. In particular I will address the influences of nominalism versus realism in textual criticism.

The Textual Situation at Qumran

Talmon aptly describes the complexity of the textual situation at Qumran:

> What makes the evidence of the Scrolls especially valuable is the fact that they present not just a horizontal cross-section of one stabilized version, such as the Massoretic *textus receptus*. Because of their diversity, the kaleidoscope of the textual traditions exhibited in them, their concurrence here with one, here with another of the known versions, or again in other cases their exclusive textual individuality, the biblical manuscripts found at Qumran, in their totality, present in a nutshell, as it were, the intricate and variegated problems of the Hebrew text and versions.[2]

This "kaleidoscope of the textual traditions" can be illustrated in nearly every biblical book that has significant textual material from Qumran. As an illustration of this situation, I will consider the evidence of the book of Exodus, for which the Qumran evidence is particularly rich.

Fragments of some sixteen Exodus manuscripts from Qumran have been discovered and published and one manuscript from Murabbaʿat.[3] Of these, several preserve only a few words and thus do not provide a

---

2. Shemaryahu Talmon, "The Old Testament Text," in *Qumran and the History of the Biblical Text*, ed. Frank Moore Cross and Shemaryahu Talmon (Cambridge: Harvard University Press, 1975), 26–27.

3. Armin Lange, *Handbuch der Textfunde vom Toten Meer.* Vol. 1, *Die Handschriften biblischer Bücher von Qumran und den anderen Fundorten* (Tübingen: Mohr Siebeck, 2009), 44–66. There is also an LXX manuscript, 7QpapLXXExod; see Eugene Ulrich, "The Septuagint Scrolls," in *The Dead Sea Scrolls and the Developmental Composition of the Bible*, VTSup 169 (Leiden: Brill, 2015), 156. An Exodus fragment of unknown provenance, with ten words or word-parts, has been published in Emanuel Tov, Kipp Davis, and Robert Duke, eds., *Dead Sea Scrolls Fragments in the Museum Collection* (Leiden: Brill, 2016), 90–109. Two other small fragments, of unknown and perhaps dubious provenance, are published in Esther Eshel and Hanan Eshel, "A

sufficient base for considering textual relationships (1QExod, 2QExod[c], 4QExod[d,e,g,h,k]), two of which are excerpted or abbreviated texts: 4QExod[d] and 4QExod[e].[4] The extent of the longer (more than fifty words or word-parts) or distinctive texts (4QExod[j]) is as follows, ordered chronologically by script.[5]

Text	Script (date)	Words/parts
4QExod-Lev[f]	Proto-cursive script (mid-third century BCE)	259
4QGen-Exod[a]	Early Hasmonean formal script (125–100 BCE)	929
4QpaleoExod[m]	Hasmonean paleo-Hebrew script (100–30 BCE)	2,050
4QpaleoGen-Exod[l]	Hasmonean paleo-Hebrew script (100–30 BCE)	804
4QExod[c]	Late Hasmonean or Early Herodian formal script (50–25 BCE)	802
4QExod[b]	Early Herodian semicursive script (30 BCE–20 CE)	389
4QExod[j]	Middle Herodian formal script (1–30 CE)	12
2QExod[b]	Middle–Late Herodian formal script (1–70 CE)	56
2QExod[a]	Late Herodian formal script (30–70 CE)	142
MurGen-Exod-Num[a]	Post-Herodian formal script (75–125 CE)	260

Preliminary Report on Seven New Fragments from Qumran," *Meghillot* 5–6 (2007): 272–74

4. Emanuel Tov, "Excerpted and Abbreviated Biblical Texts from Qumran," in *Hebrew Bible, Greek Bible, and Qumran: Collected Essays*, TSAJ 121 (Tübingen: Mohr Siebeck, 2008), 33, 38.

5. Word counts are from Lange, *Handbuch*. Other details are from the *editiones principes* in the DJD series.

Before turning to the relationships among these texts, I will address the question of appropriate methodology: How can we reliably ascertain textual relationships?

The most valuable method for determining textual relationships is the assessment of *Leitfehler* ("indicative errors") or, more precisely, shared derived innovations.[6] This approach, associated with the work of the nineteenth century classicist Karl Lachmann, operates on the premise that shared divergences from the textual ancestor are the clearest evidence of textual affiliation. These divergences—which can be regarded as either "errors" or "innovations"—are inherited along a particular branch or lineage of the textual family tree. As Sebastiano Timpanaro emphasizes, "only coincidence in error can indicate the kinship between two manuscripts."[7] In contrast, early or correct readings shared with a textual ancestor (such as the archetype, which is the earliest inferable manuscript)[8] do not indicate any particular textual relationship, since such ancient readings can be scattered across several lineages. Similarly, unique divergences—errors or innovations that occur in only one text—do not indicate textual relationships. Unique features are found in virtually every ancient manuscript. Only shared derived innovations are useful as signs of textual kinship.

A useful analogue to this method is found in the field of evolutionary biology.[9] The traits that make a new genus or species distinctive are traits that diverge from a common ancestor. Humans may share 96 percent of the genetic code with chimpanzees, but it is the other 4 percent that make

---

6. Paul Maas, *Textual Criticism*, trans. Barbara Flower (Oxford: Clarendon, 1958), 42; Paolo Trovato, *Everything You Always Wanted to Know about Lachmann's Method: A Non-standard Handbook of Genealogical Textual Criticism in the Age of Post-structuralism, Cladistics, and Copy-Text*, Storie e linguaggi 7 (Padua: Libreriauniversitaria, 2014), 54–56, 109–17. On the history of this concept, see Sebastiano Timpanaro, *The Genesis of Lachmann's Method*, trans. Glenn W. Most (Chicago: University of Chicago Press, 2005); and Michael D. Reeve, "Shared Innovations, Dichotomies, and Evolution," in *Manuscripts and Methods: Essays on Editing and Transmission* (Rome: Edizioni di storia e letteratura, 2011)," 55–69. See further, chs. 5 and 9.

7. Timpanaro, *Genesis*, 89.

8. Trovato, *Everything*, 63–67; Michael D. Reeve, "Archetypes," in *Manuscripts and Methods: Essays on Editing and Transmission* (Rome: Edizioni di storia e letteratura, 2011), 107–17; and above, ch. 1.

9. See Frank Moore Cross, "Notes on a Generation of Qumrân Studies," in *The Ancient Library of Qumran*, 3rd ed. (Minneapolis: Fortress, 1995), 179–80; Reeve, "Shared Innovations," 73–103.

our species distinctive. These "new" genes and genetic combinations are diagnostic data for identifying new groups and species. The same principle allows for the identification of genetic relationships among individuals of our (and other) species. Each person has a DNA "fingerprint" whose distinctive features serve as markers for a particular lineage or family. From the point of view of the common ancestor, these are "errors" or "innovations"—that is, indicative errors.

For texts, the indicative errors are shared scribal changes, which include inadvertent errors and deliberate revisions. Two further caveats must be made. First, since many simple kinds of scribal error and change occur spontaneously and repeatedly—such as graphic error, dittography, word misdivision, changes in spelling, and the like—an indicative error must be relatively distinctive. That is to say, it should be more distinctive than simple errors and changes that arise from what Goshen-Gottstein calls the "law of scribes" ("the ever active and repeated force of the 'law of scribes' that creates the illusion of a genetic connection").[10] These changes are spontaneously generated in every period and cannot be used as indicative errors. Second, since a single indicative error is a narrow basis for determining affiliation, the most reliable diagnostic feature is a shared pattern or collection of indicative errors.

With these methodological guidelines in mind, let us survey the relationships among the Exodus manuscripts at Qumran (and Murabbaʿat). I will group them by patterns of indicative errors where possible.

4QExod-Lev[f] is the oldest text of Exodus, dating to the mid-third century BCE[11] It shares an important indicative error with MT and SP in the secondary ordering of the fashioning of the priestly garments in Exod 39:3–24, against the arguably earlier ordering (i.e., earlier edition) preserved in LXX (at Exod 36). It also shares an indicative error in this section with SP (against MT) at Exod 39:21, where 4QExod-Lev[f] has the execution of the command to make the Urim and Thummim:

ויעש את האורים ו[את התמים ...] משה

And he made the Urim and [the Thummim ...] Moses.

---

10. Moshe H. Goshen-Gottstein, "Hebrew Biblical Manuscripts: Their History and Their Place in the HUBP Edition," in Cross, *Qumran and the History*, 74.

11. Frank Moore Cross, "4QExod-Lev[f]," in *Qumran Cave 4.VII: Genesis to Numbers*, ed. Eugene Ulrich and Frank Moore Cross, DJD XII (Oxford: Clarendon, 1994), 133–44.

Both the command and the execution are in SP (at Exod 28:30 and here), but both are lacking in MT and LXX (at Exod 28:30 and MT Exod 39:21 = LXX Exod 36:28). This double plus is arguably a harmonizing expansion, triggered by an exegetical gap in the text concerning the origin of the Urim and Thummim.[12] This is a characteristic type of expansion in SP and related texts. We may therefore agree with the editor's conclusion, "Its filiation, to judge from significant inferior readings, is with the Samaritan tradition."[13] It does not overlap with other significant expansions in SP (and 4QpaleoExod^m), but this indicative error, supplemented with some minor agreements with SP, carries weight in determining its affinity. This is the earliest text of the proto-SP family.

4QGen-Exod^a has ambiguous affinities.[14] It lacks the distinctive proto-SP harmonizing pluses at Exod 6:9 and 7:18 (based on the reconstructed space), and it lacks several small harmonizing pluses in LXX.[15] However, it seems to share an indicative error with LXX (and 4QExod^b) at Exod 1:5, where the number of Jacob's descendants going to Egypt is recalculated to be 75 (versus MT's 70). But the word order is reversed in 4QGen-Exod^a:

חמש ושבעים 4QExod^b G (πέντε καὶ ἑβδομήκοντα) [4QGen-Exod^a [שבעים] והמש

Moreover, where LXX has a corresponding change in this verse, moving וְיוֹסֵף הָיָה בְמִצְרָיִם ("Now, Joseph was in Egypt") to precede the recalculated number (therefore counting Joseph and his household in the total), 4QGen-Exod^a has this clause afterward, agreeing with the sequence in MT, SP, and 4QpaleoGen-Exod^l. The affinity with LXX is therefore ambiguous, perhaps a matter of slight mixing. The editor holds that "4QExod^a is

---

12. See William H. C. Propp, *Exodus*, AB 2 (New York: Doubleday, 1999–2006), 2:346–47; and Eugene Ulrich, "The Developmental Growth of the Pentateuch in the Second Temple Period," in *Developmental Composition*, 35; *pace* Cross, "4QExod-Lev^f," 139, and Alexander Rofé, "Digesting DJD 12: Its Contribution to the Textual Criticism of the Pentateuch," *DSD* 23 (2016): 100, who both argue for the originality of the proto-SP reading. For additional details, see below, ch. 9.

13. Cross, "4QExod-Lev^f," 136.

14. Frank Moore Cross, "4QGen-Exod^a," in Ulrich, *Qumran Cave 4.VII*, 7–30.

15. James R. Davila, "Text-Type and Terminology: Genesis and Exodus as Test Cases," *RevQ* 16 (1993): 10–14, 30–35.

most closely related to M."[16] This may be correct, but there is a margin of uncertainty.

4QpaleoExod[m] is the most extensive Exodus text from Qumran and one of the longest biblical scrolls from Cave 4.[17] It has a significant pattern of indicative errors shared with SP, which is lacking in MT, LXX, and most of the other Qumran Exodus texts (but see below on 4QExod[j]). The major expansions are due to scribal harmonization with parallel texts in Exodus (particularly in the plague narratives) or Deuteronomy (harmonizing Deut 1–3 with the previous Sinai and wilderness narratives). There is also a significant difference in textual order, with the instructions for constructing the incense altar located (secondarily) at Exod 26:35 in 4QpaleoExod[m] and SP, compared to Exod 30:1 in MT and LXX. The editors observe:

> The scroll shares all the major typological features with SP, including all the major expansions of that tradition where it is extant (twelve), with the single exception of the new tenth commandment inserted in Exodus 20 from Deuteronomy 11 and 27 regarding the altar on Mount Gerizim.[18]

4QpaleoExod[m] and SP are related texts whose common ancestor had the shared harmonizing expansions and secondary textual sequence but lacked the distinctively sectarian revisions (e.g., the new tenth commandment and some other small changes) in SP.

4QpaleoGen-Exod[l] is a relatively long text written in the paleo-Hebrew script.[19] However, it shares no indicative errors with 4QpaleoExod[m] or SP. (This demonstrates that the paleo-Hebrew script has no necessary correlation with textual affinity.) Neither does it share any clear indicative errors with other texts. The editors observe that "in smaller variants [it] sometimes agrees with MT, sometimes with SP, sometimes with Exod[m], and sometimes preserves a unique reading."[20] None of these agreements,

---

16. Ibid., 35.

17. Judith E. Sanderson, *An Exodus Scroll from Qumran: 4QpaleoExod[m] and the Samaritan Tradition*, HSS 30 (Atlanta: Scholars Press, 1986); Patrick W. Skehan, Eugene Ulrich, and Judith E. Sanderson, "4QpaleoExodus[m]," in *Qumran Cave 4.IV: Palaeo-Hebrew and Greek Biblical Manuscripts*, ed. Patrick W. Skehan, Eugene Ulrich, and Judith E. Sanderson, DJD IX (Oxford: Clarendon, 1992), 53–130.

18. Skehan, "4QpaleoExodus[m]," 66.

19. Patrick W. Skehan, Eugene Ulrich, and Judith E. Sanderson, "4QpaleoGenesis–Exodus[l]," in Skehan, *Qumran Cave 4,IV*, 17–52.

20. Ibid., 23.

however, constitutes an indicative error. There is one interesting point of affinity—4QpaleoGen-Exod[l] agrees with MT and LXX against 4Qpaleo-Exod[m] and SP at 26:36, indicating that its placement of the incense altar instructions belongs to an earlier edition than 4QpaleoExod[m] and SP.[21]

4QExod[c] shares the situation of 4QpaleoGen-Exod[l] as having a relatively small degree of variation from other texts but no clear indicative errors. The editor of 4QExod[c] states, "it agrees sometimes with MT, sometimes with SP, sometimes with another scroll, sometimes with LXX, and sometimes preserves a reading that is, so far, unique."[22] Its affiliation is ambiguous.

4QExod[b] shares four indicative errors in Exod 1:1–5 with LXX (one reconstructed on the basis of space), including the recalculation of the number of Jacob's descendants as seventy-five (with LXX and 4QGen-Exod[a] [see above], versus 70 in MT and SP).[23] It also shares fours indicative errors (all harmonizing pluses) with LXX (including one shared with SP) in Exod 2–3:

Exod 2:6: בת פרעה 4QExod[b] SP G (ἡ θυγάτηρ Φαραω) "daughter of Pharaoh"] > M

Exod 2:11: [ה]רֹבים 4QExod[b] G (πολλαῖς) "many"] > M SP

Exod 2:16: תֹ[וֹ]רֹ 4QExod[b] G (ποιμαίνουσαι) "shepherdesses"] > M SP

Exod 3:16: ואלוהי יֹשֹ[חק ואלוה]יֹ יעקוב 4QExod[b] G (καὶ θεὸς Ισαακ καὶ θεὸς Ιακωβ) "And the God of Isaac and the God of Jacob"] יצחק ויעקב M SP (+ initial ו) "(and) Isaac and Jacob"

On the basis of this cluster of shared secondary readings, the editor concludes that "4QExod[b] is a collateral witness to the textual family which provided the *Vorlage* of the Old Greek translation."[24]

---

21. Eugene Ulrich, "The Palaeo-Hebrew Biblical Manuscripts from Qumran Cave 4," in *The Dead Sea Scrolls and the Origins of the Bible*, SDSS (Grand Rapids: Eerdmans, 1999), 128–29.

22. Judith E. Sanderson, "4QExod[c]," in Ulrich, *Qumran Cave 4.VII*, 101.

23. Frank Moore Cross, "4QExod[b]," in Ulrich, *Qumran Cave 4.VII*, 79–95.

24. Ibid., 84.

4QExod[j] is a short text that arguably shares a harmonizing expansion with 4QpaleoExod[m] and SP at Exod 8:1.[25] This indicative error is inferred on the basis of space and so is not as certain as an extant reading. But the inference seems probable, placing this text in the family of 4QpaleoExod[m] and SP.

2QExod[a] is a relatively short text with some indicative errors.[26] At Exod 1:12 and 9:28, it shares harmonizing pluses with LXX:

Exod 1:12: [במאד מאד] ישרצו 2QExod[a] G (ἴσχυον σφόδρα σφόδρα)
"they swarmed more and more"] יפרץ M SP "spread"

Exod 9:28: ואש 2QExod[a] G (καὶ πῦρ) "and fire"] > M SP

On the basis of space, it may also share a plus with LXX at 1:11 (where LXX adds καὶ Ων, "and [the city of] On"). Judging from these shared secondary readings, 2QExod[a] has affinities with LXX and 4QExod[b] (although there is no overlap between 2QExod[a] and 4QExod[b]).

2QExod[b] is a relatively short text with one indicative error, a harmonizing/explicating plus shared with LXX:[27]

Exod 34:10: [י]הוה א[ל משה] 2QExod[b] G (κύριος πρὸς Μωυσῆν)
"YHWH to Moses"] > M SP

This shared error is probably too narrow a base to establish affinity. The sequence here appears to be Exod 19:9 + Exod 34:10, indicating that this either an excerpted or "rewritten" text.[28]

MurExod is a short text of Exodus dating to the beginning of the second century CE, discovered at Murabbaʿat, 11 miles from Qumran.[29] The scroll probably included MurGen[a] and MurNum, hence the current

---

25. Judith E. Sanderson, "4QExod[j]," in Ulrich, *Qumran Cave 4.VII*, 149–50.

26. Maurice Baillet, "Texts des grottes 2Q, 3Q, 6Q, 7Q à 10Q," in *Les "petites grottes" de Qumrân: Exploration de la falaise, les grottes 2Q,3Q,5Q,6Q,7Q a 10Q, le rouleau de cuivre*, ed. Maurice Baillet, Józef T. Milik, and Roland de Vaux, DJD III (Oxford: Clarendon, 1962), 49–52.

27. Baillet, "Texts des grottes," 52–55.

28. Tov ("Excerpted," 28) tentatively regards it as a "rewritten" text.

29. Józef T. Milik, "Textes Hébreux et Araméens," in *Les grottes de Murabbaʿât*, ed. Pierre Benoit, Józef T. Milik, and Roland de Vaux, DJD 2 (Oxford: Clarendon, 1961), 77–78.

designation MurGen-Exod-Num[a]. This scroll provides a partial glimpse of the textual situation a few decades after the destruction of Qumran. MurGen-Exod-Num[a] agrees in all details with MT, including spelling and paragraphing.

MurGen-Exod-Num[a]—and the other biblical texts discovered at Murabbaʿat, Naḥal Ḥever, Wadi Seyal, and Masada—seem to attest to the ascent of a narrow group of proto-M texts in at least some social groups or strata in the period before and after the Jewish Revolt against Rome (66–73 CE). These data may also suggest the recession of other types of biblical texts during this period, including most of the variety of Exodus texts represented at Qumran. The details of this apparent narrowing-down of texts remain obscure.[30]

This survey of the textual situation of Exodus at Qumran, supplemented by the Murabbaʿat text, provides a glimpse of the types and complexity of data that must be comprehended by any adequate theory of the history of the biblical text.

Text-Critical Theories

How does one comprehend this "kaleidoscope of the textual traditions"? First, we should consider some theoretical limitations. There are different possible ways to classify any set of data, depending on the criteria one adopts and the inclusions and exclusions marked by these criteria. One needs to establish cogent categories, which are both relevant and comparable (one does not want to compare apples with oranges). One also needs to gauge whether the amount and kind of data are sufficiently full to warrant the judgments and determinations necessary for reliable categorization. In the face of insufficient data, any judgment is weakly founded. Since the Qumran texts are the very epitome of incomplete data, caution is necessary.

Beyond these limitations, there is also a matter of philosophical preference or epistemological commitment in any construction of relevant categories. In particular, there is a perennial clash between the background theories of realism versus nominalism, which influences how one "sees" texts and their interrelationships. Traditionally—since at least Plato's time—realists believe that there are such things as concrete particulars *and* general or abstract categories, whereas nominalists believe that there

---

30. See below, ch. 8.

are only particulars. For a realist, words such as *red* or *infinity* refer to abstract realities, whereas for a nominalist, colors and numbers are properties of particular things. Empiricists are philosophical nominalists—so John Locke held that "All things that exist [are] particulars."[31] W. V. Quine has more recently countered, somewhat wistfully, that nominalism is an "ill-starred project," since "to the nominalists' sorrow science is saddled with abstract objects."[32] Middle grounds are being sought.

The upshot is that where one observer may see a coherent family or group, another may—with equal but opposite philosophical justification—see only a collection of individuals. This is a difference of philosophical outlook and preference. As in many such clashes, there are valid arguments on each side, and it is difficult to reconcile the two perspectives. Textual scholarship is best served by weighing the arguments—implicit and explicit—between these positions, yielding a productive dialectic. In any case, awareness of these opposed tendencies allows us to comprehend some of the unspoken issues in the theoretical arguments, as we will see below.

A THEORY OF LOCAL TEXTS

The post-Qumran discussion was inaugurated in 1955 by William F. Albright's programmatic call for a theory of local textual recensions, which he located in Babylonia (proto-M), Egypt (proto-G), and Palestine.[33] This theory was expanded and refined by Frank Cross, based on his research on Cave 4 biblical texts, which he was preparing for publication.[34] Cross differed from Albright in describing these different textual groupings as families rather than recensions, since the latter term implies systematic revision:

---

31. John Locke, *An Essay Concerning Human Understanding* (London: Holt, 1690), §3.3.1.

32. Quine, *Quiddities: An Intermittently Philosophical Dictionary* (Cambridge: Harvard University Press, 1987), 228–29.

33. William F. Albright, "New Light on Early Recensions of the Hebrew Bible," in Cross, *Qumran and the History*, 140–46.

34. See Frank Moore Cross, "The Contributions of the Qumran Discoveries to the Study of the Biblical Text," in Cross, *Qumran and the History*, 278–92; more recently, "The Fixation of the Text of the Hebrew Bible," in *From Epic to Canon: History and Literature in Ancient Israel* (Baltimore: Johns Hopkins University Press, 1998), 205–18; and below, ch. 10.

Against Albright, we should argue, however, that the local textual families in question are not properly called "recensions." They are the product of natural growth or development in the process of scribal transmission, not of conscious or controlled textual recension.[35]

Despite this qualification (to which we will return below), Cross maintained that a theory of local texts is necessary to comprehend the array of textual evidence:

Any reconstruction of the history of the biblical text before the establishment of the traditional text in the first century A.D., must comprehend this evidence: the plurality of text-types, the limited number of distinct textual families, and the homogeneity of each of these textual families over several centuries of time. We are required by these data, it seems to me, to recognize the existence of local texts which developed in the main centers of Jewish life in the Persian and Hellenistic age.[36]

Cross accepted Albright's geographical locales in general terms but charted different textual configurations for the Pentateuch and Samuel—where three or four different textual families are evident—versus other biblical books where only one or two textual families are extant. For the Pentateuch and Samuel he sketched the following map of three locales and four textual families:

Palestine   Palestinian textual family, from which stems the narrower proto-SP textual family
                characteristics: expansionistic, harmonistic, and modernizing tendencies that increase over several centuries

Egypt   proto-G textual family, which stems from an early phase of the Palestinian family
                characteristics: expansionistic, but less than later Palestinian texts

Babylonia   proto-M textual family
                characteristics: (Pentateuch) relatively little expansion or revision; (Samuel) extensive corruption, but still an unexpanded text

---

35. Cross, "Contributions," 282 n. 21.
36. Ibid., 282.

In philosophical terms this is a realist theory, in which the relationships among individual texts are comprehended by general features, which are both text-critical and historical-geographical in nature.

According to this model, the textual families in each book diverge from a common ancestor (the archetype, which is the latest common ancestor of the extant manuscripts, i.e., the one from which the branching occurred that produced the textual families). According to the local texts theory, scribal transmission in the three major centers of Jewish life allowed sufficient separation for the different textual lineages to acquire their characteristic traits, after which they were brought back into proximity in Palestine during the Hasmonean and early Roman periods. It is this latter situation that we see at Qumran. (Cross attributes this textual immigration to a widespread "return to Zion" after the restoration of a Jewish monarchy.)

According to the theory of local texts, the classification of the Qumran and Murabba'at Exodus texts is roughly as follows. (I have put question marks after four texts—4QpaleoGen-Exod[l], 4QGen-Exod[a], 4QExod[c], and 2QExod[b]—since their affiliation is unclear; see above.)

Palestine	Palestinian family: 4QGen-Exod[a] (?), 4QpaleoGenesis-Exod[l] (?), 4QExod[c] (?), 2QExod[b] (?)
	Proto-Samaritan family: 4QExod-Lev[f], 4QpaleoExod[m], 4QExod[j]
Egypt	Proto-G family: 4QExod[b], 2QExod[a]
Babylonia	Proto-M family: MurExod

Although the affinities among three of these groups are relatively clear (proto-SP, proto-G, and proto-M), a number of valid criticisms have been leveled at the local texts theory. First, since all of the Qumran (and Murabba'at, etc.) texts were found in Palestine, their differing geographical ancestry is purely conjectural. Second, the characteristics of the textual families are extremely general, making it difficult to tell, for example, what distinguishes a Palestinian text from other types. That is, the criteriology is imprecise. Third, the specification of these textual families may unfairly privilege MT, SP, and LXX.[37]

---

37. See the criticisms of Emanuel Tov, "Groups of Biblical Texts Found at Qumran," in *Time to Prepare the Way in the Wilderness: Papers on the Qumran Scrolls*, ed. Devo-

Cross's construal of the evidence in the quotation above requires further clarification and refinement: "the plurality of text-types, the limited number of distinct textual families, and the homogeneity of each of these textual families over several centuries of time." The boundary conditions, the number of categories, and the geographical origins in this classification system are all contestable to varying degrees. Nonetheless, as I have noted above, this system does comprehend several sets of clear relationships among the texts, including what Cross calls the proto-SP, proto-G, and proto-M textual families. There are many details that are conjoined in this theory, some of which are clearly warranted, and others which are impressionistic or merely conjectural. Subsequent theories have provided criticisms, refinements, and alternatives.

SOCIAL GROUPS AND PRISTINE TEXTUAL TRADITIONS

Shemaryahu Talmon has contested the local texts theory,[38] focusing on two of its central claims: (1) that there are a limited number of textual families and (2) that geographical separation is necessary to explain the growth and stability of the distinct textual families. In contrast, he raises the possibility that (1) there may once have been a much greater number of textual families, most of which did not survive, and (2) the locus for these textual families may have been distinct social groups rather than geographical locales:

> One is inclined to attribute [the limited number of textual families] to two factors: (*a*) historical vicissitudes which caused other textual families to disappear; (*b*) the necessary socio-religious conditions for the preservation of a text-tradition, namely its acceptance by a sociologically integrated and definable body.... Contradictory as it may sound, one is almost inclined to say that the question to be answered with regard to the history of the Old Testament text does not arise from the extant "plural-

---

rah Dimant and Lawrence H. Schiffman, STDJ 16 (Leiden: Brill, 1995), 85–102; and Emanuel Tov, *Textual Criticism of the Hebrew Bible*, 3rd ed. (Minneapolis: Fortress, 2012), 158–60, 173–74.

38. Talmon, "Old Testament Text," 35–40; and more recently, "Textual Criticism: The Ancient Versions," in *Text and Canon of the Hebrew Bible: Collected Studies* (Winona Lake, IN: Eisenbrauns, 2010), 403–5.

ity of text-types" but rather from the disappearance of other and more numerous textual traditions.[39]

It is entirely possible that there were once more textual families, as Talmon observes. As noted above, we need to be cognizant of the paucity of the extant evidence. However, this is a "virtual" criticism or modification of the local texts theory, since there is no extant evidence of additional textual families (see below).

More importantly, sociological context—in contrast to geographical—does play a role in textual history, particularly in the *preservation* of textual families. As Talmon observes, the MT was preserved in post-70 CE Jewish communities, the SP in the Samaritan community, and the LXX in Christian communities. Moreover, prior to 70 CE the MT textual family may have been the authorized version in particular circles, perhaps among the temple scribes, as Talmon surmises. (Note that the Chronicler in the late Persian or early Hellenistic period uses some biblical texts that arguably diverge from proto-M, so this possible inference cannot be extended back too far.)[40]

However, some social groups—such as the Qumran community (almost certainly an Essene group)—had no textual preference. The Qumran scribes, who arguably followed a distinctive scribal practice, copied proto-M, Palestinian, proto-G, proto-SP, and other biblical texts without making distinctions among them.[41] Among the Exodus texts, 2QExod[b], 4QExod[b], and 4QExod[j] were arguably written in the Qumran scribal practice, but each has affinities to a different textual family—Palestinian, proto-G, and proto-SP, respectively (see above). Further, the sectarian commentaries sometimes revel in small textual differences (e.g., 1QpHab at Hab 2:16).[42] Hence Talmon's useful emphasis on social groups in the transmission of distinct textual families is complicated by the social-textual situation at Qumran.

---

39. Talmon, "Old Testament Text," 40.

40. See Gary N. Knoppers, *I Chronicles 1–9: A New Translation with Introduction and Commentary*, AB 12A (New York: Doubleday, 2003), 69–70.

41. See Emanuel Tov, *Scribal Practices and Approaches Reflected in the Texts Found in the Judean Desert*, STDJ 54 (Leiden: Brill, 2004), 261–73, and below.

42. Timothy H. Lim, *Holy Scripture in the Qumran Commentaries and Pauline Letters* (Oxford: Oxford University Press, 1997), 50.

Another respect in which Talmon differs from the local texts theory is in his theory of divergent pristine textual traditions. He does not assume that the divergent textual families in each book descended from a common ancestor. Instead he postulates that some categories of differences among the manuscripts "may derive from divergent pristine textual traditions."[43]

It is not clear what Talmon means by "divergent pristine textual traditions." He seems to project aspects of the "kaleidoscope of the textual traditions" all the way back, without an origin or historical convergence. This is a distinctly nominalist perspective, in which individual and variants are not ranked as "preferred" or "archetypal" or "secondary," but rather each distinct reading has its own irreducible individuality and independent status. Emanuel Tov has criticized this position as unclear and historically dubious, concluding that

> [Talmon's argument] does not appear to be proven by the facts or logic....
> It appears that the parallel readings adduced as arguments in favor of this opinion were created in the course of the transmission of the biblical texts, and even though they seem to be of equal value, nevertheless, only one of them was original.[44]

That is, the two readings are not of equal value, but one must have arisen in the course of textual transmission as an error or innovation.

In his view of "divergent pristine textual traditions," Talmon posits a nominalist theory of the biblical text in which there is no apex of the textual family tree, only pristine branches. As Tov has argued, this is a dubious view. Talmon's emphasis on social groups and the once potentially greater number of textual families are, however, useful advances in the construction of a more adequate text-critical theory.

GROUPS AND NONALIGNED TEXTS

Emanuel Tov's substantial work on textual theory evinces a productive tension between nominalist and realist perspectives, which in some respects provides a synthesis of both perspectives. Because of this internal dialectic and because he continually refines his theories, his positions are ana-

---

43. Talmon, "Old Testament Text," 4; and "Textual Criticism," 406–7, 415–18.
44. Emanuel Tov, *Textual Criticism of the Hebrew Bible*, 2nd ed. (Minneapolis: Fortress, 2001), 172; similarly *Textual Criticism*, 163–65; and above, ch. 2.

lytically rich but sometimes inconsistent. I will concentrate on his more developed position in "Groups of Biblical Texts Found at Qumran" (1995) and subsequent writings.[45]

Tov's model of textual history involves several criticisms of the local texts theory, while in other respects it is a revision of it. He advances a nominalistic critique of the local texts theory, emphasizing that MT, SP, and LXX should be regarded as individual texts rather than as exemplars of three different text types: "They are just *texts*.... The textual reality of the Qumran texts does not attest to three groups of textual witnesses, but rather to a textual multiplicity displaying an unlimited number of texts."[46] However, he counters this valid nominalist caution with an admission that

> it so happens—and this is no coincidence—that many of the Qumran texts are actually close to MT, a small number to SP, and a few to LXX, so that also post factum the comparison with these texts is actually justified. But ... there are other groups of texts as well.[47]

Here Tov enters the thicket of classification. His proposed model departs from the local texts theory in several respects: (1) he rejects the geographical localization of the proto-M and proto-G groups in Babylonia and Egypt, respectively (on the latter, see further below); (2) he expands the number of textual groups to five or more; and (3) he makes important additional distinctions among the groups, defining proto-M as a textual group with no typological characteristics, pre-SP as a group with typological characteristics, and the texts related to the *Vorlage* of LXX as a group of related individual copies. He defines a fourth group of "nonaligned texts," which is not a group at all but a category of independent texts, and finally he adds (as an "appendix to the classification") a group of scrolls written with distinctive scribal features that he calls "Qumran scribal practice."[48]

This is a heterogeneous classification system in which some groups are not really comparable. The scrolls with the orthography, morphology, and

---

45. Tov, "Groups"; Tov, "The Biblical Texts from the Judean Desert: An Overview and Analysis," in *Hebrew Bible, Greek Bible, and Qumran: Collected Essays*, TSAJ 121 (Tübingen: Mohr Siebeck, 2008), 143–53; and *Textual Criticism*, 107–10, 158–60.

46. Tov, *Textual Criticism*, 159 (italics original).

47. Tov, "Groups," 88; similarly *Textual Criticism*, 108–9.

48. Tov, "Groups"; and "Overview," 143–50. The qualification that the last group is an "appendix to the classification" was added in *Textual Criticism*, 109.

scribal marks characteristic of the Qumran scribal practice include texts of various affinities, including proto-M texts (none in Exodus), pre-SP texts (4QExod^j), texts related to LXX (4QExod^b?), and nonaligned texts (2QExod^b). This group of texts is characterized by unusual accidentals (e.g., spelling and other details that are matters of scribal fashion and do not affect the text's sense) and not by their substantive readings. Only the latter are relevant for determining textual affiliation.[49] A particular system of accidentals is, in a sense, both ephemeral and transversal to the textual genealogy. The texts copied in Qumran scribal practice constitute an important category for textual study,[50] but not for assessing textual affinities. Moreover, the heterogeneity of the biblical texts copied in this scribal practice is evidence for the *lack* of preference for a particular textual family or group in the Qumran community.

The category of nonaligned texts is heterogeneous by definition. By this term Tov means that "the text does not stand in any specifically close relation to either MT, SP or LXX. It agrees with each one of these texts, though not exclusively, and by the same token it also differs from these texts."[51] As such, these texts are "not linked with any of the other texts or groups."[52] This is a group of individual texts that do not belong in any group, which is to say it is a realist notation for a nominalist set of texts.

The idea that there are such things as nonaligned texts has been aptly criticized by Bruno Chiesa.[53] He argues that Tov departs from the standard practice of textual criticism in positing independent or unaffiliated texts of a particular book, such as Exodus. Chiesa emphasizes that *all* of the manuscripts of a given book are related, and there is no such thing as a text that is "not linked with any of the other texts or groups" (Tov's formulation). I think that Tov would agree with this criticism, since he maintains

---

49. See above, ch. 5, and below, ch. 9.

50. Tov, *Scribal Practices*, 261–73; Tov, *Textual Criticism*, 100–105; and the caveats of Eibert Tigchelaar, "Assessing Emanuel Tov's 'Qumran Scribal Practice,'" in *The Dead Sea Scrolls: Transmission of Traditions and Production of Texts*, ed. Sarianna Metso, Hindy Najman, and Eileen Schuller, STDJ 92 (Leiden: Brill, 2010), 173–207.

51. Tov, "Groups," 98.

52. Ibid., 101.

53. Bruno Chiesa, "Textual History and Textual Criticism of the Hebrew Old Testament," in *The Madrid Qumran Congress: Proceedings of the International Congress on the Dead Sea Scrolls, Madrid, 18–21 March, 1991*, ed. Julio Trebolle Barrera and Luis Vegas Montaner, STDJ 11 (Leiden: Brill, 1992), 257–72.

that all of our biblical manuscripts descend from earlier texts, including an original text for each book or edition.[54]

The term *nonaligned* seems to conflate several issues: (1) the (logically unwarranted) idea that a text of a work can lack affinities with other texts of that work, (2) the absence of evidence for a text's affinities, and (3) a text with mixed affinities. (A text can have mixed affinities if, for example, it was copied from one text and subsequently corrected according to a text of a different group.) Tov's use of nonaligned seems to denote the first category, a text that lacks affinities, which (as Chiesa observes) is impossible. However, the term may legitimately denote the other categories: texts whose affinities are unknown (because of insufficient data) or whose affinities are mixed (because of "horizontal" transmission, i.e., corrections toward other texts). Hence I suggest that Tov's group of nonaligned texts is best replaced by two groups, "texts of unknown affiliation" and "texts of mixed affiliation." In Exodus, given our fragmentary evidence, these two groups are difficult to differentiate. In the absence of a pattern of mixed indicative errors, one should favor "unknown affiliation."

In sum, we may not know a text's alignment or it may be complexly aligned, but it cannot be nonaligned in theory. The nominalist impulse behind the concept of independent or nonaligned texts generates a flawed category.

According to Tov's categories (but omitting the category of texts written in Qumran scribal practice, and revising the nonaligned category), the Exodus texts from Qumran and environs can be classified roughly as follows:[55]

Proto-MT: 4QGen-Exod[a], 4QpaleoGen-Exod[l], 4QExod[c], MurExod
Pre-SP: 4QpaleoExod[m], 4QExod[j] (?)
Texts Related to the *Vorlage* of LXX: none
Nonaligned: 4QExod-Lev[f], 4QExod[b], 2QExod[b], 2QExod[a]

The chief differences in manuscript classification between the groups theory and the local texts theory concern the existence of the nonaligned category in one and the Palestinian category in the other. For example, Cross classifies 4QExod-Lev[f] as an Old Palestinian text, whereas Tov clas-

---

54. Tov, *Textual Criticism*, 161–69.
55. After Tov, *Textual Criticism* and Tov, "Biblical Texts."

sifies it as nonaligned. Two texts that Cross classifies as proto-G are also classified by Tov as nonaligned (2QExod[a] and 4QExod[b]). Three other manuscripts that I tentatively placed in Cross's Palestinian class are listed under proto-M by Tov (4QpaleoGenesis-Exod[l], 4QGen-Exod[a], 4QExod[c]). While these different placements depend on the different configurations of groups, they also point to the problem of imprecise boundary conditions, a problem shared by the local texts theory and the groups theory.

Despite Tov's differences in detail and theory from the local texts theory, there is a good deal of overlap, as the classification of many of the Exodus texts illustrates. In many respects Tov's model is a revision of the local texts theory, stripping away some of its more speculative features and adding precision to the definition of textual relationships within a group (e.g., textual family in the case of proto-M, recension in the case of pre-SP).

Although Tov rejects the geographical localizations of the local texts theory as lacking evidence, he has provided a new argument for *a* theory of local texts (i.e., a revised theory), with respect to the provenance of the texts related to the *Vorlage* of LXX:

> We should … draw attention to another aspect of the LXX which provides positive evidence for *a* theory of local texts…. When analyzing differences between textual traditions, it is helpful to start from typologically different textual traditions, e.g., the short text of the LXX of Jeremiah (also reflected in 4QJer[b, d]) and of the story of David and Goliath (1 Samuel 17–18), chronological differences between the LXX and MT in 1–2 Kings, as well as other elements which bear on the literary growth of the Hebrew Bible…. It may be suggested that where such disparities existed, geographical separation perpetuated in one center textual traditions that had become obsolete in another or others.[56]

Although Tov argues that there is no evidence to indicate an Egyptian location for the development of texts related to the *Vorlage* of LXX, he suggests that some form of local texts theory would account for the preservation of earlier editions in such texts. In other words, these local texts preserved features (i.e., an earlier edition) that had been displaced elsewhere. Tov writes, "such changes were not inserted in the copies of the biblical books used in centers remote from those where the changes were

---

56. Emanuel Tov, *The Text-Critical Use of the Septuagint in Biblical Research*, 2nd ed. (Jerusalem: Simor, 1997), 187.

made."[57] This situation is analogous to the relationships of language dialects between center and periphery, where peripheral communities may preserve old features that have been displaced in the central community (e.g., Shakespearean features of English preserved in Appalachia).

With regard to the local factors in the LXX, Jan Joosten has recently deepened the argument that the pentateuchal translators were "Jews of the Egyptian diaspora writing for a local Jewish audience."[58] The LXX lexicon is colloquial Egyptian Greek, with occasional doses of Egyptian Aramaic, and is characteristic of "nonelite" Egyptian society. The local identity of the translators plausibly suggests that their biblical texts were also local. (This contrasts with the extravagant picture drawn in the Letter of Aristeas, in which the translators were Jerusalem sages, and the pentateuchal texts were precious scrolls "written in gold" [§176] sent as a gift from the high priest of Jerusalem.) As a local and relatively lowbrow translation, it is plausible that the LXX translation was made from local texts from the Egyptian diaspora community.

Tov's contribution to textual theory includes both a critique of previous theories and an evolving new synthesis. While there are flaws in some portions of his theory—such as the text-critical relevance of the texts written in Qumran practice and the category of nonaligned texts—his careful and nuanced discussions have significantly advanced many aspects of text-critical theory. He has refined the categories of texts related to MT, LXX, and SP, and has carefully explored texts that are not as closely (or as identifiably) allied. His groups theory is in some ways a refinement of the local texts theory and in other ways an alternative.

Consecutive Literary Editions

Eugene Ulrich has further advanced the theoretical discussion by more thoroughly incorporating the implications of multiple editions of biblical texts.[59] These editions play a role in the other theories (as with Tov's com-

---

57. Ibid.

58. Jan Joosten, "Language as Symptom: Linguistic Clues to the Social Background of the Seventy," in *Collected Studies on the Septuagint: From Language to Interpretation and Beyond*, FAT 83 (Tübingen: Mohr Siebeck, 2012), 194.

59. Eugene Ulrich, "Double Literary Editions of Biblical Narratives and Reflection on Determining the Form to Be Translated," in *Origins*, 34–50; Ulrich, "Pluriformity in the Biblical Text, Text Groups, and Questions of Canon," in *Origins*, 79–98;

ments about local texts regarding the early editions in LXX), but Ulrich has placed them at the center of his theory. He proposes that

> The main lines in the picture of the history of the biblical text were formed by the deliberate activity of a series of creative scribes who produced the new or multiple literary editions of the books of the Bible.... The emergence of each fresh literary edition occasioned variant versions of the literature that would coexist for some time. Variant text types were thus caused by revised literary editions.[60]

He defines the major axes of textual history as the editions (i.e., recensions) of various texts, which constitute discernible criteria for establishing textual affinity. This is the most extensive type of textual change, and as such deserves a central place in text-critical theory. For the purpose of determining affiliation, the new editions constitute large-scale patterns of indicative errors (using "error" as a cover term for textual change, not as a value judgment).

In some respects this model revives Albright's idea of early recensions but provides clear evidence for such recensions. For Exodus, Ulrich defines three editions: the earliest (known) textual form, which Ulrich calls the "base text," and two subsequent editions.[61] Edition I or the base text is the form of Exodus preserved in the LXX, which differs from later editions in its short version of the construction of the tabernacle in Exod 35–40.[62] Edition II was created from Edition I by systematically harmonizing the commands and executions in the tabernacle text. This is the form of the text found in MT and allied texts. Edition III was created from Edition II by the extensive additional harmonizations that are found in 4QpaleoExod^m, SP, and allied texts (see above).

Ulrich "Multiple Literary Editions," in *Origins*, 99–120; and Ulrich, "Developmental Growth," 29–45.

60. Ulrich, "Multiple Literary Editions," 107–8.

61. Ulrich, "Double Literary Editions," 38–39; Ulrich, "Multiple Literary Editions," 114.

62. Anneli Aejmelaeus, "Septuagintal Translation Techniques: A Solution to the Problem of the Tabernacle Account?" in *On the Trail of the Septuagint Translators: Collected Essays*, 2nd ed., CBET 50 (Leuven: Peeters, 2007), 107–21; Brandon E. Bruning, "The Making of the Mishkan: The Old Greek Text of Exodus 35–40 and the Literary History of the Pentateuch" (PhD diss., University of Notre Dame, 2014).

By focusing on the sequence of editions, Ulrich's model provides clear criteria for the determination of textual affiliation. This is an advantage over the local texts theory and the groups theory, where the criteria for affiliation are less clearly defined. However, this advantage is in other respects a weakness, since (1) it allows for classification only where sufficient text is preserved to determine which edition a text contains, and (2) it does not pertain to books where only one edition is extant. In such cases, "one can skip to the level of individual textual variants to refine the interrelationship of preserved manuscripts."[63] That is, where there is only one edition or where the textual evidence is insufficient to determine its edition, one reverts to the type of criteria emphasized in the other theories.

Hence Ulrich's theory is eclectic, incorporating the classifications of the previous theories within it. He describes the stemmatic (i.e., genealogical) form of his classification system as follows:

> On an ideal stemma (which is different for each book), the main lines would be drawn according to variant editions ... while the secondary lines would be drawn according to the pattern of individual variants between or within text families.[64]

For Exodus, Ulrich's model would look roughly as follows, with the editions as the major axes and the other textual groupings nested within each edition:

Edition I
    Proto-G Texts: 4QExod^b (?), 2QExod^a (?), *Vorlage* of LXX

Edition II
    Proto-M Texts: MurExod, MT
    Other (Palestinian): 4QpaleoGenesis-Exod^l (?), 4QGen-
        Exod^a (?), 4QExod^c (?), 2QExod^b (?)

Edition III
    Pre-S Texts: 4QExod-Lev^f, 4QpaleoExod^m, 4QExod^j
    SP

---

63. Ulrich, "Multiple Literary Editions," 114.

64. Eugene Ulrich, "Two Perspectives on Two Pentateuchal Manuscripts from Masada," in *Emanuel: Studies in Hebrew Bible, Septuagint and Dead Sea Scrolls in Honor of Emanuel Tov*, ed. Shalom M. Paul et al., VTSup 94 (Leiden: Brill, 2003), 461.

There is a good deal of guesswork in the assignation of texts (marked by question marks), since many of the Qumran fragments are not extant at places where changes of edition occur. For example, 4QExod[b] and 2QExod[a] are not extant at Exod 35–40, but are otherwise affiliated with LXX. Similarly, most of the texts listed under Edition II are not extant at the places where Edition III differs from Edition II. Among the subgroupings, I have used the ambiguous designation "other (Palestinian)" for texts in Edition II that are arguably outside of the proto-M textual family. (The boundaries are imprecise, as seen by the disagreements in the classification of manuscripts by Cross and Tov, see above).

This classification system has the advantage of clear criteria in its major axes. But there are some further problems in the relationships among the segments. Whereas Edition II is chronologically later than Edition I, there are arguably textual relationships that cut across these editions. For example, Cross proposes that the proto-G texts in the Pentateuch derive from the Old Palestinian textual family. We might imagine, therefore, that a text like 4QExod-Lev[f] is an older relation of 4QExod[b], but that the latter's textual precursor escaped the insertion of Edition II in the tabernacle section (Exod 35–40), perhaps because it was a local (Egyptian) text (see above). In other words, the (or a) local texts model has some advantages in specifying genealogical relationships that the editions model lacks.

Nonetheless, the editions model makes an important contribution to text-critical theory. It clarifies that we could—in theory—determine the affiliation of many of the biblical manuscripts by their edition. This provides a coherent axis of large-scale criteria. There are arguably sixteen books for which there is evidence of multiple editions: Genesis, Exodus, Numbers, Joshua, Judges, Samuel, Jeremiah, Ezekiel, the Minor Prophets, Psalms, Proverbs, Song of Songs, and Daniel.[65] The editions model provides some clear advantages for these books, although as noted above, there are practical difficulties, given the fragmentary nature of many of our texts.

Ulrich's proposal integrates the implications of multiple editions into text-critical theory. The challenge is how best to integrate the advantages of this model with the different virtues of the other models.

---

65. Tov, *Textual Criticism*, 283–326.

Conclusions

I concur with Ulrich's judgment that each of the post-Qumran text-critical theories has validity in explaining particular periods or qualities of the textual data:

> Cross has focused on the *origins* or originating causes of the different text types—how the different types came to be or were produced. Talmon has focused on the *final stages*—how we end up with only three main texts or text-types. Tov has focused on the *complexity* of the textual witnesses in the manuscript remains.[66]

This is an apt amalgamation of the three theories, which charitably sidesteps their criticisms of each other and their internal flaws. Ulrich's theory can be seen as complementary as well—he has added a focus on *editions*, which figure importantly in the textual genealogy of many biblical books.

The idea of mapping the virtues of each theory onto a composite model is attractive. To achieve this goal, we may need to imagine an eclectic or multidimensional set of representations, which include cross-cutting and independent criteria. Textual relationships should be mapped according to several axes, including locale, social group, textual groups and subgroups, and editions. Ideally one could envision a holographic or mathematical model, which can accommodate different layers and clusters of relationships.[67]

Since this essay is limited to two dimensions, I offer the diagram below as a tentative eclectic minimal stemma of Exodus, which incorporates details of each of the text-critical theories discussed above, and which provides an intelligible frame for the relationships among the relevant data.

This stemma includes multiple classificatory layers: editions, locales, social setting, and textual groups. It includes vertical transmission (i.e., genealogical lineages and branching) and horizontal transmission (i.e., contemporaneous exchange, as in the replacement of Edition I by Edition II in some lineages). As in the case of language, change may be inherited (vertical transmission) or superimposed (horizontal transmission, comparable to wave theory in linguistics). Variables of time, place, social loca-

---

66. Ulrich, "Pluriformity," 82–83 (italics original).

67. See Michael P. Weitzman, *The Syriac Version of the Old Testament: An Introduction* (Cambridge: Cambridge University Press, 1999), 319–22.

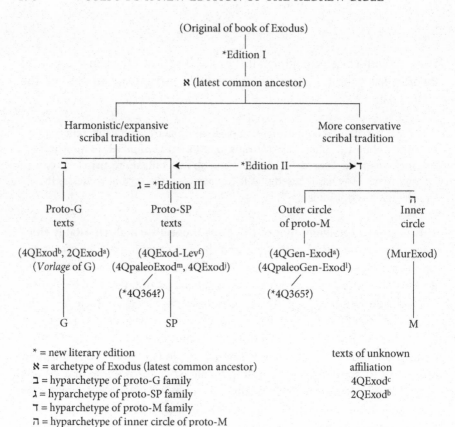

(Original of book of Exodus)

*Edition I

א (latest common ancestor)

Harmonistic/expansive   More conservative
scribal tradition   scribal tradition

ב ◄——————— *Edition II———————► ד

ג = *Edition III

| Proto-G | Proto-SP | Outer circle | ה |
| texts | texts | of proto-M | Inner circle |

(4QExod^b, 2QExod^a)   (4QExod-Lev^f)   (4QGen-Exod^a)   (MurExod)
(*Vorlage* of G)   (4QpaleoExod^m, 4QExod^j)   (4QpaleoGen-Exod^l)
(*4Q364?)   (*4Q365?)

G   SP   M

* = new literary edition   texts of unknown
א = archetype of Exodus (latest common ancestor)   affiliation
ב = hyparchetype of proto-G family   4QExod^c
ג = hyparchetype of proto-SP family   2QExod^b
ד = hyparchetype of proto-M family
ה = hyparchetype of inner circle of proto-M

tion, and recensional activity are accommodated (in broad strokes) in this eclectic model.

The diagram includes an extrastemmatic category of "texts of unknown affiliation," which I have argued is necessary in our situation of incomplete data. I have listed SP separately from the pre-SP texts because of its few but important sectarian changes. MT is a narrow subgroup of the proto-M lineage or family. The LXX of Exodus was translated from a proto-G text.

There is no doubt that the internal branchings in this historical stemma were more complex than indicated in the diagram. Any theoretical model requires simplification of variables. As the saying goes, map is not territory—if it were, it would be infinite in its complexity.[68] This

---

68. See Jorge Luis Borges, "On Exactitude in Science," in *Collected Fictions*, trans.

stemma is a map of what we are warranted to surmise about the textual relationships among our earliest Exodus texts and versions. As Paolo Trovato observes, "A stemma is simply the most effective depiction of the relationships ... of the mss. still in existence at the time when the philologist creates the stemma."[69]

I should mention that drawing a map of such relationships is itself a realist endeavor. It is an abstract model—a historical reconstruction—that attempts to explain the affinities among the individual texts. The theory embedded in this model is a realist theory, which hypothesizes that the textual reality transcends the collection of individual texts. Further, it posits a textual archetype, which is the latest common ancestor of the extant manuscripts—and an exemplar of Edition I. This too is an abstraction, but a logically and historically necessary one. Several of these concepts are inimical to a pure nominalist position, as noted above. Hence we need to realize that there are underlying philosophical assumptions and epistemological commitments in any text-critical theory.[70] This is not a matter of regret, but pertains to the nature of textual scholarship.

Andrew Hurley (New York: Penguin, 1998), 325; cf. Alfred Korzybski, *Science and Sanity: An Introduction to Non-Aristotelian Systems and General Semantics*, 5th ed. (Brooklyn: Institute of General Semantics, 1994), 58: "A map *is not* the territory it represents, but, if correct, it has a *similar structure* to the territory, which accounts for its usefulness" (italics original).

69. Trovato, *Everything*, 135.

70. See David C. Greetham, *Theories of the Text* (Oxford: Oxford University Press, 1999); and above, ch. 5.

8

THE (PROTO-)MASORETIC TEXT OF THE PENTATEUCH

> I see plurality around the ancient mainstream which finally led to our
> Masoretic *textus receptus*.
> —Moshe Goshen-Gottstein, "The Rise of the Tiberian Bible Text"

The term *Masoretic Text* conventionally refers to the vocalized, accented,
and annotated biblical codices produced by late medieval Hebrew scribes
and their modern heirs. There are three branches of MT—Tiberian, Babylonian, and Palestinian—which differ according to their vocalization systems.[1] The consonantal text does not differ in major details among these
branches.[2] Nonetheless, the consonantal text of each medieval MT manuscript differs in minor details, due to the fluidity of spelling and common
types of scribal error. The premedieval scrolls belonging to the MT textual
family will be designated proto-M. The proto-M textual family can be further subdivided into an inner circle and an outer circle (see below).

The oldest complete or nearly complete codices of the MT Pentateuch
are from the tenth or early eleventh century CE:[3]

---

1. See Geoffrey Khan, *A Short Introduction to the Tiberian Masoretic Bible and
Its Reading Tradition*, GHand (Piscataway, NJ: Gorgias, 2012), 43–62; Khan, "Biblical
Hebrew: Pronunciation Traditions," in *Encyclopedia of Hebrew Language and Linguis-
tics*, ed. Geoffrey Khan (Leiden: Brill, 2013), 1:341–52.

2. The variants (all minor) in the Cairo Geniza Pentateuch fragments with Palestinian vocalization are listed in Bruno Chiesa, *L'Antico Testamento ebraico secundo la
tradizione palestinense* (Turin: Erasmo, 1978), 125–42.

3. Early codices are listed in Michèle Dukan, *La Bible hébraïque: Les codices copiés
en Orient et dans la zone séfarade avant 1280* (Turnhout: Brepols, 2006), 71–76; Malachi Beit-Arié, "The Damascus Pentateuch: MS Jerusalem, Jewish National and University Library Heb. 4° 5702: Orient, ca. 1000," in *The Makings of the Medieval Hebrew
Book: Studies in Palaeography and Codicology* (Jerusalem: Magnes, 1993), 111, 125;

+ St. Petersburg Bible Codex I B19a (L = National Library of Russia I Firkovitch B19a)[4]
+ St. Petersburg Pentateuch Codex II B17 (L[1] = National Library of Russia II Firkovitch B17)[5]
+ St. Petersburg Pentateuch Codex II B10 (L[3] = National Library of Russia II Firkovitch B10)[6]
+ Cairo Pentateuch Codex (C3 = Gottheil 18)[7]
+ Damascus Pentateuch Codex (S = Sassoon 507 = National Library of Israel MS Heb. 24°5702)[8]
+ London Pentateuch Codex (B = British Library Or. 4445)[9]

L is the oldest codex that contains the complete Pentateuch. Most of the Pentateuch is lacking in the Aleppo Codex (A), ca. 930, which is the most accurate MT codex from the Tiberian Ben Asher family with respect to vocalization, accentuation, and Masorah.[10] Another important early Pentateuch codex is Vatican ebr. 448 (V), ca. eleventh–twelfth century.[11]

---

and Israel Yeivin, *Introduction to the Tiberian Masorah*, ed. and trans. E. J. Revell, MasS 5 (Missoula, MT: Scholars Press, 1980), 15–29.

4. Dated in colophon to 1008/9 CE; David Noel Freedman, *The Leningrad Codex: A Facsimile Edition* (Grand Rapids: Eerdmans, 1998); Malachi Beit-Arié, Colette Sirat, and Mordechai Glatzer, *Codices Hebraicis Litteris Exarati quo Tempore Scripti Fuerint Exhibentes*, vol. 1, *Jusqu'à 1020* (Turnhout: Brepols, 1997), 114–31.

5. Dated in colophon to 929 CE; extant from Gen 2:6 with many lacunae. The scribe, Solomon ben Buyaʿa, was also the scribe of A; the *naqdan* was his brother Ephraim. See Beit-Arié, *Codices*, 53–64; Dukan, *Bible hébraïque*, 238–39.

6. Tenth century; Yeivin, *Introduction*, 23; Dukan, *Bible hébraïque*, 314–15.

7. Tenth century; Jordan S. Penkower, "A Tenth-Century Pentateuchal MS from Jerusalem (MS C3), Corrected by Mishael Ben Uzziel" [Hebrew] *Tarbiz* 58 (1988): 49–74.

8. Ca. 1000 CE; extant from Gen 9:26, lacking Exod 18:1–23; Beit-Arié, "Damascus Pentateuch"; David S. Loewinger and Malachi Beit-Arié, *The Damascus Pentateuch*, 2 vols., EHMF 1–2 (Copenhagen: Rosenkilde and Bagger, 1978–1982); http://tinyurl.com/SBL7010q.

9. Tenth–early eleventh century: extant from Gen 39:20 to Deut 1:33, lacking Num 7:46–73; 9:12–10:18; Dukan, *Bible hébraïque*, 296–97; Aron Dotan, "Reflections towards a Critical Edition of Pentateuch Codex Or. 4445," in *Estudios Masoréticos (X Congreso de la IOMS): En memoria de Harry M. Orlinsky*, ed. Emilia Fernández Tejero and Maite T. Ortega Monasterio (Madrid: Instituto de Filología, 1993), 39–50.

10. Extant from Deut 28:17; Beit-Arié, *Codices*, 65–72; http://tinyurl.com/SBL7010r. The Pentateuch text in Menachem Cohen, *Miqraʾot Gedolot Ha-Keter*

The codex format was adopted in the eighth or ninth century for scholarly study.[12] Previously, all known texts of the Hebrew Bible were written in scroll format. Medieval Torah scrolls, written on leather (parchment), contain the consonantal text of MT with the inevitable small variants.

The oldest complete Torah scroll is the Bologna Torah Scroll, dated to the twelfth or early thirteenth century CE.[13] The oldest fragments of late antique and early medieval Torah scrolls or scrolls of individual books date roughly from the third to the seventh centuries CE.[14] They are on leather or papyrus (marked by P below) and contain the consonantal text of MT with minor variants:

- Oxford, Bodleian Library MS Heb. D.89 (P) frag. i, portions of Exod 2:23–25[15]
- Cambridge University Library T-S NS 3.21 and 4.3 (Cairo Geniza), portions of Gen 4:14–6:5 and 13:10–17:9[16]
- Berlin Staatliche Museen P. 10598, portions of Exod 3:13–4:9[17]

(Ramat Gan: Bar Ilan University Press, 1992–2013) is based on Yemenite codices that are elsewhere very close to A.

11. Extant from Gen 7:11; Alejandro Díez Macho, *The Pentateuch with the Masorah Parva and the Masorah Magna and with Targum Onkelos, MS. Vat. Heb. 448* (Jerusalem: Makor, 1977); http://tinyurl.com/SBL7010s.

12. Colette Sirat, *Hebrew Manuscripts of the Middle Ages* (Cambridge: Cambridge University Press, 2002), 35, 42–47; the oldest dated biblical codex (with fragments of Ruth and Nehemiah) is from 903/904 CE (pl. 20); Dukan, *Bible hébraïque*, 234.

13. Mauro Perani, "Il più antico rotolo del Pentateuco ebraico integro: Una scoperta alla Biblioteca Universitaria di Bologna," *TECA* 4 (2013): 87–97.

14. Dukan, *Bible hébraïque*, 32.

15. Dated to ca. third century CE by Ada Yardeni, *The Book of Hebrew Script: History, Palaeography, Script Styles, Calligraphy and Design* (London: British Library, 2002), 73 and fig. 90; see Colette Sirat, *Les papyrus en caractères hébraïques trouvés en Égypte*, MMCH (Paris: Centre National de la Recherche Scientifique, 1985), 31–32, 123, and pl. 83; and Sirat, *Hebrew Manuscripts*, 29, pl. 12.

16. Dated to ca. eighth century CE by Yardeni, *Hebrew Script*, 79 and fig. 97; see Colette Sirat, Michèle Dukan, and Ada Yardeni, "Rouleaux de la Tora antérieurs à l'an mille," *CRAI* 138 (1994): 861–64; Sirat, *Hebrew Manuscripts*, 27–28 and pl. 11; images in Ben Outhwait, "The Oldest Hebrew Fragment in the Collection? T-S NS 3.21," *Fragment of the Month: November 2010*, http://tinyurl.com/SBL7010g. There is a variant at Gen 17:1, where this MS has the singular שׁנה, versus the plural שׁנים in other MT (and SP) manuscripts.

17. Sirat, *Papyrus*, 34–35 and pl. 9; the text is mistakenly identified as Num 3–4.

◆   MS London-Ashkar, portions of Exod 9:18–16:1[18]

The Oxford scroll, written in small characters and format, was presumably used for study.[19] The other scrolls have larger formats, which were suitable for synagogue use.

The earliest pentateuchal texts, all fragmentary, are from the Judean Desert, dating from the mid-third century BCE to the early second century CE. The earliest, 4QExod-Lev[f] (mid-third century BCE), has affinities with the proto-SP family. The earliest proto-M fragment, 4QLev-Num[a], is from the early Hasmonean period (ca. 150–100 BCE, see below). It is unclear whether complete Torah scrolls existed in the Second Temple period, but the multibook scrolls from the Judean Desert—notably MurGen-Exod-Num[a] (below)—suggests that this was possible.[20]

TYPOLOGICAL FEATURES, SCRIBAL ERRORS, AND ORTHOGRAPHY

The (proto-)MT Pentateuch has certain typological features that distinguish it from the other identifiable textual families in the Pentateuch (proto-SP and proto-G).[21] These features include several substantive editorial revisions by scribes in the proto-M tradition. These revisions contrast with the earlier or parallel editions preserved in proto-SP and/or proto-G:

1.   A revised edition of the chronologies of Gen 5 and 11.[22]

---

18. Edna Engel and Mordechay Mishor, "An Ancient Scroll of the Book of Exodus: The Reunion of Two Separate Fragments," *Israel Museum Studies in Archaeology* 7 (2015): 24–60; Paul Sanders, "The Ashkar-Gilson Manuscript: Remnant of a Proto-Masoretic Model Scroll of the Torah," *JHS* 14 (2014): art. 7, http://tinyurl.com/SBL7010h.

19. Sirat, *Papyrus*, 32.

20. Emanuel Tov, *Scribal Practices and Approaches Reflected in the Texts Found in the Judean Desert*, STDJ 54 (Leiden: Brill, 2004), 75–77.

21. See below, ch. 9. I use the prefix *proto-* for these families (following Cross) to indicate that they are contemporary and related textual families. One should not attach teleological value to these sigla or see them as privileging their eponyms; they are merely conventions.

22. Ronald Hendel, *The Text of Genesis 1–11: Textual Studies and Critical Edition* (New York: Oxford University Press, 1998), 61–80; Ronald Hendel, "A Hasmonean Edition of MT Genesis? The Implications of the Editions of the Chronology in Genesis

MT, SP, and LXX have three different editions of these chronologies. All three are responses to exegetical problems in the text.
2. An expanded edition of the tabernacle text of Exod 35–40.[23]
    LXX has a shorter account of the construction of the tabernacle. The MT edition is expanded, harmonized, and reordered to correspond more closely with God's instructions to Moses in Exod 25–30.
3. Sequence differences at Gen 47:5–6 and Num 10:34–36.[24]
    The MT of Gen 47:5–11 is reordered and truncated due to problems in the narrative (see below). LXX preserves the earlier text. The MT and LXX have different locations for the "Song of the Ark" in Num 10:34–36. It is unclear whether one placement is secondary or whether the Song was a late editorial insertion in both textual traditions.
4. Theologically motivated revisions at Deut 27:4, 32:8, and 32:43.[25]
    An anti-Samaritan revision occurs at Deut 27:4, where MT reads "Ebal," replacing "Gerizim" in SP and LXX (restored from the Old Latin). An antipolytheistic revision occurs at Deut 32:8, where proto-M reads "sons of Israel," replacing the original "sons of

---

5," *HBAI* 1 (2012): 1–17; Emanuel Tov, "The Genealogical Lists in Genesis 5 and 11 in Three Different Versions," in *Textual Criticism of the Hebrew Bible, Qumran, Septuagint: Collected Essays*, VTSup 167 (Leiden: Brill, 2015), 221–38.

23. Anneli Aejmelaeus, "Septuagintal Translation Techniques: A Solution to the Problem of the Tabernacle Account?," in *On the Trail of the Septuagint Translators: Collected Essays*, 2nd ed., CBET 50 (Leuven: Peeters, 2007), 107–21; Brandon E. Bruning, "The Making of the Mishkan: The Old Greek Text of Exodus 35–40 and the Literary History of the Pentateuch" (PhD diss., University of Notre Dame, 2014).

24. Emanuel Tov, "Some Sequence Differences between the Masoretic Text and the Septuagint and Their Ramifications for Literary Criticism," in *The Greek and Hebrew Bible: Collected Essays on the Septuagint*, VTSup 72 (Leiden: Brill, 1999; repr., Atlanta: Society of Biblical Literature, 2006), 414–15.

25. Eugene Ulrich, "Joshua's First Altar in the Promised Land," in *The Dead Sea Scrolls and the Developmental Composition of the Bible*, VTSup 169 (Leiden: Brill, 2015), 47–65; Stefan Schorch, "The Samaritan Version of Deuteronomy and the Origin of Deuteronomy," in *Samaria, Samarians, Samaritans: Studies on Bible, History and Linguistics*, ed. József Zsengellér, SJ 66 (Berlin: de Gruyter, 2011), 23–37; Gary N. Knoppers, *Jews and Samaritans: The Origins and History of Their Early Relations* (New York: Oxford University Press, 2013), 184–87, 201–12; Alexander Rofé, "The End of the Song of Moses (Deuteronomy 32:43)," in *Deuteronomy: Issues and Interpretation*, OTS (London: T&T Clark, 2002), 47–54.

> God," preserved in 4QDeut^{j} and LXX. Another antipolytheistic revision occurs in Deut 32:43, where proto-M omits a poetic line referring to the "sons of God" and in the parallel line replaced "heaven" with "nations." The original readings are preserved, with variants and expansions, in 4QDeut^{q} and LXX.

These revisions are sufficiently distinctive to count as typological features of the proto-M textual family in the Pentateuch.[26] They provide a contrast with the respective typological features of the other pentateuchal textual families. Aside from these typological features, there are many other smaller-scale scribal revisions in the proto-M textual family, including harmonizations and explicating glosses.[27] In general, the proto-M Pentateuch is a less revised text than proto-SP and proto-G, but still has the notable revisions above.

Besides these typological features and smaller revisions, there are many small scribal errors in the (proto-)MT Pentateuch. These are the inevitable product of scribal transmission of texts. The following is a small sample of the kinds of scribal errors in the MT Pentateuch. These are found in all the early MT codices. Many additional scribal errors occur in the MT codices and printed editions of the early modern period, as demonstrated in the collations of Benjamin Kennicott (1776–1780) and Giovanni de Rossi (1788).[28] The correct readings below (listed first) are either attested in non-MT pentateuchal texts and versions or are cogent conjectures.

---

26. In contrast, Emanuel Tov argues ("The Textual Development of the Torah," in *Collected Essays*, 248–49) that the proto-MT Pentateuch does not have typological or secondary features and is essentially the archetype: MT Pentateuch "do[es] not display secondary features.… All other texts branched off from MT or a similar text.… In the Torah the proto-Masoretic texts stand at the top of the *stemma*." Presumably he would hold that the MT editions in Gen 5 and Exod 35–40 are the first (or base) editions, or that they are too small or localized to have bearing on the stemma. See below, ch. 9.

27. E.g., בני ענק מן הנפלים ("the Anakites are from the Nephilim") at Num 13:33; see Reinhard Müller, Juha Pakkala, and Bas ter Haar Romeny, *Evidence of Editing: Growth and Change of Texts in the Hebrew Bible*, RBS 75 (Atlanta: Society of Biblical Literature, 2014), 35–38; additional examples in Hendel, *Text of Genesis*, 40–60.

28. See Moshe H. Goshen-Gottstein, "Hebrew Biblical Manuscripts: Their History and Their Place in the HUBP Edition," in *Qumran and the History of the Biblical Text*, ed. Frank Moore Cross and Shemaryahu Talmon (Cambridge: Harvard University Press, 1975). 42–89.

Graphic Confusion: Gen 10:4

רֹדָנִים SP G (Ῥόδιοι) "Rhodians" also 1 Chr 1:7

דֹּדָנִים M "Dodians" (ד → ר)

Metathesis: Deut 31:1

ויכל (משה לדבר) 1QDeut[b] G (συνετέλεσεν) "Moses *finished* speaking"

וַיֵּלֶךְ (מֹשֶׁה וַיְדַבֵּר) M SP "Moses *went* to speak" (לכ → לב)

Transposition: Gen 27:5

(לצוד ציד) *לאביה(ו) G (θηρεῦσαι θήραν τῷ πατρὶ αὐτοῦ) "to hunt game *for his father*"

(לָצוּד צָיִד) לְהָבִיא M SP "to hunt game *to bring*" (לאביה[ו] → להביא)[29]

Dittography: Lev 20:10

(רֵעֵהוּ) וְאִישׁ אֲשֶׁר יִנְאַף אֶת־אֵשֶׁת conjecture "And a man who commits adultery with the wife of (his neighbor)"

(רֵעֵהוּ) וְאִישׁ אֲשֶׁר יִנְאַף אֶת־אֵשֶׁת אִישׁ אֲשֶׁר יִנְאַף אֶת־אֵשֶׁת M SP G "And a man who commits adultery with the wife of *a man who commits adultery with the wife of* (his neighbor)" (איש אשר ינאף את אשת → written twice)

Haplography: Lev 22:18

(בישראל) הגר הגר 4QLev[b] SP G (τῶν προσηλύτων τῶν προσκειμένων) "the sojourner *who sojourns* (in Israel)"

(בְּיִשְׂרָאֵל) הַגֵּר M "the sojourner (in Israel)" (הגר הגר → הגר)

Word Misdivision: Gen 49:19–20

עקבם אשר SP "*their* heels. Asher"

עָקֵב מֵאָשֵׁר M "heel. *From* Asher" (במ#מ→ במ#)[30]

Reminiscence: Gen 9:7

(פרו ורבו שרצו בארץ) *ורדו בה conjecture "(Be fruitful and multiply, spread on the earth,) and *rule* it" (cf. Gen 1:28)

---

29. It is also possible that this is a near-haplography: להביא לאביהו → להביא לאביהו (MT).

30. The misdivision occurred prior to the consistent use of final letters in the post-Herodian era; see Tov, *Scribal Practices*, 230–34.

פְּרוּ וּרְבוּ שִׁרְצוּ בָאָרֶץ) וּרְבוּ־בָהּ) M SP G (καὶ πληθύνεσθε ἐπ᾽ αὐτῆς)
"(Be fruitful and multiply, spread on the earth,) and *multiply* on it"
(reminiscence of וּרְבוּ, "multiply" three words previously)[31]

Graphic Confusion and Near-Haplography: Gen 47:21
וְאֶת הָעָם) הֶעֱבִיד אֹתוֹ לַעֲבָדִים) SP G (κατεδουλώσατο αὐτῷ εἰς παῖδας)
"(As for the people,) he *enslaved* them into *slavery*"
וְאֶת־הָעָם) הֶעֱבִיר אֹתוֹ לֶעָרִים) M "(As for the people,) he *transferred*
them to the *cities*" (ד → ר [2x] and ר→בר)

The orthography of (proto-)MT Pentateuch reflects roughly the practices of the earliest Qumran biblical scrolls, which date to the third century BCE.[32] The distribution of *matres lectionis* in the MT Pentateuch is
slightly fuller than 4QSam^b but not as full as 4QExod-Lev^f or 4QJer^a (all
third-century scrolls). For instance, the use of *waw* to mark word-internal
long *ō* is infrequent in 4QSam^b, more frequent in the MT Pentateuch, and
regular in 4QExod-Lev^f and later scrolls. Compare the distribution of full
and defective spelling of *'ēpōd* ("ephod"): 4QSam^b: אפד; MT Pentateuch:
אפד and אפוד; 4QExod-Lev^f and later texts (e.g., 4QSam^a): אפוד.
The MT Pentateuch also preserves an unusual number of preexilic
spellings, such as occasionally marking final *ō* with *he* (rather than the
later extension of *waw* to this position);[33] for example, אהלה ("his tent")
in the *ketiv* of Gen 9:21, 12:8, 13:3, and 35:21. There are also a smattering
of late spellings in the MT Pentateuch, for example, the occasional final
he in the 2ms pronominal suffix: ידכה ("your hand," Exod 13:16); כמכה
("like you," Exod 15:11, twice); לכה ("to you," Gen 27:37).[34] Generally, in
orthography as well as substantive readings, the inner circle of the proto-

---

31. Hendel, *Text of Genesis*, 56–57.

32. David Noel Freedman, "The Massoretic Text and the Qumran Scrolls: A Study
in Orthography," in Cross, *Qumran and the History*, 196–211.

33. The earliest epigraphic instance of *waw* mater in this position is בו ("in him")
in the Ketef Hinnom inscription (I.11), late seventh–early sixth century BCE; Gabriel
Barkay et al., "The Amulets from Ketef Hinnom: A New Edition and Evaluation,"
BASOR 334 (2004): 54, 60.

34. On regularities and irregularities in MT spelling practices, see James Barr, *The
Variable Spellings of the Hebrew Bible*, Schweich Lectures (Oxford: Oxford University
Press, 1989).

M Pentateuch (see below) is less expansionistic than the outer circle or the non-MT pentateuchal texts.

History of the (Proto-)MT Pentateuch

There are three general models of the history of the (proto-)MT Pentateuch.[35] The first, formulated by Johann Gottfried Eichhorn, and refined by Paul de Lagarde, holds that MT derives from a particular textual family (Eichhorn) or a particular text (Lagarde; see below), which in turn descends from the textual original (*Urtext*). The original text of the Pentateuch is loosely identified with Ezra's ספר תורת משה ("scroll of the Torah of Moses") in Neh 8:1, which portrays events of the mid-fifth century BCE. The second model, formulated by Paul Kahle, holds that MT derives from editorial efforts in the first century CE to create a standard version out of the plethora of "vulgar" texts in circulation at the time. A pentateuchal *Urtext* of the fifth century BCE is not excluded from this scenario. Kahle argued that the MT is itself a "kritischen Reduktion des Vulgärtextes,"[36] essentially a work of ancient textual criticism. A third model, which derives from Kahle's, was formulated by Talmon, who holds that MT is a written crystallization of one of many oral versions of the Pentateuch in circulation during the Persian period. In his view, "the process culminating in the practically total substitution of written transmission for oral tradition [occurred] toward the end of the Persian age."[37] He holds that many variants in the ancient biblical texts stem from independent oral versions, and that there was no *Urtext* behind these textual crystallizations.

---

35. Cf. the overviews in Armin Lange, "'They Confirmed the Reading' (*y. Taʿan.* 4.68a): The Textual Standardization of Jewish Scriptures in the Second Temple Period," in *From Qumran to Aleppo Aleppo: A Discussion with Emanuel Tov about the Textual History of Jewish Scriptures in Honor of His 65th Birthday*, ed. Armin Lange, Matthias Weigold, and József Zsengellér, FRLANT 230 (Göttingen: Vandenhoeck & Ruprecht, 2009), 31–45; Emanuel Tov, "The History and Significance of a Standard Text of the Hebrew Bible," in *Hebrew Bible/Old Testament: The History of Its Interpretation*, ed. Magne Saebø (Göttingen: Vandenhoeck & Ruprecht, 1996), 1.1:49–66; and Bruno Chiesa, *Filologia storica della Bibbia ebraica*, Studi biblici 125 (Brescia: Paideia, 2000), 420–26.

36. Paul Kahle, "Untersuchungen zur Geschichte des Pentateuchtextes," in *Opera Minora* (Leiden: Brill, 1956), 35–36.

37. Shemaryahu Talmon, "Textual Criticism: The Ancient Versions," in *Text and Canon of the Hebrew Bible: Collected Studies* (Winona Lake, IN: Eisenbrauns, 2010), 393.

While each of these models is theoretically possible, and others are imaginable, the genealogical textual model of Eichhorn and Lagarde has gained currency in light of the data from the Qumran biblical texts. Against Kahle, there is no reason to regard the MT Pentateuch as the product of systematic editing.[38] Against Talmon, the variants among MT, the biblical Dead Sea Scrolls, SP, and LXX are consistently analyzable as scribal errors or revisions made while copying texts (as in the instances above), and are unlikely to stem from independent oral variants. There is no evidence in favor of Talmon's theory of "multiple pristine texts."[39]

Lagarde, following the historical text-critical method of Karl Lachmann and others, observed that the MT Pentateuch has certain paratextual elements that allow us to trace its textual history into premedieval times. These features include the *puncta extraordinaria* (dotted letters), *nun suspensa*, and other unusual scribal marks, which are written in all medieval and early modern scrolls and codices.[40] Lagarde argued that such distinctive secondary features must ultimately derive from a single manuscript, since such a complex cluster of scribal features cannot have arisen independently in unrelated texts. He inferred that all exemplars of MT descend from a manuscript that he designated (after Lachmann's usage) the "archetype of the Masoretic Text" ("archetypus des masoretischen textes"). Noting that the scribal dots are correction marks that mean "delete," he writes:

> Our Hebrew manuscripts of the Old Testament go back to one single exemplar, and have even reproduced as true corrections the correction [marks] of its scribal errors and taken over its random imperfections.[41]

---

38. Bertil Albrektson, "Reflections on the Emergence of a Standard Text of the Hebrew Bible," in *Text, Translation, Theology: Selected Essays on the Hebrew Bible* (Farnham, UK: Ashgate, 2010), 47–62; Emanuel Tov, *Textual Criticism of the Hebrew Bible*, 3rd ed. (Minneapolis: Fortress, 2012), 174–80.

39. See the critiques by Tov, *Textual Criticism*, 163–67; and above, ch. 2.

40. Tov, *Scribal Practices*, 187–98, 214–18.

41. Paul de Lagarde, *Anmerkungen zur griechischen Übersetzung der Proverbien*, (Leipzig: Brockhaus, 1863), 2: "unsere hebräischen handschriften des alten testaments auf ein einziges exemplar zurückgehn, dem sie sogar die korrektur seiner schreibfehler als korrektur treu nachgeahmt und dessen zufällige unvollkommenheiten sie herübergenommen haben."

Lagarde maintained that the archetype of MT, that is, the first manuscript with this cluster of secondary features, existed in the first century CE, primarily since these features are already known in rabbinic literature.[42]

Another set of secondary features that can arguably be used to elucidate the history of the MT Pentateuch is the *qere perpetuum* in the Pentateuch in which הוא (3ms pronoun) is the *ketiv* and היא (3fs pronoun) is the *qere*. This textual feature occurs around 120 times in the Pentateuch, versus 11 instances where היא is correctly written. This textual phenomenon is either (1) a retention of a dialectal feature in which the old feminine singular independent pronoun was replaced by an epicene pronoun, הוא,[43] or (2) a systematic graphic confusion of *yod* and *waw* in a proto-M Torah scroll or scrolls.[44] Since the oldest proto-M scroll, 4QLev-Num[a] (early Hasmonean period; see below), correctly reads היא where the MT *ketiv* is הוא (at Num 5:6),[45] a systematic graphic error subsequent to the Early Hasmonean period is the more likely solution. Cross has argued that this systematic graphic error stems from the script of the Early Herodian period:

> The most plausible explanation of this is that the manuscript or manuscripts copied for the Pentateuchal Recension was a manuscript in which *waw* and *yod* were not distinguished in the Jewish script. This occurs at only one time in the development of the Jewish scripts: in the Early Herodian Period (30–1 BCE).[46]

---

42. This date was advocated by scholars on other grounds, e.g., the Talmudic account of the three scrolls in the Temple Court, or the hermeneutical rules of Rabbis Hillel, Aqiba, and Ishmael; see Emanuel Tov, "The Text of the Hebrew/Aramaic and Greek Bible Used in the Ancient Synagogues," in *Hebrew Bible, Greek Bible, and Qumran: Collected Essays*, TSAJ 121 (Tübingen: Mohr Siebeck, 2008), 177–84.

43. Recently advocated by Steven E. Fassberg, "The Kethiv/Qere הוא, Diachrony, and Dialectology," in *Diachrony in Biblical Hebrew*, ed. Cynthia L. Miller-Naudé and Ziony Zevit, LSAWS 8 (Winona Lake, IN: Eisenbrauns, 2012), 171–80.

44. So John A. Emerton, "Was There an Epicene Pronoun *Hūʾ* in Early Hebrew?" *JSS* 45 (2000): 267–76 (his answer is "not likely").

45. Eugene Ulrich, "4QLev-Num[a]," in *Qumran Cave 4.VII: Genesis to Numbers*, ed. Eugene Ulrich and Frank Moore Cross, DJD XII (Oxford: Clarendon, 1994), 166–67; SP also (correctly) reads היא. Ulrich (157–58) tentatively reads [א]וֹהִ at Lev 14:44, but the text is fragmentary.

46. Frank Moore Cross, "The Stabilization of the Canon of the Hebrew Bible," in *From Epic to Canon: History and Literature in Ancient Israel* (Baltimore: Johns Hopkins University Press, 1998), 223.

These two genealogical arguments, based on widespread innovations or *Leitfehler* (indicative errors, *errores significativi*) in the proto-M Pentateuch converge on the period that is illuminated by the Dead Sea Scrolls.

PROTO-M PENTATEUCH: THE INNER CIRCLE

Emanuel Tov has usefully distinguished between two categories of proto-M texts in the Dead Sea Scrolls, an inner and an outer circle:

> We should posit two types of Masoretic scrolls, an inner circle of proto-rabbinic scrolls that agree precisely with codex L and a second circle of scrolls that are very similar to it.... Most scrolls found at Qumran belong to this second circle, with only a few texts belonging to the first group. On the other hand, all the scrolls found at sites in the Judean Desert other than Qumran belong to the inner circle of proto-rabbinic scrolls.[47]

Tov's distinction between the inner circle and outer circle of proto-M texts corresponds to Armin Lange's distinction between proto-Masoretic and semi-Masoretic texts.[48] Since proto-M conventionally refers to all of the premedieval scrolls in this textual family, I will adopt Tov's terminology. I will, however, criticize Tov's use of the term *protorabbinic* (following Cross's usage) to designate the proto-M family.[49]

The criterion for determining the inner circle scrolls is relatively simple: they are scrolls that "differ from the medieval manuscripts no more than the latter differ among themselves."[50] The following list of inner circle scrolls (in roughly chronological order) includes only scrolls with more than fifty words.[51] These scrolls were written in Herodian or post-Herodian script, dating from ca. 30 BCE to 125 CE. The earliest are from

---

47. Tov, "Ancient Synagogues," 176. On the distinctive character of the pentateuchal scrolls from Masada and the Bar Kokhba caves, see Ian Young, "The Stabilization of the Biblical Text in the Light of Qumran and Masada: A Challenge for Conventional Qumran Chronology?" *DSD* 9 (2002): 370–76.

48. Lange, "Textual Standardization," 47; Lange, *Handbuch*, 16.

49. See Emanuel Tov, "The Biblical Texts from the Judean Desert: An Overview and Analysis," in *Hebrew Bible, Greek Bible*, 146–47; Cross, "Fixation of the Text," 213.

50. Tov, "Ancient Synagogues," 173.

51. Word-counts are from Lange *Handbuch*; other details are from the *editiones principes* in DJD. Lange (*Handbuch*, 16) agrees on the assignment of these scrolls to the inner circle/proto-M.

Qumran and Masada. The later scrolls are from the Bar Kokhba caves at Murabbaʿat, Naḥal Ḥever, and Wadi Sdeir (perhaps including 4QGen[b]), and a Byzantine-era synagogue at En-Gedi (ca. 300–600 CE).[52]

Text	Script (date)	Words or Partials
MasLev[a]	Early Herodian formal script (30–1 BCE)	63
MasDeut	Early Herodian formal script (30–1 BCE)	68
MasLev[b]	Middle Herodian formal script (1–30 CE)	457
4QDeut[g]	Middle Herodian formal script (1–30 CE)	151
XḤev/SeNum[b]	Late Herodian formal script (30–75 CE)	95
Mur/ḤevLev	Late or post-Herodian formal script (50–100 CE)	107
4QGen[b]	Late or post-Herodian formal script (50–100 CE)	358
SdeirGen	Late or post-Herodian formal script (50–100 CE)	117
MurGen-Exod-Num[a]	Post-Herodian formal script (75–125 CE)	260
En-Gedi Lev	Post-Herodian formal script (75–125 CE)	185

The differences between these inner circle scrolls and our early MT codices are purely orthographic, with no substantive variants. The variants listed in the *editiones principes* (relative to L) are below, collated with

---

52. According to Cross, the coarse and poorly prepared leather of 4QGen[b] suggests that it did not come from Qumran Cave 4 but from one of the other Judean desert caves "and was inadvertently mixed with the Cave 4 manuscripts by the Bedouin," apud James R. Davila, "4QGen[b]," in Ulrich, *Qumran Cave 4.VII*, 31. For Mur/ḤevLev (formerly XLev[c]), see Torleif Elgvin, Michael Langlois, and Kipp Davis, eds., *Gleanings from the Caves: Dead Sea Scrolls and Artefacts from the Schøyen Collection*, LSTS 71 (London: T&T Clark, 2016), 159–67. For En-Gedi Lev, see Michael Segal, Emanuel Tov, William B. Seales, Clifford S. Parker, Pnina Shor, Yosef Porath, with an appendix by Ada Yardeni, "An Early Leviticus Scroll from En-Gedi: Preliminary Publication," *Textus* 26 (2016): 1–20.

the early MT codices A, S, B, V, and the Second Rabbinic Bible (Rab) of 1524–1525.

Gen 1:15 למארת 4QGen[b] Rab] למאורת L B
Lev 4:7 ישפוך MasLev[a]] ישפך L S B V Rab
Lev 11:28 הסה MasLev[b]] המה L S B V Rab
Deut 33:19 ושפני MasDeut A S V Rab] ושפוני L

The differences in Gen 1:15, Lev 4:7, and Deut 33:19 are cases of *plene* versus *defectiva* spelling. The difference in Lev 11:28 is another kind of orthographic variant: a final *mem* in medial position. This phenomenon occurs once in MT (למרבה, Isa 9:6), but it is relatively frequent (ca. 40 times) in the biblical Dead Sea Scrolls.[53]

Of these inner circle proto-M scrolls, only the longest, MasLev[b], has text that corresponds to the indicative errors that Lagarde or Cross adduce to approximate the date of the archetype of the MT Pentateuch. MasLev[b] has two readings that overlap the MT perpetual *qere* of היא/הוא. At Lev 10:17 and 11:6 MasLev[b] reads הוא, agreeing with the MT *ketiv*.[54] At Lev 11:39, it agrees with the MT *ketiv* in reading היא, one of the eleven correct readings of the third feminine singular pronoun in the MT Pentateuch. The implications are worth considering. As Cross notes, the early Herodian script is the likely source for the *yod*/*waw* confusion in the third feminine singular pronoun. MasLev[b], written in the middle Herodian script, is from the era when a scribe would have had to disambiguate the script of an Early Herodian scroll. MasLev[b] may therefore be roughly contemporary with the MT archetype, but it is not identical to it—note the final *mem* in medial position at Lev 11:28 (above). MasLev[b] may provide a partial view of the scribal origins of the MT archetype within the proto-M family.

There are two scrolls not in my list that Tov or Lange assign to the inner circle of proto-M. Tov assigns MasGen to this category.[55] MasGen is written in a Hasmonean semicursive script (ca. 150–50 BCE) and preserves eleven words or partials. It is the oldest biblical scroll from Masada. If Tov's attribution is correct, then MasGen would be the earliest pentateuchal scroll of this type. However, as Ulrich has observed, the variants in MasGen do not cohere with Tov's (and previously Talmon's) categori-

---

53. Tov, *Scribal Practices*, 232–34.
54. At Lev 10:17, הוא is a superlinear insertion.
55. Tov, "Texts from the Judean Desert," 135.

zation.[56] In Gen 46:7–8, MasGen twice reads מצרים against MT מצרימה (with *he*-locale). The second מצרים in MasGen agrees with a variant in the (lost) Severus Scroll, whose unusual readings are listed in some rabbinic texts.[57] In Gen 46:8, MasGen reads את יעקוב ("with Jacob"), against MT יעקב. Talmon reconstructs this phrase as את יעקוב [אביהם] ("with Jacob [their father]"), a reading reflected in Jub. 44:11–12.[58] I note that this phrase, את יעקוב אביהם, occurs in 4QExod[b] and LXX of Exod 1:1, where it is a scribal expansion of MT's את יעקב. The reading in MasGen is arguably a harmonization with the parallel Exodus text. In view of these substantive variants and their affinities, MasGen should be categorized as either an outer circle or a non-MT type text.[59] In sum, this is the only Masada biblical scroll that probably does *not* belong to the inner circle of proto-M. It is an outlier, which highlights the predominance of the inner circle of proto-M Pentateuch scrolls at Masada.

Lange assigns 4QDeut[e] to this inner circle.[60] 4QDeut[e] is another relatively early text, written in late Hasmonean formal script (ca. 50–25 BCE), and it preserves 126 words or partials. However, it has a notable agreement with LXX in a secondary reading: בידך versus לפניך (MT) in Deut 7:23, probably a harmonization with בידך in the following verse. This is not a large percentage of variation from MT, and hence it falls within Lange's threshold of 2 percent variation from MT for inner circle/proto-M texts. However, it is a larger variation than exists among the early MT codices.

---

56. Eugene Ulrich, "The Masada Scrolls," in *Developmental Composition*, 252–54.

57. Shemaryahu Talmon, "Hebrew Fragments from Masada," in *Masada VI: The Yigael Yadin Excavations 1963–1965 Final Report*, ed. Talmon and Yigael Yadin, Masada Reports (Jerusalem: Israel Exploration Society, 1999), 32, slightly misstates the data; see Jonathan P. Siegel, *The Severus Scroll and 1QIsaa*, MasS 2 (Missoula, MT: Scholars Press, 1975), 31; Armin Lange, "The Severus Scroll Variant List in Light of the Dead Sea Scrolls," in *Tradition, Transmission, and Transformation from Second Temple Literature through Judaism and Christianity in Late Antiquity: Proceedings of the Thirteenth International Symposium of the Orion Center for the Study of the Dead Sea Scrolls and Associated Literature*, ed. Menahem Kister et al., STDJ 113 (Leiden: Brill, 2015), 187.

58. Talmon, "Masada," 33–34.

59. On the orthography of MasGen, its plene reading of יעקוב (twice) is rare in the MT Pentateuch, occurring only at Lev 26:42. At Gen 46:9, MasGen has a medial *kap* in final position: חנוכ.

60. Lange, *Handbuch*, 154.

This shared secondary reading with proto-G may be sufficiently weighty to exclude this text from the inner circle of proto-M scrolls.

Another notable feature is the format of the inner circle proto-M scrolls. Tov observes that many scrolls belonging to the inner circle are what he calls "*de luxe* scrolls," characterized by ample top and bottom margins (more than 3 cm) and long columns of text.[61] The inner circle scrolls do not all feature fine workmanship and materials.[62] They do, however, conform to the later requirement in rabbinic literature for the vertical margins of single books of the Pentateuch: "in the Five Books, (the margin) below is three fingerbreadths, (the margin) above is two fingerbreadths" (b. Menaḥ. 30a).[63] Most or all of the inner-circle MT Pentateuch scrolls listed above conform to this standard. The only uncertain cases are MasLev[a] and MasLev[b], whose extant margins are slightly less than 3 cm, but they are broken; and Sdeir-Gen, which has no preserved top or bottom margins.

While there is a tendency for inner circle scrolls to be deluxe scrolls, there is not a fixed correlation between format and text-type. 4Qpaleo-Exod[m] and 4QSam[a] are also deluxe scrolls, and they belong, respectively, to the proto-SP and the proto-G family. The oldest deluxe pentateuchal scroll is an outer circle proto-M scroll, 4QpaleoGen-Exod[l] (see below). Although ample vertical margins are only one indicator of textual status, the distribution of this format arguably indicates a high status for the inner circle proto-M scrolls from at least the early Herodian period.

PROTO-M PENTATEUCH: THE OUTER CIRCLE

The criteria for determining the outer circle of the proto-M Pentateuch (what Lange calls "semi-Masoretic") are not well defined. It consists of scrolls that have a greater variance from the medieval MT manuscripts than the latter vary among themselves, but which are still affiliated with

---

61. Tov "Ancient Synagogues," 176; Tov, *Scribal Practices*, 125–129. On deluxe Greek scrolls, see William A. Johnson, *Bookrolls and Scribes in Oxyrhynchus*, SBPC (Toronto: University of Toronto Press, 2004), 155–56: such scrolls, written in fine script, were "likely to be a roll of middling height with a narrow band of text bordered by dramatic large bands of blank space at top and bottom."

62. Compare the well-prepared leather of 4QDeut[g] with the coarse and poorly prepared leather of 4QGen[b].

63. בחומשין מלמטה שלש אצבעות מלמעלה שתי אצבעות; cited in Talmon, "Masada," 21–22.

the proto-M family. Tov regards roughly half of the Qumran pentateuchal scrolls as belonging to this category.[64] However, as several scholars have observed, Tov's method for determining textual affiliation is biased in favor of the proto-M group, since he includes in this category manuscripts with mixed MT/SP affinities.[65] Moreover, his statistics rely predominantly on minor variants—those produced by the "law of scribes," the variants that are liable to be polygenetic—which are not reliable indicators of textual affinity. Lange describes this category (which he calls "semi-Masoretic") as consisting of scrolls with more than 2 percent variation from MT but does not specify the other boundary conditions.[66]

The only reliable indicators of textual affinity are shared derived innovations (*Leitfehler*). Unfortunately, none of the plausibly proto-M texts (including the outer and inner circle) include portions that overlap with the distinctive innovations of the proto-M family (see above). To discern the outer circle of proto-M texts we are left with two less conclusive measures: (1) quantitative agreement or disagreement with nonindicative readings of MT, and (2) disagreement with typological (indicative) features of the other known textual families, proto-SP and proto-G. The use of such conjunctive and disjunctive variants provides a rough measure to establish affiliation, but with this group of scrolls it is the best we can do.

Using these criteria, we can plausibly identify the following scrolls with substantial text as belonging to the outer circle of the proto-M Pentateuch:[67]

Text	Script (date)	Words or Partials
4QLev-Num[a]	Early Hasmonean formal script (150–100 BCE)	1173
4QGen-Exod[a]	Early Hasmonean formal script (125–100 BCE)	929

---

64. Tov, "Texts from the Judean Desert," 145.

65. James C. VanderKam and Peter Flint, *The Meaning of the Dead Sea Scrolls: Their Significance for Understanding the Bible, Judaism, Jesus, and Christianity* (San Francisco: Harper, 2002), 146; Lange, *Handbuch*, 15; Hans Debel, "Greek 'Variant Literary Editions' to the Hebrew Bible?," *JSJ* 41 (2010): 170; Sidnie White Crawford, "Understanding the Textual History of the Hebrew Bible: A New Proposal," in *The Hebrew Bible in Light of the Dead Sea Scrolls*, ed. Nóra Dávid et al., FRLANT 239 (Göttingen: Vandenhoeck & Ruprecht, 2012), 68.

66. Lange, *Handbuch*, 16, lists only 4QGen-Exod[a] and 4QpaleoGen-Exod[l] as semi-Masoretic pentateuchal scrolls.

67. As above, word counts are from Lange, *Handbuch*.

4QpaleoGen-Exod[l]   Hasmonean paleo-Hebrew script (100–30 BCE)   804

In light of our rough criteria, the details below make it likely, but not demonstrable, that these scrolls belong to the outer circle of the proto-M Pentateuch.

4QLev-Num[a], as Nathan Jastram observes, has roughly forty variants, of which three are disjunctive readings from distinctive innovations in proto-SP and/or proto-G.[68] In Num 3:12 and Num 32:29–33, it lacks small harmonizations shared by G and SP, and in Num 4:3, it lacks a small harmonization with G. There are sufficient small disagreements with MT to indicate that it does not belong to the inner circle of proto-M. Among the disagreements, it correctly reads היא where MT has הוא (at Num 5:6). As noted above, this feature (a *qere perpetuum*) in MT may derive from the period after this scroll was written. 4QLev-Num[a], written in early Hasmonean script, is the oldest scroll in either circle (outer or inner) of the proto-M Pentateuch.

4QGen-Exod[a] lacks distinctive proto-SP harmonizing pluses at Exod 6:9 and 7:18 (based on the reconstructed space), and it lacks several harmonizing pluses in G.[69] However, it agrees with G and 4QExod[b] on the recalculated number seventy-five in Exod 1:5 (versus seventy in MT/SP). In light of this divergence and numerous small disagreements with MT, it *may* belong in the outer circle of proto-M.

4QpaleoGen-Exod[l] lacks the distinctive pluses of the proto-SP family at Exod 8:19; 10:2; and 26:35 and lacks three distinctive proto-G readings in the tabernacle text at Exod 27:11.[70] It has numerous small disagreements with MT, hence it does not belong to the inner circle of proto-M Pentateuch. There are two notable features of this early proto-M scroll. As Tov observes, it is a deluxe scroll, indicated by ample vertical margins. It is the earliest extant proto-M pentateuchal scroll in this format. Second, it

---

68. Nathan Jastram, "Numbers, Book of," in *EDSS* 2:616; see also Ulrich, "4QLev-Num[a]," 154–57, on two possible large omissions by eye-skip at Lev 14:24, 45, the latter filled in supralinearly.

69. James R. Davila, "Text-Type and Terminology: Genesis and Exodus as Test Cases," *RevQ* 16 (1993): 10–14, 30–35.

70. Patrick W. Skehan, Eugene Ulrich, and Judith E. Sanderson. "4QpaleoGenesis-Exodus[l]," in *Qumran Cave 4.IV: Palaeo-Hebrew and Greek Biblical Manuscripts*, ed. Patrick W. Skehan, Eugene Ulrich, and Judith E. Sanderson, DJD IX (Oxford: Clarendon, 1992), 23–25.

is also the only proto-M pentateuchal scroll written in paleo-Hebrew. At some point scribes transmitting proto-M scrolls seem to have abandoned this script, perhaps as a reaction to the exclusive use of the paleo-Hebrew script in the Samaritan Pentateuch.[71]

The more fragmentary Qumran scrolls (i.e., the vast majority) lack sufficient distinctive readings to identify them as outer circle proto-M scrolls. For example, aside from 4QGen^b (addressed above), the fragmentary Genesis texts from Qumran Cave 4 that contain portions of Gen 1 (i.e., 4QGen^{d,g,h,k}) sometimes lack the distinctive features of the highly harmonized text in proto-G, but there is insufficient evidence to determine whether they belong to the proto-M or the proto-SP textual family. As a default position, Tov characterizes such texts as proto-M.[72] But this decision masks our inability to make such a determination. Where we cannot ascertain the textual affinities of a scroll due to its fragmentary state, we should acknowledge the limits of our knowledge and describe it as a text of unknown or undetermined affiliation.

Who Promulgated the Inner Circle of the Proto-M Pentateuch?

Most textual critics have attributed the rise of the inner circle of proto-M texts to the influence of the early rabbinic or Pharisaic sages. For instance, Tov writes, "the text that was carefully transmitted through the centuries was previously embraced by rabbinic circles."[73] He follows Cross in referring to the proto-M family as proto-rabbinic.[74] However, as Lange has recently argued, "whether the Pharisees played an important role in the development of the proto-Masoretic standard text during the early first century CE—maybe due to the influence of Hillel—remains doubtful."[75] As Lange correctly emphasizes, both Josephus and rabbinic texts indicate that "the Jerusalem temple played a key role in the process of tex-

---

71. See Frank Moore Cross, "The Fixation of the Text of the Hebrew Bible," in *From Epic to Canon: History and Literature in Ancient Israel* (Baltimore: Johns Hopkins University Press, 1998), 215.

72. Tov, "Texts from the Judean Desert," 144.

73. Tov, "Ancient Synagogues," 175, 177.

74. Cross, "Fixation," 213.

75. Lange, "Textual Standardization," 80.

tual standardization."[76] He concludes that "the standard text was created by priests in the Jerusalem temple."[77] In contrast, I would emphasize the agency of a particular scribal guild in promulgating the proto-M Pentateuch. But it is likely, as I will argue below, that this guild was institutionally allied at some point with the Jerusalem temple and its priests.[78]

Lange argues that "the Jerusalem priests employed the principle of majority readings to create a standard text."[79] This is a variant of Kahle's model of the recensional origins of MT. However, Albrektson and Tov have cogently argued against the idea that the "standard text" was created by deliberate editorial activity.[80] The view that the MT was created by editorial activity derives from rabbinic narratives about the sages selecting among textual variants in "three scrolls in the temple court" (שלושה ספרים ... בעזרה) by adopting the majority reading.[81] These stories revolve around ancient variants—real and imagined—and are not likely to be reminiscences of ancient textual activity. Talmon aptly describes these tales as reflecting rabbinic discussions that are, in a sense, "a very early case of Masoretic-type notation," which "do not relate to the creation of a *textus receptus*."[82] These are the three sets of variants under discussion:

Deut 33:27: מעון versus מענה (M) "dwelling place"
Exod 24:5: זעטוטי versus נערי (M) "young men"[83]

---

76. Ibid., 76.

77. Ibid., 79.

78. The situation is more complicated for biblical books outside the Pentateuch, whose transmission history is more complex; see Crawford, "Textual History," 67; Trebolle Barrera, "Qumran Evidence," 89–100; Ulrich, "Canonical Process," 56–61.

79. Lange, "Textual Standardization," 79.

80. See above, n. 38.

81. Sipre Deut 356; Y. Ta'an. 4:2, 68a (and parallels); Sop. 6:4; 'Abot R. Nat. B 46; see Shemaryahu Talmon, "The Three Scrolls of the Law That Were Found in the Temple Court," in *Text and Canon*, 329–46; Albrektson, "Reflections," 52–54; Tov, "Ancient Synagogues," 178–79; Lange, "Textual Standardization," 75–76.

82. Talmon, "Three Scrolls," 336, 346. Talmon does, however, regard the stories as historically reliable, from which I demur.

83. The word זעטוט ("young men') is attested in Qumran Hebrew; see ibid., 345; Elisha Qimron, *The Hebrew of the Dead Sea Scrolls*, HSS 29 (Atlanta; Scholars, 1986), 116.

Qere perpetuum (3fs pronoun): היא written nine times versus היא written eleven times (M)[84]

The first is a difference of gender (m versus f), a common category in *ketiv-qere*, although מעון is here unattested.[85] The second is a late Aramaism (known from Qumran Hebrew) versus an ordinary Hebrew word. The third describes the *qere perpetuum* of היא for הוא (*ketiv*) in the MT Pentateuch, in which היא is correctly written eleven times (see above). In one version of the story, the minority readings (i.e., those in only one scroll) provide the names for that scroll: ספר מעון (the *Maʿon* Scroll), ספר זעטוטי (the *Zaʿṭuṭê* Scroll), and ספר היא (the *Hiʾ* Scroll). The idea that these were the three authoritative scrolls in the Jerusalem Temple is fabulous. The stories provide an etiology for the origin of the *textus receptus* and its odd features (e.g., the *qere perpetuum*) and for the textual authority of the rabbis. These cultural memories serve to anchor rabbinic authority in the prestigious past of temple and Torah.

The actual historical context, to the degree that we can discern it, is different. In the Second Temple period, the high priest was generally the authority in religious affairs, and the Jerusalem temple was the locus of priestly authority. This authority extended to sacred texts. Josephus, who proudly asserted his priestly lineage, asserted that Moses handed over the books of the Torah to the priests, who ensured their accurate transmission (*Ant.* 4.304; *Ag. Ap.* 1.28–29). According to Philo of Alexandria, priestly authority regarding sacred texts extended to the synagogue. He writes: "Some priest who is present or one of the elders reads the Holy Law to them and expounds them point by point" (*Hypoth* 7.13). It is plausible, as David Goodblatt suggests, that "Philo may indicate here a preference for a priestly reader while allowing a lay elder to teach if no priest is available."[86] The Mishnah recalls a similar procedure: "A priest reads [the Torah] first, and after him a Levite, and after him an Israelite" (m. Giṭ. 5.8). The priests had textual authority that extended from the temple to the synagogue, in theory if not always in practice. It may be relevant to note that in an early synagogue inscription, from the Theodotos synagogue of pre-70 Jerusalem, the benefactor identifies himself as a

---

84. Following the earlier versions in the Sipre and y. Taʿanit.

85. Cf. Gen 27:3, צידה (*ketiv*) versus ציד (*qere*); Talmon, "Three Scrolls," 342.

86. David Goodblatt, *Elements of Ancient Jewish Nationalism* (Cambridge: Cambridge University Press, 2006), 81.

priest and the head of the synagogue, as were his father and grandfather before him.[87]

It is reasonable to surmise that the priests exercised authority over the copyists of sacred books, whom Josephus calls ἱερογραμματεῖς, "sacred scribes." If there were Torah scrolls at the Jerusalem temple, as Josephus and rabbinic texts recall, then the copying of these scrolls would have been under priestly authority. [88] According to the Talmud, the מגהים ("correctors") of Torah scrolls in Jerusalem were paid from the תרומת הלשכה ("Temple funds," b. Ketub. 106a; y. Šeq. 4.48a). As Meir Bar-Ilan observes, "most of the scribes of the end of the Second Temple period whose genealogy is known were priests,"[89] and Daniel Schwartz plausibly argues that many of the scribes were Levites or Sadducees.[90] These details and inferences indicate a link between the priests' textual authority and the scribes' textual activity.

However, the Jerusalem priests did not have textual power at Qumran, which defined itself as a breakaway sacred enclave, in contrast to the defiled Jerusalem priesthood. This split may account for the different profile of the biblical texts at Qumran versus the texts at Masada and the Bar Kokhba caves. Since Qumran and Masada were both destroyed in the First Jewish Revolt, the contrast in the textual affinities of the scrolls at these sites is salient. According to Josephus, the occupants of Masada were originally the Sicarii ("dagger-man") from Jerusalem, who were later joined by other refugees.[91] The Sicarii were not priests, although one of

---

87. Lee I. Levine, *The Ancient Synagogue: The First Thousand Years* (New Haven: Yale University Press, 2005), 57–59.

88. See Arie van der Kooij, "Preservation and Promulgation: The Dead Sea Scrolls and the Textual History of the Hebrew Bible," in Dávid, *Light of the Dead Sea Scrolls*, 29–40.

89. Meir Bar-Ilan, "Scribes and Books in the Late Second Commonwealth and Rabbinic Period," in *Mikra: Text, Translation, Reading and Interpretation of the Hebrew Bible in Ancient Judaism and Early Christianity*, ed. Martin J. Mulder and Harry Sysling, CRINT 2.1 (Assen: Van Gorcum, 1988), 22.

90. Daniel R. Schwartz, " 'Scribes and Pharisees, Hypocrites:' Who are the 'Scribes' in the New Testament?" in *Studies in the Jewish Background of Christianity*, WUNT 60 (Tübingen: Mohr Siebeck, 1992), 89–101; cf. Martin Goodman, "Texts, Scribes and Power in Roman Judaea," in *Judaism in the Roman World: Collected Essays*, AGJU 66 (Leiden: Brill, 2007), 79–90.

91. The Sicarii should not be conflated with the Zealots, as Yigael Yadin and others have done; see Mark A. Brighton, *The Sicarii in Josephus's Judean War: Rhe-*

their founders, Zadok, may have been the scion of a priestly family. These refugees carried their biblical scrolls to Masada, predominantly scrolls from the inner circle of proto-M.[92] The Qumran library, in contrast, has few inner circle proto-M texts, perhaps only one from the Pentateuch (4QDeutᵍ). The Qumran community had a wide range of texts outside of this circle, including proto-SP and proto-G pentateuchal scrolls. This textual contrast arguably corresponds to a sociological contrast in the locus of textual authority. The Qumran enclave was outside of the textual authority of the Jerusalem priests, whereas the Masada group was, at least originally, inside it.[93]

Notice that the Pharisees or proto-rabbis have no role in this textual situation. Their religious authority was located elsewhere, perhaps as popular interpreters of law in the public domain, including matters of purity, marriage laws, calendar, and tithes.[94] There is no warrant for assuming their authority in the production, dissemination, or public reading of Torah scrolls in the period from the Maccabees to the Mishnah. According to rabbinic texts, some rabbinic sages were scribes (e.g., R. Meir), but this does not argue for proto-rabbinic authority over scribes. The earliest rabbinic text about the Torah scrolls in the temple court says that the sages (חכמים) made the textual decisions (Sipre Deut 356), but this is what

---

torical Analysis and Historical Observations, EJL 27 (Atlanta: Society of Biblical Literature, 2009).

92. Among the nonbiblical scrolls, two may indicate the presence of refugees from Qumran: MasQumran-type Text (Mas 1n, written in Qumran orthography) and MasShirShabb (Mas 1k, Songs of the Sabbath Sacrifice); see Emanuel Tov, "A Qumran Origin for the Masada Non-Biblical Texts?" DSD 7 (2000): 57–67. On the difficulty in determining whether ShirShabb is sectarian, Carol A. Newsom, " 'Sectually Explicit' Literature from Qumran," in The Hebrew Bible and Its Interpreters, ed. William H. Propp, Baruch Halpern, and David Noel Freedman, BJSUCSD 1 (Winona Lake, IN: Eisenbrauns, 1990), 178–85.

93. The Samaritan community is another example of a sociological context outside the authority of the Jerusalem priests, and the SP (specifically the sectarian revisions) exemplifies their independence; see Stefan Schorch, "Which Kind of Authority? The Authority of the Torah during the Hellenistic and Roman Periods," in Scriptural Authority in Early Judaism and Ancient Christianity, ed. Isaac Kalimi, Tobias Nicklas, and Géza G. Xeravits, DCLS 16 (Berlin: de Gruyter, 2013), 1–11.

94. Shaye J. D. Cohen, "The Place of the Rabbi in the Jewish Society of the Second Century," in The Significance of Yavneh and Other Essays in Jewish Hellenism, TSAJ 136 (Tübingen: Mohr Siebeck, 2010), 282–96. Note that these include the topics of Jesus's arguments with the Pharisees in the New Testament.

Bertil Albrektson calls "rabbinic embroidery" and cannot be relied on as historical evidence.[95] Torah scrolls in the temple court would have been textual icons of priestly authority. It is to be expected that rabbinic texts would assert a memory of the sages' ancient textual authority, a historiographic *Tendenz* that Jacob Neusner and Shaye Cohen aptly call the "rabbinization of Jewish history."[96]

Who were the scribes who transmitted and promulgated the inner circle of the proto-M Pentateuch? We do not know. All we can say is that it was a relatively conservative tradition, whose scribal philosophy at some point narrowed to minimal intervention in the text. As noted above, the orthography of the MT Pentateuch preserves spelling practices of the third century BCE; this may be the era when other kinds of textual change were curtailed in this scribal lineage. Another possibility is that a later scribal group used third-century pentateuchal scrolls as model scrolls. Under either scenario, the third century BCE may have been the *terminus ad quem* for substantive changes in the inner circle of the proto-M Pentateuch. (An exception is the change of Gerizim to Ebal in MT Deut 27:4, which, as noted above, is probably a revision from the Hasmonean era.) The correct readings in the MT Pentateuch, of course, stem from an earlier period still, when the Pentateuch was compiled and made public, which returns us to the portrait of Ezra reading the Torah in Jerusalem in the fifth century BCE (Neh 8). This is the Bible's own representation of the "publication" of the Pentateuch.

Excursus: Value for Literary (Source) Criticism

Some features of the MT Pentateuch are valuable for discerning the earlier compositional history of the Pentateuch, particularly where proto-M scribes found contradictions in the narrative and attempted to repair them. For example, two of the typological features noted above—the revision of chronologies in Gen 5 and 11, and the sequence revision at Gen 47:5–11—are exegetical responses to source-critical problems. The chronological revision in Gen 5 was motivated by a contradiction between the date of the flood in P and the lifespans of three of Noah's ancestors (Lamech, Methuselah, and Jared) in the ספר תלדת אדם ("Book of the

---

95. Albrektson, "Reflections," 54.

96. Shaye J. D. Cohen, "Parallel Historical Tradition in Josephus and Rabbinic Literature," in *Significance of Yavneh*, 158–59.

Generations of Adam," Gen 5:1), which was probably a source document of P.[97] The chronological revisions in proto-M, proto-SP, and proto-G are independent attempts to solve what was, in origin, a source-critical problem within P: the overlap between the lifespans of three patriarchs and the onset of the flood.

The revision at Gen 47:5–6 in proto-M is an attempt to overcome a problem of narrative continuity caused by the combination of J and P. The proto-G reading is arguably the superior text.[98] The following quote begins in verse 4, with Joseph's brothers speaking. Pharaoh's two speeches are indicated below by italics and bold italics.

LXX
[J] And the brothers said to Pharaoh ... "Now let your servants dwell in the land of Goshen." And Pharaoh said to Joseph, *"Let them dwell in the land of Goshen, and if you know that there are capable men among them, appoint them as overseers of my livestock."* [P] And Jacob and his sons came into Egypt to Joseph, and Pharaoh, king of Egypt, heard. And Pharaoh spoke to Joseph, saying, **"Your father and your brothers have come to you. Behold, the land of Egypt is before you. Settle your father and your brothers in the best land."**[99]

MT
And the brothers said to Pharaoh ... "Now let your servants dwell in the land of Goshen." And Pharaoh said to Joseph, saying, **"Your father and your brothers have come to you. The land of Egypt is before you. In the best land settle your father and your brothers.** *Let them dwell in the land of Goshen, and if you know that there are capable men among them, appoint them as rulers of my livestock."*

The revision in proto-M eliminates the problem of discontinuity by two revisions: (1) erasing the second arrival of Jacob and his sons, which comes from the P source; and (2) combining into one Pharaonic speech what were originally two speeches, one from J and the other from P. A cor-

---

97. See above, n. 22.

98. See John Skinner, *A Critical and Exegetical Commentary on Genesis*, 2nd ed., ICC (Edinburgh: T&T Clark, 1930), 497–98.

99. Translation adapted from Robert J. V. Hiebert, "Genesis," in *A New English Translation of the Septuagint: And the Other Greek Translations Traditionally Included under That Title*, ed. Albert Pietersma and Benjamin G. Wright (New York: Oxford University Press, 2007), 39.

roborating clue for the secondary recombination of sources in MT is the doublet of ארץ גשן ("the land of Goshen," J) and ארץ רעמסס ("the land of Rameses," P; see Gen 47:11), which is consistent in the LXX reading but not in MT. The restructured text in MT is an exegetical response to a problematic source-critical seam in the Pentateuch.

As these examples show, the textual history of the proto-M Pentateuch is in some measure a consequence and continuation of the Pentateuch's literary history. These late literary interventions—after the separation of the proto-G and proto-M textual families—show that the proto-M scribes were, in Talmon's sense, "minor partner[s] in the creative literary process."[100]

---

100. Talmon, "Textual Study," 381.

9
PROBLEMS OF CLASSIFICATION
AND OTHER TEXTS OF THE PENTATEUCH

> The origin of the various readings could be investigated and represented by individual codices, by pairs of codices, by lesser and greater groups, and by their families, tribes, and nations; and from their affinities and separations the codices can be reduced to certain configurations.
> —Johann A. Bengel, *Novum Testamentum Græcum*

There are many possible ways to classify ancient Hebrew manuscripts of the Pentateuch. For instance, one could use any or all of the following criteria, generating a series of intersecting classifications:

♦ square script versus paleo-Hebrew script
♦ iron-based versus carbon-based ink
♦ conventional orthography versus Qumran orthography
♦ excerpted or abbreviated book versus complete book
♦ scrolls with more than one book versus a single book
♦ has interlinear corrections versus none
♦ has unique readings versus none
♦ has affinities with the Samaritan Pentateuch, and/or Septuagint, and/or MT, or none
♦ has top and bottom margins of more than three cm. versus less than three cm.
♦ written by the same scribe as 1QS and 4QTestimonia versus a different scribe
♦ published versus unpublished

Most of these criteria have been used to good effect in scholarly studies.[1]

For any particular classificatory task, one must identify the relevant criteria for classification and eliminate the irrelevant ones; otherwise the results will be misleading. To ascertain the textual history of the Pentateuch—in contrast to the history of its scribal production, sometimes called textual bibliography—one must first abstract the "text" from its material manifestations. This requires a series of reductions. First, one must bracket the physical features of a manuscript and focus on its purely semiotic features. Second, one must distinguish between the substantive semiotic features—the sequence of words (or lexemes)—and the "accidental" (or presentational) features, such as spelling or script, which vary according to local scribal practice. The primary evidence for textual history consists of the substantive linguistic features irrespective of their physical manifestations. These features are abstract (i.e., semiotic) but in a way that competent readers recognize.

A further reduction is required for textual history. As textual critics have long established, one must distinguish between substantive features that descend from a common ancestor (monogenetic features) from those that are likely to be independently produced (polygenetic features).[2] Only monogenetic features are useful for classifying manuscripts according to their textual history. A precise designation for such monogenetic features is *shared derived innovations*. This term, borrowed from biology and linguistics, requires some unpacking. *Shared* means that the relevant traits exist among two or more manuscripts. Traits that exist in only one manuscript (*lectiones singulares*, "unique readings") are irrelevant for genealogi-

---

1. See, e.g., Emanuel Tov, *Scribal Practices and Approaches Reflected in the Texts Found in the Judean Desert*, STDJ 54 (Leiden: Brill, 2004); Ada Yardeni, *The Book of Hebrew Script: History, Palaeography, Script Styles, Calligraphy and Design* (London: British Library, 2002); Eibert Tigchelaar, "In Search of the Scribe of 1QS," in *Emanuel: Studies in Hebrew Bible, Septuagint and Dead Sea Scrolls in Honor of Emanuel Tov*, ed. Shalom M. Paul et al., VTSup 94 (Leiden: Brill, 2003), 439–52.

2. See Paolo Trovato, *Everything You Always Wanted to Know about Lachmann's Method: A Non-standard Handbook of Genealogical Textual Criticism in the Age of Post-structuralism, Cladistics, and Copy-Text*, Storie e linguaggi 7 (Padua: Libreriauniversitaria, 2014), 49–56, 73; and, in our discipline, Bruno Chiesa, "Textual History and Textual Criticism of the Hebrew Old Testament," in *The Madrid Qumran Congress: Proceedings of the International Congress on the Dead Sea Scrolls, Madrid, 18–21 March, 1991*, ed. Julio Trebolle Barrera and Luis Vegas Montaner, STDJ 11 (Leiden: Brill, 1992), 1:256–72.

cal classification.[3] For instance, nearly all of our pentateuchal manuscripts contain unique innovations. But these features, since they are unique, have no implications for their genealogical relationships. *Derived* means that the trait descends from a common ancestor. Like unique innovations, traits that are likely to be nonderived (polygenetic) are unreliable or irrelevant for establishing genealogical relationships. *Innovation* refers to any type of substantive textual change, including both accidental error and deliberate revision. Since innovations are not limited to errors, the usual text-critical terms for shared derived innovations—*Leitfehler, errores significativi,* indicative error—are somewhat misleading. The term *innovation* is more felicitous than *error* for this designation, as textual critics have noted.[4]

The procedure for ascertaining historical relationships among texts by means of shared derived innovations (called the Lachmann, genealogical, or common-error method) is aptly characterized by Michael Reeve:

> When copies share an innovation absent from the rest, they are related (more closely, that is, than by being copies of the same work); if none of those that share the innovation can plausibly be regarded as the one where it originated, it must have originated in a lost ancestor common to them all. With luck, the extant copies and their postulated ancestors can be arranged in a family tree.[5]

A degree of luck is necessary for the task of textual history because we often lack sufficient evidence to discern the historical patterns of shared derived innovations. For ancient texts, the extant manuscripts are only a small portion of the once-existing evidence; hence the patterns we can discern are only partial glimpses of the full textual history. The genealogy that we can discern is, as Paolo Trovato observes, "the genealogy of the surviving tradition."[6] It is a reduced and truncated version of the whole family tree.

---

3. Paul Maas, *Textual Criticism,* trans. Barbara Flower (Oxford: Clarendon Press, 1958), 5–6.

4. Trovato, *Everything,* 54; Michael D. Reeve, "Shared Innovations, Dichotomies, and Evolution," in *Manuscripts and Methods: Essays on Editing and Transmission,* (Rome: Edizioni di storia e letteratura, 2011), 58, quotes Paul Lejay: "une faute ou plutôt une innovation."

5. Michael D. Reeve, foreword to Trovato, *Everything,* 9–10.

6. Trovato, *Everything,* 232.

A further complicating factor is that some shared innovations may be the result of copying or correcting parts of a book from manuscripts that belong to different branches of the family tree (stemma). This is called horizontal transmission, contamination, or conflation, in contrast to the historical process of vertical transmission, where one manuscript is wholly copied from another.[7] (In linguistics the parallel to horizontal transmission is language contact; in biology the approximate parallel is hybridization.) The possibility of horizontal transmission complicates the task of textual history, since such innovations indicate synchronic contact rather than common descent.

The character of polygenetic innovations—traits that are similar but independently generated—requires further clarification. In textual criticism, many kinds of scribal change are characteristically polygenetic and therefore are unreliable—or useless—for ascertaining genealogical affinity. Moshe Goshen-Gottstein aptly ascribed such polygenetic innovations to "the ever active and repeated force of the 'law of scribes' that creates the illusion of a genetic connection."[8] The law of scribes generates such textual changes as haplography, dittography, word misdivision, graphic confusion, and the addition or subtraction of simple particles (e.g., conjunctive *waw*). The effects of this law are richly documented in the medieval and early modern manuscripts of the Hebrew Bible, all of which belong to the same (Masoretic) textual family.[9] To ascertain genealogical relationships, one must exclude the background noise of the law of scribes. Most of the small variants in the ancient and medieval pentateuchal scrolls belong to this category and are therefore not useful for classification.

The genealogical method of ascertaining textual genealogy assumes that all the manuscripts of a given book belong to a single multibranched community of descent. Each manuscript of a book—for example, the book of Genesis—belongs to the genealogy of that book and not to independent genealogies that generated more-or-less identical books of Genesis. This assumption seems self-evident, but it has been contested by some schol-

---

7. Ibid., 128–38.

8. Moshe H. Goshen-Gottstein, "Hebrew Biblical Manuscripts: Their History and Their Place in the HUBP Edition," in *Qumran and the History of the Biblical Text*, ed. Frank Moore Cross and Shemaryahu Talmon (Cambridge: Harvard University Press, 1975), 74.

9. Although one cannot exclude the possibility of the occasional transmission of some extra- or non-MT readings; see ibid., 84–85.

ars. Talmon has influentially argued for the existence of "divergent pristine textual traditions" that descend from variant oral traditions.[10] In this view, a particular manuscript of Genesis may be textually unrelated to other manuscripts of Genesis. However, as Emanuel Tov and others have pointed out, there is no evidence for such a phenomenon in biblical books.[11] The manuscripts are simply too similar to warrant this hypothesis, and their variants are accountable by the normal mechanisms of scribal change.[12] The variations among the manuscripts do not correspond to the types and degree of variance characteristic of oral transmission or manuscripts derived from oral formulaic composition. As I have argued, the idea of "divergent pristine textual traditions" for the books of the Hebrew Bible is a scholarly chimera.[13]

Each textual family within the genealogy is distinguished by a shared cluster of derived innovations. These innovations are *conjunctive* with respect to that textual family, and they may also be regarded as *disjunctive* with respect to other textual families or groups. Yet it is important to note that there are no objective boundaries between textual families or other nested genealogical units—what Bengel calls "lesser and greater groups, ... families, tribes, and nations"[14]—just as there are no objective boundaries between languages or species. As with linguistic and biological distinctions, the analytical boundaries are based on the identification of innovations or clusters of innovations within the broader field of derived traits. As John Huehnergard states for Semitic linguistics, "the most useful criteria for establishing genetic relatedness are shared features that are innovative with respect to the bundle of features inherited from the common family stock."[15] These criteria are clues for establishing historical relationships, but they are not objectively marked in the data themselves.

As Eugene Ulrich aptly argues, the most useful criteria (i.e., the largest clusters of shared derived innovations) are editions of biblical books: "the

10. Talmon, "Textual Criticism: The Ancient Versions," in *Text and Canon of the Hebrew Bible: Collected Studies* (Winona Lake, IN: Eisenbrauns, 2010), 406–7, 413–18.

11. Emanuel Tov, *Textual Criticism of the Hebrew Bible*, 3rd ed. (Minneapolis: Fortress, 2012), 163–65.

12. See above, ch. 6.

13. See above, ch. 1.

14. Johann A. Bengel, *Novum Testamentum Græcum* (Tübingen: Cotta, 1734), 387: "per syzygias minores majoresque, per familias, tribus, nationesque."

15. John Huehnergard, "What Is Aramaic?" *Aram* 7 (1995): 263.

main lines in the picture of the history of the biblical text were formed by the deliberate activity of a series of creative scribes who produced the new or multiple literary editions of the books of the Bible."[16] The next best criteria are smaller-scale clusters of innovations, for example, patterns of harmonizations or explications. The least useful—but not negligible—criteria are shared secondary readings that are not particularly distinctive. Trovato describes the latter as "characteristic readings" or "confirmatory readings," in other words, "reading which characterize, besides indicative errors, a group of witnesses."[17] Such readings are useful for confirming or supplementing the primary evidence of indicative errors.

The genealogical (common-error) method is not widely used in textual criticism of the Hebrew Bible. A prominent example is Tov, who articulates his own eclectic approach to textual history based in part on his distrust of the genealogical method:

> There is no generally accepted method of determining the relation between the scrolls and the other witnesses. Some North American scholars pay more attention to the comparative (primary/secondary) value of readings than others. Other scholars pay more attention to the mere counting of readings (the statistical method).... In my own thinking, editorial differences carry more weight than other variants. I take agreements as well as disagreements and independent readings into consideration. Further, I realize that shared errors carry more weight than shared common readings, but nevertheless I do not rely much on this type of reasoning because of its subjective aspects.[18]

He criticizes the genealogical method primarily because of its subjectivity, since it requires the identification of shared errors. Elsewhere he emphasizes the "absence of objective criteria for classifying the Qumran scrolls."[19] His criticism is correct: the genealogical method involves text-critical judgment,

---

16. Eugene Ulrich, "Multiple Literary Editions: Reflections toward a Theory of the History of the Biblical Text," in *The Dead Sea Scrolls and the Origins of the Bible*, SDSS (Grand Rapids: Eerdmans, 1999), 107; see above, ch. 6.

17. Trovato, *Everything*, 116–17.

18. Emanuel Tov, "The Hebrew Qumran Texts and the Septuagint: An Overview," in *Hebrew Bible, Greek Bible, and Qumran: Collected Essays*, TSAJ 121 (Tübingen: Mohr Siebeck, 2008), 355.

19. Tov, *Textual Criticism*, 107.

since it relies on the logic of shared derived innovations. This requirement, of course, also applies to classification in linguistics and biology.

I submit that this is not a compelling criticism of the genealogical method. Objectivity, as I have emphasized above, is not an applicable standard for textual criticism and other kinds of historical inquiry. The epistemology of textual criticism relies on the procedures of the evidential paradigm, the logic of error and innovation, and inference to the best explanation, not on an elusive (and illusory) objectivity. As Trovato rightly emphasizes, the task of textual criticism involves "the ineluctability of critical judgment."[20] We cannot escape this condition, nor should we want to. There is no objective method for textual history, only more or less rational methods. As far as I am aware, the genealogical method is the only logically warranted method for textual history, as it is in linguistics, biology, and other historically oriented disciplines. It is worth emphasizing that purely statistical methods require a genealogical "rooting" to determine the historical arrow of textual relationships.[21] In the task of textual history, as Michael Weitzman writes, "the notion of error cannot be sidestepped."[22]

Typological Features: Editions and Harmonizations

In recent years textual critics have focused on two kinds of shared derived innovations that are prominent in ancient pentateuchal manuscripts: editions and harmonizations. Both of these features are useful for discerning textual history and categorizing textual families. Editions and harmonizations are complementary and crosscutting features in the Pentateuch, illuminating the surviving branches of its textual genealogy.

A new edition of a book or a portion of a book can be defined as a systematic revision, such as resequencing of text (verses, pericopes, or larger sections), the insertion of new compositions, and/or systematic exegetical revisions (e.g., revisions of chronology).[23] Harmonization can be defined

---

20. Trovato, *Everything*, 243.

21. Ibid., 185–224.

22. Michael P. Weitzman, "The Analysis of Open Traditions," *SBib* 38 (1985): 97.

23. See Ulrich, "Multiple Literary Editions"; Eugene Ulrich, "The Developmental Growth of the Pentateuch in the Second Temple Period," in *The Dead Sea Scrolls and the Developmental Composition of the Bible*, VTSup 169 (Leiden: Brill, 2015); Tov, *Textual Criticism*, 283–323; Zipora Talshir, "Textual Criticism at the Service of Literary Criticism and the Question of an Eclectic Edition of the Hebrew Bible," in *After*

as a transfer of textual details or blocks of text between two parallel texts, with the aim to reduce perceived dissonance, whether the parallel texts are in the same pericope or in different textual units or books.[24] In the Pentateuch, multiple editions and harmonizations are intersecting phenomena, since some new editions of pentateuchal books were created by systematic large-scale harmonizations (see below). But small harmonizations also exist in each textual family. To differing degrees, a general tendency toward harmonization is characteristic of two of the three major textual families in the Pentateuch (proto-SP and proto-G; see below).

The cases of multiple editions in the Pentateuch are as follows:

(1) Revised editions of the chronologies of Gen 5 and 11.[25] MT, SP, and LXX have three different editions of these chronologies. All three are responses to exegetical problems in the text, including the apparent survival of three antediluvian patriarchs after the flood. Jubilees has affinities with the SP genealogy in Gen 5, indicating that this innovation was wider than the SP alone and pertains to its textual family.

Qumran: Old and Modern Editions of the Biblical Texts; The Historical Books, ed. Hans Ausloos, Bénédicte Lemmelijn, and Julio Trebolle Barrera, BETL 246 (Leuven, Peeters 2012); Talshir, "Texts, Text-Forms, Editions, New Composition and the Final Products of Biblical Literature," in *Congress Volume Munich 2013*, ed. Christl M. Maier, VTSup 163 (Leiden: Brill, 2014); and above, ch. 1.

24. See Emanuel Tov, "The Nature and Background of Harmonizations in Biblical Manuscripts," *JSOT* 31 (1985): 3–29; Esther Eshel, "4QDeut^n—A Text That Has Undergone Harmonistic Editing," *HUCA* 62 (1991): 120–23; Esther Eshel and Hanan Eshel, "Dating the Samaritan Pentateuch's Compilation in Light of the Qumran Biblical Scrolls," in Paul, *Emanuel*, 215–40; Michael Segal, "The Text of the Hebrew Bible in Light of the Dead Sea Scrolls," *MG* 12 (2007): 11–17; Molly M. Zahn, *Rethinking Rewritten Scripture: Composition and Exegesis in the 4QReworked Pentateuch Manuscripts*, STDJ 95 (Leiden: Brill, 2011), 143–56; Sidnie White Crawford, "Scribal Traditions in the Pentateuch and the History of the Early Second Temple Period," in *Congress Volume Helsinki 2010*, ed. Martti Nissinen, VTSup 148 (Leiden: Brill, 2012), 167–84.

25. Ronald Hendel, *The Text of Genesis 1–11: Textual Studies and Critical Edition* (New York: Oxford University Press, 1998), 61–80; Ronald Hendel, "A Hasmonean Edition of MT Genesis? The Implications of the Editions of the Chronology in Genesis 5," *HBAI* 1 (2012): 1–17; Emanuel Tov, "The Genealogical Lists in Genesis 5 and 11 in Three Different Versions," in *Textual Criticism of the Hebrew Bible, Qumran, Septuagint: Collected Essays*, VTSup 167 (Leiden: Brill, 2015), 221–38.

(2) An expanded edition of the tabernacle text of Exodus 35–40.[26] LXX has a shorter account of the construction of the tabernacle. The MT edition is expanded, harmonized, and reordered to correspond more closely with God's instructions to Moses in Exod 25–30.

(3) A distinctive cluster of large-scale harmonizations in a group of texts including SP and several Qumran biblical manuscripts.[27] There are roughly forty such harmonizations, in which significant blocks of textual details have been transferred between parallel texts. Most notably, large harmonizations were made in the correspondence between the divine commands and executions in the plague stories (Exod 7–11) and between events recalled by Moses in Deut 1–3 and the description of those events in Exodus and Numbers.

Using the criterion of multiple editions to organize the manuscript evidence into textual families, we find the following results:

	Base Edition	New Edition(s)
Genesis 5 and 11	(archetype)	proto-M, proto-SP, proto-G
Exodus 35–39 (±large harms.)	proto-G	proto-M ≈ proto-SP
± Sequence of large harms. (ca. 40)	proto-M ≈ proto-G	proto-SP

Only the last revised edition includes all the pentateuchal books. However, as we will see below, other confirmatory features (e.g., the layer of small harmonizations shared by LXX and SP) also include all the pentateuchal books. Hence it seems warranted to treat the Pentateuch as a single unit in this schema of textual families.

---

26. Anneli Aejmelaeus, "Septuagintal Translation Techniques: A Solution to the Problem of the Tabernacle Account?," in *On the Trail of the Septuagint Translators: Collected Essays*, 2nd ed., CBET 50 (Leuven: Peeters, 2007), 107–21; Brandon E. Bruning, "The Making of the Mishkan: The Old Greek Text of Exodus 35–40 and the Literary History of the Pentateuch" (PhD diss., University of Notre Dame, 2014).

27. Listed in Magnar Kartveit, *The Origin of the Samaritans*, VTSup 128 (Leiden: Brill, 2009), 276–88, 310–12; Emanuel Tov, "Rewritten Bible Compositions and Biblical Manuscripts, with Special Attention Paid to the Samaritan Pentateuch," in *Hebrew Bible, Greek Bible*, 60–68.

A note on terminology. I use the prefix *proto-* for these textual families (following Cross) to indicate that they are contemporary and related textual families. These terms should not be seen as privileging MT, SP, or G. We could as easily designate these textual families by other sigla (e.g., א, ב, and ג) but there is no advantage in obscure terminology. Tov uses the term *pre-Samaritan* in order to indicate that SP has some unique (sectarian) readings that are not shared by the other members of this family.[28] However, since unique readings are not relevant for genealogical classification, this is not a compelling argument. Moreover, as Tov observes, the orthography of SP "reflects a typologically earlier stage in the development of the ﬡﬡ-group,"[29] indicating that the manuscript that was the hyparchetype of SP was an early member of this group. Some manuscripts in this family, for example, 4QNum[b], have substantive features that are typologically later than SP (i.e., new harmonizing expansions). In sum, it seems inapt to call this group pre-SP, since all the other biblical manuscripts in it are typologically post-SP, orthographically and/or substantively. Esther Eshel proposes that we call this group the "harmonistic text group."[30] However, this term is ambiguous, since there are also harmonistic tendencies in the proto-G family (see below).

In this schema, there is no fixed correlation between the editions and the textual families. The proto-M family has a later edition in the Genesis chronologies and Exodus tabernacle text, but the earlier edition in the case of the large-scale harmonizations. The proto-G family has a later edition in the Genesis chronologies, but the earlier edition in the tabernacle text and the large-scale harmonizations. Only the proto-SP family has the later edition in all three cases. These results—which produce a schema that is not predictable—seem to support Ulrich's proposal that editions should have priority in classification.

---

28. Tov, *Textual Criticism*, 91: "The use of the term *pre-Samaritan* is … based on the assumption that while the connections between ﬡﬡ and the pre-Samaritan texts are exclusive, they reflect different realities. The pre-Samaritan texts are *not* Samaritan documents, as they lack the specifically Samaritan readings, but they share with ﬡﬡ its major features" (emphasis original).

29. Tov, *Textual Criticism*, 93 n. 152; similarly Emanuel Tov, "The Samaritan Pentateuch and the Dead Sea Scrolls: The Proximity of the Pre-Samaritan Qumran Scrolls to the SP," in *Collected Essays*, 401.

30. Eshel, "4QDeut[n]," 121; and Eshel and Eshel, "Dating," 228–29.

Two Scribal Approaches

Aside from its sequence of large harmonizations, the proto-SP family also shares a layer of small harmonizations with the proto-G family. According to the research of Kyungrae Kim, there are roughly 330 small harmonizations shared by LXX and SP in the Pentateuch.[31] Many may have been made independently by scribes (i.e., polygenesis, the law of scribes), but the density of these shared innovations indicates a genealogical affinity between the two families.

This layer of small harmonizations allow us to infer a more general distinction between these families and the proto-M family in the Pentateuch. The proto-M Pentateuch has far fewer harmonizations and other small changes (e.g., explicating pluses, linguistic modernizations) than the other textual families. This distinction of scribal tendencies indicates a general typological distinction. As Crawford emphasizes, "there were two scribal traditions or approaches to Scripture at work in Second Temple period Palestine, transmitting the books that became the Hebrew Bible."[32] The two approaches have been characterized by various binary terms: "pristine" versus "expansionistic" (Cross),[33] "careful approach" versus "free approach" (Tov),[34] nonharmonistic versus "harmonistic" (Eshel),[35] "exact/conservative approach" versus "creative/free approach" (Crawford),[36] and "exact" versus "facilitating" (Teeter).[37]

---

31. Kyungrae Kim, "Studies in the Relationship between the Samaritan Pentateuch and the Septuagint" (PhD diss., Hebrew University, 1994), 288–91; see also Hendel, *Text of Genesis*, 81–92; Emanuel Tov, "Textual Harmonization in the Stories of the Patriarchs," in *Collected Essays*, 166–88; and Emanuel Tov, "Textual Harmonizations in the Ancient Texts of Deuteronomy," in *Hebrew Bible, Greek Bible*, 271–82.

32. Crawford, "Scribal Traditions," 175.

33. Frank Moore Cross, "The Contributions of the Qumran Discoveries to the Study of the Biblical Text," in *Qumran and the History of the Biblical Text*, ed. Frank Moore Cross and Shemaryahu Talmon (Cambridge: Harvard University Press, 1975), 283.

34. Tov, *Textual Criticism*, 184.

35. Eshel, "4QDeut[n]," 121; Eshel and Eshel, "Dating," 228–30.

36. Crawford, "Scribal Traditions," 175–77.

37. David Andrew Teeter, *Scribal Laws: Exegetical Variation in the Textual Transmission of Biblical Law in the Late Second Temple Period*, FAT 92 (Tübingen: Mohr Siebeck, 2014), 254–60.

Two distinctive scribal traditions or hermeneutical tendencies can be discerned *grosso modo*, one that was antiquarian and conservative and one that allowed for inner-textual explication by various means, including large- and small-scale harmonization and linguistic modernization. As scholars have cogently argued, the expansionist tradition has distinctive procedures, and hence should not be characterized as "vulgar" or "free."[38] We may infer a scale of tacit scribal knowledge of what constitutes right transmission, varying along a gradient between verbatim copying and actively enhancing intelligibility and formal perfection. The procedures of the latter tendency constitute, as Andrew Teeter emphasizes, "an accepted *exegetical method* of sorts within textual transmission."[39] Different scribal schools during the Second Temple period adopted varying positions in this scale of exegetical approaches to the textual transmission of the Pentateuch.

It remains unclear whether there are social, geographical, or functional distinctions that correspond to these different scribal approaches. An interesting point of comparison is two leather *tefillin* cases from Qumran, one containing harmonistic excerpted texts (XQPhyl 1, 2, 3) and the other containing proto-M excerpted texts (4QPhyl D, E, F).[40] This contrast may reflect different geographical or sociological origins for these *tefillin*, but it also suggests that there was no functional distinction between these two kinds of pentateuchal text at Qumran.

Proto-SP Texts at Qumran

In 1955, Patrick Skehan announced the discovery of "Exodus in the Samaritan Recension from Qumran."[41] This manuscript, later named 4QpaleoExod[m], has all the large harmonizations characteristic of SP where the manuscript is preserved (twelve), with the notable exception of the expanded tenth commandment in SP (at Exod 20:17, which is har-

---

38. Ibid., 265–67; Jonathan Ben-Dov, "Early Texts of the Torah: Revisiting the Greek Scholarly Context," *JAJ* 4 (2013): 224–26.

39. Teeter, *Scribal Laws*, 178 (italics original).

40. Yonatan Adler, "Identifying Sectarian Characteristics in the Phylacteries from Qumran," *RevQ* 23 (2007): 88–89; *contra* Eshel and Eshel's characterization ("Dating," 238) of XQPhyl 1 and 2 as proto-M texts.

41. Patrick W. Skehan, "Exodus in the Samaritan Recension from Qumran," *JBL* 74 (1955): 182–87.

monized with Deut 11 and 27), which celebrates Mount Gerizim as the holy mountain.[42] The obvious implication is that 4QpaleoExod^m contains the same edition of the Pentateuch as SP, but without the thin sectarian overlay. The discovery of 4QNum^b, announced the following year, clarified this situation, since it also has the large SP harmonizations where the manuscript is preserved (five, plus a large harmonization at Num 36 not in SP).[43] As Frank Cross summarized in 1958, the SP "differs from the 'proto-Samaritan' text at Qumrân only slightly; these differences would include, no doubt, the specifically sectarian readings.... There is not the slightest reason to suppose that the 'proto-Samaritan' is in any sense a sectarian recension."[44]

There are several Qumran manuscripts that belong to this family or are close affines with it.[45] Those that are identifiable according to the criterion of editions (i.e., the shared sequence of large-scale harmonizations) are 4QpaleoExod^m, 4QExod-Lev^f, and 4QNum^b among the biblical scrolls, and two scrolls of 4QReworked Pentateuch (4QRP^a = 4Q158; and 4QRP^b = 4Q364), which are either biblical scrolls or "parabiblical" scrolls (see below). 4QpaleoExod^m is a "deluxe" scroll, indicating its high status.[46] An anthological text, 4QTestimonia (4Q175), quotes from a proto-SP scroll. All of the proto-SP scrolls exemplify the harmonizing/facilitating scribal approach, as do other Qumran biblical texts (such as 4QDeut^n; see below) that lie outside of the proto-SP family.

---

42. On this instance of harmonization/conflation in SP, see Jeffrey H. Tigay, "Conflation as a Redactional Technique," in *Empirical Models for Biblical Criticism*, ed. Jeffrey H. Tigay (Philadelphia: University of Pennsylvania Press, 1985), 78–83; Kartveit, *Origin*, 290–94.

43. See Nathan Jastram, "4QNum^b," in *Qumran Cave 4.VII: Genesis to Numbers*, ed. Eugene Ulrich and Frank Moore Cross, DJD XII (Oxford: Clarendon, 1994), 215, 262–64. On the relationship between 4QNum^b and 4QpaleoExod^m, see Nathan Jastram, "A Comparison of Two 'Proto-Samaritan' Texts from Qumran: 4QpaleoExod^m and 4QNum^b," *DSD* 5 (1998): 264–89.

44. Frank Moore Cross, *The Ancient Library of Qumran and Modern Biblical Studies* (Garden City, NY: Doubleday, 1958), 144 (unchanged in subsequent editions).

45. See Tov, *Textual Criticism*, 90–93; Emanuel Tov, "The Samaritan Pentateuch and the Dead Sea Scrolls: The Proximity of the Pre-Samaritan Qumran Scrolls to the SP," in *Collected Essays*, 387–410; Crawford, *Rewriting Scripture in Second Temple Times*, SDSS (Grand Rapids: Eerdmans, 2008), 22–36.

46. Tov, *Scribal Practices*, 126.

The following examples—from Genesis, Exodus, and Numbers—illustrate the major typological feature of this family, that is, the sequence of verbatim or near-verbatim blocks of text transferred from one parallel text to another. In these examples the harmonizing expansions in the (fragmentary) Qumran texts are presented in Hebrew, followed by a restored text in translation (with lacunae supplied from SP), with brackets around the broken portions of the Qumran manuscripts. The restorations follow the careful textual analyses and estimations of space by the editors in the DJD series. Orthographic variants with SP are underlined.

Gen 30:36 fin] + Gen 31:11–13 SP 4QRP[b]

ויואמ[...] ה[...]ה ֹ[...]כֹּה[...] דֹּים[...] שר[...]מ[...]א[...]⁴⁷

And [the angel of God] sai[d to Jacob in a dream, saying "Jacob," and he said,] "He[re I am." And he said, "Lift up] your [eyes and see all the goats that go up to the flocks are striped, spe]ckled, [and mottled, for I have seen all that Laban has done to you. I am the God of Bethel, wh]ere [you anointed a stone pillar and where you swore an oath to me. And now, rise and go out] fr[om this land and return to the land of your] fa[thers."]

This addition harmonizes the narrative in Gen 30 with the following chapter, where Jacob recounts a previous dream revelation. The revision inserts a narration of the dream at an appropriate point in the prior narrative. This solves the exegetical problem of Jacob's reminiscence of an event that was not previously narrated. The origin of this problem is source-critical: the reminiscence in Gen 31 is from the E source, whereas the story in Gen 30 is from the J source. The harmonizing expansion smooths over the narrative gap between these stories.

Exod 7:18 fin] + Exod 7:16–18 SP 4QpaleoExod[m]

וי[...]וֹמר אליו יה[...] שלח את עמי ויעבד[...] כה אֹמר יהוה
בז[...] מֹ[...]הֹ במטה אשר [...] וֹ[...]גה אשר בת[...] מֹ[...]ריַם
לֹש[...]⁴⁸

---

47. Emanuel Tov and Sidnie White (Crawford), "Reworked Pentateuch," in *Qumran Cave 4. VIII: Parabiblical Texts, Part I*, ed. Harold W. Attridge et al., DJD XIII (Oxford: Clarendon, 1994), 211.

48. Patrick W. Skehan, Eugene Ulrich, and Judith E. Sanderson. "4QpaleoGenesis-Exodus[m]," in *Qumran Cave 4.IV: Palaeo-Hebrew and Greek Biblical Manuscripts*,

[Moses and Aaron went to Pharaoh,] and he (var. they) said to him, "Yah[weh, the god of the Hebrews, sent us to you, saying,] 'Let my people go that they may serve [me in the desert,' but you did not hear until now.] Thus says Yahweh, 'By th[is you shall know that I am Yahweh. I] am going to stri[k]e with the rod that is [in my hand the water of the Nile, and it will turn to blood.] And [the f]ish that are in the mid[st of (var. in) the Nile will die, and the Nile will stink. And the] E[g]yptians [will be unable] to dr[ink water from the Nile.]

4QpaleoExod[m] has the same plus as SP, with two variants: singular וי[א]וֹמר ("and he said") versus plural ויאמרו in SP; and the fuller בת[וך היאר] ("in the midst of the Nile") versus ביאר ("in the Nile") in SP. The large expansion consists of a verbatim repetition of the words of Yahweh's command to Moses in Exod 7:16–18, with a simple change in the initial verb from the command ואמרת ("And you shall say") to a completed action, the singular וי[א]וֹמר ("And he said") in 4QpaleoExod[m],[49] and the plural ויאמרו ("And they said") in SP, the latter including Moses and Aaron.[50] The hermeneutical technique of near-verbatim repetition to fill a perceived gap—here in the relationship of the divine command and its execution—is characteristic of the major expansions in the proto-SP family.

Exod 39:21 fin] + Exod 28:30 SP 4QExod-Lev[f]

ויעש את האורים ו[...] משה[51]

---

ed. Patrick W. Skehan, Eugene Ulrich, and Judith E. Sanderson, DJD IX (Oxford: Clarendon, 1992), 75.

49. The internal *waw* mater in the 4QpaleoExod[m] reading reflects the quiescence of *'aleph*; see Elisha Qimron, *The Hebrew of the Dead Sea Scrolls*, HSS 29 (Atlanta: Scholars Press, 1986), 23.

50. The change to the plural to include Aaron is a frequent harmonization in SP; see Judith E. Sanderson, *An Exodus Scroll from Qumran: 4QpaleoExod[m] and the Samaritan Tradition*, HSS 30 (Atlanta: Scholars Press, 1986), 201–3, 215–16.

51. Cross, "4QExod-Lev[f]," in Ulrich, *Qumran Cave 4.VII*, 139. On the secondary nature of this plus, I agree with the analyses of Ulrich, "Developmental Growth," 35; and William H. Propp, *Exodus: A New Translation with Introduction and Commentary*, AB 2 (New York: Doubleday, 2006), 2:346–47; against Cross ("4QExod-Lev[f]," 139) and Alexander Rofé ("Digesting DJD 12: Its Contribution to the Textual Criticism of the Pentateuch," *DSD* 23 [2016]: 100). It is easier to attribute this variation to the characteristic harmonizing/explicating *Tendenz* of proto-SP than to an error (Cross) or deliberate omission (Rofé).

And he (var. they) made the Urim and [the Thummim as Yahweh had commanded] Moses.

This plus, shared with SP (with a variation in the verb, plural in SP), is a harmonization with a matching plus at SP Exod 28:30: ועשית את האורם ואת התמים ("And you shall make the Urim and the Thummim"). That plus is in the verse where the Urim and Thummim are first mentioned (Exod 28:30 [MT = LXX = SP], "You shall place in the breastplate of judgment the Urim and the Thummim"). The absence of a command to make the Urim and the Thummim motivated a proto-SP harmonizing scribe to fill the gap by inserting a command and its execution. In the execution in Exod 39:21, the previous command ועשית ("you shall make") is turned into a completed action, the singular ויעש ("and he made") in 4QExod-Lev^f, and the plural ויעשו ("and they made") in SP, including Moses and Aaron. This two-fold plus, adding a command and its execution, is a striking instance of the gap-filling hermeneutics of the proto-SP scribal tradition.

Num 27:23 fin] + Deut 3:21–22 SP 4QNum^b

[...המ] h̊ אליו עיניכַה הרֹאֹות את אשר עשה יהוה לשני המ[...][52]

[And] Mo]ses (var. he) [said] to him, "Your own eyes have seen what Yahweh did to the two ki[ngs]"

This plus is shared with SP, with one variant: מ(ו)שה ("Moses") is lacking in SP. The new text is a near-verbatim harmonization with Deut 3:21–22, where Moses recalls this speech to Joshua. As in the previous expansions, this plus fills a perceived gap in the text, making the event and its recollection conform exactly.

4QDeut^n, an excerpted biblical text, has a large harmonization in the Sabbath command in Deut 5:15, imported from the parallel text in Exod 20:11.[53] This is a unique harmonization, not found in SP, indicating that the scribal approach of inserting large harmonizations was not limited

---

52. Jastram, "4QNum^b," 243.

53. Sidnie White Crawford, "4QDeut^n," in *Qumran Cave 4.IX: Deuteronomy to Kings*, by Eugene Ulrich et al., DJD XIV (Oxford: Clarendon, 1995), 125–26; Eshel, "4QDeut^n," 142–47; Elizabeth Owen, "4QDeut^n: A Pre-Samaritan Text?" *DSD* 4 (1997): 162–78; Crawford, "A Response to Elizabeth Owen's '4QDeut^n: A Pre-Samaritan Text?" *DSD* 5 (1998): 92–94.

to the proto-SP family. Similar tendencies are found in some *tefillin* and *mezuzah* texts and in a number of "rewritten Bible" texts.[54]

PROTO-G PENTATEUCHAL TEXTS AT QUMRAN

The distinctive profile of the proto-G Pentateuch brings in the issue of harmonization at another level. While the LXX and related manuscripts lack the large-scale harmonizations of the proto-SP family and preserves the earlier (unharmonized) edition of the tabernacle text, it has an extensive number of small-scale harmonizations from Genesis through Deuteronomy. As Tov observes, "The Hebrew source of the LXX [Pentateuch] reflects the largest number of contextual small harmonizations among the textual witnesses, more than the SP group.... This feature is the most prominent among the textual features of the Hebrew source of the LXX."[55] Other distinctive characteristics are "the chronologies in Genesis 5 and 11, the different sequence of the verses in Genesis 31, and the greatly deviating version of Exodus 35–40."[56] Tov rightly emphasizes that "there is no evidence for a Septuagintal text-type" across all the biblical books,[57] but the Pentateuch is an exception. These typological features indicate that the proto-G Pentateuch is an identifiable textual family.

The many small harmonizations shared with the proto-SP family indicate that the proto-G and proto-SP branches descend from a common ancestor (hyparchetype), after which the proto-G texts accumulated further small harmonizations, and the proto-SP texts acquired an extensive cluster of large-scale harmonizations. According to Kim's study of the relationship between LXX and SP, there are roughly 1,500 harmonizations in the LXX Pentateuch, of which 328 are shared with SP.[58] The large quantity of small harmonizations in LXX constitute a consistent pattern across all the pentateuchal books.[59]

---

54. Crawford, *Rewriting Scripture*, 30–56; Eshel, "4QDeut^n," 122–23.

55. Tov, "The Textual Development of the Torah," in *Collected Essays*, 244–45; see above, n. 31.

56. Ibid., 245 n. 21; and see above, ch. 8.

57. Tov, "The Hebrew Qumran Texts and the Septuagint: An Overview," in *Collected Essays*, 364.

58. Kim, "Studies," 288–91.

59. A striking example is the harmonization of command and execution in Gen 1, which parallels the proto-SP approach but with smaller harmonizations; see Hendel, *Text of Genesis*, 20–35.

The Qumran scrolls that are likely members or close affines of the proto-G family are 4QExod[b] and 4QDeut[q] (an excerpted text). Other Qumran pentateuchal texts share some harmonizing pluses with LXX, notably 4QDeut[b] and 4QLev[d], but it is difficult to be confident about their affinity based on relatively sparse details.[60] Since none of these texts overlap with Gen 5, 11, 31, or Exod 35–40, these specific proto-G features are not in sight.

4QExod[b] shares a notable exegetical revision with LXX at Exod 1:5–6.[61] It reads חמש ושבעים נפש וימת ("seventy-five people, and [Joseph] died"), the same reading as LXX (πέντε καὶ ἑβδομήκοντα. ἐτελεύτησεν δὲ Ιωσηφ). MT and SP read שבעים נפש ויוסף היה במצרים וימת יוסף ("seventy people, and Joseph was in Egypt, and Joseph died"). The 4QExod[b]/LXX reading is the result of a recalculated number by a proto-G scribe, who inserted Joseph's five grandsons and great-grandsons from the Joseph lineage (LXX Num 26:32–41 = MT Num 26:28–37, Machir, Gilead, Shuthelah, Tahan, and Edan) into LXX Gen 46:20.[62] This may have been motivated by the inclusion of Judah's grandsons and great-grandsons in Gen 46:12; by analogy, the reviser applied the genealogical depth of four generations to Joseph's line. The new total, "seventy-five," was inserted at LXX Gen 46:27, Exod 1:5, and Deut 10:22.[63] The recalculating scribe also moved ויוסף היה במצרים ("and Joseph was in Egypt") to the end of Exod 1:4, presumably to clarify that Joseph's household was included in the count.[64] 4QExod[b] at Exod 1:5 provides valuable testimony that this innovation existed in Hebrew manuscripts belonging to (or with close affinity to) the proto-G family.[65]

---

60. See Tov, "Hebrew Texts and the Septuagint," 356, 362; Armin Lange, *Handbuch der Textfunde vom Toten Meer*, vol. 1: *Die Handschriften biblischer Bücher von Qumran und den anderen Fundorten* (Tübingen: Mohr Siebeck, 2009), 16.

61. Cross, "4QExod[b]," in Ulrich, *Qumran Cave 4.VII*, 84–85.

62. In Num 26, MT/SP has an additional grandson, בכר, who is lacking in LXX.

63. LXX Gen 46:27 recalculates the total of Joseph's descendants as nine, whereas there are only seven listed in LXX Gen 46:20. The enhanced number, added to the total of sixty-six descendants of Jacob in Gen 46:26, yields seventy-five. This seems to be an alternative strategy for reaching this total. As elsewhere, a scribal revision can generate internal disharmonies; for other examples, see Segal, "Text," 12–13.

64. For other analyses of these variants, see Cross, "4QExod[b]," 85 (who regards 75 as a recalculated number); Rofé, "Digesting," 100 (who regards 70 as the revised number); and Propp, *Exodus*, 1:121–23 (who is agnostic).

65. 4QGen-Exod[a] partially preserves the recalculated number at Exod 1:5, with

4QDeutq (an excerpted text) is also a close affine to the proto-G family.[66] At Deut 32:43 it reads:

הרנינו שמים עמו / והשתחוו לו כל אלהים
כי דם בניו יקום / ונקם ישיב לצריו
ולמשנאיו ישלם / ויכפר אדמת עמו[67]

Rejoice, O heavens, with Him,
and let all the gods bow to Him.
For He will avenge the blood of His sons,
and He will turn back vengeance on His foes,
And He will repay His enemies,
and He will cleanse His people's land.

The LXX has the same reading, with the following variants: "sons of God" instead of "gods" in the second verse; the insertion of Yahweh in the last clause, and an additional couplet after the first couplet: "Gladden, O nations, His people / and let all the sons of God prevail for him." This additional LXX couplet may be a conflate text or a double translation. In any case, the LXX is an expanded version of the reading in 4QDeutq, which contrasts with the shorter version of only two couplets in MT/SP. In this verse, none of the witnesses preserves the ancestral reading, which Alexander Rofé plausibly argues was approximately the following:[68]

Rejoice, O heavens, with Him,
and let the sons of God exult;
For He will avenge the blood of His servants,
and He will cleanse His people's land.

---

the words reversed, followed by the MT/SP reading: וחמש נפש ויוסֵף ("[seventy-]five people, and Joseph"). This fragment seems to have mixed affinities; see above, ch. 7.

66. Patrick W. Skehan and Eugene Ulrich, "4QDeutq," in Ulrich, *Qumran Cave 4.IX*, 138; Tov, "Hebrew Texts and the Septuagint," 356–57; Alexander Rofé, "The End of the Song of Moses (Deuteronomy 32:43)," in *Deuteronomy: Issues and Interpretation*, OTS (London: T&T Clark, 2002), 47–54.

67. Skehan and Ulrich, "4QDeutq," 141–42; the text is written in poetic stichometry.

68. Rofé, "Song of Moses," 54.

The reading in 4QDeut^q has a harmonizing expansion, with two clauses imported from Deut 32:41 and changed from first person to third person. This expansion creates a doubling effect of divine intention followed by poetic proclamation:

I will turn back vengeance on my foes, / and I will repay my enemies (32:41)
And he will turn back vengeance on his foes, / and he will repay his enemies (32:43)

The proto-G reading includes this secondary harmonizing expansion, which counts as a shared derived innovation. 4QDeut^q is therefore testimony to a relatively early stage of the proto-G family.

4QDeut^b shares an expansion with LXX at Deut 31:28 in a list of Israelite leaders, adding ושפטיכם [וזקניכם], "[and your elders] and your judges."[69] This duplicates the expansion in a similar list at LXX Deut 29:9. Although this is a small plus, it has the same character as harmonizing expansions elsewhere in proto-G. This fragment arguably provides another witness to the proto-G family.

4QLev^d has a short exegetical/harmonizing plus shared with LXX at Lev 17:3 and a long exegetical/harmonizing plus shared with LXX and SP at 17:4.[70] On the basis of this sample, the manuscript is a member of or close affine to the proto-G family. It also illustrates the harmonizing/explicating approach that is shared, in different degrees, by proto-G and proto-SP texts.

There are several other Qumran fragments that share readings with LXX against MT/SP, but in the following cases these readings are arguably earlier (archetypal) readings, and as such do not have implications for textual affinity. Original readings can be preserved at multiple locations in the genealogy. If more of these texts had been preserved, we would be able to ascertain their relationship with the proto-G family or to other hitherto undiscovered textual families and genealogical branches:

---

69. Julie A. Duncan, "4QDeut^b," in Ulrich, *Qumran Cave 4.IX*, 13–14.

70. Emanuel Tov, "4QLev^d," in Ulrich, *Qumran Cave 4.VII*, 194–95; Teeter, *Scribal Laws*, 76–94; Reinhard Müller, Juha Pakkala, and Bas ter Haar Romeny, *Evidence of Editing: Growth and Change of Texts in the Hebrew Bible*, RBS 75 (Atlanta: Society of Biblical Literature, 2014), 19–25.

4QGen[h] at 1:9: מקוה G (συναγωγήν) "gathering"] מקום 4QGen[b] M SP ("place")[71]

4QGen[k] at 1:9: [שה היב]ותרא G (καὶ ὤφθη ἡ ξηρά) "and the dry land appeared"] > M SP[72]

4QDeut[j] at 32:8: בני אלוהים G (υἱῶν [var. ἀγγέλων] θεοῦ) "sons of God"] בני ישראל M SP "sons of Israel"[73]

4QDeut[h] at 33:8: [הבו ללו[י] G (Δότε Λευι) 4QTest "Give to Levi"] > M SP[74]

INDEPENDENT (NONALIGNED) TEXTS?

Tov has argued that many of the Qumran pentateuchal texts should be classified as *independent* or *nonaligned*. By this he means texts that "follow an inconsistent pattern of agreements and disagreements with MT, LXX, and SP and ... also contain readings not known from other sources."[75] He cites as an example 11QpaleoLev[a], a sizeable manuscript that has many small variants and one large unique reading (see below), but has no consistent pattern of affinity with MT, LXX, or SP. Therefore, Tov maintains, it "must be regarded as a *fourth* source of the book, previously unknown."[76] Including this scroll, Tov lists seventeen pentateuchal manuscripts as indepen-

---

71. James R. Davila, "4QGen[h]," in Ulrich, *Qumran Cave 4.VII*, 61–62; Hendel, *Text of Genesis*, 24–25.

72. James R. Davila, "4QGen[k]," in Ulrich, *Qumran Cave 4.VII*, 76; Hendel, *Text of Genesis*, 25–27.

73. Julie A. Duncan, "4QDeut[j]," in Ulrich, *Qumran Cave 4.IX*, 90 (an excerpted text); see also Jan Joosten, "A Note on the Text of Deuteronomy xxxii 8," *VT* 57 (2007): 548–55; Sidnie White Crawford; "Deuteronomy 32:1–9," in Sidnie White Crawford, Jan Joosten, and Eugene Ulrich, "Sample Editions of the Oxford Hebrew Bible: Deuteronomy 32:1–9, 1 Kings 11:1–8, and Jeremiah 27:1–10 (34 G)," *VT* 58 (2008): 357.

74. Julie A. Duncan, "4QDeut[h]," in Ulrich, *Qumran Cave 4.IX*, 68–69; Julie A. Duncan, "New Readings for the 'Blessing of Moses' from Qumran," *JBL* 114 (1995): 280.

75. Tov, *Textual Criticism*, 109.

76. Emanuel Tov, "A Modern Textual Outlook Based on the Qumran Scrolls," *HUCA* 53 (1982): 20, emphasis original; see Emanuel Tov, "The Textual Character of 11QpaleoLev" [Hebrew], *Shnaton* 3 (1978–79): 238–44; and *Textual Criticism*, 159–60.

dent (some with question marks).[77] Lange lists twenty-one pentateuchal manuscripts as independent (including four manuscripts of 4QRP; see further below).[78] Ten manuscripts are on both lists: 4QExod^b, 4QExod-Lev^f, 11QpaleoLev^a, 4QDeut^b, 4QDeut^c, 4QDeut^h, 4QDeut^j, 4QDeut^{k1}, 4QDeut^{k2}, 4QDeut^m, and 4QDeut^n.

However, as we have noted above, several of these manuscripts have affinities with one or another textual family. 4QExod-Lev^f has affinities with the proto-SP family, and 4QExod^b and 4QDeut^b have affinities with the proto-G family. Eshel has argued that 4QDeut^j, 4QDeut^{k1}, and 4QDeut^n (all excerpted texts) should be grouped with the "harmonistic" text group."[79]

Aside from these differences in identifying the affiliation of these texts, there are some general problems regarding the cogency of Tov's category of "independent/nonaligned texts."[80] He bases this category on "an inconsistent pattern of agreements and disagreements with MT, LXX, and SP" and "readings not known from other sources." But these are arguably not the right criteria for ascertaining textual affinity.

As Chiesa observes, "in textual criticism what matters is not the *number* of agreements and disagreements between the various witnesses, but the *nature* of their variant readings and/or errors."[81] Many or most of the variants in the putative independent/nonaligned texts are kinds that are polygenetic, that is, within the range of the law of scribes. Other variants may be original or archetypal readings, which have no value for establishing affinity. Unique readings (*lectiones singulares*) are also of no value for establishing affinity (or, in this case, nonaffinity). In sum, the logical

---

77. Tov, *Scribal Practices*, 332–33: 4QGen^k, 2QExod^b?, 4QExod^b, 4QExod^d, 4QExod^e?, 4QExod-Lev^f, 11QpaleoLev^a, 11QLev^b?, 4QDeut^b, 4QDeut^c, 4QDeut^h, 4QDeut^j, 4QDeut^{k1}, 4QDeut^{k2}, 4QDeut^m, 4QDeut^n, 5QDeut.

78. Lange, *Handbuch*, 155: 4QGen^f, 2QExod^a, 4QExod^b, 4QExod^c, 4QExod-Lev^f, 4QLev-Num^a, 4QLev^b, 11QpaleoLev^a, 1QDeut^b, 4QDeut^b, 4QDeut^c, 4QDeut^h, 4QDeut^i, 4QDeut^{k1}, 4QDeut^{k2}, 4QDeut^n, 4QpaleoDeut^r.

79. Eshel, "4QDeut^n," 122. On the text-critical complications of the excerpted texts, see Brent A. Strawn, "Excerpted Manuscripts at Qumran: Their Significance for the Textual History of the Hebrew Bible and the Socio-religious History of the Qumran Community and Its Literature," in *The Dead Sea Scrolls and the Qumran Community*, vol. 2 of *The Bible and the Dead Sea Scrolls*, ed. James H. Charlesworth (Waco, TX: Baylor University Press, 2006), 130–47.

80. See above, ch. 7.

81. Chiesa, "Textual History," 267 (italics original).

structure of the category of independent/nonaligned texts is flawed. All biblical manuscripts are dependent or aligned with respect to their history. Even a manuscript that is "mixed," that is, copied and/or corrected from two or more manuscripts from different places in the stemma, is still aligned, albeit complexly so. For many of the manuscripts placed in this category by Tov, there is simply insufficient evidence to determine their place in the textual genealogy.

11QpaleoLev[a], Tov's prime example of this category, is one of the better preserved pentateuchal scrolls.[82] Since Leviticus has a relatively stable textual history, with few major expansions, one does not expect considerable textual drama.[83] In 11QpaleoLev[a] there are only two shared derived innovations that clearly rise above the level of the law of scribes. At Lev 15:3, the scroll shares a medium-size harmonizing/explicating plus with SP and LXX, lacking in MT:[84]

[טמאתו היא] בו כל ימי ז[ב בשרו]
[This is his impurity] in him all the days that [his member] dischar[ges]

There is one variant between SP and LXX in the initial sequence, which is broken in 11QpaleoLev[a]. SP reads טמא הוא ("he is impure") where LXX probably reads טמאתו היא (αὕτη ἡ ἀκαθαρσία αὐτοῦ, "this is his impurity").

Teeter has cogently argued that this plus is "an explanatory gloss on the difficult formulation of the original verse."[85] The original verse, which is attested in all the witnesses, begins (MT pointing): וְזֹאת תִּהְיֶה טֻמְאָתוֹ בְּזוֹבוֹ רָר בְּשָׂרוֹ אֶת־זוֹבוֹ ("And this will be his impurity in his discharge, [whether] his member runs with his discharge"). (The last clause is a par-

---

82. Tov, "11QpaleoLev"; David Noel Freedman and Kenneth A. Matthews, *The Paleo-Hebrew Leviticus Scroll (11QpaleoLev)* (Winona Lake, IN: American Schools of Oriental Research, 1985).

83. Sarianna Metso, "Evidence from the Qumran Scrolls for the Scribal Transmission of Leviticus," in *Editing the Bible: Assessing the Task Past and Present*, ed. John S. Kloppenborg and Judith H. Newman, RBS 69 (Atlanta: Society of Biblical Literature, 2012), 67–79.

84. See Teeter, *Scribal Laws*, 94–99.

85. Teeter, *Scribal Laws*, 98. Cf. Tov, "11QpaleoLev," 244, who regards this as the earlier text, lost by homoioteleuton in MT/SP; so also David Noel Freedman, "Variant Readings in the Leviticus Scroll from Qumran Cave 11," *CBQ* 36 (1974): 528–29.

enthetical aside.) As Teeter observes, a harmonizing/exegetical scribe imported wording from the parallel text of female genital discharge in Lev 15:25, כָּל־יְמֵי זוֹב ("all the days that [it] discharges"), into this verse in order to explicate the duration of the male discharge impurity. As elsewhere in the scribal tradition of the proto-SP and proto-G families, the strategy is near-verbatim transfer of language between parallel passages. This shared innovation indicates the affinity of 11QpaleoLev[a] with the common substrate (or hyparchetype) of the proto-SP and proto-G families.

11QpaleoLev[a] also shares a small harmonizing plus with LXX at Lev 26:24, reading חמת קרי ("angry hostility") versus MT/SP קרי ("hostility"). This is a harmonization with the parallel passage in Lev 26:28, which has חמת קרי.[86] This harmonization—and the identical harmonization in LXX Lev 26:41—creates a verbally consistent divine discourse. Notably, SP is not harmonistic in these passages.

In these two shared innovations, at Lev 15:3 and 26:24, 11QpaleoLev[a] has affinities with the harmonistic substrate of proto-SP/proto-G and with the proto-G family, respectively. In sum, 11QpaleoLev[a] is not an independent or nonaligned text but has notable affinities when examined by the genealogical method.

Most of the putatively independent scrolls lack sufficient diagnostic features to place in a particular textual genealogy. If we had the scrolls in their entirety, their affinities would be more apparent. For instance, the affinities of the Genesis scrolls would be clarified if they contained Gen 5 and 11; the Exodus scrolls if they contained Exod 35–40; and so on. For many of the scrolls in their present condition, we cannot infer their affiliation because of the paucity of data. This is a condition of our fragmentary evidence, and does not warrant an extra category of independent/nonaligned texts. The fragmentary manuscripts whose affinities we cannot detect are best designated texts of unknown affiliation or, in some cases, of mixed affiliation.

Is 4QRP a Pentateuchal Text?

The five fragmentary scrolls called 4QReworked Pentateuch (4QRP[a] = 4Q158; 4QRP[b–e] = 4Q364–367) have been characterized by modern scholars either as "rewritten" pentateuchal texts, that is, exegetical com-

---

86. Freedman and Matthews, *Leviticus Scroll*, 47.

positions that retell portions of the Pentateuch, or as new edition(s) of the Pentateuch. This dichotomy was already expressed by the initial editors. This group of texts was originally assigned to Cross, under the assumption that they were biblical texts. Cross decided that they were not and handed them over to John Strugnell. Strugnell described 4Q365 as a "copy of a wildly aberrant text of the whole Pentateuch containing several non-Biblical additions, some identical with the Samaritan Pentateuch pluses, others unattested elsewhere."[87] But he named these texts 4QPentateuchal Paraphrase, indicating that they are not pentateuchal texts but exegetical works. This question—are they pentateuchal texts or a reworked Pentateuch—continues to perplex. The final editors, Tov and Crawford, have changed their minds on this issue, both recently concluding that the scribes who wrote them meant them to be pentateuchal texts.[88] Ulrich characterizes it as a "variant literary edition of the Pentateuch."[89] Segal maintains that the manuscripts represent different compositions, one of which is a "rewritten Bible" text (4Q158), another possibly an excerpted Leviticus text (4Q367), and the others texts of the Pentateuch.[90] These issues are probably undecidable, due to the fragmentary nature of the scrolls and the lack of any contextual information (e.g., citations in other sources). Zahn aptly questions whether "in the current state of the texts we are able to decide with any confidence whether the 4QRP texts represent copies of the Pentateuch or compositions belonging to the rewritten Bible genre."[91]

The 4QRP scrolls, some of which may be independent works, have the following characteristics: (1) extensive reproduction of pentateuchal texts;

---

87. Quoted in Sidnie White Crawford, "4QTemple? (4Q365A) Revisited," in *Prayer and Poetry in the Dead Sea Scrolls and Related Literature: Essays in Honor of Eileen Schuller Schuller on the Occasion of Her 65th Birthday*, ed. Jeremy Penner, Ken M. Penner, and Cecilia Wassen, STDJ 98 (Leiden: Brill, 2012), 88 n. 6.

88. Crawford, *Rewriting Scripture*, 56; Emanuel Tov, "From 4QReworked Pentateuch to 4QPentateuch (?)," in *Collected Essays*, 45–59.

89. Eugene Ulrich, "'Nonbiblical' Scrolls Now Recognized as Scriptural," in *Developmental Composition*, 193.

90. Segal, "4QReworked Pentateuch or 4QPentateuch?," in *The Dead Sea Scrolls: Fifty Years after Their Discovery: Proceedings of the Jerusalem Congress, July 20–25, 1997*, ed. Lawrence H. Schiffman, Emanuel Tov, and James C. VanderKam (Jerusalem: Israel Exploration Society, 2000), 391–99.

91. Molly M. Zahn, "Problem of Characterizing the 4QReworked Pentateuch Manuscripts: Bible, Rewritten Bible, or None of the Above?," *DSD* 15 (2008): 333.

(2) large harmonizations; (3) rearrangement or linkage of noncontiguous pentateuchal texts; and (4) new compositions. The collocation of features (1) and (2) are characteristic of many pentateuchal texts (see above), but features (3) and (4) are not. Feature (3) is characteristic of excerpted texts. Feature (4) is characteristic of "rewritten Bible" texts such as Jubilees and the Temple Scroll. Some of the new compositions in the 4QRP scrolls are closely related to portions of Jubilees and the Temple Scroll (cf. 4Q364 3 with Jub. 27; 4Q365 23 with 11QTª xxiii–xxiv).[92]

Two of the 4QRP scrolls (4Q158 and 4Q364) have affinities with the proto-SP family, sharing three large harmonizations with this family (4Q158 at Exod 20:17 [20:21 MT]; 4Q364 at Gen 30:36 and Deut 2:7).[93] However, another scroll (4Q365) lacks affinity with proto-SP (no harmonization at Exod 26:35, and no sequence difference at Exod 29:21). The 4QRP compositions seem to have varying textual affinities.[94]

The arrangement of noncontiguous pentateuchal texts in 4QRP is often motivated by thematic triggers, such as the dangerous encounters with God in Gen 32 and Exod 4 (4Q158), the care of the tabernacle in Num 4 and 7 (4Q365), and the story of Zelophehad's daughters in Num 27 and 36 (4Q365). The harmonistic expansion of the Decalogue (4Q158) is a well-known phenomenon from the proto-SP family and the other harmonistic pentateuchal texts (see above).

The fragmentary state of these scrolls leaves undecidable the question of whether the omitted texts in these sections were reinserted elsewhere. If they were not, then it is difficult to imagine that any ancient Jew—Essene or not—would have regarded them as pentateuchal scrolls. As Bernstein observes, "the phenomenon of large-scale deletion (as opposed to rearrangement) of legal material is totally anomalous and unexpected in a biblical text."[95] Falk plausibly comments, "it seems likely there were significant omissions in the presentation of the Pentateuch—thus possibly a sort

---

92. Crawford, *Rewriting*, 47, 50–51; Crawford, "4QTemple"; Zahn, *Rethinking*, 77–81, 102–7.

93. Zahn, *Rethinking*, 29–34; Tov and White (Crawford), "Reworked Pentateuch," 209–11, 230–31.

94. Tov, "4QPentateuch," 54.

95. Bernstein, "What Has Happened to the Laws? The Treatment of Legal Material in 4QReworked Pentateuch," *DSD* 15 (2008): 49.

of excerpted Pentateuch."[96] Leviticus without all the laws would certainly be, in Strugnell's terms, a "wild" book.[97]

Whether the 4QRP scrolls were viewed as new editions of the Pentateuch or an exegetically rewritten Pentateuch—or some combination of these genres—these texts could have been regarded as authoritative at Qumran, as were other rewritten Pentateuch compositions (e.g., Jubilees and the Temple Scroll). 4QRP may best be characterized, in Najman's term, as a "Mosaic discourse," an interpretation of the revelation at Sinai that responds to new circumstances and to exegetical imperatives within the Pentateuch.[98] It is a Mosaic discourse in a gray area bridging textual transmission and new composition. Perhaps due to its hybridity, it soon became extinct. As Crawford observes, "We may have in the Reworked Pentateuch group the end of a very long tradition of inner-scriptural scribal exegesis, soon to be replaced by another tradition of separating the authoritative text from its commentary."[99]

---

96. Daniel K. Falk, *The Parabiblical Texts: Strategies for Extending the Scriptures in the Dead Sea Scrolls*, LSTS 63 (London: T&T Clark, 2007), 111.

97. See further above, ch. 4.

98. Najman, *Seconding Sinai Sinai: The Development of Mosaic Discourse in Second Temple Judaism*, JSJSup 77 (Leiden: Brill, 2003), 1–40.

99. Crawford, *Rewriting*, 57.

10

The Contribution of Frank Cross
to Textual Criticism, with Special Attention
to 4QSam^a

I found myself forced into a new world requiring new critical thinking,
new methods. Most extraordinary, I found myself for the first time interested in textual criticism.
> —Frank Moore Cross, "Reminiscences of the Early Days
> in the Discovery and Study of the Dead Sea Scrolls"

For fifty years, Frank Moore Cross was the doyen of textual criticism of the
Hebrew Bible. As the original editor of the biblical scrolls from Qumran
Cave 4 (later joined by Patrick Skehan) and as the first to synthesize the
data from the biblical scrolls with the discipline of textual criticism, Cross's
scholarship informed all aspects of the field and continues to play a major
role. Many of the current practitioners of the discipline are Cross's students (including myself), and all are in his intellectual debt. Progress in
the field often comes by finding a gap or inconcinnity in Cross's arguments, and reanalyzing the data until a clearer solution is at hand. In this
way, textual critics have created new layers of understanding, by thinking
with, through, and against Cross's text-critical scholarship. As with all of
his work, he combined mastery of details with a talent for synthesis, in
which the data are made intelligible within the larger historical and disciplinary horizons. In this oscillating scope, joining small details within a
broad synthetic sweep, Cross rivaled the erudition of his great predecessor
Julius Wellhausen, whom he regarded as the master of textual criticism of
the Hebrew Bible. Through his oeuvre, his teaching, and his nurturing of
younger talent, Cross ushered in a new era and a new intellectual standard
in the discipline.

In the following, I briefly describe and evaluate Cross's contributions to this field, using as an organizing thread his work on his favorite Qumran scroll, 4QSam[a]. This scroll was his first and last contribution to the field, from his discovery and publication of the first fragments in 1953 to his 2005 *editio princeps* in the DJD series.[1] These were the initial and final publications of the biblical scrolls from Qumran Cave 4. After addressing 4QSam[a] as a perspicuous example of Cross's contributions to textual criticism, I turn to Cross's general views on the theory and practice of textual criticism. These topics continue to be debated in contemporary scholarship, which is ample testimony to the continuing relevance of his work. I will include my own views, of course, and those of other current researchers on these topics, with the keen awareness that they are, where viable, firmly perched on the shoulders of a giant.

THE ADVENTURES OF 4QSAM[a]

As the first member of the team of scholars assigned to study the manuscripts of Qumran Cave 4, Cross was initiated into the discipline of textual criticism by necessity. He arrived in Jerusalem in 1953 at the tender age of thirty-two, three years after earning his PhD. He was assigned to clean and decipher a batch of recently excavated manuscript fragments from Cave 4. Among these were the first fragments of 4QSam[a]. In 2000, Cross vividly recalled these events:

> The summer of 1953 was wonderful. I was alone in the scrollery working on the materials excavated by Harding and de Vaux after the plundering by the Taʿâmireh Bedouin was halted. I had a cross section of Cave 4 manuscripts, eloquent evidence of the chaotic mix of fragments surviving in the cave.... The document which most seized my interest ... consisted of some twenty-seven illegible fragments, some backed by papyrus. The leather was darkened and mostly covered in yellow crystals—evidently dried animal urine, but very old urine. The fragments were found under roughly a meter of deposit in Cave 4. I cleaned these with a camel's hair brush and castor oil. The document seemed to have material concerning Samuel but it did not follow the Masoretic Text. Cleaning the fragments

---

1. Frank Moore Cross, "A New Qumran Biblical Fragment Related to the Original Hebrew Underlying the Septuagint," *BASOR* 132 (1953): 15–26; Frank Moore Cross, Donald W. Parry, and Richard J. Saley, "4QSam[a]," in *Qumran Cave 4. XII: 1–2 Samuel*, ed. Frank Moore Cross et al., DJD XVII (Oxford: Clarendon, 2005), 1–216.

was tedious and unpleasant, so I laid the task aside after a while. From the few legible places on the fragments it appeared to be a biblical story book. Or, I dreamed, a source of the Deuteronomist. Later, I returned to the task and by whimsy opened the Brooke-McLean edition of the Greek Bible to Samuel. I had brought up the Larger Cambridge Septuagint from the library stacks in the basement of the museum to compare its readings with other biblical scrolls. Perusing the Greek text, I came upon certain readings in my manuscript. I suddenly realized with a shock that I had a manuscript of biblical Samuel but not the text preserved in the received Hebrew text.[2]

He had discovered, as he stated in the title of an article published a few months later, "A New Qumran Biblical Fragment Related to the Original Hebrew Underlying the Septuagint." In this article, he concluded: "these materials will profoundly influence the direction of textual criticism."[3] In particular he emphasized:

This fragment and the others yet to be published sharply underline the seriousness with which the LXX dealt with the Hebrew text in their hands, and confirms most emphatically the usefulness of the LXX for the establishment of a more nearly original Hebrew text.[4]

In order to appreciate the magnitude of this discovery and its implications for the discipline, it is useful to take a step back and consider the state of the textual criticism of the Hebrew Bible at the mid-twentieth century.[5] The optimism of Julius Wellhausen, Carl Heinrich Cornill, and others in the late nineteenth century concerning the utility of the LXX in the task of reconstituting a better text of the Hebrew Bible had eroded. Paul de Lagard's exacting work toward a critical edition of the LXX had demonstrated the complexity of the Septuagintal manuscripts and history.

---

2. Frank Moore Cross, "Reminiscences of the Early Days in the Discovery and Study of the Dead Sea Scrolls," in *The Dead Sea Scrolls Fifty Years after Their Discovery: Proceedings of the Jerusalem Congress, July 20–25, 1997*, ed. Lawrence H. Schiffman, Emanuel Tov, and James C. VanderKam (Jerusalem: Israel Exploration Society, 2000), 935.

3. Cross, "Qumran Biblical Fragment," 23.

4. Ibid., 25.

5. See Frank Moore Cross, *The Ancient Library of Qumran*, 3rd ed. (Minneapolis: Fortress, 1995), 125–30; Moshe H. Goshen-Gottstein, "The Textual Criticism of the Old Testament: Rise, Decline, Rebirth," *JBL* 102 (1983): 382–84.

By the mid-twentieth century, many scholars concluded that if one could not reach the Old Greek translation through the welter of manuscript evidence, then perhaps one could not use the LXX for textual criticism at all. In 1940, Leo Seeligman, a superb textual critic, despaired of constituting a viable critical edition of the Septuagint: "The endeavor to reconstruct, or even only come close to an Urtext of the LXX is, so we fear, no more than an illusion."[6]

Moreover, many scholars came to regard the LXX, where it diverged from MT, as a loose, periphrastic translation. For instance, in his 1938 monograph on the text of Samuel, P. A. H. de Boer concluded: "we in G have to do with the same Hebrew text as the one offered by M." The differences were due to the translator:

> On the grounds of our research, this part of G can be considered of little value for the determination of the "original" Hebrew text. The divergences give important material for the determination of the intrinsic value of the translation and point out the difficulties which M has not smoothed out, but they cannot amend the Hebrew text.[7]

He rejected "any suggestion from [the ancient versions] to emend the Hebrew text, that treats them as variants to the Hebrew text and not as translations with their own purpose and history."[8] At midcentury, the use of the LXX in the textual criticism of the Hebrew Bible seemed, in the eyes of many biblical scholars, to be unwarranted.

In 1958, with 4QSam[a] and other Qumran Cave 4 manuscripts in hand, Cross announced a sea-change:

> It now becomes clear ... that the Septuagint's divergent text was due less to "translation idiosyncrasies" than to the type of text which it translated. These manuscripts established once for all that in the historical books the Septuagint translators faithfully and with extreme literalness reproduced their Hebrew *Vorlage*. And this means that the Septuagint of the historical books must be resurrected as a primary tool of the Old Testament critic. This is a repudiation of much of the textual theory and

---

6. Isaac L. Seeligman, "Problems and Perspectives in Modern Septuagint Research," *Textus*15 (1990): 201.

7. P. A. H. de Boer, *Research into the Text of Samuel I–XVI: A Contribution to the Study of the Books of Samuel* (Amsterdam: Paris, 1938), 69.

8. P. A. H. de Boer, "Research into the Text of 1 Samuel xviii–xxxi," *OtSt* 6 (1949): 4.

method developed and applied to the Hebrew text of Samuel during the last generation.[9]

With these data and arguments, a new era in the textual criticism of the Hebrew Bible began, reviving on a new level the path pioneered by Wellhausen and others. Careful study of the LXX and other ancient versions yield primary data for, in Cross's words, "the establishment of a more nearly original Hebrew text." The twin text-critical tasks of textual history and emendation—*historia textus* and *constitutio textus*—could recommence on a new evidentiary foundation.

In order to illustrate and refine Cross's arguments, let us return to 4QSam[a]. Of all the Cave 4 biblical manuscripts, this scroll is "the most important as well as the most extensively preserved."[10] In his DJD edition, Cross described its close affinities with the LXX:

> 4QSam[a] stands in the same general tradition as the Hebrew text upon which the Old Greek translation was based. The divergences between 4QSam[a] and the Old Greek are sufficiently explained by the century or so between the translation of Samuel into Greek, and the copying of our manuscript.[11]

In various works he characterized the general textual features of the major versions of Samuel:

> The Hebrew underlying the Septuagint is a full text, sometimes conflate, frequently original.[12]

> [4QSam[a] is a] much fuller text ... than the *textus receptus*. Many of [its] pluses are expansionistic."[13]

---

9. Cross, *Ancient Library*, 132–33 (unchanged from first edition, 1958).

10. Frank Moore Cross, "The History of the Biblical Text in the Light of Discoveries from the Judaean Desert," in *Qumran and the History of the Biblical Text*, ed. Frank Moore Cross and Shemaryahu Talmon (Cambridge: Harvard University Press, 1975), 180.

11. Cross, "4QSam[a]," 25.

12. Cross, *Ancient Library*, 133 n. 2.

13. Frank Moore Cross, "The Evolution of a Theory of Local Texts," in Cross, *Qumran and the History of the Biblical Text*, 311.

The [Masoretic] text of Samuel is remarkably defective, and its shortness is the result of a long history of losses by haplography.[14]

In Cross's view, these opposite textual characteristics—expansionist (LXX and 4QSamᵃ) versus haplographic (MT)—are "a most fortunate circumstance for the critic who wishes to reconstruct their common ancestor and thereby press back to an extremely early form of the Hebrew text."[15] By comparing expansionistic readings of LXX and 4QSamᵃ with the defective text of MT, one can make progress in reconstructing the history of the readings and in establishing a superior text.

Let us consider a clear example. First Samuel 1:24 displays many of the characteristic textual features described by Cross, and it has some much-discussed problems.[16] My analysis is informed by the preliminary work of Zipora Talshir for her HBCE edition of Samuel.[17] In the parallel texts below, the middle column is an approximation of the Hebrew *Vorlage* of the LXX,[18] surrounded by 4QSamᵃ and MT.

---

14. Cross, "History of the Biblical Text," 185.

15. Cross, *Ancient Library*, 133 n. 2.

16. Valuable treatments of this passage include Otto Thenius, *Die Bücher Samuelis erklärt*, 2nd ed. (Leipzig: Hirzel, 1864), 8; Julius Wellhausen, *Der Text der Bücher Samuelis untersucht*, (Göttingen: Vandenhoeck & Ruprecht, 1871), 41; Moshe H. Segal, *The Books of Samuel* [Hebrew] (Jerusalem: Kiryat Sefer, 1964),יד–יג ; Eugene Ulrich, *The Qumran Text of Samuel and Josephus*, HSM 19 (Chico, CA: Scholars 1978), 48–49, 71–72; Kyle P. McCarter Jr., *1 Samuel: A New Translation with Introduction, Notes, and Commentary*, AB 8 (Garden City, NY: Doubleday, 1980), 57; Stephen Pisano, *Additions or Omissions in the Books of Samuel: The Significant Pluses and Minuses in the Massoretic, LXX and Qumran Texts*, OBO 57 (Fribourg: Universitätsverlag; Göttingen: Vandenhoeck & Ruprecht, 1984), 157–60; Jürg Hutzli, *Die Erzählung von Hanna und Samuel: Textkritische und literarische Analyse von 1. Samuel 1–2 unter Berücksichtigung des Kontextes*, ATANT 89 (Zurich: TVZ, 2007), 80–83; Anneli Aejmelaeus, "Corruption or Correction? Textual Development in the MT of 1 Samuel 1," in *Textual Criticism and Dead Sea Scroll Studies in Honour of Julio Trebolle Barrera: Florilegium Complutense*, ed. Andrés Piquer Otero and Pablo A. Torijano Morales, JSJSup 157 (Leiden: Brill, 2012), 7. I prescind from discussing the end of the verse, which is complicated.

17. My thanks to Talshir for her guidance and insights. I miss her deeply. On her model of the textual history of Samuel, see below.

18. My thanks to Anneli Aejmelaeus for allowing me to quote her preliminary Göttingen critical text: καὶ ἀνέβη μετ᾿ αὐτοῦ εἰς Σηλὼμ ἐν μόσχῳ τριετίζοντι καὶ ἄρτοις καὶ οἰφὶ σεμιδάλεως καὶ νέβελ οἴνου. On the *status quaestionis* of the OG of Samuel, see Anneli Aejmelaus, "How to Reach the Old Greek in 1 Samuel and What to Do with

4QSamᵃ	Proto-G	MT
<u>ותעל אותו שילה כאשר</u>	<u>ותעל עמו/אתו שילה</u>*	וַתַּעֲלֵהוּ עִמָּהּ כַּאֲשֶׁר גְּמָלַתּוּ
[...]		
<u>[בפר בן] בקר משלש</u> <u>ולחם [ואיפה</u>	<u>בפר משלש ולחם</u>	בְּפָרִים שְׁלֹשָׁה
אחת קמח ונבל יין]	ואיפה אחת קמח ונבל יין	וְאֵיפָה אַחַת קֶמַח וְנֵבֶל יַיִן

<u>And she brought him to Shiloh</u> when [... <u>with a]</u> <u>three-year-old</u> [bull, son of] <u>the herd, and bread</u> [and an *ephah* of flour and a skin of wine]	<u>And she went up with him to Shiloh with a three-year-old bull and bread</u> and an *ephah* of flour and a skin of wine.	And she brought him with her when she had weaned him with three bulls and an *ephah* of flour and a skin of wine.

I have designated with single underlining the readings where proto-G differs from MT. The unique readings in 4QSamᵃ are designated with double underlining. The close relationship of 4QSamᵃ and proto-G is illustrated by their shared readings (single underlining) against MT. Although one of the shared readings is a reconstruction [בפר] in 4QSamᵃ,[19] the preserved readings—ותעל, שילה, משלש, and ולחם—are sufficient to establish this close relationship.

Cross's observation about the affinities of 4QSamᵃ with LXX are clearly illustrated by this passage. In nearly every place where LXX diverges from MT, 4QSamᵃ agrees with LXX. There are two exceptions, both at the beginning of verse 24. 4QSamᵃ reads אותו instead of proto-G's עמו/אתו* (LXX: μετ᾽ αὐτοῦ),[20] while MT has עמה. That is, 4QSamᵃ reads 'ôtô, the direct object marker with third masculine singular pronominal suffix, whereas proto-G is reading either 'ittô ("with him") or 'immô ("with him"), and

---

It," in *Congress Volume Helsinki 2010*, ed. Martti Nissinen, VTSup 148 (Leiden: Brill, 2012), 185–205.

19. The reconstructions are from Cross, "4QSamᵃ," 31, but I have left the second line blank, with discussion below.

20. Cross's treatment here ("4QSamᵃ," 33) is ambiguous; the lemma suggests that proto-G and 4QSamᵃ had the same reading (אותו), but then he clarifies, "One suspects that the *Vorlage* of G read אתו."

MT reads *'immâ* ("with her"). The history of these readings seems to involve the following steps, although only the first and last are secure: עמה → עמו (reinterpretation of final vowel letter) → אתו (synonym) → אותו (reinterpretation as direct object marker).

The second divergence of 4QSam[a] from LXX, later in the same line, is the clause beginning with כאשר. (The remainder of the clause is not preserved on the parchment.) The word כאשר is in MT but is lacking in LXX. Cross observes, "We know that [גמלתו] כאשר is too short to fill out the line in the scroll," hence, he tentatively proposes a longer reconstructed clause: [יעלה אלקנה לזבח ליהוה] כאשר.[21] This possible reconstruction is a harmonization with 1 Sam 1:3 and with the large plus later in our verse in 4QSam[a] (which is mostly shared with proto-G). However one restores this clause, it corroborates the notion that 4QSam[a] is a more expanded text than proto-G.

4QSam[a] has one additional unique plus: the phrase [בן] בקר. This is an expansion of the well-known variant in proto-G, which was correctly analyzed in the pre-Qumran era by Thenius and Wellhausen:[22]

MT	בפרים שלשה ("with three bulls")
proto-G	בפר משלש* (ἐν μόσχῳ τριετίζοντι, "with a three-year-old bull")
4QSam[a]	בפר בן] בקר משלש ("[with a] three-year old [bull, son of] the herd")

Since verse 25 refers to the sacrifice of הפר ("the [aforementioned] bull"), not three bulls, it is clear that the MT reading has suffered a common scribal error, a word misdivision. This error likely occurred in a proto-M manuscript prior to the consistent use of final letters (ca. late first century CE),[23] so that the *mem* at the beginning of משלש could easily be reanalyzed as the last letter of the preceding word, בפר. The adjectival form of משלש is rare in Biblical Hebrew, providing a motive for the scribal error in proto-MT.

---

21. Ibid., 35.

22. See n. 16; Cross, "Qumran Biblical Fragment," 19 n. 8; Emanuel Tov, *Textual Criticism of the Hebrew Bible*, 3rd ed. (Minneapolis: Fortress, 2012), 236, 278.

23. Emanuel Tov, *Scribal Practices and Approaches Reflected in the Texts Found in the Judean Desert*, STDJ 54 (Leiden: Brill, 2004), 231.

The correct reading בפר משלש ("with a three-year old bull") is preserved in proto-G, 4QSam[a] (partially reconstructed), and the Syriac Peshiṭta. As Cross comments: "That the original reading here was בפר משלש has generally been accepted by commentators since Thenius.... The addition of בן בקר in 4QSam[a] is readily understandable in light of the frequent use of the expression in the Pentateuch."[24]

Notably, both proto-G and 4QSam[a] are expansive in this passage. Among the ancient variants we can detect three different textual changes, including the corruption in MT:

בפרים שלשה → בפר משלש		word-misdivision, MT
→ בפר משלש ולחם		addition of ולחם ("and bread"), proto-G
→ בפר בן בקר משלש ולחם		addition of בן בקר ("son of the herd"), 4QSam[a]

The history of readings begins with the archetype (i.e., the latest common ancestor), which had the correct reading, בפר משלש. The first expansion, the appended ולחם in proto-G, is further expanded by [בן] בקר in 4QSam[a]. Clearly 4QSam[a] is the fullest text. Yet, although proto-G and 4QSam[a] are expansionistic, this instance illustrates that they also preserve old readings that have become corrupt in MT.

Alexander Rofé has refined Cross's analysis by observing that the addition of בן בקר in 4QSam[a] is a "nomistic" feature, a characteristic type of expansion in Second Temple scribal circles.[25] The scribes responsible for these additions were concerned with making the sacrifice conform to the Levitical laws, and hence supplied some "missing" details. As Rofé observes, in 1 Sam 1–2 "we find traces of nomistic revision in all of our textual witnesses."[26] Proto-G adds ולחם* (καὶ ἄρτοις, "and bread") imported from Lev 7:13.[27] 4QSam[a] further adds the designation בן בקר, "son of (i.e., belonging to) the herd," which seems to "denote a single ox, calf, etc." for

---

24. Cross, "4QSam[a]," 33.

25. Alexander Rofé, "The Nomistic Correction in Biblical Manuscripts and Its Occurrence in 4QSam[a]," *RevQ* 14 (1989): 252.

26. Ibid., 250.

27. Rofé fails to comment on ולחם in proto-G and 4QSam[a], although it clearly fits his category. Segal (*Samuel*, יד) cogently suggests that the addition of ולחם is a harmonization with the instructions for the תודה-offering in Lev 7:13.

food or sacrifice,[28] as in Lev 1:5; 4:3; and Num 15:8–9. Further nomistic pluses include the addition of "tithes" to Elkanah's annual offering in LXX of 1 Sam 1:21; in the specification of the priestly portion of the sacrifice (breast and right thigh) in 4QSam[a] of 1 Sam 2:16; and in the references to Nazirite rules in LXX and 4QSam[a] of 1 Sam 1:11 and 4QSam[a] of 1 Sam 1:22.[29] The inclusion of nomistic details is one of the motives for expansion in proto-G and its more fully expanded congener, 4QSam[a].

Other instances can be adduced where 4QSam[a] expands on prior expansions in proto-G. For example, in 1 Sam 6:2, when the Philistine chiefs call out to their religious specialists, MT, LXX, and 4QSam[a] differ on the list of specialists. (I am following Cross's retroversion of proto-G and his restoration of 4QSam[a].)

MT	לַכֹּהֲנִים וְלַקֹּסְמִים ("to the priests and diviners")
proto-G	*לכהנים ולקסמים ולחרטמים (τοὺς ἱερεῖς καὶ τοὺς μάντεις καὶ τοὺς ἐπαοιδούς, "to the priests, diviners, and enchanters")
4QSam[a]	לכהנים ולקסמים ולחרטמים [ולמעונ]נִי[ם] ("[to the priests, diviners, enchanters,] and soothsayers")

As Cross observes, "The short text of M is superior, most probably, to both the expansive text of G and the doubly expansive text of 4QSam[a]."[30]

These examples illustrate a general feature of the textual history of Samuel. Although MT has suffered many small corruptions (as in 1 Sam 1:24, above) and some large losses from homoioteleuton (as at 1 Sam 10:1 and 14:41), in many or most cases the pluses in LXX/4QSam[a] are arguably exegetical expansions or clarifications.[31]

Recently Zipora Talshir has argued that the fuller text of the LXX is best construed as representing a second edition of Samuel. 4QSam[a] is an exemplar of a later, fuller expansion of this edition. MT is an (imperfect) exemplar of the first edition.[32] I concur with Talshir's description:

---

28. BDB, 133a.

29. Rofé, "Nomistic," 251–53.

30. Cross, "4QSam[a]," 53.

31. I note that MT Samuel also has exegetical expansions, including the nomistic plus in 1 Sam 2:22 (Rofé, "Nomistic," 250–51) and the longer edition of the David and Goliath story in 1 Sam 17–18.

32. Zipora Talshir, "Texts, Text-Forms, Editions, New Composition and the

The perception of the MT as a vastly damaged text emerged from the over-estimation of readings preserved in 4QSam[a] and the LXX, readings which turn out to be part of an edition later than the edition preserved in the MT.... The edition of Samuel whose copy found its way to Egypt and was translated there into Greek—that is, the translation crystallized one of the texts that circulated in the middle of the 3rd century B.C.E.—also lived on in Judah, and attracted further changes.[33]

Talshir's description of the relationships among MT, LXX, and 4QSam[a] constitutes a revision of Cross's views. It differs from his model, but it does so by working with and through his scholarship, both concerning the details and the larger picture. Cross was, as Tov asserts, "the master of the biblical scrolls."[34] His legacy, however, is not set in amber. He encouraged his students and colleagues to argue with him and to refine his work, based on careful analysis of the evidence and clear thinking. This is his larger legacy. In the integration of the data from the scrolls into the history of the biblical text, he wrote, "the ground is not yet sure, and many missteps will be taken before certain results can be hoped for."[35] It is incumbent on our generation and those that follow to continue the work.

THEORY AND PRACTICE OF TEXTUAL CRITICISM

Cross's contributions to the theory of textual criticism of the Hebrew Bible stem from the paradigm shift that occurred with the discovery of the scrolls. One could now construct new models of the history of the biblical text, and one could envision kinds of textual scholarship that had previ-

---

Final Products of Biblical Literature," in *Congress Volume Munich 2013*, ed. Christl M. Maier, VTSup 163 (Leiden: Brill, 2014), 49–60; cf. the position of Eugene Ulrich, "The Samuel Scrolls," in *The Dead Sea Scrolls and the Developmental Composition of the Bible*, VTSup 169 (Leiden: Brill, 2015), 73–108. On Rofé's proposal that 4QSam[a] is best described as a midrash on Samuel ("4QMidrash Samuel? Observations Concerning the Character of 4QSam[a]," *Textus* 19 [1998]: 63–74), see Talshir, "Text-Forms," 59–60; and Zipora Talshir, "The Relationship between Sam-MT, 4QSam[a], and Chr and the Case of 2 Sam 24," in *In the Footsteps of Sherlock Holmes: Studies in the Biblical Text in Honour of Anneli Aejmelaeus*, ed. Kristin De Troyer, Timothy M. Law, and Marketta Liljeström, CBET 72 (Leuven, Peeters, 2014), 297–98.

33. Talshir, "Text-Forms," 50, 55.

34. Emanuel Tov, foreword to Cross, *Qumran Cave 4.XII*, xi.

35. Cross, *Ancient Library*, 138.

ously been dismissed as impossible. Here too we are still working out the implications and possibilities contained in Cross's scholarship.

Based primarily on the diverse textual evidence for Samuel and the Pentateuch, Cross developed a theory of local texts, which posited separate geographical locales for the distinctive text-types or families. For Samuel, he posited an initial split between the proto-MT text-type and an Old Palestinian text-type and then a split of the proto-G text-type from the Old Palestinian. This yielded three local text-types, which Cross tentatively located in Egypt (for proto-G), Palestine (for the Qumran scrolls of Samuel), and Babylonia (for proto-MT). Although the reasons for the geographical locales are circumstantial (and nonexistent for the Babylonian locale of MT), this model does account for the long-term preservation of differences among the texts.

However, there are other ways to construe the evidence.[36] Talmon proposed that the different text-types developed in different social locations within Palestine, rather than in different geographical locales, and that there could have been a plethora of additional text-types that have been lost.[37] Tov argued that the diversity of data is not explicable by a model of different text-types; rather we have an abundance of texts, only some of which can be classified as belonging to one textual group or another.[38] For instance, Tov maintains that proto-G of Samuel is simply a text, not a member of a distinctive textual group or stemmatic lineage.[39] Ulrich has argued, correctly in my view, that differences of edition should be central to our models of textual history.[40] Such engagements with and revisions of Cross's theory of local texts continue apace.

---

36. See above, ch. 7.

37. Shemaryahu Talmon, "The Old Testament Text," in Cross, *Qumran and the History of the Biblical Text*, 40–41; Shemaryahu Talmon, "Textual Criticism: The Ancient Versions," in *Text and Canon of the Hebrew Bible: Collected Studies* (Winona Lake, IN: Eisenbrauns, 2010), 415–18.

38. Tov, *Textual Criticism*, 180–90.

39. Tov, "The Hebrew Qumran Texts and the Septuagint: An Overview," in *Textual Criticism of the Hebrew Bible, Qumran, Septuagint: Collected Essays*, VTSup 167 (Leiden: Brill, 2015), 353–67, esp. 367: "the Qumran scrolls that were close to the LXX did not form a close-knit textual family and a Septuagintal text-type never existed."

40. Ulrich, "Multiple Literary Editions: Reflections toward a Theory of the History of the Biblical Text," in *The Dead Sea Scrolls and the Origins of the Bible*, SDSS (Grand Rapids: Eerdmans, 1999), 99–120; Eugene Ulrich, "The Developmental Growth of the

On the larger implications of the scrolls for textual criticism, Cross was a consistent advocate of a renewal of the classical task of the discipline, in which the inquiry into textual history (*historia textus*) informs the constitution of a critical text (*constitutio textus*). In 1953, he pointed to the implications of the scrolls for "the establishment of a more nearly original Hebrew text."[41] In 1979, he made his position crystal clear:

> The existence of identifiable textual families makes possible genuine progress in establishing an eclectic text, that is to say a critically established text, progress on the way to establishing a text of biblical works closer to their archetypes.... The sole way to improve a text, to ferret out error, is to trace the history of readings, to determine an archetype which explains or makes transparent the introduction of error or corruption.[42]

He diagnosed the inevitable resistance to this aim:

> The prestige of the *textus receptus* is formidable. Probably a greater obstacle is the inertia which slows scholars from changing methods and perspectives in which they were trained and which have grown habitual in their scholarly practice. The potentialities for progress in the new discoveries will be fully realized only in a new generation of textual critics. Even in major text-critical projects of relatively recent date, we note a persistence of an older perspective.[43]

Finally, he offers an exhortation:

> The plea must be made for eclectic method in the textual study of the Hebrew. All manuscripts and all textual traditions including the Massoretic text must be examined freely, reading by reading, without prejudice, and superior readings, whenever they appear, firmly chosen. Many barriers hindering the practice of a genuine eclectic criticism have fallen in our day, and new opportunities may be seized.[44]

Pentateuch in the Second Temple Period," in *The Dead Sea Scrolls and the Developmental Composition of the Bible*, 29–46.

41. See above, n. 4.

42. Frank Moore Cross, "Problems of Method in the Textual Criticism of the Hebrew Bible," in *The Critical Study of Sacred Texts*, ed. Wendy Doniger O'Flaherty, BRSS 2 (Berkeley: Graduate Theological Union, 1979), 50.

43. Ibid.

44. Ibid., 54.

Cross's vision of the task of textual criticism of the Hebrew Bible is eloquent and bold. I recall reading this essay while a graduate student and thinking that a fully critical text of the Hebrew Bible would be a marvelous resource, but I pitied the scholar who would have the audacity to do it. It would surely be a massive and interminable project. Some years later, to my surprise, I organized such a project, the HBCE, dedicated to the production of critical texts, with abundant text-critical commentary, for each book of the Hebrew Bible.

This is indeed a complicated venture, with many issues of method and theory that we have had to examine closely. The project has been subjected to intensive criticism by many textual scholars. Happily, these criticisms have pushed us to think more deeply about the contested issues, and to construct richer and more suitable solutions. The efforts by the editorial team will yield significant fruits, contributing to the renewal of textual scholarship in our field. This project is unthinkable without Cross's vision of a future textual criticism.

CONCLUSIONS

As John Sandys-Wunsch dryly observes, "textual criticism makes its decisions after a careful and tedious comparison of different texts, compared to which accounting looks exciting." On the plus side, he notes, it has a sound epistemology and aim: "it is tied to how texts are written and what they actually contain, and, like accounting, it is a study where the obligation is to search for the truth, not the convenience of the searcher."[45] Among the virtues of Cross's contributions is that he made textual criticism lively and challenging, far more exciting than accounting. Of course, the discovery of ancient manuscripts in the Dead Sea caves will do that. With the exacting standards of his intellect and scholarship, Cross was the right scholar at the right time to integrate the scrolls into biblical scholarship. His work renewed textual criticism in the post-Qumran era. He taught his students and colleagues to think clearly about complex matters and to be willing to go beyond conventional wisdom in the advancement of scholarship.

Cross always encouraged innovation. Against the position of the Moshe Goshen-Gottstein, founding editor of the Hebrew University Bible

---

45. John Sandys-Wunsch, *What Have They Done to the Bible? A History of Modern Biblical Interpretation* (Collegeville, MN: Liturgical Press, 2005), 93.

Project, whose goal was to "present nothing but facts,"[46] Cross argued that this represents "a curiously ambiguous and tentative posture, poised to enter a new, vibrant realm of risk, too cautious to let go of traditional assumptions."[47] In contrast to a critical edition of the Bible as a vast collection of real and pseudo-variants, Cross argued for the classical task of the discipline, which requires *interpreting* the facts and the careful marshaling of erudition, judgment, and philological tact. Cross was severe in his criticism of those who would avoid the difficult work of textual criticism:

> Once the textual critic has established the existence of variant textual families, and of genuine variant readings, it would seem natural for him to get on with the task of investigating the variant readings and establishing the superior readings. Not at all. One should never underestimate the resources of the textual critic in finding ways to avoid work.[48]

By such programmatic formulations and animadversions, Cross sought to clear away the accumulation of bad habits in what he called the "miasmal precincts of text-critical labors."[49] He conceived of textual criticism in the post-Qumran era as "a new, vibrant realm of risk," ripe for new investigations and new initiatives. In particular I note—with a sense of intellectual debt and gratitude—that he created the conceptual space for a new kind of critical edition of the Hebrew Bible.

---

46. Moshe H. Goshen-Gottstein, *The Book of Isaiah: Sample Edition with Introduction* (Jerusalem: Magnes, 1965), 7.

47. Cross, "Problems of Method," 51.

48. Ibid.

49. Cross, "History of the Biblical Text," 177.

11

THE DREAM OF A PERFECT TEXT:
TEXTUAL CRITICISM AND THEOLOGY
IN EARLY MODERN EUROPE

Variants are arts of the devil.
—Laurentius Fabricius, letter to Johannes Buxtorf, 1625

Textual criticism and theology have a curiously intertwined history. In the early modern period, textual variants were mobilized as weapons in theological controversies about authority, heresy, and salvation. The early modern obsession with textual variants produced monumental effects, giving rise to a new critical method in biblical scholarship and a new doctrine of biblical inerrancy in orthodox Christian theology. It may not seem obvious how the analysis of textual variants could simultaneously yield modern scholarship and fundamentalism. But, as historian Richard Muller observes, "the high orthodox doctrine of Scripture was framed by debate over the critical approach to the text."[1] The clashing discourses of biblical philology and biblical inerrancy were born out of the same matrix of theological controversy, engendered by the Protestant heresy and intensified by arguments over variants in MT, LXX, and SP. In this period, text-critical details were tightly bound with theological disputes. Their mixture had unexpected consequences.

The story I will tell has three phases: (1) the rise of early modern textual criticism in the era of Christian humanism; (2) the intensified stakes of textual criticism in the Protestant-Catholic controversy after Trent; and (3) the dialectic between the rise of modern textual criticism and the formation of the orthodox Protestant doctrine of biblical inerrancy. The story

---

1. Richard A. Muller, *Holy Scripture: The Cognitive Foundation of Theology*, vol. 2 of *Post-Reformation Reformed Dogmatics*, 2nd ed. (Grand Rapids: Baker, 2003), 372.

has many more players and details than I can address, hence this is a broad brush account of these mostly forgotten events, which nonetheless still resound in our present academic and theological discourses.[2]

TEXTUAL CRITICISM AND CHRISTIAN HUMANISM

The first work that systematically applied the Renaissance model of textual criticism to the Hebrew Bible was Agostino Steuco's *Veteris Testamenti ad Veritatem Hebraicam Recognitio* ("The Old Testament Revised to the Hebrew Truth"), published in 1529.[3] It provides a systematic comparison of textual variants in the Pentateuch—focused on the Vulgate, MT, and the Septuagint, and with reference to the Targums and medieval commentaries—in order to lay the foundation for a corrected edition of the Vulgate. Like Jerome and most of Steuco's contemporaries, he regarded the MT as the unchanging and perfect original text, the *Hebraica veritas*, and he argued for correcting the Vulgate readings accordingly. Steuco was an excellent Hebraist and was well-versed in the techniques of classical textual criticism formulated by Italian Renaissance textual critics, most notably Angelo Poliziano.[4]

An example of Steuco's text-critical skill is his discussion of a variant in Gen 14:7, presented in modern form as follows:

שדה MT V (*regionem*) "field"] שרי* LXX (ἄρχοντας) "rulers" (graph ד → ר)

---

2. The Hebrew Bible is more important than that of the New Testament in the second and third phases; on the importance of New Testament in the first phase, see below, ch. 12.

3. Agostino Steuco, *Veteris Testamenti ad Veritatem Hebraicam Recognitio* (Venice: Aldine, 1529); 2nd ed. (Lyons: Gryphium, 1531). Pagination is to the second edition. On Steuco, see Ronald K. Delph, "Emending and Defending the Vulgate Old Testament: Agostino Steuco's Quarrel with Erasmus," in *Biblical Humanism and Scholasticism in the Age of Erasmus*, ed. Erika Rummel, BCCT 9 (Leiden: Brill, 2008), 297–317.

4. On Poliziano's importance in the history of textual criticism, see Anthony Grafton, "The Scholarship of Poliziano and Its Context," in *Defenders of the Text: The Traditions of Scholarship in an Age of Science, 1450–1800* (Cambridge: Harvard University Press, 1991), 47–75; Anthony Grafton, *Textual Criticism and Exegesis*, vol. 1 of *Joseph Scaliger: A Study in the History of Classical Scholarship* (Oxford: Clarendon, 1993), 9–44.

Following Poliziano's method, Steuco's astutely observes that this is a paleographical variant, triggered by a graphic confusion between *dalet* and *reš*. He writes:

> Consider, I urge you, the variety that is discovered even in the Hebrew manuscripts. For without a doubt the Septuagint translators seemed to have read not שדה but שרי with the letter *resh*. For as has often been said, there is the greatest similarity between these two letters.... Most certainly then they did not read the word with a *dalet* but with a *resh*. I myself marvel at this variety, and this causes me to suspect that many other things throughout the Bible have been altered.[5]

I note that the Greek reading reflects not only the graphic confusion of *dalet* and *reš*, but also a secondary change of *he* to *yod*, yielding the construct plural form שרי. This two-step development indicates that the variant was more likely a product of a Hebrew scribe than the Greek translator. This observation supports Steuco's conclusion.[6] But the main point is Steuco's "marvel at this variety" as he perceives the possible extent of readings that were affected by such scribal slips.

Despite his text-critical skills, Steuco presupposes that the MT is a perfect text, always correct, and therefore any variants in the LXX or Vulgate are translators' or copyists' errors. This assumption of textual perfection—the equation of the *textus receptus* with the "Hebrew truth"—is a philological and historical impossibility. Scribal errors and changes occur in all of the manuscript traditions of the Hebrew Bible, and in any given case it is impossible to forecast which manuscript or version—if any—preserves the best (or the earliest inferable) reading. But the assumption that one text of the Bible was correct and all the others corrupt was widespread in Steuco's time, and it persists in some circles to this day. It is difficult to think about the Hebrew Bible as a text that is dispersed among

---

5. Trans. Delph, "Emending," 309. Steuco, *Veteris Testamenti*, 229: "Animadvertite quaeso varietatem, quae etiam in codicibus Hebraicis reperitur. Nam Septuaginta procul dubio, non שדה, sed שרי per resc legisse videntur. Est enim ut saepe dictum est, maxima inter eas duas literas similitude.... Certissime igitur non dalet, sed resc legerunt. Mirorque ipse hanc varietatem. Eaque res facit etiam ut suspicer, pleraque alia tota Biblia immutata esse."

6. The Samaritan Pentateuch, which was not available in 1529, agrees with MT in reading שדה. The Syriac Peshiṭta, which was similarly unavailable, reads ܪܝܫܐ ("chief"), agreeing with LXX.

many manuscripts and versions, and whose readings, in some cases, are lost forever.

Steuco was a Catholic humanist in the early years of the Protestant Reformation, which entails certain theological commitments. He occasionally peppered his philological discussions with theological invective against the Protestants, as when he defends the ritual "sacred offices" (*sacris officiis*) in the Bible that provide warrant for Catholic institutions.[7] He also defended the authority of the Vulgate, which he aimed to improve, not replace. He criticized on theological grounds his colleague Sante Pagnini's Latin translation of the Hebrew Bible (1527), which could be seen as replacing the Vulgate. Paul Grendler summarizes Steuco's objection: "[it] gave the enemies of true religion, especially Jews, the impression that Christians were weak in their faith."[8] Clearly, textual criticism was bound up with theological affirmations of authority and truth. Textual perfection and power were thoroughly intertwined.

Despite his conventional theological views, Steuco's textual criticism had vocal opponents. The scholastic theologians at the universities of Paris, Louvain, Salamanca, and elsewhere resisted the pull of sacred philology. As Erika Rummel comments, "the [scholastic] defenders of the Vulgate Bible argued that it was an inspired text and thus flawless in every respect."[9] Hence there was no reason to improve its text. Knowledge of the original languages was not necessary—and indeed an impediment—to its full understanding. As Pierre Cousturier, a theologian at the Sorbonne, fulminated (against Erasmus):

> We do not need a knowledge of foreign languages for an understanding of Holy Writ and for this reason it is vain and frivolous to spend time on learning them. Nor is it necessary to learn them for the purpose of producing a new translation of Scripture, for the Vulgate translation is quite sufficient…. It is completely insane and smacks of heresy for anyone to affirm that one should sweat over foreign languages for this purpose.[10]

---

7. Steuco, *Veteris Testamenti*, 557, at Num 8.

8. Paul F. Grendler, "Italian Biblical Humanism and the Papacy, 1515–1535," in Rummel, *Biblical Humanism*, 247.

9. Erika Rummel, *The Humanist-Scholastic Debate in the Renaissance and Reformation*, HHS 120 (Cambridge: Harvard University Press, 1995), 125.

10. Ibid., 113.

Linguistic and philological knowledge were a lure to heresy, not a means to textual (or doctrinal) purification. The text's perfection was guaranteed by theology. Textual criticism was beyond the pale, an unthinkable concept except by the "completely insane." The rhetorical tone indicates the importance of the underlying issues involving the text's authority and the institutional authority that derives from the perfect text.

Erasmus, the most acute textual critic of the age, had a different criticism of Steuco's work. In a letter to Steuco in 1531, he argued that some variants in the LXX, reflecting old Hebrew readings, were superior to the readings in MT. In other words, MT is not in every instance the *Hebraica veritas*. We can discern superior Hebrew readings elsewhere. Erasmus supports his philological point with a characteristic polemical thrust, which offers a preemptive defense against the accusation of impiety. He writes:

> Now if the Hebrew words are not ambiguous, then one must believe that the Septuagint translators read something different than we have. Indeed is it any wonder if anywhere I follow the Septuagint version, since in a number of places the apostles and evangelists do likewise?[11]

Erasmus positions his textual criticism in a way that seems to be supported by the evangelists and apostles. But Erasmus's philological method was theologically explosive, since it was subversive of the theological authority of the Vulgate and of its orthodox defenders. Yet Erasmus was not a Hebraist, and therefore to Steuco goes the laurel for initiating a new era in the textual criticism of the Hebrew Bible.

Erasmus correctly notes that Steuco's text-critical method is marred by his allegiance to the "Hebrew truth" of MT. He rightly saw that the best readings are distributed among multiple texts. At this time the issue of textual variants was relatively minor, mostly confined to the desire of Christian humanists to improve the Vulgate. But the theological stakes surrounding these text-critical issues were about to shift. The controversies within Christian humanism (e.g., between Erasmus and Steuco) were eclipsed by controversies with the Protestant heresy. Textual criticism became an explosive agent in the Catholic-Protestant religious wars.

---

11. Trans. Delph, "Emending," 316.

TEXTUAL WARS

In response to the schismatic Protestants, the Council of Trent issued the following decree in 1546 concerning the authoritative version of Scripture:

> This holy Council ... ordains and declares that the old Vulgate edition, which has been approved for use in the Church for so many centuries, is to be taken as authentic in public lectures, disputations, sermons, and expositions, and that no one should dare or presume to reject it under any circumstances whatsoever.[12]

The decree was carefully worded to avoid the complicated issue of textual corruptions in the Vulgate and to avoid denigrating the Hebrew text of the Old Testament and the Greek text of the New Testament.[13] The Council's position was that the Vulgate had been the customary Bible of the Roman Catholic Church for roughly a thousand years and by long usage was held to be reliable in matters of faith and doctrine. Because it was the traditional text—and thereby linked with church tradition and authority—it had earned its status as the authoritative text. The decree essentially raised the Vulgate's *de facto* status to *de jure*. The main purpose of the decree was to assert the authority of the traditional Scripture—and, by extension, the traditional authority of the Roman Catholic Church—against the Protestants and their bevy of vernacular translations.

Behind the scenes there was controversy over the omissions and ramifications of this decree. The Commission of Cardinals in Rome was highly critical. According to a letter by Cardinal Alessandro Farnese:

> In its opinion it would have been better to leave out the chapter on the authenticity of the Vulgate, but since it has been drawn up we must look for ways and means to tone it down, that is, to explain it further, for it is

---

12. Trans. Richard J. Blackwell, *Galileo, Bellarmine, and the Bible: Including a Translation of Foscarini's Letter on the Motion of the Earth* (Notre Dame: University of Notre Dame Press, 1991), 182. The decree, issued on April 8, 1546, reads: "Insuper eadem sacrosancta synodus ... statuit et declarant, ut haec ipsa vetus et vulgata editio, quae longo tot saeculorum usu in ipsa ecclesia probate est, in publicis lectionibus, disputationibus, praedicationibus et expositionibus pro authentica habeatur, et ut nemo illam rejicere quovis praetextu audeat vel praesumat."

13. See Hubert Jedin, *A History of the Council of Trent*, vol. 2, *The First Sessions at Trent, 1545–47*, trans. Ernest Graf (London: Nelson, 1961), 75–98.

impossible to deny that in many passages the Vulgate departs from the certain Hebrew and Greek text and fails to render its meaning.[14]

But the Vulgate decree was not toned down. Its status as "authentic" (*authentica*) was affirmed, notwithstanding its corruptions and variants.

The Protestant critique was severe. In his 1547 pamphlet presenting his "Antidote" to the Council of Trent, John Calvin denounced the Vulgate decree as "erroneous" and "barbarous":

> The sacred oracles of God were delivered by Moses and the Prophets in Hebrew, and by the Apostles in Greek.... [Those] who are acquainted with the languages perceive that this version [the Vulgate] teems with innumerable errors; and this they make manifest by the clearest evidence. On the other hand, the Fathers of Trent contend that, although the learned thus draw the pure liquor from the very fountain and convict the infallible Vulgate of falsehood, they are not to be listened to.[15]

Calvin concludes his treatise with the damning conclusion: "The sum is, that the spirit of Trent wished, by this decree, that Scripture should only signify to us whatever dreaming monks might choose."[16] The textual wars had begun.

The first wave of Catholic responses to Protestant criticism of Trent tended to radicalize the Vulgate decree. In his 1558 treatise, *De Optimo Scripturas Interpretandi Genere* ("On the Best Way of Interpreting Scripture"), Dutch theologian William Lindanus (Guillaume Van der Linden) revived the scholastic argument that the Vulgate was *the* reliable text of the Bible.[17] He asserted that the Hebrew and Greek texts had been corrupted by Jews and other heretics, whereas the Vulgate, made from uncorrupted manuscripts, had been faithfully preserved in the Catholic Church.[18] He offered as evidence a portion of Ps 13 in Hebrew that he

---

14. Quoted in Jedin, *History*, 96–97.

15. John Calvin, "Acts of the Council of Trent: With the Antidote" (1547), in *Tracts Relating to the Reformation*, trans. Henry Beveridge (Edinburgh: Calvin Translation Society, 1849), 3:71.

16. Ibid., 76.

17. William Lindanus, *De Optimo Scripturas Interpretandi Genere* (Cologne: Cholinum, 1558). On Lindanus, see Victor Baroni, *La Contre-Réforme devant la Bible: La question biblique* (Lausanne: Concorde, 1943), 139–41.

18. The title of ch. 3, book 1, is indicative (Lindanus, *De Optimo*, 19): "Hebraicam

believed had escaped corruption, since it agreed with the Vulgate. However, as the Hebraists Johannes Isaac Levita and Benito Arias Montano subsequently demonstrated, this was a medieval Christian Psalter that had Latin readings retroverted into Hebrew.[19] The Vulgate remained vulnerable to criticism.

Lindanus recycled the traditional Christian calumny against the Jews—that they falsified Scripture out of hatred for Christianity—and redirected it against the Protestants. Interestingly, this calumny (formulated first by Justin Martyr in his *Dialogues with Trypho*) was originally an explanation for the textual variants between the LXX and MT.[20] Now it was mobilized in defense of the Vulgate against MT. Lindanus added a notable scholarly argument: as Elijah Levita had carefully argued in 1538, the vowel points in MT were an invention of the medieval Masoretes.[21] Lindanus cited the lateness of the vocalization in his denunciation of MT: "What more harsh could be said against Hebrew codices deformed in various ways by the Jews through the efforts of Rabbis maddened by hatred of Christ, and those Jews who punctuated the Bible who are not trustworthy enough that you may safely believe them?"[22] The controversy

---

Lectionem hodiernam non esse germanam [et] genuinam, sed adulteratam" ("The Hebrew Readings of Today Are Not Authentic and Genuine, But Adulterated").

19. Johannes Isaac (Levita), *Defensio Veritatis Hebraicae Sacrarum Scripturarum* ("Defense of the Truth of the Hebrew Sacred Scriptures") (Cologne: Soter, 1559); Benito Arias Montano, "De Psalterii Anglicani Exemplari Animadversio" ("Critique of the English Manuscript of the Psalter"), in volume 8 of *Biblia Polyglotta* (Antwerp: Plantin, 1569–1573); see Theodor W. Dunkelgrün, "The Multiplicity of Scripture: The Confluence of Textual Traditions in the Making of the Antwerp Polyglot Bible (1568–1573)" (PhD diss., University of Chicago, 2012), 296–319. This "English Psalter" is Leiden University Library Ms. Or. 4725, from the twelfth century.

20. Lindanus, *De Optimo*, 28; see Justin Martyr, *Dial.* 71–73, 83; and Irven M. Resnick, "The Falsification of Scripture and Medieval Christian and Jewish Polemics," *MedEnc* 2 (1996): 353–54.

21. Lindanus, *De Optimo*, 18; see *The Massoreth Ha-Massoreth of Elias Levita: Being an Exposition of the Massoretic Notes on the Hebrew Bible; or the Ancient Critical Apparatus of the Old Testament in Hebrew*, ed. and trans. Christian D. Ginsburg (London: Longmans, 1867), 121–34.

22. Ibid., 32: "Quid enim contra Hebraicos codices a Iudaeis varie Rabbinorum Christi odio rabidorum opera deformatos dicatur durius, Iudaeos istos punctorum Biblis afficatorum authores non satis fidos, ut eis tuto credas?"

about the vowel points became a flashpoint in subsequent Protestant-Catholic polemics.[23]

There is irony in Catholic polemicists arguing for the corruption of MT in favor of Jerome's Vulgate, for it was Jerome who sought to return to the *Hebraica veritas* of MT. But this irony was lost on these religious controversialists. The high stakes in the Catholic-Protestant polemics created contorted positions on both sides.

The most accomplished and influential Catholic polemicist was Robert Bellarmine, whose multivolume *Disputationes de Controversiis Christianae Fidei Adversus Hujus Temporis Haereticos* ("Disputations on the Controversies over Christian Faith against the Heretics of This Time") set a new standard of erudition in this debate.[24] The first book, *De Verbo Dei* ("On the Word of God," 1586), addressed the issue of the Vulgate versus the Hebrew and Greek texts. Bellarmine sensibly dismissed the argument that the variants were due to Jewish connivance. He correctly argued that there are scribal errors in all biblical texts and versions:

> The Hebrew Scriptures have not been generally corrupted by the efforts or malice of the Jews; nor, however, are they absolutely intact and pristine. Rather, they do contain some errors, which crept in partly through the negligence or ignorance of the copyists, especially since in Hebrew it is easy to make errors in some similar letters, such as ב and כ; ד and ך; ה, ח, and ת; and ו and ז; and partly through the ignorance of the Rabbis who added the vowel points.[25]

---

23. Richard A. Muller, "The Debate over the Vowel Points and the Crisis in Orthodox Hermeneutics," in *After Calvin: Studies in the Development of a Theological Tradition*, OSHT (New York: Oxford University Press, 2003), 146–54.

24. Robert Bellarmine, *Disputationes de Controversiis Christianae Fidei Adversus Hujus Temporis haereticos*, 3 vols. (Ingolstadt: Sartorius, 1586–1593). Citations are to Robert Bellarmine, *Opera Omnia*, 6 vols. (Naples: Giuliano, 1856–1862). On Bellarmine, see Joseph de la Servière, *La Théologie de Bellarmin* (Paris: Beauchesne, 1908); and Blackwell, *Bellarmine*.

25. Trans. adapted from Noel Malcolm, "Hobbes, Ezra, and the Bible: The History of a Subversive Idea," in *Aspects of Hobbes* (Oxford: Oxford University Press, 2002), 417; Bellarmine, *De Verbo* 2.2 (*Opera*, 1:65): "Scripturas hebraicas non esse in universum depravatas, opere vel malitia Judaeorum; nec tamen esse omnino integras et puras, sed habere suos quosdam errores, qui partim irrepserint negligentia vel ignorantia librariorum, praesertim cum in hebraeo facile sit errare ob literas quasdam simillimas, quales sunt; ב and כ: ד and ך: ה, ח, and ת: ו and ז partim ignorantia Rabbinorum qui addiderunt puncta."

This more sober position was still aimed against the Protestants, for if the Hebrew Bible was sometimes unreliable, then the Protestant principle of *sola scriptura* was flawed. One needed a theological authority behind the text. For Bellarmine, this authority was the Roman Catholic Church and its traditional doctrines. The problem of textual errors was solved by an inerrant church.

Perhaps surprisingly, Bellarmine raised the stakes in the textual wars by investing the *contents* of the Bible with more, not less, perfection. Whereas the Council of Trent had repeatedly referred to the Bible as authoritative *in rebus fidei et morum* ("in matters of faith and morals/mores"), Bellarmine argued that the Bible was without error in all matters: "There can be no error in Scripture, whether it deals with faith or with morals/mores, or whether it states something general and common to the whole Church, or something particular and pertaining to only one person."[26] This expands the traditional concept of biblical authority, which previously—both in Catholic and Protestant tradition—was focused on *fides et mores*.

Bellarmine anticipates the objection to his novel expansion of doctrine by arguing as follows: "In Scripture there are many things which of themselves do not pertain to the faith, that is, which were not written because it is necessary [for salvation] to believe them. But it is necessary to believe them because they were written."[27] He further explains: "In the Scriptures not only the opinions expressed, but each and every word pertains to faith. For we believe that not one word is useless or not used correctly."[28]

As Richard Blackwell observes, this was a novel expansion of Scriptural authority:

> His remarks expand the concept of "matters of faith" considerably by introducing a startling standard of exegesis, which was new to the debate. We will call this the principle of *de dicto* truth. *The mere fact that*

---

26. Trans. Blackwell, *Bellarmine*, 31; Bellarmine, *De Conciliis* 2.12 (*Opera*, 2:62): "in Scriptura nullus potest esse error, sive agatur de fide, sive de moribus, et sive affirmetur aliquid generale, et toti Ecclesiae commune, sive aliquid particulare, et ad unum tantum hominem pertinens."

27. Trans. Blackwell, *Bellarmine*, 32; Bellarmine, *De Verbo* 4.12 (*Opera*, 1:140): "in Scripturis plurima sunt, quae ex se non pertinent ad fidem, id est, quae non ideo scriptua sunt, quia necessario credenda erani, sed necessario creduntur, quia scripta sunt."

28. Trans. Blackwell, *Bellarmine*, 31; Bellarmine, *De Conciliis* 2.12 (*Opera*, 2:62): "in Scriptura non solum sentential, sed etiam verba omnia, et singular ad fidem pertinent. Credimus enim nullum esse verbum in Scriptura frustra, aut non recte positum."

something has been said in the Scriptures makes it not only certainly true but a "matter of faith," assuming that its meaning is clearly established.... As a result every statement in Scripture, once its correct literal meaning has been established is a *de fide* truth. And, of course, the power to determine the correct literal meaning is ultimately located in the Church.[29]

As Blackwell notes, Bellarmine's high view of biblically authorized truth was crucial in his later condemnation of Galileo, which concerned matters of astronomy, not faith or morals.[30] The new principle of *de dicto* truth had major consequences in the Catholic-Protestant debate.[31]

Previously, the Protestants had not held a doctrine of uniform biblical inerrancy. As Roland Bainton observes, for Luther "inspiration did not insure inerrancy in all details. Luther recognized mistakes and inconsistencies in Scripture and treated them with lofty indifference because they did not touch the heart of the Gospel."[32] Where minor errors occur, as when Matt 27:9 mistakenly cites Jeremiah instead of Zechariah, Luther responds: "Such points do not bother me particularly."[33] Similarly, in his commentaries Calvin is not bothered by errors in the text where they

---

29. Blackwell, *Bellarmine*, 105 (italics original).

30. Ibid., 105–9.

31. Bellarmine was not the only post-Tridentine theologian working out this principle; e.g., the Salamanca theologian Domingo Bañez, *Scholastica Commentaria in Primam Partem Angelici Doctoris D. Thomae* (Venice: Concordiae, 1585), 63–64: "Spiritus Sanctus non solum res in Scriptura contentas inspiravit, sed etiam singular verba quibus scriberentur, dictavit atque suggessit" ("The Holy Spirit not only inspired the things contained in Scripture, but also dictated and suggested every word with which it was written"); cited in Ulrich Horst, *Der Streit um die Autorität der Vulgata: Zur Rezeption des trienter Schriftdekrets in Spanien* (Coimbra: Coimbra Editora, 1983), 163. See also Aidan Nichols, *The Shape of Catholic Theology: An Introduction to Its Sources, Principles, and History* (Collegeville, MN: Liturgical Press, 1991), 117: "Thomas' [Aquinas'] theory could have been developed in either a maximalizing or a minimalizing direction. Either one could stress that God really is the principal efficient cause, or one could stress that the human writer really is the instrumental efficient cause. In fact, his teaching was developed in a maximalizing direction and so was turned into the theory of verbal dictation" during the sixteenth–seventeenth centuries.

32. Roland H. Bainton, "The Bible in the Reformation," in *The West from the Reformation to the Present Day*, vol. 3 of *The Cambridge History of the Bible*, ed. Stanley L. Greenslade (Cambridge: Cambridge University Press, 1963), 12.

33. Ibid., 13.

are unrelated to matters of faith and salvation.[34] He acknowledges minor errors without anxiety, as in the contradictions among the gospels: "It is well known that the Evangelists were not very concerned with observing the time sequences."[35]

Calvin and Luther also accepted the traditional doctrine of accommodation, which holds that God simplified his biblical discourse in order for it to be understandable to uneducated people.[36] Regarding the cosmology of Gen 1–3, Calvin commented, "Moses is by no means to be blamed, if he, considering the office of schoolmaster as imposed upon him, insists on the rudiments suitable to children."[37] As Paul Helm explains, "It is an accommodation because Calvin believes that such a statement is not strictly true."[38] A comparable flexibility occurs, as Brian Gerrish observes, in those "interesting places where Calvin speaks not of the fallibility of the text, but of its historical relativity," including directives in the New Testament that are no longer relevant in Calvin's time, such as "Christian communism, the regulation of usury, and Paul's directives on masculine hairstyle."[39] In sum, for the Reformers the Bible's inerrancy is where it needs to be: on matters of faith and doctrine and on historical events basic to the history of salvation.[40] The doctrine of uniform inerrancy in

---

34. See Brian A. Gerrish, "The Word of God and the Words of Scripture: Luther and Calvin on Biblical Authority," in *The Old Protestantism and the New: Essays on the Reformation Heritage* (Chicago: University of Chicago Press, 1982), 62–63.

35. John Calvin, *Commentaires sur le Nouveau Testament. Tome premier: Sur la concordance ou harmonie composée de trois évangélistes* (Paris, Meyrueis, 1854), 319 (at Luke 8:19): "On sçait bien que les Evangélistes ne se sont pas guères arrestez à observer l'ordre des temps." Cited in William J. Bouwsma, *John Calvin: A Sixteenth Century Portrait* (New York: Oxford University Press, 1988), 121–22.

36. See generally, Stephen D. Benin, *The Footprints of God: Divine Accommodation in Jewish and Christian Thought* (Albany: State University of New York Press, 1993).

37. John Calvin, *Genesis*, trans. John King (Edinburgh: Calvin Translation Society, 1847; repr. 1984), 141 (at Gen 3:1); see similarly at Gen 1:5–6, 14–16, 22, 31; 2:8, 10; 3:23.

38. Paul Helm, *John Calvin's Ideas* (Oxford: Oxford University Press, 2004), 394.

39. Gerrish, "Word," 300 n. 76.

40. I do not mean to imply that the Reformers had a consistent view of inspiration or Scripture. Luther could also say, "Gott ist in allen seinen Worten, ja Syllaben" ("God is in every word, every syllable;" *Tischreden*, no. 1983). As Gerrish comments (*Old Protestantism*, 177): "Neither of them [Luther and Calvin] had a comprehensive theory of religious language: Calvin's principle of accommodation, for instance, was used chiefly as a problem-solving device, to be rolled out only when needed."

the literal sense across all details is an innovation of the Catholic-Protestant polemics after Trent.

Protestant theologians responded to Bellarmine's innovation in kind, affirming the uniform inerrancy of Scripture for their own apologetic ends. The most distinguished Protestant response to Bellarmine was by William Whitaker, the Regius Professor of Divinity at Cambridge. His 1588 *Disputatio de Sacra Scriptura; Contra Huius Temporis Papistas* (translated as *Disputation on Holy Scripture, Against the Papists, Especially Bellarmine and Stapleton*) was widely influential among Protestant and Catholic theologians.[41] As a counterpoint to Bellarmine's nesting of the Bible's inerrancy with the church's, Whitaker emphasized the sovereignty of an inerrant Scripture: "Scripture is as it were the queen and mistress which ought to rule and govern human infirmity, and to which our whole intellect, all teaching, every thought and opinion, should be conformed in dutiful submission."[42] He agreed on the high perfection of the Bible but rejected the interpretive authority of the Roman Catholic Church. The Protestant high doctrine of biblical inerrancy was formulated as a polemical rejoinder—an inverse echo—of the Catholic position. Whitaker avers: "Say they, the church never errs; the pope never errs. We shall shew both assertions to be false in the proper place. We say that scripture never errs."[43]

Whitaker extended the inerrancy of Scripture to include the detailed perfection of the Hebrew text. He argued that the Vulgate is a tissue of scribal and translational errors, while the Hebrew Bible is perfect. He responded point by point to Bellarmine's examples of scribal errors in the MT, arguing that in each the Hebrew is correct (at Isa 9:6; Jer 23:6; Ps 22:17; Ps 19:5; and Exod 2:22).[44] For instance, Whitaker correctly observes that the birth and naming of Moses's second son, Eliezer, in some versions

---

41. William Whitaker, *Disputatio de Sacra Scriptura; Contra Huius Temporis Papistas*, (Cambridge: Thomas, 1588); William Whitaker, *Disputation on Holy Scripture, Against the Papists, Especially Bellarmine and Stapleton* trans. William Fitzgerald (Cambridge: Cambridge University Press, 1849); pagination is from the latter. On Whitaker, see Peter Lake, *Moderate Puritans and the Elizabethan Church* (Cambridge: Cambridge University Press, 1982), 58–66, 93–115; Muller, *Holy Scripture*, 107–8; John D. Woodbridge, *Biblical Authority: A Critique of the Rogers/McKim Proposal* (Grand Rapids: Zondervan, 1982), 74–76.

42. Whitaker, *Disputation*, 663–64.

43. Ibid., 476.

44. Ibid., 158–60.

of Exod 2:22 (LXX[mss], Peshiṭta, and Vulgate) is a secondary harmonizing expansion based on Exod 18:4. I submit that Whitaker is wrong on Ps 19:5, where קַוָּם ("their line") in MT is a simple corruption of קוֹלָם ("their voice"), as reflected in the Greek ὁ φθόγγος αὐτῶν (cf. Ps 19:4). However, Whitaker has the better argument in the other instances.

Whitaker concludes: "These then are the passages which Bellarmine was able to find fault with the originals; and yet in these there is really nothing to require either blame or corrections."[45] The only textual change he acknowledges is the shift from the old Hebrew script to the square script. Hence he affirms that we possess the original text of the Hebrew Bible: "We must hold, therefore, that we have now those very scriptures which Moses and the other prophets published, although we have not, perhaps, precisely the same forms and shapes of the letters."[46]

Whitaker held that the Hebrew Bible in the MT is inerrant in all things, including text and vocalization. The perfection of the text supported a perfect divine discourse. Here we see the leveling of the whole Bible to a state of perfection. The previous distinction between "matters of faith and morals/mores" and matters unconnected to salvation was no more. It was all one divine discourse, each word dictated by God and necessarily true.

The textual wars put at risk the Reformation doctrine of sola scriptura, which entailed the clarity, self-sufficiency, and self-interpreting quality of Scripture. Orthodox Protestants mounted a defense behind a uniform doctrine of inerrancy, including the sense, the words, and even the vowels of the Hebrew text. Amandus Polanus enunciated the mature orthodox doctrine in his Syntagma Theologiae Christianae ("System of Christian Theology"): "The Old Testament Scripture was transmitted by God through the prophets, not only with respect to the sense, but also with respect to the words, and therefore also with respect to the vowels, without which the words cannot be clear."[47] The perfection of Scripture goes all the

---

45. Ibid., 160.

46. Ibid., 117.

47. Amandus Polanus, Syntagma Theologiae Christianae (Hanover: Aubrii, 1615), 486: "Quia Scriptura Veteris Testamenti est a Deo per Prophetas tradita, non tantum quoad sensum, sed etiam quoad verba, ac proinde etiam quoad vocales, sine quibus verba nulla constare possunt." On Polanus, see Heiner Faulenbach, Die Struktur der Theologie des Amandus Polanus von Polansdorf (Zurich: EVZ-Verlag, 1967), and on this passage, 110.

way down. In all of its details, Polanus proclaims, "Sacred Scripture … is infallibly certain."[48]

Polanus's colleague, the Hebraist Johannes Buxtorf, affirms the truth and perfection of the Hebrew text in his edition of the *Biblia Rabbinica* (1619): "We have left the Hebrew text in the most ancient truth of its purity and substance…. It is impious either to add or remove anything, or to change it in any way whatsoever." [49] Buxtorf eschewed textual criticism of the Hebrew Bible because it clashed with his orthodox commitments. For Buxtorf and the orthodox Protestant theologians, the attribution of error of any kind opened a theological abyss. As Laurentius Fabricius wrote in a letter to Buxtorf in 1625, "Variants are arts of the devil."[50]

Sacred Criticism and Its Discontents

The Catholic scholar Jean Morin, who produced the *editio princeps* of the Samaritan Pentateuch for the Paris Polyglot (1645), acidly described the Protestant problem concerning the Hebrew text: "if mistakes abound in that which is the only foundation of their faith, this faith is certainly completely ruined and absolutely sterile."[51] This is, in retrospect, a clear exaggeration. However, orthodox Protestant theologians and scholars agreed in the main with this proposition. Thus, when Morin published his *Exercitationes Ecclesiasticae in Utrumque Samaritanorum Pentateuchum* ("Ecclesiastical Engagements in the Samaritan Pentateuch," 1631), in which he argued that the Samaritan Pentateuch was older than and superior to MT, turmoil ensued.[52] Morin's chief argument was paleographical: the Samari-

---

48. Polanus, *Syntagma*, 17: "Sacrae Scripturae … est infallibiliter certa."

49. Quoted in Stephen G. Burnett, *From Christian Hebraism to Jewish Studies: Johannes Buxtorf (1564–1629) and Hebrew Learning in the Seventeenth Century*, SHCT 68 (Leiden: Brill, 1996), 227 n. 111: "Textum Hebraeum in antiquissima & verissima sua puritate & substantia … reliquimus. Impius enim, quisquis ei aliquid vel addiderit vel detraxerit, aut quovis modo in eo quid mutaverit."

50. Letter to Buxtorf, August 24, 1625; quoted in Burnett, *Hebraism*, 237 n. 167: "Variae sunt artes Diaboli."

51. Letter of 1653; quoted in Dominique Barthélemy, *Studies in the Text of the Old Testament: An Introduction to the Hebrew Old Testament Text Project*, trans. Stephen Pisano et al., TCT 3 (Winona Lake, IN: Eisenbrauns, 2012), 23.

52. See Pierre Gibert, "The Catholic Counterpart and Response to the Protestant Orthodoxy," in *Hebrew Bible/Old Testament: The History of Its Interpretation*, ed. Magne Saebø (Göttingen: Vandenhoeck & Ruprecht, 2008), 2:768–72.

tan text is written in old Hebrew script, which preceded the square (Aramaic) script used in MT. This script chronology is correct, but the inference that the Samaritan text is necessarily older than MT is not. In any case, Morin joined his philological argument to the old calumny: the Protestants were using a Hebrew text (MT) that was corrupted by the Jews.[53]

The solution to the quandary of variants—now including old Hebrew variants from the Samaritan Pentateuch—was meticulously detailed in Louis Cappel's *Critica Sacra, sive de Variis quae in Sacris Veteris Testamenti Libris Occurrunt Lectionibus Libri Sex* ("Sacred Criticism, or On the Various Readings that Occur in the Sacred Old Testament, in Six Books") completed in 1634 but not published until 1650.[54] Cappel was a Protestant Hebraist, but more importantly a brilliant philologist who had absorbed the latest methods of textual criticism as practiced by Joseph Scaliger, Isaac Casaubon, and their students.[55] As Steuco had done a century earlier, Cappel put textual criticism of the Hebrew on a new scholarly level. Cappel collected and analyzed the many variant readings in the MT (including parallel texts and the *ketiv/qere*), the Samaritan Pentateuch, the Septuagint, and other versions (Targums, Peshiṭta, Vulgate) and argued that one should use all of these sources in an analytically rigorous way to reconstitute the original text. His reasoning is exemplary:

> It is not possible to define with certainty which Codex should be preferred to the other.... That is to say, the arguments cannot be derived from extrinsic factors, but are intrinsic and inherent.... The reading is undoubtedly better and preferred, which in itself produces a truer sense,

---

53. Morin added an eccentric wrinkle, arguing that kabbalistic exegesis motivated many of the scribal changes; see Robert T. Anderson and Terry Giles, *The Samaritan Pentateuch: An Introduction to Its Origin, History, and Significance for Biblical Studies*, RBS 72 (Atlanta: Society of Biblical Literature, 2012), 154–59.

54. See François Laplanche, *L'Écriture, le sacré et l'histoire: Érudits et politiques protestants devant la Bible en France au XVIIe siècle* (Amsterdam: Holland University Press, 1986), 181–290; Bruno Chiesa, *Filologia storica della Bibbia ebraica*, Studi biblici 125 (Brescia: Paideia, 2000), 356–75.

55. Laplanche, *L'Écriture*, 91–100; Grafton, *Scaliger*, 176: "Scaliger transformed the art of criticism. He showed that a critical edition could not rest on a genealogical examination of the extant manuscripts alone. Rather, it had to rest on a reconstructed history of the textual tradition; and where the oldest manuscripts were no longer extant, errors in the surviving ones and even literary evidence had to be called into play. He had thus arrived at the fundamental insight of nineteenth-century German critics ... who made Scaliger's method the accepted one."

plainer, more suitable, consonant, commodious, more coherent in its consequences and antecedents, and closer to the writer's mind and scope of instruction.[56]

Cappel here rejects the concept of one manuscript as the perfect text, and formulates the principle that internal factors—including style and contextual fit—govern the text-critical evaluation of variants and conjectures. In his book, Cappel invents the modern method of textual criticism of the Hebrew Bible. He clearly enunciates the hermeneutical orientation of critical scholarship: "We are not here contending with authority, but with reason."[57]

Cappel granted that the Hebrew Bible was a sacred and authoritative text. In this he was a perfectly pious Protestant. However, he correctly maintained that it was humanly transmitted, and therefore susceptible to scribal errors, which it was the task of the textual critic to detect and, where possible, correct. This injected a human dimension into the biblical text that was unsettling to the orthodox. Further, it meant that theologians had to cede some of their authority to scholars. Both points were resisted. The Protestant orthodox now had to contend not only with Catholics, but also with a Protestant scholar who elevated reason to an unprecedented position. Correcting the text of Homer or Cicero was one thing, but correcting the Word of God was something new and different. As Muller observes, "It seemed now as if the textual underpinnings of the Reformation's *sola scriptura* were being chipped away from within the ranks of the Reformed."[58]

In some respects this rift replays and deepens the previous clash between scholastics and humanists. The former saw no use for languages when studying Scripture, because the Holy Spirit was sufficient. A century later, no one contested the value of knowing the languages. That battle had been lost. Bellarmine and Whitaker were arguing about the Latin,

---

56. Louis Cappel, *Critica Sacra, sive de Variis quae in Sacris Veteris Testamenti Libris Occurrunt Lectionibus Libri Sex* (Paris: Cramoisy, 1650; repr., Halle: Hendel, 1775), 303: "Cum itaque hac ratione certo definiri non possit uter Codex alteri sit praeferendus ... quarenda nempe sunt argumenta non extrinsecus assumpta, sed intrinseca & insita.... Ea nempe lectio indubitato melior est, atque praeferenda, quae sensum parit in se veriorem, planiorem, aptiorem, concinniorem, commodiorem, consequentibus [et] antecedentibus magis cohaerentem, menti & scopo scriptoris propiorem atque congruentiorem." See Chiesa, *Filologia*, 364–65.

57. Ibid., 396: "Non enim hic auctoritate sed ratione pugnamus."

58. Muller, "Vowel Points," 149.

Greek, and Hebrew. So were Cappel and his opponents, both Protestant and Catholic. Since his position impugned the authority of the Vulgate and church tradition, Rome placed his books on the *Index of Prohibited Books*. The Protestant response was even more intense.

Buxtorf's son, Johannes Jr., also an eminent Hebraist, described Cappel's book as "most pestilential poison" in his critique, *Anticritica: seu Vindiciae Veritatis Hebraicae: Adversus Ludovici Cappelli Criticam quam Vocat Sacram, eiusq. Defensorem: Quibus Sacrosanctae Editionis Bibliorum Hebraicae Authoritas, Integras, & Sinceritas, a Variis eius Strophis, [et] Sophismatis* ("Anti-Critica, or Vindication of the Hebrew Truth against the Criticism called Sacred by Louis Cappel and his Defenders, by Whom the Sanctity of the Authoritative Hebrew Edition of the Bible, Complete and Sincere, [is Impugned] by His Various Tricks and Sophistry," 1653).[59] The orthodox had a learned champion, but the polemics overshadowed the philology.

The harsh orthodox response to Cappel's work was codified in a doctrinal confession issued by the Swiss Reformed Church in 1675, the *Formula Consensus Ecclesiarum Helveticarum* (The Helvetic Formula Consensus).[60] It reads in part:

> The Hebrew original of the Old Testament which we have received and to this day do retain as handed down by the Hebrew Church ... is, not only in its consonants, but in its vowels ... not only in its matter, but in its words, inspired by God. It thus forms, together with the original of the NT the sole and complete rule of our faith and practice; and to its standard, as to a Lydian stone, all extant versions, eastern or western, ought to be applied, and wherever they differ, be conformed....Therefore, we are not able to approve of the opinion of those who believe that the text which the Hebrew original exhibits was determined by man's will alone, and do not hesitate at all to remodel a Hebrew reading which they consider unsuitable, and amend it from the versions of the LXX and other Greek versions, the Samaritan Pentateuch, by the Chaldaic Targums, or even from other sources. They go even to the point of following the corrections that their own rational powers dictate from the various readings of the Hebrew original itself—which, they maintain, has been corrupted

---

59. The quote is from the dedication: "pestilentissimum Venenum." On Buxtorf's response to Cappel, see Laplanche, *L'Écriture*, 299, 307–13.

60. See Martin I. Klauber, "The Helvetic Formula Consensus (1675): An Introduction and Translation," *TJ* 11 (1990): 103–23.

in various ways; and finally, they affirm that besides the Hebrew edition of the present time, there are in the versions of the ancient interpreters which differ from our Hebrew text, other Hebrew originals. Since these versions are also indicative of ancient Hebrew originals differing from each other, they thus bring the foundation of our faith and its sacred authority into perilous danger.[61]

This is a repudiation of textual criticism of the Hebrew Bible, because any change to the text—"corrections that their own rational powers dictate from the various readings"—creates a double problem: it elevates human judgment and rational inquiry to a place unreachable by theology, and it defines the Bible as an imperfect source of salvation. This is impiety or worse, which "bring[s] the foundation of our faith and its sacred authority into perilous danger."

The Helvetic Formula Consensus was the last Reformed Orthodox confession. As Muller observes, "the level of dogmatic detail … manifests, if nothing else, the profound trauma experienced by the orthodox theories of the inspiration, interpretation, and authority of Scripture in the face of a rising tide of textual and historical criticism of the Bible."[62] Even the vowel points were sacrosanct, for, as Muller notes, "If the vowel points were in fact a late invention, then tradition had invaded Scripture!"[63] If the authority of the Bible rested on the veracity of medieval Jewish Masoretic sages, then the "foundation of our faith" was indeed in peril. If the vowel points were a late addition, the Hebrew Bible was perspicuous only if Jewish tradition was reliable. The doctrine of *sola scriptura* rested on tradition after all—but it was a Jewish tradition. The extreme orthodox response was, perhaps ironically, a Masoretic fundamentalism, buttressed by a rejection of text-critical scholarship.

However, the Helvetic Consensus Formula was never actually a consensus. Many Swiss divines refused to sign, and it was eventually with-

---

61. Ibid., 115–16.

62. Muller, *Post-Reformation*, 92.

63. Ibid., 94. See Jan Joosten, "Le débat sur la vocalisation massorétique de la Bible d'Élie Levita à Louis Cappel," in *Les hébraïsants français au seizième siècle*, ed. Annie Noblesse Rocher and Gilbert Dahan (Geneva: Droz, forthcoming), where he emphasizes Cappel's distinction between the vowel signs (which are medieval) and the vocalization tradition (which is ancient). The importance of this distinction was generally lost in the heat of Catholic-Protestant controversy.

drawn.[64] It was the high mark of biblical inerrancy in Protestant orthodoxy, but it quickly faded into obscurity.

A revised version of inerrancy, formulated by the Swiss theologian
Francis Turretin (François Turretini), a cowriter of the Helvetic Consensus
Formula, became instead the orthodox standard. Many of its arguments
remain in place today in conservative evangelical doctrine.[65] In his *Institutio Theologiae Elencticae* ("Institutes of Disputational Theology"),[66] Turretin presents a detailed defense of inerrancy that takes into account the
existence of variants in the MT manuscripts. He does not concede much
to Cappel, but he modifies the extreme Masoretic fundamentalism of the
Helvetic Consensus by granting a limited validity to textual criticism.

Turretin grants that scribal errors happen, even in MT. But God has
prevented their proliferation to the point that the original is unrecover-
able. Because of divine providence, textual criticism can recover the original inspired text of Scripture. He writes:

> Although we attribute absolute integrity to Scripture, we do not hold
> that the copyists and printers have been inspired, but only that the provi-
> dence of God has so watched over the copyists that, although many
> errors could have entered, they did not, or at least they did not enter
> the codices in such a manner that they cannot easily be corrected by
> comparison with other copies or with [other parts of] Scripture itself. So

---

64. See Martin I. Klauber, "The Demise of Reformed Scholasticism and the Abrogation of the Helvetic Formula Consensus of 1675," in *Between Reformed Scholasticism
and Pan-Protestantism: Jean-Alphonse Turretin (1671–1737) and Enlightened Orthodoxy at the Academy of Geneva* (Cranbury, NJ: Associated University Presses, 1994),
143–64.

65. The current standard, the 1978 "Chicago Statement on Biblical Inerrancy,"
blends Turretin's views with those of the nineteenth-century Princeton theologians,
although it denies these historical roots (Article 16): "We deny that inerrancy is a doctrine invented by Scholastic Protestantism, or is a reactionary position postulated in
response to negative higher criticism." On the relationship between Turretin and the
Princeton theologians, see Mark A. Noll, *The Princeton Theology 1812–1921: Scripture,
Science, and Theological Method from Archibald Alexander to Benjamin Breckinridge
Warfield* (Grand Rapids: Baker, 1983), 28–30.

66. *Institutio Theologiae Elencticae*, 3 vols. (Geneva: Tournes, 1679–1685). Cited
from Francis Turretin, *The Doctrine of Scripture: Locus 2 of Institutio Theologiae Elencticae*, ed. and trans. John W. Beardslee (Grand Rapids: Baker, 1981). On Turretin, see
also Richard A. Muller, "Scholasticism Protestant and Catholic: Francis Turretin on
the Object and Principles of Theology," in *After Calvin*, 137–44.

the basis of the purity and integrity of the sources does not rest on the inerrancy of human beings but on the providence of God.[67]

For Turretin, textual criticism is valid because it is fully *sacred* criticism, superintended by divine providence. God limits the extent of error, such that it may be easily remedied and the perfect text restored.

But Turretin makes an important caveat. Only variants in manuscripts and printed editions of MT are valid evidence for the original Hebrew text. The variants in the Samaritan Pentateuch and the old translations (Septuagint, Vulgate, etc.) are deviations from the Hebrew original. Here Turretin maintains the exclusions detailed in the Helvetic Consensus Formula. He denies the possibility that "discrepancies between the old versions and the present Hebrew text were variant readings of Hebrew manuscripts different from ours."[68] Textual criticism is an inner-MT affair.

As a consequence of the efficacy of a (limited) textual criticism, Turretin maintains that the Catholic critics of *sola scriptura* are wrong. The existence of textual variants does not make the Hebrew Bible an imperfect vessel of faith. Through the restorative effect of an orthodox *critica sacra*, the Bible retains its inerrant authority:

> The question is whether the original text, in Hebrew or in Greek [for the New Testament], has been so corrupted, either by the carelessness of copyists or by the malice of Jews and heretics, that it can no longer be held as the judge of controversies and the norm by which all versions without exception are to be judged. The papists affirm this; we deny it.[69]

Turretin accepts the legitimacy of a limited, inner-MT textual criticism that restores the perfection of the original text.

But there remains a problem. What if textual criticism does not always succeed in restoring the original text? What if one cannot determine whether a *waw* or a *yod* is correct in a given reading? Turretin gives no ground to this objection. For the orthodox, the text must be perfect, and therefore if errors exist, its perfect state *must* be restorable. God's providence is the causal nexus that ensures this end. But there remains a hint of anxiety in Turretin's emphatic response to this problem:

---

67. Turretin, *Doctrine*, 62–63 (§5.10).
68. Ibid., 140 (§12.8).
69. Ibid., 113–14 (§10.3).

> Unless unimpaired integrity is attributed to Scripture, it cannot be regarded as the sole rule of faith and practice, and a wide door is opened to atheists, libertines, enthusiasts, and others of that sort of profane people to undermine its authority and overthrow the foundation of salvation. Since error cannot be part of the faith, how can a Scripture which is weakened by contradictions and corruptions be regarded as authentic and divine? Nor should it be said that these corruptions are only in matters of little significance, which do not affect the fundamentals of faith. For as soon as the authenticity of Scripture has been found wanting, even if it be in a single corruption that cannot be corrected, how can our faith any longer be sustained? If corruption is conceded in matters of little importance, why not also in others of more significance?[70]

All error must be uprooted, else Scripture loses its "unimpaired integrity." Atheists and libertines are at the door, and not a single unremedied textual corruption can be conceded. Turretin's orthodoxy requires an inerrant text. If it cannot be achieved, then chaos ensues. In this weighty formulation of Reformed orthodoxy, textual criticism carries a heavy load. It must be hedged by divine providence in order to reproduce a perfect text.

Conclusions

The dream of a perfect text in the sixteenth and seventeenth centuries is a story worth telling—although I have only sketched the highlights— because the discipline of biblical scholarship still works largely within the conceptual space carved out by these controversies. In particular, the modern discipline of textual criticism and the orthodox Protestant doctrine of biblical inerrancy have a shared origin in early modern arguments about textual variants in the Hebrew Bible. Since then, textual criticism has become institutionalized as a (mostly) nontheological practice, and most theologians are unaware of its inner workings. Yet the empirical *realia* of texts and variants were once central in theological discourse, providing a fulcrum for deep rifts in early modern culture. These conceptual changes were long lived.

As Muller observes, approaches to the biblical text were affected by many factors, including the return to the sources (*ad fontes*) in Renaissance thought and the loss of the multiple figural senses of Scripture:

---

70. Ibid., 60 (§5.7).

The alteration of approach to the text brought on by the combination
of Renaissance and Reformation mastery of ancient languages with the
loss, over many centuries, of the *quadriga* [the four senses of Scripture]
and related "allegorical" patterns of exegesis, pressed hard against the
received doctrines.[71]

As a consequence of the loss of Scripture's figural senses, the orthodox
were hard-pressed to defend their traditional doctrines. The rise of a concept of uniform inerrancy of the plain sense was a response to these and
similar forces. As Cardinal Bellarmine asserted, biblical authority and
truth now extended across every verse, irrespective of its relation to faith
and morals. The Protestant orthodox seconded this doctrinal innovation.
Muller writes: "The orthodox response ... included the insistence that
'there is nothing in Holy Scripture of no importance' and that even in relatively minor details, the Holy Spirit had preserved his 'amenuenses' free
from error, leading them 'always and in all things ... into a most certain,
unfailing, and constant truth.'"[72]

This response was new to the Post-Tridentine era. It was not wholly
discontinuous with previous views, but was a heightening beyond the previous insistence on inerrancy in matters of faith and morals/mores. The
Catholic-Protestant controversy, based in part on the problem of textual
variants, yielded the high doctrine of biblical inerrancy. As Philip Benedict
sums up, "Controversy with Catholicism and the need to defend established positions had produced the doctrine of the literal inerrancy of the
biblical text."[73] Text-critical issues were at the center of these fraught discourses about the perfect text.

"Clearly," Muller observes, "certainty had to be grounded some-
where—and the options offered were the individual exegete, the church
and its tradition, and the Bible."[74] The assertion that the Bible is absolutely
inerrant in all details betrays the anxiety of the Protestant orthodox in
their desire for certainty. Their view of biblical authority—and of their
own authority—was threatened by the claims of textual critics and other
heretics. Their defensive response was to intensify the doctrine of *sola*

---

71. Muller, *Holy Scripture*, 523.

72. Ibid., 306, quoting Johannes Hoornbeeck.

73. Philip Benedict, *Christ's Churches Purely Reformed: A Social History of Calvinism* (New Haven: Yale University Press, 2002), 301.

74. Muller, *Holy Scripture*, 307.

scriptura such that every word, construed as a plain fact, and even every vowel point, must be immune from error.

Ironically, this position was mirrored by those on the opposite side of the theological spectrum. The freethinkers of the early Enlightenment turned the orthodox position into an argument *against* Christianity. If any detail in the Bible is in error, they argued, then the whole system fails. Jonathan Swift ridiculed this radical Enlightenment position in his 1708 pamphlet, *An Argument Against Abolishing Christianity*.[75] The following anecdote hinges on a textual variant in the New Testament, the Johannine Comma in 1 John 5:7–8, which is a late scribal insertion referring to the Trinity.[76] Swift writes:

> The freethinkers consider it [the Bible] as a sort of edifice, wherein all the parts have such a mutual dependence on each other, that, if you happen to pull out one single nail, the whole fabric must fall to the ground. This was happily expressed by him, who had heard of a text brought for proof of the Trinity, which in an ancient manuscript was differently read; he thereupon immediately took the hint, and, by a sudden deduction of a long *sorites* [a string of syllogisms], most logically concluded, Why, if it be as you say, I may safely whore and drink on, and defy the parson.[77]

This outcome is what the freethinkers hoped for and the orthodox feared. If the masses found errors in the Bible they would "defy the parson." But it is a ridiculous attitude in either case. The Bible is not a system of logical propositions, which is falsifiable by a single error. It is a different kind of book.

The dream of a perfect text is simply that, a dream. None of our texts are perfect, and textual criticism is not an inquiry that yields perfect results. It is a historical and philological discipline whose results are always

---

75. Jonathan Swift, *An Argument to Prove that the Abolishing of Christianity in England May, as Things Now Stand, be Attended with Some Inconveniences, and Perhaps Not Produce Those Many Good Effects Proposed Thereby* (1708), in *The Works of Dr. Jonathan Swift* (Edinburgh: Donaldson, 1774), 1:225–41.

76. See Bruce M. Metzger and Bart D. Ehrman, *The Text of the New Testament: Its Transmission, Corruption, and Restoration*, 4th ed. (New York: Oxford University Press, 2005), 148: "The *Comma* probably originated as a piece of allegorical exegesis of the three witnesses [spirit, water, and blood] and may have been written as a marginal gloss in a Latin manuscript of 1 John, whence it was taken into the text of the Old Latin Bible during the fifth century."

77. Swift, *Argument*, 239–40.

corrigible, subject to refinement and further argument and analysis. This is why critical editions need to be redone periodically. Our techniques do not guarantee perfection, only probable or warranted arguments. At the risk of stating the obvious, it is not superintended by divine providence. Cappel's position, that textual criticism is a human enterprise based on reason and scholarship, weathered the orthodox attempt (by Turretin and others) to subordinate it to a theological standard of perfection.

Textual critics do what we can, but it is wrong to expect or demand a perfect text. If a doctrine of biblical inerrancy requires a perfect text, then this requirement cannot be met by textual critics or a modern critical edition. We live in a world where perfection is a passing dream, and uncertainty—Heisenbergian or otherwise—is our epistemic condition. This is not a negative, since perfection is arguably boring. In textual criticism as in life, as Wallace Stevens writes, "the imperfect is our paradise."[78]

---

78. Wallace Stevens, "The Poems of Our Climate," in *The Palm at the End of the Mind: Selected Poems and a Play*, ed. Holly Stevens (New York: Vintage, 1972), 158.

THE UNTIMELINESS OF BIBLICAL PHILOLOGY

A little more philology, a little more knowledge, a little more lack of knowledge, are not impossible wishes.
—Julius Wellhausen, in Friedrich Bleek, *Einleitung in das Alte Testament*

In the second of his *Untimely Observations* (*Unzeitgemässe Betrachtungen*), Friedrich Nietzsche, a professor of classical philology at Basel, called for a new kind of philology, one that disturbs contemporary culture: "I do not know what meaning classical philology would have for our age if not to have an untimely effect within it, that is, to act against the age and so have an effect on the age to the advantage, it is to be hoped, of a coming age."[1] Nietzsche practiced this kind of philology: painstakingly close readings of the meaning and internal contradictions of European culture and thought. However, as his fellow classicist Ulrich Wilamowitz vigorously noted, Nieztsche's "future philology" was far from the canons of academic discourse.[2] While classical philology as such has rarely been untimely since Nietzsche, I wish to make the case that biblical philology has consistently been so, since at least the Renaissance, often despite the explicit

---

1. Friedrich Nietzsche, *On the Advantage and Disadvantage of History for Life*, trans. Peter Preus (Indianapolis: Hackett, 1980), 8; Nietzsche, *Unzeitgemässe Betrachtungen, Zweites Stück: Vom Nutzen und Nachteil der Historie für das Leben* (Leipzig: Fritzsch, 1874), vi: "Ich wüsste nicht, was die classische Philologie in unserer Zeit für einen Sinn hätte, wenn nicht den, in ihr unzeitgemäss—das heisst gegen die Zeit und dadurch auf die Zeit und hoffentlich zu Gunsten einer kommenden Zeit—zu wirken."
2. Ulrich von Wilamowitz-Moellendorff, "Future Philology!" trans. Gertrude Postl, Babette Babich, and Holger Schmid, *New Nietzsche Studies* 4 (2000): 1–33. See further, James I. Porter, *Nietzsche and the Philology of the Future* (Stanford: Stanford University Press, 2000), 1–31; and Sheldon Pollack, "Future Philology: The Fate of a Soft Science in a Hard World," *CrInq* 35 (2009): 931–61.

intentions of its practitioners. There is something about biblical philology that is disruptive, that acts "against the age" (*gegen die Zeit*), even when it addresses the most banal of textual details, such as small scribal errors like dittography or haplography.

The disruptive power of such details is emphatically voiced in rabbinic literature, as when a young scribe meets Rabbi Ishmael (b. ʿErub. 13a):

> When I came to Rabbi Ishmael, he said to me, "My son, what is your occupation"? I said to him, "I am a copyist." He said to me, "My son, be careful in your work, for your work is heaven's work; for should you omit one letter or add one letter, you will destroy the entire universe."

Such consequences—even if only imagined or exaggerated—indicate the potentially disruptive power of biblical philology, even in the precincts of textual criticism, in which diagnosing scribal errors is normal practice. When trafficking with a textually-based regime of knowledge, philology can be most untimely. As the following examples will illustrate, biblical philology can raise epistemic doubts and disrupt networks of authority. These effects are often marked, as we will see, by accusations of hubris and heresy.

The work of textual criticism has a tendency to open new vistas by disrupting the *doxa* of everyday knowledge, the tacit "consensus on the sense of the world," in Pierre Bourdieu's formulation.[3] These disruptive effects often set into motion the discourses of heterodoxy and orthodoxy, which reinforce each other by their contesting claims. This dialectic of disturbed (and hence focalized) *doxa* and consequent conflicts of heterodoxy and orthodoxy surrounds the practice of biblical philology in the modern era, even when its practitioners are innocent of such intentions. The work of biblical philology entails, to echo Jeremiah and Ecclesiastes, a tearing down and a building up. Given the status of the Bible in western culture, the untimeliness of this dialectic is perhaps inevitable.

My brief genealogy of the disruptive effects of biblical philology begins with Erasmus's 1516 edition of the New Testament, continues with Louis Cappel's establishment of the discipline of textual criticism of the Hebrew Bible, and ends with controversies about the HBCE project. In the *longue durée* of biblical scholarship, the making of critical editions is an untimely

---

3. Pierre Bourdieu, *Outline of a Theory of Practice*, trans. Richard Nice, CSSA 16 (Cambridge: Cambridge University Press, 1977), 167.

act, bordered with imagined and real fears. In tracing the untimeliness of these philological works, I hope to contribute to Nietzsche's call to "pose philology itself as a problem,"[4] and to promote a philological practice that is self-reflective and aware of its own contradictions.

THE NEW INSTRUMENT

In 1516 Erasmus published the first critical edition of the Greek New Testament, titled *Novum Instrumentum* ("The New Instrument").[5] The Greek text was accompanied by a Latin translation that differed in many details from the Vulgate, which at this time was a more or less corrupted version of Jerome's fourth-century translation. The variants from the Vulgate caused much furor. Among the readings omitted by Erasmus from his critical text and translation were a verse from the Epistle of John (1 John 5:7) that is the sole New Testament attestation of the Trinity, and a sentence in Matt 6:13 that is the conclusion of the Lord's Prayer ("For thine is the kingdom, and the power, and the glory, forever. Amen."). These missing verses, along with other less sensational differences, raised controversy. Popular preachers and learned theologians accused Erasmus of heresy; some likened him to the antichrist.[6]

Prior to publication, Erasmus's friend Martin van Dorp cautioned him, "My dear Erasmus, much evil could come of this! Many people will begin to discuss the integrity of the text of the Sacred Scriptures, and many will begin to doubt even if only a small part appears to be false."[7] Here is the fingerprint of biblical philology's untimeliness: it disturbs

---

4. Friedrich Nietzsche, *Wir Philologen* (an unpublished section of *Unzeitgemässe Betrachtungen*); see *Unmodern Observations,* trans. William Arrowsmith (New Haven: Yale University Press, 1990), 372; Nietzsche, *Digitale Kritische Gesamtausgabe: Werke und Briefe,* http://tinyurl.com/SBL7010f: "stellen … die Philologie als Problem hin." See also Pollack, "Future Philology," 937.

5. Erasmus, *Novum Instrumentum* (Basel, Froben, 1516). See Jerry H. Bentley, *Humanists and Holy Writ: New Testament Scholarship in the Renaissance* (Princeton: Princeton University Press, 1983), 112–93.

6. Erika Rummel, *Erasmus and His Catholic Critics,* BHRef 45 (Nieuwkoop: de Graaf, 1989), 1:117, 128, 137.

7. Trans. Cecilia Asso, "Martin Dorp and Edward Lee," in *Biblical Humanism and Scholasticism in the Age of Erasmus,* ed. Erika Rummel, BCCT 9 (Leiden: Brill, 2008), 172; *Opus Epistolarum Des. Erasmi Roterodami,* vol. 2, *1514–1517,* ed. Percy S. Allen (Oxford: Clarendon, 1910), 15 (Ep. 304, 1514): "Officiet mehercle, Erasme. Nam de

unquestioned *doxa*, such as the integrity—and by extension, the author-ity—of the biblical text. "Even if only a small part" is in question, the fact of raising this issue to popular consciousness is a clear danger: "many people will begin to discuss ... and many will begin to doubt." The unset-tling of biblical *doxa* and the ensuing critical discourse lead to hetero-doxy. Philology, whether intentionally or not, disrupts the unquestioned habits of Christian faith.

Dorp also rightly asserted that Erasmus's philological method under-mines the institutional authority of the church theologians. As Cecilia Asso observes:

> This is the substance of Dorp's accusation: You have ridiculed the theo-logical profession as a whole, denigrating them and lowering their prestige in the eyes of the people, and now you take on a task which is traditionally theirs. Would that not indicate that you desire to eliminate their *raison d'être*?[8]

The interpretation of Scripture was the theologians' domain. Now a mere philologist was usurping their authority. This, Dorp cautioned, was an obvious danger to the church.

Erasmus was not shy about asserting his philological claim to author-ity in the domain of biblical interpretation against the scholastic theo-logians. The preface to the *Novum Instrumentum* included a section on method, *Methodus Verae Theologiae* ("The Method of True Theology"). In it he made clear that philology undercuts the authority of the theologians. Philology, he argued, offered the only reliable avenue to biblical truth. The prerequisite was not institutional authority but linguistic facility, which excluded virtually all the professional theologians of his time:

> The first concern must be the thorough learning of the three languages, Latin, Greek and Hebrew, because it is agreed that all the mystery of scripture is made known by them.... I do not think that these men deserve attention who, while they rot in sophistical trifles until senility are accustomed to say, "Jerome's translation is enough for me."... Those who have invested a good part of their life in Bartolus, Averroes, Aris-

---

sacrarum litterarum integritate disputabunt plurimi, ambigent multi, si vel tantillum in iis esse falsi."

8. Asso, "Dorp," 171.

totle and the Sophistical cavilings do not savor the divine letters as they really are but only as they think they are.[9]

These remarks on method are addressed to "the future theologian"—they clearly exclude the current crop of theologians who "rot in sophistical trifles until senility." Erasmus contrasts the true path to knowledge of Scripture, which is linguistic and philological, with the false path, which is the delusive sophistry of the theologians. Erasmus was not trying to convince contemporary theologians of the value of philology; he was trying to bury them. He aimed to plant the seed for a philologically literate Christianity.

As Asso emphasizes, Dorp's criticism of Erasmus highlights "the essence of Erasmus' religious work: he sought to define a new type of theology and a new type of theologian."[10] The new theology was one that grants and incorporates philology's claim to be the preliminary method for interpreting Scripture.

The establishment theologians were scandalized. They derided Erasmus as a mere *grammaticus*, who had no business making biblical editions and translations. The reactions of theologians associated with the University of Paris were particularly fierce. In 1525 Pierre Cousturier (Petrus Sutor) published a book castigating Erasmus, *De Tralatione Bibliae et Novarum Reprobatione Interpretationum* ("On Translation of the Bible and Rejection of New Interpretations"). He insisted that philological knowledge was unnecessary, since God has preserved the original texts and translations intact:

> We do not need a knowledge of foreign languages for an understanding of Holy Writ and for this reason it is vain and frivolous to spend time on learning them. Nor is it necessary to learn them for the purpose of producing a new translation of Scripture, for the Vulgate translation is quite

---

9. Trans. by Alan K. Jenkins and Patrick Preston, *Biblical Scholarship and the Church: A Sixteenth Century Crisis of Authority* (Aldershot: Ashgate, 2007), 250, 253; Erasmus, *Novum Instrumentum*: "Prima cura debetur, per discendis tribus linguis, latinae, graecae, hebraicae, quod constet omnem scripturam mysticam hisce proditam esse.... Nequem audiendos arbitror, istos quosdam, qui cum in sophisticis tricis, useque ad decrepitam aetatem computrescant, dicere solent, Mihi satis est interpretatio Hieronymi.... Ita qui bonam vitae partem, in Bartholo, in Averroe, in Aristotele, in Sophisticis cauillationibus posuerunt ijs divinae literae non sapiunt id quod sunt, sed quod illi secum ad ferunt."

10. Asso, "Dorp," 171.

sufficient.... It is completely insane and smacks of heresy for anyone to affirm that one should sweat over foreign languages for this purpose.[11]

The vehemence of this critique of biblical philology is a symptom of *doxa* disrupted.

In the following year the theologian Nöel Beda published his *Annotations* against Erasmus, decrying Erasmus and his fellow "theologizing humanists" as heretics

> who have undertaken to expound on all things holy, trained only in the aids of the humanities and languages ... with no small loss of souls. Indeed the illness is all the more incurable because these theologizing humanists ... spurn the healers of this type of disease, namely the teachers of Holy Scripture, as if they were utterly unskilled in their own art, inasmuch as they preach that the scholastics spend their whole lives on philosophical trifles and a tangled mess of pretentious arguments.[12]

Erasmus, in his sharp reply, *Notatiunculae quaedam Extemporales ad Naenias Bedaicas* ("Some Little Notes against the Trifling Ditties of Beda," 1529), characterized Beda as "the most stupid of bipeds" and declared, "Far be it from me to worry about a hot-headed monster that is also impotent, stupid, doting, and out of his mind."[13] Philology's defender had

---

11. Trans. Erika Rummel, *Humanist-Scholastic Debate in the Renaissance and Reformation*, HHS 120 (Cambridge: Harvard University Press, 1995), 113; Cousturier, *De Tralatione Bibliae et Novarum Reprobatione Interpretationum* (Paris: Petit, 1525), 63: "Pro intelligendis sacris scripturis nihil nunc opus esse peregrinarum linguarum cognitione, eamque obrem cassum ac frivolum esse in eis propterea discendis operam sumere.... Conficiamus denique insanum penitus esse heresim que redoler, si in ipsis linguis peregrinis ad eum finem discendis quisquam desudandum affirmarit."

12. Trans. Mark Crane, "A Scholastic Response to Biblical Humanism: Nöel Beda against Lefèvre d'Etaples and Erasmus (1526)," *HumLov* 59 (2010): 62–63: "qui solis humanitatis ac linguarum praesidiis instruci, sacra omnia edisserere sunt aggressi ... in non parvam animarum iacturam maiores semper vires suscipere, et eo quidem incurabilius, quo eiusmodi aegritudinum medicos—id est Sacrarum literarum professores—, isti humanistae theologizantes ... velut suae artis plane imperitos aspernarentur, utpote quos praedicant in solis philosophicis ac argumentorum sophismatumque tricis consenescere."

13. Trans. James K. Farge, "Nöel Beda and the Defense of the Tradition," in Rummel, *Biblical Humanism*, 160; Erasmus, *Opera Omnia*, ed. Jean Le Clerc (Leiden: van der Aa, 1703–1706), 9:717: "bipedum stupidissimus"; 9:718: "Sed absit, ut ego propter unum portentum, cerebrosum, impotens, stupidum, delirum ac demens."

a wicked pen, not unlike his nineteenth century heirs (e.g., Wilamowitz and Nietzsche). The intensity of the rhetoric indicates the high stakes in this debate. Who has true knowledge of Scripture? Who merits theological authority? The clash between philology and tradition involved a fundamental struggle over the prerogatives of knowledge and power.

It is fair to say that Erasmus—and humanist philology—won this debate. The "theologians of the future" had to learn some Latin, Greek, and Hebrew as a prerequisite to interpreting Scripture. But it is also fair to say that the philological critique of church practice—that linguistic facility trumps theological system—fueled heterodoxy and dissent. Another critic of Erasmus, Edward Lee, predicted "tumults, factions, quarrels, and tempests" because of Erasmus's edition of the New Testament.[14] A century of sectarian schism and religious war did indeed ensue. This was not the fault of philology, yet philology was not wholly innocent in the chaos unleashed on the world.[15]

SACRED CRITICISM

In 1650 Louis Cappel published his *Critica Sacra* ("Sacred Criticism"), which established on a sound philological basis the principles and procedures of textual criticism of the Hebrew Bible. The publication was literally untimely—it took sixteen years for Cappel to find a willing publisher for his theologically explosive work.[16] Cappel systematically analyzed all the extant texts and ancient versions and provided copious treatments of the

---

14. Edward Lee, *Annotationum Libri Duo, Alter in Annotationes Prioris Aeditionis Novi Testamenti Desiderij Erasmi, Alter in Annotationes Posterioris Aeditionis Eiusdem* (Paris: Gourmant, 1520), 128 (§25): "Quod si hic fiet: quid non sequet tumultuum: quid non factionum: quid non rixarum: quid non tempestatum?" See Roland H. Bainton, *Erasmus of Christendom* (New York: Scribner's Sons, 1969), 136–37.

15. On Erasmus's legacy among radical reformers, heretics, and freethinkers, see Peter G. Bietenholz, *Encounters with a Radical Erasmus: Erasmus' Work as a Source of Radical Thought in Early Modern Europe*, Erasmus Studies (Toronto: University of Toronto Press, 2009).

16. On the travails of Cappel's manuscript, see François Laplanche, *L'Écriture, le sacré et l'histoire: Érudits et politiques protestants devant la Bible en France au XVIIe siècle* (Amsterdam: Holland University Press, 1986), 224–29; and Peter T. Van Rooden, *Theology, Biblical Scholarship, and Rabbinical Studies in the Seventeenth Century: Constantijn L'Empereur (1591–1648), Professor of Hebrew and Theology at Leiden* (Leiden: Brill, 1989), 222–27.

causes and categories of scribal variants that had accumulated in the transmitted texts, including the Hebrew *textus receptus*, the MT. He concluded:

> According to the universal fate and condition of all books, because of human frailty in the transcription of copies, one after another in the long succession of centuries, by men subject to error and fault, a multiplicity of variant readings came into the extant Sacred Codices.[17]

To rectify this condition, Cappel proposed the production of a new edition of the Hebrew Bible, in which the MT is supplemented by a presentation of the best readings (including conjectures):

> In our day, taking note of the variant readings, we could expect and prepare a new and refined edition of the Old Testament, in which are presented the best readings (annotated in the outer margin or at the end of the individual chapters). [18]

Cappel was introducing a rigorous philological method—based on the advances of Scaliger and Causabon in Greek texts—into the study of the Hebrew Bible. Cappel, like Erasmus, did not seek the theologians' favor in his philological work. He insisted as a matter of principle: "we are not here contending with authority, but with reason."[19] Naturally, the orthodox scholars and theologians were furious.

In 1653 Johannes Buxtorf Jr. published his *Anticritica*, which, as the subtitle says, is a "Vindication of the Hebrew Truth" (*Vindiciae Veritatis Hebraicae*). In the foreword, he informs his discerning readers that he has "prepared a health-giving antidote against the most pestilent poison handed to less cautious and resolute readers."[20] *Anticritica* is the cure for

---

17. Cappel, *Critica Sacra, sive de Variis quae in Sacris Veteris Testamenti Libris Occurrunt Lectionibus Libri Sex* (Paris: Cramoisy, 1650; repr., Halle: Hendel, 1775), 384: "Sed (quae fuit omnium omnino in universum librorum sors & conditio) humana fragilitate in transcriptione tot exemplariorum, quae alia ex aliis, tam longo tot saeculorum curriculo, descripta sunt ab hominibus errori & lapsui obnoxiis, irrespsisse in Sacros Codices, qui iam exstant."

18. Ibid., 434: "Ex eadem hac nostra de variis lectionibus obseruatione sperari & adornari posset noua & exquisita Vetus Testamenti editio arque Versio, in quam conferrentur optimae quaeque lectiones (ad marginem e regione, vel in singulorium Capitum calce, annotatae)."

19. Ibid., 396: "Non enim hic auctoritate sed ratione pugnamus."

20. Trans. John Sandys-Wunsch, *What Have They Done to the Bible? A History of*

Cappel's noxious *Critica*. Buxtorf held there were no errors in the *textus receptus* of the Hebrew Bible: "The current Hebrew text is pure and uncorrupt."[21] The defense of Scripture's perfection was necessary, in the view of orthodox Protestant scholars and theologians, to support their doctrine of *sola scriptura*.[22] The authority of Scripture—and the authority of orthodoxy—were at stake.

Buxtorf made some apt criticisms of individual analyses, but he evidently failed in administering the full antidote. In the prolegomena to the London Polyglot of 1657, Brian Walton adopted Cappel's method, as did virtually all subsequent textual critics of the Hebrew Bible. Cappel's philology became normal practice in Hebrew Bible scholarship.

Cappel attempted to defuse the orthodox rejection of his critical philology by pointing to the illogic in their defense of the textual perfection of Scripture. Variant readings are demonstrable in the texts, and there are obvious scribal errors in the Hebrew *textus receptus*; hence the authority of Scripture should be defended in such a way as to allow for these facts. Cappel was a progressive Calvinist who saw no conflict between philology and theology. Both, in his view, should be informed by reason. He defended his philology accordingly:

> Away with this unsafe, slippery, and dangerous opinion that the entire authority of the word of God and the sacred text will be endangered and destroyed if it is conceded that various and multiple readings have crept into it in the course of time, by the fault and carelessness of copyists. For when that is proposed and accepted, the entire authority of God's word is overturned and plainly falls down, for it is easy and obvious to demonstrate those various and multiple readings, as I have done and will do further.[23]

Modern Biblical Interpretation (Collegeville, MN: Liturgical Press, 2005), 92; Johannes Buxtorf Jr., *Anticritica: Seu Vindiciae Veritatis Hebraicae* (Basel: Regis, 1653), [*Dedicatio*], 9: "Contra pestilentissimum Venenum, poculo aureo Lectoribus minus cautis & confirmatis propinatum, Antidotum salutare præparandum."

21. Ibid., 28: "Hodiernum textum Hebraeum esse purum & incorruptum."

22. A distinctive feature of this doctrine as it evolved in the heat of these controversies was the high orthodox view of biblical inerrancy, as Buxtorf exemplifies (ibid., 911): "Omnia etiam minima verba, scripserint ex pari Spiritus Sancti illuminatione et infallibilate" ("Everything, even the smallest of the words, [were] written under the equal illumination and infallibility of the Holy Spirit"); see Laplanche, *L'Écriture*, 311; and above, ch. 11.

23. Cappel, *Critica Sacra*, 301: "Facessat ergo non satis tuta, nimisque lubrica

Orthodox theologians were not swayed. John Owen, a Puritan divine, vigorously contested these claims of philology:

> Lay but these two principles together, namely, that the points are a late invention of some Judaical Rabbins (on which account there is no reason in the world that we should be bound unto them), and that it is lawful to gather various lections by the help of translations ... and for my part I must needs cry out δός ποῦ στῶ ["Give (me) a place to stand"] as not seeing any means of being delivered from utter uncertainty in and about all sacred truth.... By the subtlety of Satan, there are principles crept in even amongst Protestants, undermining the authority of the Hebrew verity.[24]

Owen spoke for many in seeking a "place to stand" as a pious Christian if the textual foundation of scriptural religion was unstable. The orthodox Calvinist theologians of Switzerland made a last stand against Cappel's heresy in a short-lived doctrinal confession, the Helvetic Consensus Formula of 1675. In it they denounced Cappel's philology:

> The Hebrew original of the Old Testament which we have received and to this day do retain as handed down by the Hebrew Church ... is, not only in its consonants, but in its vowels ... not only in its matter, but in its words, inspired by God.... Therefore, we are not able to approve of the opinion of those who believe that the text which the Hebrew original exhibits was determined by man's will alone, and do not hesitate at all to remodel a Hebrew reading which they consider unsuitable, and amend it from the versions of the LXX and other Greek versions, the Samaritan Pentateuch, by the Chaldaic Targums, or even from other sources. They go even to the point of following the corrections that their own rational powers dictate from the various readings of the Hebrew original itself....

---

atque periculosa sententia, Periclitari & concidere omnem verbi Dei & sacri textus auctoritatem, si concedatur in eum irrepsisse, lapsu temporis, & Descriptorum vitio atque incuria varias & multiplices lectiones, ea enim posita, atque recepta evertitur plane & concidit omnis verbi Dei auctoritas, facile enim & obvium est demonstrare varias illas & multiplices lectiones, quod hactenus fecimus, & porro in sequentibus facturi adhuc sumus."

24. John Owen, *Of the Divine Original, Authority, Self-Evidencing Light, and Power of the Scriptures* (Oxford: Hall, 1659) in *The Works of John Owen*, ed. Thomas Russell (London: Baynes, 1826), 4:383–85.

They thus bring the foundation of our faith and its sacred authority into perilous danger.[25]

Cappel's textual criticism endangered "the foundations of our faith" by raising doubts about the textual perfection of Scripture and by substituting the philologists' "own rational powers" for the authority of the church. This is an institutional and epistemological conflict, based on how one knows about Scripture and who is qualified to produce such knowledge. Power and knowledge are intertwined in the disruptive claims of philology.

The Helvetic Consensus collapsed after a few years. Many theologians refused to sign on, considering it overreach to prescribe such a detailed reactionary position. But the antipathy to biblical philology among the orthodox did not disappear. The rise of Protestant fundamentalism in the late nineteenth century has roots in the doctrines and controversies over Cappel's textual criticism. As church historian Richard Muller observes:

> The level of dogmatic detail [in the Helvetic Consensus Formula] manifests, if nothing else, the profound trauma experienced by the orthodox theories of the inspiration, interpretation, and authority of Scripture in the face of a rising tide of textual and historical criticism of the Bible.[26]

The rising tide of biblical philology came to a crest in nineteenth-century German biblical scholarship, which in turn led to the rise of modern fundamentalism. Philology was a proximate cause of fundamentalism—along with other surprises from geology and biology. Philology is not wholly culpable for fundamentalism, but it was the chief irritant that caused it to crystallize. Biblical philology gave rise to both theological liberalism and fundamentalism, the two alter egos of modernity. Like Jacob and Esau, they are twins from the same mother, perpetually contesting each other for authority.

---

25. Trans. Martin I. Klauber, "The Helvetic Formula Consensus (1675): An Introduction and Translation," *TJ* 11 (1990): 115–16.

26. Richard A. Muller, *Holy Scripture; The Cognitive Foundation of Theology*, vol 2 of *Post-Reformation Reformed Dogmatics*, 2nd ed. (Grand Rapids: Baker, 2003), 92.

PHILOLOGY OF THE PRESENT

In 1871 Julius Wellhausen introduced his monograph, *Der Text der Bücher Samuelis untersucht*, with this statement: "In this book I want to make a contribution to a future edition of the Old Testament."[27] By this he meant an eclectic edition, which had not been attempted previously. The great Semitist, Theodor Nöldeke, responded in a review of Wellhausen's book with vigorous opposition to this goal:

> It is unfortunate that even in this book the critic proceeds in an absolutely eclectic fashion, so that the decision between two readings often wholly depends on subjective judgment.... I hope that no one will be tempted thereby to put his or anyone else's corrected readings into an edition of the Hebrew text.... I even think that a Hebrew edition of the Old Testament should never go beyond the Masoretic text. Because, after all, this is a text that once actually had to be reckoned with.[28]

Unlike the opposition to Erasmus or Cappel, Nöldeke's reservations were not theological but historical. The Masoretic text existed as a positive fact, whereas an eclectic text, constructed by means of "subjective judgment" would arguably lack historical authenticity. If any of its constitutive readings were incorrect, the whole enterprise would collapse. This is, in some respects, a secularization of the earlier theological objections to biblical philology. Nöldeke concludes with a visceral response: the project "provokes a gentle shudder in my philological sensibility."[29]

Nöldeke's shudder indicates the untimeliness of Wellhausen's philology. There is no cry of theological heresy, but rather philological hubris. The standard of orthodoxy has been replaced by historicity. If a critical text were not demonstrably historical, if the restored readings did not coexist simultaneously in a past manuscript, then the result would be a chimera (or another fictional monster), an affront to philology. What Nöldeke was not willing to grant, in the heyday of historicism, was that all historical scholarship, including textual criticism, entails subjective judgments. It is a probabilistic enterprise, not an objective procedure. This is why it is

---

27. Julius Wellhausen, *Der Text der Bücher Samuelis untersucht* (Göttingen: Vandenhoeck & Ruprecht, 1871), iii.

28. Theodor Nöldeke, review of *Der Text der Bücher Samuelis untersucht*, by Julius Wellhausen, *ZWT* (1873): 118.

29. Ibid.

called "criticism," κριτική. As E. J. Kenney states: "There is no escape from *ratio et res ipsa* ["reason and the case itself"], from the commitment of the critic to do what his name implies—to judge, to decide, to discriminate."[30] Nöldeke's shudder reveals, I submit, an unphilological sensibility, one that holds a commitment to positivism and objectivity that no historical inquiry can sustain. Textual criticism entails the possibility of failure, as do all our scholarly labors. To expect certainty is arguably a theological criterion, transposed into the language of historicism. In his classic essay on the method of textual criticism, Paul Maas rightly states, "Anyone who is afraid of … an uncertain text had best confine himself to dealing with autograph manuscripts."[31]

Despite its internal contradictions, Nöldeke's dictum, that one should not depart from the Masoretic Text in a critical edition of the Hebrew Bible, held sway for a century. The kind of text-critical work advocated by Wellhausen continued in articles, monographs, and critical commentaries, but the major critical editions were diplomatic presentations of the MT, with variants presented in the margins, as Cappel had called for in 1650.

When I proposed the creation of a critical eclectic edition of the Hebrew Bible at a conference in 1997, the reaction was mixed. The distinguished editor of the Hebrew University Bible Project, Shemaryahu Talmon, told me unequivocally, "This must not be done." When I asked why, he responded, with a slight increase in volume, "This must not be done." My proposal was, it seems, untimely.

Talmon's response was, at least in part, impelled by his reverence for the Hebrew *textus receptus*. He regarded the early (or proto-)Masoretic text as the product of "normative Judaism" of the pre-70 CE period, which was promulgated to unite Jews after the destruction of Jerusalem. He writes: "In the wake of these events, it became imperative to propagate a uniform version of the biblical books which would be accepted and hallowed by all Jews, in Palestine as well as in the Diaspora, and would serve as a unifying factory of Jewry."[32] The belief that the *textus receptus* unified

---

30. E. J. Kenney, *The Classical Text: Aspects of Editing in the Age of the Printed Book*, SCL 44 (Berkeley: University of California Press, 1974), 136 (invoking Richard Bentley).

31. Paul Maas, *Textual Criticism*, trans. Barbara Flower (Oxford: Clarendon, 1958), 17.

32. Shemaryahu Talmon, "The Transmission History of the Text of the Hebrew Bible in the Light of Biblical Manuscripts from Qumran and Other Sites in the Judean

Judaism in antiquity—whether or not this is historically credible—illuminates Talmon's, "No." An eclectic critical edition, not bound to the *textus receptus*, represents a return to chaos, an undoing of the unifying legacy of normative Judaism. Talmon adds the weight of Jewish tradition to Nöldeke's philological shudder.

But normativity is a theological criterion, not a philological one. For textual criticism it is a matter of indifference if particular, more or less corrupt, versions of a work were declared authoritative by religious authorities (cf. above on the authority of the Vulgate in Western Christianity). As Cappel insisted in his *Critica Sacra*, "we are not here contending with authority, but with reason." Biblical philology disturbs the authority of the *textus receptus*—and its attending theological and textual guardians—precisely because they are irrelevant to its operations. This elicits shudders of various intensities.

After my rationale for a new edition of the Hebrew Bible (now called The Hebrew Bible: A Critical Edition) was published, a harsh critique appeared by another distinguished scholar, Hugh Williamson, then Regius Professor of Hebrew at Oxford.[33] I have responded to Williamson's substantive criticisms elsewhere, some of which are well-founded and others less so.[34] My interest here is the emotional tone of his response, which further illustrates the untimeliness of this philological project. He decries an eclectic edition of the Hebrew Bible as "hazardously hypothetical" and "misguided." He argues that it is "not a Bible" because it would not be "regarded as scriptural" by any believing community. The inclusion of certain textual details "shows a sorry lack of understanding." He concludes, "I regret its adoption as a purported Bible text."[35] To the question in his article's title, "Do We Need a New Bible?" his answer is emphatically no. Nonetheless, he admits some professional curiosity: "I am intrigued to see what our learned colleagues will produce from a narrowly academic point of view."[36]

Desert," in *The Dead Sea Scrolls: Fifty Years after Their Discovery*, ed. Lawrence H. Schiffman, Emanuel Tov, and James C. VanderKam (Jerusalem: Israel Exploration Society, 2000), 42.

33. H. G. M. Williamson, "Do We Need a New Bible? Reflections on the Proposed Oxford Hebrew Bible," *Bib* 90 (2009): 153–75.

34. See above, chs. 1–2.

35. Williamson, "Reflections," 169, 174–75.

36. Ibid., 170.

The tone of Williamson's critique, it seems to me, is illuminated by the phrase, "from a narrowly academic point of view." As a philologist, Williamson is naturally interested in—and quite adept at—textual criticism. His objection is not to philology as such, which he practices in his critical commentaries, articles, and monographs. The vehemence stems from his convictions outside of "a narrowly academic point of view." I am not certain what those convictions are, but they seem to involve shielding the masses from the perils of philology. Williamson warns that the edition will not be well-received by "some who may be wedded to a conservative textual approach for religious or other reasons."[37] This recalls Dorp's caution to Erasmus, "Many people will begin to discuss the integrity of the text of the Sacred Scriptures, and many will begin to doubt." Philology is best done discreetly, limited to specialist literature and dusty library stacks. Otherwise it will disrupt the slumber of the faithful. Biblical philology, it seems, remains untimely in the present age.

Conclusion: After Philology?

As these examples show—from Erasmus's edition of the New Testament to the new edition of the Hebrew Bible—biblical philology is untimely. It goes against the grain of habitual and unexamined *doxa*; it brings to thought what usually goes without thinking. As E. A. Housman bitingly observes of lazy text-critical habits, "thought is irksome and three minutes is a long time."[38] Biblical philology makes people think hard thoughts for a long time. This makes it most untimely.

In part because of its untimeliness, biblical philology is becoming an endangered species within the field of biblical studies. This follows a wider trend across the humanities, as Sheldon Pollack has eloquently lamented.[39] Most graduate programs in Hebrew Bible do not teach textual criticism and ancillary philological topics. They are becoming rare arts. Moreover, the loss is often celebrated. A bias against philology is a concomitant of many of the new approaches in biblical scholarship in recent decades, which

---

37. Ibid.
38. A. E. Housman, "Preface to Juvenal" (1905), in *Selected Prose*, ed. John Carter (Cambridge: Cambridge University Press, 1961), 56.
39. Pollack, "Future Philology."

tend to be ideologically antihistoricist.[40] There is a lamentable tendency to proclaim new methods as supersessionist, as replacing older practices rather than complementing or complicating them. This claim reproduces the biblical rhetoric of supersessionism—where Judaism replaces Canaanite religion and, in the New Testament, Christianity replaces Judaism—and is therefore perhaps not surprising, since scholarship often mimics the discourse it studies. But it is a problem in a field that is shrinking in academia and needs to justify—to itself and others—its continued support and existence. The balkanization of biblical studies is a recipe for oblivion.

To take a perspicuous example, I recently read a postmodern critique of biblical textual criticism that claims it to be outdated because of its "ontology of presence." This is a common trope of postmodernism. Brennan Breed writes:

> Text criticism has a difficult time thinking of identity and difference because its logic, method and vocabulary derives from a metaphysical system that determines things in terms of presence. For instance, the term "variant" presupposes that there is some positive, present, and knowable constant from which one may measure deviance. By thinking in terms of differences, we can say that there is no positive, unified transcendental work by which one can measure variances in particular empirical manuscripts—because there are only variants.[41]

This is an interesting argument, but interestingly wrong in several ways. Let us do some philology. The noun clause, "a metaphysical system that determines things in terms of presence," is imprecise and possibly meaningless. The binary contrast of "presence" and "difference" to categorize how two distinctive ontologies "determine things" is breathtakingly vague, and arguably derives from a misapplication (or misyoking) of concepts from Saussurean linguistics and Heideggerian philosophy. The assertion that "there is no positive, unified, transcendental work by which one can measure variances" also combines several complicated topics

---

40. Note Porter's comment (*Philology*, 6): "Ahistoricity being, Nietzsche will hold, the form in which the present experiences its historicity."

41. Brennan W. Breed, *Nomadic Text: A Theory of Biblical Reception History*, ISBL (Bloomington: Indiana University Press, 2014), 71. Breed here develops the position of David J. A. Clines, "The Pyramid and the Net: The Postmodern Adventure in Biblical Studies," in *On the Way to the Postmodern: Old Testament Essays 1967–1998*. vol. 1, JSOTSup 292 (Sheffield: Sheffield Academic, 1998), 146–47.

into a uniform negation, which oversimplifies the conceptual issues and arguably denies the historicity of any text or work. In sum, these claims are cognitively weak or vacuous. They convey a postmodern *attitude*, not a warranted proposition. Like Noam Chomsky's famous sentence, "Colorless green ideas sleep furiously," the collocation of words, while grammatical (and perhaps even beautiful), is an infelicitous proposition.

Consider Breed's conclusion: "there is no reason to be call any version of a text corrupt."[42] As a philologist, I note that this sentence is marred by a scribal error: the word "be" is an excrescence. In other words, this text, which denies the possibility of corrupt texts, is a corrupt text. The textual error could be the result of an intentional authorial or editorial revision ("to be" partially replaced by "to call"), or it could be a random typo. Fortunately, this corrupt text is easily corrected. In fact, our normal linguistic competence leads us to correct it unconsciously. This linguistic tendency may be termed a "principle of charity" that facilitates communication.[43] It is an internal property of human communication. In other words, in our daily lives we are all textual critics, whether we know it or not. As Nietzsche wrote to his mother and sister, "We are all, for the most part, philologists."[44]

The postmodern critique of textual criticism undermines its own plausibility when subjected to careful philological analysis. There is much more to be said about the problems of "strong" postmodernism,[45] but it suffices here to observe that the text of this critique enacts a performative contradiction—a speech-act that contradicts its propositional content—which undermines the grounds of its own assertion. To put it differently, this critique of philology fails under the gaze of philological critique.

But there is a larger issue at play. The postmodern critique of textual criticism—based on the assertion that "there are only variants" and therefore "no original or final … form of a text but only differential

---

42. Breed, *Nomadic Text*, 67.

43. Variations of this principle are articulated by W. V. Quine, *Word and Object*, Studies in Communication (Cambridge: MIT Press, 1960), 59; and Donald Davidson, *Inquiries into Truth and Interpretation* (Oxford: Clarendon, 1984), 27, 136–37, 197–201.

44. Letter to Franziska and Elisabeth Nietzsche, October 24–25, 1864, in Nietzsche, *Gesamtausgabe*: "Wir sind alle zum grössten Theile Philologen."

45. See Ronald Hendel, "Mind the Gap: Modern and Postmodern in Biblical Studies," *JBL* 133 (2014): 422–43.

networks"[46]—relegates philology to a passing phase in the history of reading. This is part of an attempt to formulate a postmodern theory of biblical reception history. As Breed concludes, "everything is reception history."[47] But to lump together philology with other forms of reception in this fashion is mistaken, because philology has distinctive epistemological features that give it the capacity to be untimely. Classicist Margalit Finkelberg aptly articulates this point:

> A significant flaw in reception theory [is] its disregard for critical inquiry into the text as practiced by the scholar. The assumption which underlies this attitude is that scholarship is a variety of reception and is therefore subject to the same laws. Yet [this] … is patently wrong. In a sense, assuming that scholarship is indistinguishable from reception would be equivalent to assuming that there is no difference between the results of a physicist's or a biologist's research on natural phenomena and the way these phenomena appear to us in our everyday experience.… The scholar's way is not merely to adapt the text to its interpretive attitudes prevailing in their own time but to approach it analytically.[48]

It is this capacity to read texts and history analytically, and potentially against the age (*gegen die Zeit*), that allows philology to be, in Luciano Canfora's phrase, "the most subversive discipline."[49] The postmodern critique, since it abjures the analyticity of critical scholarship, arguably reduces itself to being a passing phase in the history of reception.

As the "old philologist" Nietzsche argued, philology is at its root "the art of reading well," the practice of which extends far beyond the reading of ancient texts. He writes:

> What is here meant by philology is, in a very broad sense, the art of reading well—of reading facts without falsifying them by interpretation, without losing caution, patience, delicacy, in the desire to understand. Philology as *ephexis* ["holding back, hesitating"] in interpretation—

---

46. Breed, *Nomadic Text*, 73.

47. Ibid., 115, and the book's subtitle, *A Theory of Biblical Reception History*.

48. Margalit Finkelberg, "The Original Versus the Received Text with Special Emphasis on the Case of the *Comma Johanneum*," *IJCT* 21 (2014): 196.

49. Luciano Canfora, *Filologia e libertà: La più eversiva delle discipline, l'indipendenza di pensiero e il diritto alla verità* (Milan: Mondadori, 2008).

whether it is a matter of books, the news in a paper, destinies, or weather conditions, not to mention "salvation of the soul."[50]

The patient, self-reflective practice of philology is, in Nietzsche's evaluation, the only reliable path to warranted knowledge, since it is inherently perspectival, viewing phenomena from multiple angles, weighing the merits of alternative interpretations. It involves "the ability to have one's For and Against *under control* and to engage and disengage them, so that one knows how to employ a *variety* of perspectives and affective interpretations in the service of knowledge."[51] The discipline of philology is, in essence, a development of our natural philological skills in interpreting— and surviving—the world.

I find the philologist Nietzsche to be a welcome corrective to the fuzzy thinking of postmodernism. This is, of course, ironic, since Nietzche (in another of his moods) is a hero of postmodernism. But throughout his oeuvre, Nietzsche extols the powers of philology. For instance, he praises the Greeks (with extravagant excess) over his contemporaries for their aptitude for philology:

> The great, the incomparable art of reading well had already been established.... The *sense for facts*, the last and most valuable of all the senses, had its schools and its tradition of centuries. Is this understood? Everything *essential* had been found, so that the work could be begun: the methods, one must say it ten times, *are* what is essential, also what is most difficult, also what is for the longest time opposed by habits and

---

50.Friedrich Nietzsche, *The Antichrist* §52; trans. Walter Kaufmann, *The Portable Nietzsche* (New York: Viking Press, 1968), 635; Nietzsche, *Gesamtausgabe*: "Unter Philologie soll hier, in einem sehr allgemeinen Sinne, die Kunst, gut zu lesen, verstanden werden,—Tatsachen ablesen können, ohne sie durch Interpretation zu fälschen, ohne im Verlangen nach Verständnis die Vorsicht, die Geduld, die Feinheit zu verlieren. Philologie als Ephexis in der Interpretation: handle es sich nun um Bücher, um Zeitungs-Neuigkeiten, um Schicksale oder Wetter-Tatsachen,—nicht zu reden vom 'Heil der Seele.'" Nietzsche refers to himself as "einem alten Philologen" ("an old philologist") in *Beyond Good and Evil* §22.

51. Nietzsche, *Genealogy of Morals* §3.12; trans. Cox, *Nietzsche*, 111–12; Nietzsche, *Gesamtausgabe*: "das Vermögen, sein Für und Wider *in der Gewalt zu haben* und aus- und einzuhängen: so dass man sich gerade die *Verschiedenheit* der Perspektiven und der Affekt-Interpretationen für die Erkenntniss nutzbar zu machen weiss" (emphasis original).

laziness ... the free eye before reality, the cautious hand, patience and seriousness in the smallest matters, the whole *integrity* of knowledge.[52]

This sense of genuine philology must be recovered in order to reverse the downward spiral of our humanistic disciplines. We must continue to be untimely, to work against the grain of our institutions and reclaim the *integrity* of knowledge, including especially the disruptive bits. We must use philology to solve the problem of philology and to elucidate the worth of future philology in our lives and intellectual disciplines.

---

52. Nietzsche, *Antichrist* §59; trans. Kaufman, *Portable Nietzsche*, 650; Nietzsche, *Gesamtausgabe*: "Man hatte die grosse, die unvergleichliche Kunst, gut zu lesen, bereits festgestellt ... der *Thatsachen-Sinn*, der letzte und werthvollste aller Sinne, hatte seine Schulen, seine bereits Jahrhunderte alte Tradition! Versteht man das? Alles *Wesentliche* war gefunden, um an die Arbeit gehn zu können:—die Methoden, man muss es zehnmal sagen, *sind* das Wesentliche, auch das Schwierigste, auch das, was am längsten die Gewohnheiten und Faulheiten gegen sich hat ... den freien Blick vor der Realität, die vorsichtige Hand, die Geduld und den Ernst im Kleinsten, die ganze *Rechtschaffenheit* der Erkenntniss" (emphasis original).

13
FROM POLYGLOT TO HYPERTEXT

A book is not an isolated thing: it is a relationship, an axis of innumerable relationships.
— Jorge Luis Borges, "A Note on (toward) Bernard Shaw"

The Hebrew Bible is a text that is not one. First, it is a library of books, as
the Greek τὰ βιβλία ("the books") announces. Second, for each book there
is a plurality of manuscripts and translations, which are related in a diz-
zyingly complex genealogical web. Part of the task of the biblical textual
critic is to explore this network of manuscripts and versions in order to
make sense of it, to historicize the relationships, and to uncover what we
can of each book's *historia textus*. This is an attempt to manage diversity,
to tame the sheer abundance of biblical texts. Yet while we seek to master
the plethora of manuscripts, we also savor their very unmanageability. The
textual critic's heart yearns for even more abundance and leaps at the discovery of new manuscripts. It does not matter whether they were molder-
ing in caves or a synagogue *genizah* or miscataloged in an air-conditioned
library. We crave new texts, even as they drive us to distraction. The super-
abundance of texts is our joy and our burden.

So we make editions of the Hebrew Bible. This is a way of taming
diversity, in which we attempt to make the relationships among the texts
intelligible and, to the extent possible, restore the earliest readings of each
book (including, ideally, the earliest inferable state of each edition of a
book). The idea of a critical edition of the Hebrew Bible has taken many
forms over the centuries, and it continues to evolve. In the following, I
explore the aims and intellectual context of the first modern critical edition, the Complutensian Polyglot (1514–1517), whose quincentennial

we celebrate, and latest one, the HBCE, whose first volume has recently appeared.[1] Given the passage of a half-millennium, it is illuminating to observe the points of convergence and divergence in the ways the two projects represent and manage diversity, both with respect to the plurality of the biblical text and the plural aims of a critical edition.

As we imagine the possibilities of the HBCE digital edition, we are in some respects returning to the Polyglot's strategic mobilization of a new technology—in its case, the printing press—in a novel representation of the biblical text. Digital technology raises the prospect of a new kind of polyglot, since it multiplies the possibilities of representing parallel and plural texts.[2] But while we are reviving the idea of a polyglot, our understanding of textual plurality contrasts markedly with the conceptual orientation of the Complutensian Polyglot. Our textual concepts have been thoroughly historicized, such that we now see an array of scribal and exegetical developments where the Polyglot's editors saw different manifestations of the *sensus plenior* and/or a clash between truth and heresy. The axis of relationships that constitutes the concept of textual plurality has shifted radically, even as we return to the question of how to present the plural forms of the biblical text. In the following I will trace some of changes and continuities between the mental landscapes of the Complutensian Polyglot and the HBCE hypertext, which will illuminate the shifts in textual scholarship over the last five hundred years, over the *longue durée* of modern textual scholarship.

The Complutensian Polyglot: A Cultural Polyphony

The diverse—and in part contradictory—aims of the Complutensian Polyglot are presented in two prologues, one addressed to the pope and the second to the reader.[3] The prologues were probably jointly written but are

---

1. Michael V. Fox, *Proverbs: An Eclectic Edition with Introduction and Textual Commentary*, HBCE 1 (Atlanta: SBL Press, 2015).

2. Emanuel Tov has long advocated the model of electronic parallel texts without a critical text or apparatus; see Tov, "Hebrew Scripture Editions: Philosophy and Praxis," in *Hebrew Bible, Greek Bible, and Qumran: Collected Essays*, TSAJ 121 (Tübingen: Mohr Siebeck, 2008), 268–69.

3. On the Polyglot and its texts, see Luis Alonso Schökel et al., *Anejo a la edición facsimile de la Biblia Políglota Complutense* (Valencia: Fundación Biblica Española/ Universidad Complutense de Madrid, 1987); for the intellectual context, see also Adrian Schenker, "The Polyglot Bible of Alcalá 1514–17," in *Hebrew Bible, Old Testa-*

signed by the founder and patron of the project, Francisco Jiménez de Cisneros, whose titles are listed proudly: "Cardinal Priest of St. Balbina of the
Holy Roman Church, Cardinal of Spain, Archbishop of Toledo, Archchan-
cellor of the Kingdom of Castille."[4] He was also the Inquisitor General,
but this title is not mentioned. The prologues are fascinating documents,
which mix a variety of motives for the production of the Polyglot.

The first prologue presents a series of characteristic ideas of Renaissance humanism. These include, in Felipe Fernández-Armesto's paraphrase, the following notions:

> Translation cannot express the full force of the original, especially in
> the case of the language which Christ actually spoke; the studious need
> to have the original documents to hand; one should drink from the
> fountainhead, not the rivulets, to assuage one's thirst for eternal life; in
> existing translations, *mendositas* ["error"] is found, though Jerome's is
> the best because of its accuracy and clarity; the text has to be redeemed
> from the confusion created by a large number of rival translations.[5]

All these points illustrate the Renaissance desire to return to the sources—
ad fontes.[6]

The production and publication of expertly edited Hebrew, Aramaic,
Greek, and Latin texts—including linguistic aids—contribute to the cardinal's pedagogical aim: "so that the hitherto dormant study of Holy Scripture may now at last begin to revive."[7] The revival of scriptural study was

---

ment: *The History of Its Interpretation*, ed. Magne Saebø (Göttingen: Vandenhoeck &
Ruprecht, 2008), 2:286–91; and Theodor W. Dunkelgrün, "The Multiplicity of Scrip-
ture: The Confluence of Textual Traditions in the Making of the Antwerp Polyglot
Bible (1568–1573)" (PhD diss., University of Chicago, 2012), 26–43.

4. *Biblia Polyglotta Complutensis*, 6 vols. (Alcalá de Henares: Brocar, 1514–1517),
vol. 1, 3a. Translations of the first prologue are adapted from John C. Olin, *Catholic
Reform: From Cardinal Ximenes to the Council of Trent, 1495–1563; An Essay with
Illustrative Documents and a Brief Study of St. Ignatius Loyola* (New York: Fordham
University Press, 1990), 61–64.

5. Felipe Fernández-Armesto, "Cardinal Cisneros as a Patron of Printing," in *God
and Man in Medieval Spain: Essays in Honour of J. R. L. Highfield*, ed. Derek W. Lomax
and David Mackenzie (Warminster: Aris & Phillips, 1989), 157.

6. Arjo Vanderjagt, "*Ad fontes!* The Early Humanist Concern for the *Hebraica
veritas*," in Sæbø, *Hebrew Bible*, 2:154–89.

7. *Biblia Polyglotta*: "incipient divinarum litterarum studia hactenus intermortua
nunc tandem reviviscere."

part of his general plan to reform the church. The Polyglot and the founding of the University of Alcalá (*Complutum* in Latin) were twin enterprises to this end, producing a more educated and more pious clergy and, ultimately, a purified Christendom.

Other points in the two prologues, as Fernández-Armesto observes, are "drawn from diverse traditions and sometimes seem to sit uneasily together."[8] These traditions reflect the esoteric side of the Renaissance, including kabbalistic speculation and mystical-ascetic devotion. The cardinal embraced both. He was an important supporter of the Spanish movement of spiritual asceticism, the *Alumbrados* ("Illuminati"), which included a dose of millenarian fervor.[9] In the first prologue, these esoteric practices are also enhanced by a return to the sources:

> From this source, those to whom it has been given "to behold the glory of the Lord with an unveiled face and thus be transformed into that very image" [2 Cor 3:18] can continually draw the marvelous secrets of his divinity. [mystical devotion][10]

> Indeed, there can be no diction and no combination of letters from which the most hidden meanings of heavenly wisdom do not emerge abundantly.[11] [kabbalah]

> The main part of interpretation depends on proper names, which are foreseen from eternity; they are of incredible help in revealing spiritual and abstruse meanings and uncovering arcane mysteries that the Holy Spirit has veiled under the shadow of the literal text.[12] [kabbalah]

---

8. Fernández-Armesto, "Cisneros," 158.

9. Marcel Bataillon, *Érasme et l'Espagne: Recherches sur l'histoire spirituelle du XVIe siècle* (Geneva: Droz, 1998; corrected repr. of 1937 ed.), 65–75.

10. *Biblia Polyglotta*, 3a: "unde hi quibius datum est revelata facie gloriam dei speculari: ut in eadem imaginem transformentur: possint assidue haurire mira divinitatis eius arcana."

11. Ibid.: "Quippe cum nulla diction nulla litterarum connexio esse possit: ex qua non emergant et veluti pullulent reconditissimi coelestis sapientiae sensus."

12. Ibid.: "huius praecipua pars ex propriorum nominum interpretation dependeat: quorum ab aeterno praevisa imposition incredibilem opem affert ad propalados spirituals abstrusos que sensus et detegenda arcana mysteria: quae sub ipso litteralis textus umbraculo spiritus sanctus velavit."

The mix of cryptic senses and spiritual discipline provide a rationale for the Polyglot beyond the imperatives of Renaissance philology. Mysticism fuses with humanism in Cisneros's polyglot.

Surprisingly, as scholars have noted, the second prologue contains a striking statement of antihumanism, asserting the ideology of late medieval scholasticism. In its explanation of the layout of the pages, the prologue defends the perfection of the Vulgate against the Scriptures of the Jews (the MT) and the Greek church (the LXX). The pages place the Latin in the central column, flanked by the Hebrew in the outside column and the Greek in the inside column:

> We have placed the Latin translation of the blessed Jerome as though between the Synagogue and the Eastern Church, placing them like the two thieves one on each side, and Jesus, that is the Roman or Latin Church, between them. This one alone is built on solid rock (whenever the others deviate from the true understanding of Scripture), and it always remains immovable in truth.[13]

This statement seems to undermine the previous rationales for the Polyglot, as if the non-Vulgate versions were criminals compared to Christ. This reflects the view that the Jews and Greeks deliberately altered—for reasons of malice or heresy—the true words of Scripture, which were preserved correctly by Jerome. If this were the case, then why include the Hebrew and Greek alongside the Vulgate? The moral and veridical contrast of versions directly contradicts the previously stated aims of the Polyglot.

In part, this internal contradiction reflects fissures among the editors and Cisneros's own ambivalence. Antonio de Nebrija, Spain's greatest scholar, had argued that the Latin should be corrected to the Hebrew or Greek where the "rivulet" diverged from its sources, but Cisneros forbade it. According to Nebrija, the cardinal said to him, "God forbid that I should

---

13. Translation adapted from Basil Hall, "Biblical Scholarship: Editions and Commentaries," in *The Cambridge History of the Bible*, vol. 3, *The West from the Reformation to the Present Day*, ed. Stanley L. Greenslade (Cambridge: Cambridge University Press, 1963), 51; *Biblia Polyglotta*, 3b: "Mediam autem inter has latinam beati Hieronymi translationem velut inter Synagogam et Orientalem Ecclesiam posuimus: tanque duos hinc et inde latrones medium autem Iesum hoc est Romanam sive latinam Ecclesiam collocantes. Haec enim sola supra firmam petram aedificata (reliquis a recta Scripturae intelligentia quamdoque deviantibus) immobilis semper in veritate permansit."

alter a word of the Blessed Jerome's."[14] Cisneros allowed the collation of different Vulgate manuscripts, but no further corrections of the Latin. This was a limited textual criticism, in which the Vulgate's authority was scrupulously policed. But why include the Greek or Hebrew at all, if they were thieves on either side of the Blessed Lord? How could the Hebrew text—collated from good Spanish manuscripts, which the cardinal acquired at great expense—be the *veritas*, as the prologue asserts, if only the Latin Vulgate is "immovable in truth"?

This contradiction exposes some of the cultural contradictions of the Polyglot project. The Polyglot was a Christian edition, authorized (belatedly in 1520) by the pope, but it incorporated texts preserved and transmitted in heretical communities—the Jews and the Greek church. The Polyglot's textual plurality carried with it the stain of heterodoxy from the infidels who transmitted the original sources. Seth Kimmel has argued that the denunciation of these textual communities was a tactic to appropriate the texts while distancing them from their heterodox contexts: "As the Latin Vulgate became just one in a series of available biblical texts … biblical scholars labored to distinguish the dangerous heresies of the Jews and schismatic early Christians from their useful Hebrew and Greek manuscripts."[15] The Polyglot goes back to the sources to purify the church, but purification comes at the risk of pollution, since the MT and the LXX belong to heretics and schismatics. By making these homologies and their moral relations explicit (Vulgate = Roman Church, MT = Jews, LXX = Eastern Church), the second prologue strategically distances the Polyglot from the heresies of Jews and Greeks.

This theological distancing prevents potential "leakage" of Jewish and Eastern texts onto the firm foundation of the Roman Church. But this strategic position is fraught with contradiction. The Polyglot's visual form does resemble Christ surrounded by thieves. But why should thieves have interlinear Latin translation and helpful marginal aids? The pages visually complicate this theological hierarchy and seem to present the three columns as a polyphony of biblical discourses, with the familiar Latin translation as a rivulet flowing alongside its sources.

---

14. Quoted in Fernández-Armesto, "Cisneros," 157. See also Carlos del Valle Rodríguez, "Antonio Nebrija's Biblical Scholarship," in *Biblical Humanism and Scholasticism in the Age of Erasmus*, ed. Erika Rummel, BCCT 9 (Leiden: Brill, 2008), 66–69.

15. Seth Kimmel, *Parables of Coercion: Conversion and Knowledge at the End of Islamic Spain* (Chicago: University of Chicago Press, 2015), 7.

The Council of Trent would later revisit these issues in its doctrinal affirmation of the Vulgate as the sole biblical authority (1546), by reason of its long use in the church. But, as the Polyglot and its successors illustrate, this defense was weakened from within, as the perception of textual diversity undermined the adamantine authority of the Vulgate.

The polyphony of the Polyglot's aims is compounded when we turn from the prologues to the motives of the Hebraists on the editorial team. The three known editors of the Hebrew Bible (and the Targum Onqelos, which was printed below the three columns of the Pentateuch) were all first-generation *conversos*: Pablo Colonel, Alfonso de Alcalá, and Alfonso de Zamora. Their motives, although mostly invisible to us, must have differed from the views in the prologues. Some hints are contained in Zamora's writings.

Zamora was the first professor of Hebrew at the University of Alcalá, where he begat an impressive lineage of Christian Hebraists.[16] As a yeshiva-educated *converso* teaching Jewish languages at a Catholic university, he was obviously a man between worlds, a "divided soul" in Elisheva Carlebach's evocative phrase.[17] In an era when biblical humanism was an elite avocation, he earned extra money copying biblical and targumic manuscripts for Christian patrons. In the colophon to a targum commissioned by Cardinal Cisneros, he writes:

נשלם ... על יד אלפונשו די סאמורה במאמר דון פראנסישקו שימיניז
די סישנירוש כהן גדול של טליטולה

It was finished ... by Alfonso de Zamora by order of Don Francisco Jiménez de Cisneros, high priest of Toledo"[18]

---

16. On Zamora, see Adolf Neubauer, "Alfonso de Zamora," *JQR* 7 (1895): 398–417; Jesús de Prado Plumed, "La enseñanza del hebreo en Alcalá: La búsqueda complutense de Dios/Teaching Hebrew in Alcalá: The Complutense Search for God," in *V Centenario de la Bíblia Políglota Complutense*, ed. José L. G. Sánchez-Molero (Madrid: Universidad Complutense, 2014), 452–86; Jesús de Prado Plumed, "The Commission of Targum Manuscripts and the Patronage of Christian Hebraism in Sixteenth-Century Castile," in *A Jewish Targum in a Christian World*, ed. Alberdina Houtman, Eveline van Staalduine-Sulman, and Hans-Martin Kirn, JCPS (Leiden: Brill, 2014), 146–65.

17. Elisheva Carlebach, *Divided Souls: Converts from Judaism in Germany, 1500–1750* (New Haven: Yale University Press, 2001).

18. Plumed, "Targum Manuscripts," 149–50.

Zamora renders Cisneros's title as כהן גדול ("high priest") of Toledo, translating the title of archbishop into a biblical idiom. The Hebrew, as it were, Judaizes Cisneros, holding a distorting mirror to the head of the Spanish church and the Inquisition. To call someone a high priest is a term of honor and respect, but the flavor of the Hebrew may—possibly—convey a hint of irony and perhaps a glimpse of Zamora's divided soul.

Zamora makes clear elsewhere that the Latin Vulgate had, in his eyes, no authoritative status. In a poem celebrating the Hebrew translation of the Pentateuch in 1536 by his fellow *converso*, Pedro Ciruelo, Zamora extols the *Hebraica veritas* at the expense of the Vulgate and the Septuagint:

כי שתי הלשונות   יון ורומי עונות
וגם כן משנות   לפעמים באשורים
ולשון עבראן נכון   ולא יחליף מכון
כי לנצח תכון   ודבריה ישרים

> For the two languages   Greek and Latin testify
> And also distort   at times the Assyrian script.
> But the Hebrew language is correct,   and it never changes its solidity
> For it is firm forever,   and its words are right.[19]

If for Cardinal Cisneros the translation of Jerome was immovable like a rock, for Zamora the Latin distorts, while the Hebrew "never changes its solidity." The firmness of the Hebrew text is emphasized in the rhyming repetition of תכון... מכון ... נכון, which are permutations of *kwn* ("be firm"). I do not imagine that Zamora ever raised this issue with the cardinal (or vice-versa), but one can see the divergence of viewpoints and the dangerous—at times lethal—discourse of "Judaizing" in Zamora's advocacy of the Hebrew against the Latin and Greek.

Toward the end of his career, Zamora wrote a Hebrew letter to Pope Paul III complaining about the aggressive policies of the Inquisition toward the university faculty. In it he writes poignantly, אני נשארתי לבדי מכל חכמי ספרד ("I alone am left of all the sages of Spain").[20] Is this a rhe-

---

19. Carlos del Valle, "Un poema hebreo de Alfonso de Zamora en alabanza de la versión latina bíblica de Pedro Ciruelo," *Sefarad* 59 (1999): 435 (lines 12–13).

20. Neubauer, "Zamora," 414; Plumed ("Teaching Hebrew," 457) reports that there is no record of this letter (dated 1544) in the Vatican library or the national archives in Madrid, so it may never have been sent.

torical flourish in a letter to the pontiff or the cry of a divided soul? We cannot be sure.

In the Polyglot, Zamora and his fellow *conversos*—the last Jewish sages of Spain—preserved Jewish texts and learning for posterity. The first Polyglot was the last one on which Jewish converts labored. The chief Hebraist of the Antwerp Polyglot (1568–1573), Benito Arias Montano, was educated at the University of Alcalá by Zamora's Christian Hebraist successors.[21]

The confluence of Christian humanism, mysticism, scholasticism, and Jewish texts and erudition—embodied in the partnership of the cardinal and the *converso*—creates a multifaceted mix of motives in the production of the Complutensian Polyglot. As a cultural product, it brought together all the contradictions of Renaissance Spain after the *Reconquista* and expulsion. The management of diversity in the Polyglot pertains not only to the variety of biblical texts but also to the diversity of the peoples of the book. By mobilizing new technology (the printing press), the Polyglot realized new representational possibilities, including the massive inclusion of Jewish texts in a Christian Bible. The purification of Christendom entailed the incorporation of Jewish knowledge, but without Jews or Judaism.

Within a dozen years after the Polyglot's completion and the death of Cisneros (both occurred in 1517), the program of cultural reform represented by the Polyglot was in trouble. Due to Luther's heresy and the harsh logic of the Inquisition, Hebrew philology came under suspicion as a symptom of Judaizing heresy. As Rodrigo Manrique, the son of an Inquisitor-General, wrote to the humanist Luis Vives in 1533, "For now it is clear that no one can possess a smattering of letters without being suspect of heresy, error, and Judaism."[22] The monotone of reactionary zeal interrupted the polyphony of the Polyglot.

The HBCE Hypertext: A Return to Polyglossia

The age of the great Polyglots—of Alcalá, Antwerp, Paris, and London—came to an end with a new kind of *critica sacra* announced in the work of

---

21. The Antwerp Polyglot was originally planned as a reprint of the Complutensian Polyglot but grew to include additional versions and scholarly commentary; see Dunkelgrün, "Multiplicity of Scripture."

22. David Nirenberg, *Anti-Judaism: The Western Tradition* (New York: Norton, 2013), 245.

Louis Cappel and Richard Simon.[23] Both proposed that a critical edition of the Hebrew Bible should consist of a single Hebrew text and an apparatus of variant readings and conjectures. As Peter Miller writes, "Precisely that element of testimony which was central to the great Polyglots ... was discarded. The Age of Criticism had arrived."[24] The apparatus of variants was the critically winnowed remainder of the Polyglots, a lingering trace of textual plenitude. The logic of the new philology mandated that only the sources count, with the rivulets valued only for what they might preserve of the sources, not for their own distinctive swerves.

Another step was taken when Hebrew philology became sufficiently confident to consider the possibility of an eclectic edition, following the model of the New Testament and the Greek and Latin classics. Johann Gottfried Eichhorn first raised this possibility in a review of Benjamin Kennicott's *Vetus Testamentum Hebraicum, cum Variis Lectionibus* (1776), which published the Hebrew *textus receptus* with an apparatus of variants from nearly seven hundred late medieval and early modern Hebrew manuscripts and printed editions.[25] The apparatus is impressive, but, as Eichhorn acidly notes, there is little textual criticism in the edition: "On every page of his Bible one sees that he knows little of the art called Criticism, and even less does he strive for that great idea, a critical edition of the Bible."[26] Eichhorn expanded on this "great idea" in his *Einleitung in das Alte Testament*.[27] In fits and starts, Eichhorn's idea of a critical eclectic edition of the Hebrew Bible has become viable.

---

23. Louis Cappel, *Critica Sacra, sive de Variis quae in Sacris Veteris Testamenti Libris Occurrunt Lectionibus Libri Sex* (Paris: Cramoisy, 1650; repr., Halle: Hendel, 1775); Richard Simon, *Histoire critique du Vieux Testament*, 2nd ed. (Rotterdam: Leers, 1685).

24. Miller, "Antiquarianization," 472.

25. Kennicott's edition also presents variants from the Samaritan Pentateuch in a parallel column.

26. Johann Gottfried Eichhorn, review of *Vetus Testamentum Hebraicum cum Variis Lectionibus*, by Benjamin Kennicott, *Jenaische Zeitungen von Gelehrten Sachen* (1776): 827: "Über auf allen Seiten seiner Bibel blikt der Mann durch, der wenig von der Kunst, Kritik genannt, weiss; noch weniger sich bis zu dem grosen Gedanken: kritische Bibel Ausgabe versteigen kan." Cited in Jonathan Sheehan, *The Enlightenment Bible: Translation, Scholarship, Culture* (Princeton: Princeton University Press, 2005), 184.

27. Johann Gottfried Eichhorn, *Einleitung in das Alte Testament*, 3 vols. (Leipzig: Weidmanns, Erben & Reich, 1780–1783).

Another important step toward a more fully historicized textual criticism was taken when scholars began to regard variants as not simply corruptions (although visual and aural errors certainly are corruptions), but began to explore textual variation for evidence of scribal exegesis. Deliberately composed variants, even if historically secondary, deserve to be objects of study, rather than textual debris consigned to the "prison house" of the apparatus. This interpretive turn was pioneered by Abraham Geiger[28] and has been revived by the discovery of ancient textual variants in the biblical Dead Sea Scrolls.

Many kinds of textual variants—including variant literary editions—are evidence of scribal interpretation, opening a new window onto the intellectual horizons of scribal culture in the Second Temple period. This is a central part of the process by which the books were "scripturalized," that is, transformed into a Bible. They are also phenomena of inner-biblical interpretation, since they are in the books themselves. This is a dimension of textual criticism that expands its traditional scope and promises to expand its importance within biblical scholarship generally. A fully historicized textual criticism engages with the whole textual life of the Bible's books, not just its initial phases. In this respect, a new kind of *sensus plenior* emerges from our textual inquiry. Not the mystical or anagogical senses extolled by Polyglot prologue, but a fine-grained understanding of the plural ways that the biblical books were understood, revised, and even rewritten by successive generations of scribes.

The HBCE project responds to each of these imperatives: the restoration of the earliest inferable state of a book's text and variant editions, and the study of the life of the book through its scribal interpretations. As Michael V. Fox's edition of Proverbs makes clear, these twin goals are viable and mutually illuminating. The fullest possible understanding of a book's textual plurality—its manuscripts, variants, editions, and scribal tendencies—enables the textual critic more adequately to recuperate the historical life of the text from its earliest inferable state (or states) to the plethora of the extant versions.

The new digital technology allows for further innovation. The electronic HBCE, as we envision it, will reproduce the critical edition of the print volumes and will supplement it with a hypertext of all the relevant

---

28. Abraham Geiger, *Urschrift und Uebersetzungen der Bibel in ihrer abhängigkeit von der inner Entwickelung des Judenthums* (Breslau: Hainauer, 1857).

texts and versions, including photographs of important manuscripts and other text-critical aids. The user will be able to construct a virtual polyglot of any or all of these texts. For instance, one can assemble a polyglot with parallel columns of the Hebrew, Greek, Latin, and Aramaic of a particular passage, like the Complutensian Polyglot, but including modern critical editions of each version. One can add other texts unknown to the Complutensian Polyglot, including the Samaritan Pentateuch, the Syriac Peshiṭta, and the Qumran biblical texts, along with photographs of manuscripts. With the new digital media, we can compose a virtual polyglot with no limits. Textual criticism, codicology, the history of the book, and early biblical interpretation—all these disciplines will be enhanced by the virtual polyglot, which will be free and open access.

The electronic HBCE represents a return to the Polyglot's ideal of presenting the textual plurality of the Hebrew Bible. But it does so on a different level of conceptual complexity. Whereas the Polyglot's aims were shaped by the ideals of Renaissance humanism and spirituality—return to the sources, purifying the church's Vulgate, renewing the study of the Bible to create a more educated and pious clergy, purifying Christianity, revealing hidden mysteries—the HBCE is shaped by a different set of concerns. The return to the sources is expanded to the whole history and life of the text. The condition of textual plurality opens up vistas of cultural, religious, and literary history, not the history of salvation (and damnation). To be sure, as Geiger surmised, there is a dialectic of orthodoxy and heterodoxy *within* the textual diversity—such as some sectarian variants in the SP and the MT, and a larger number of theologically "purifying" revisions—but this is a dialectic within history, not in our normative or constructive theology. As Louis Cappel clearly articulated, philology has a logic of justification which is not that of theology. He insisted: "we are not here contending with authority, but with reason."[29]

The HBCE editors are a diverse team, including (unlike the Polyglot) women and men, Jews, Catholics, and Protestants, atheists, and agnostics, from Europe, America, Asia, and Africa. Unlike the Polyglot project, this diversity does not require divided souls, since our inquiries are guided by the standards of critical scholarship rather than the authority of the church, the crown, or the Inquisition. Like the transnational Republic of Letters of the Renaissance, our project relies on the international com-

---

29. Cappel, *Critica Sacra*; 396: "Non enim hic auctoritate sed ratione pugnamus."

munity of scholars, which has its own code of discursive rules. Its commitments are to erudition, critical analysis, and cogent argumentation. It allows for mistakes and wrong conclusions, which ideally are correctable through the critical conversation of scholarly discourse, and which are not susceptible to accusations of heresy. The HBCE is an attempt to make textual diversity intelligible and to produce a new kind of critical edition of the Hebrew Bible.

The medium of the hypertext poses new possibilities for biblical philology. As Theodor Dunkelgrün comments about the great Polyglots: "The technology of the printing press did not only enable an immense acceleration of production and distribution of knowledge, it made new kinds of textual scholarship possible."[30] The new modern technology also makes possible a wider distribution of knowledge and, one may hope, new kinds of textual scholarship. At a time when the humanities are in decline in a long trajectory since the Renaissance, the powers of philology may yet surprise us. With a new medium, whose entailments and implications are still being explored, we may be able to reimagine the axis of innumerable relationships in a very old book.

---

30. Dunkelgrün, "Multiplicity of Scripture," 43.

APPENDIX
COMPARING CRITICAL EDITIONS:
BHQ PROVERBS AND HBCE PROVERBS

It is difficult to compare critical editions of a biblical book. There will always be cases where editors agree and others where their judgments differ. The differences are usually more interesting. As Michel de Montaigne writes, "Resemblance does not make things so much alike as difference makes them unlike."[1] The differences, in this instance, go beyond individual text-critical judgments to broader conceptual and practical issues. The BHQ and the HBCE editions of Proverbs represent different but related genres—BHQ is a diplomatic edition, the HBCE is an eclectic edition—and they present differing concepts of Proverbs as a book.

The BHQ edition, ably edited by Jan de Waard, is primarily a critical companion and commentary on the Masoretic Text, as instantiated in its oldest complete manuscript, the St. Petersburg (formerly Leningrad) Codex B19A. The Greek Septuagint (cited, in the absence of a Göttingen edition, from Rahlfs/Hanhart) is relevant only where it translates a Hebrew text that basically corresponds to MT. Readings in LXX that diverge widely from MT are regarded as irrelevant for the task at hand, but are indicated in the apparatus for the sake of completeness. As de Waard writes, "The other extra material in G, even if irrelevant for Hebrew textual criticism, has, for completeness sake, been included."[2] This follows the series guidelines. The "other extra material in G" is tersely indicated in the apparatus, with ample ellipses, as in Prov 9:12, where LXX (and the Syriac) has seven

---

1. Michel de Montaigne, *Les Essais*, ed. Pierre Villey and Verdun-Louis Saulnier (Paris: Presses universitaires, 1965), 1065: "La ressemblance ne faict pas tant un comme la différence faict autre"; Michael de Montaigne, *The Complete Essays of Montaigne*, trans. Donald M. Frame (Stanford: Stanford University Press, 1958), 815.
2. Jan de Waard, *Proverbs*, BHQ 17 (Stuttgart: Deutsche Bibelgesellschaft, 2008).

stichoi not in MT. There is no text-critical commentary on these "other extra" materials, since they diverge from MT and are, as such, outside the scope of the volume.

In the HBCE edition, ably edited by Michael V. Fox, the places where LXX diverges from MT are treated fully. Where LXX differs by expanding on an item that exists in MT, that material is treated in the apparatus and the commentary. Where LXX has material that does not even loosely correspond to MT, that material is treated only in the commentary. For instance, the LXX and Syriac plus in Prov 9:12*a–c* is indicated in the apparatus, reproduced in the commentary, and fully discussed for three and a half pages. Fox argues that the first four *stichoi* (Prov 9:12*a–*12*b*) represent a Hebrew *Vorlage* that can be approximately retroverted, which he then does. This is an instance where the book of Proverbs—in Hebrew—continued to develop in the proto-G family after the branching of the proto-M and proto-G textual families. The book of Proverbs and its Hebrew textual history extends beyond the bounds of MT.

As Fox writes in his extensive eighty-three-page introduction, Proverbs is a "multiplex" book with a complex textual history. His edition has three intertwined goals: (1) "to reconstruct the hyparchetype of proto-M," (2) "to recover ancient Hebrew variants (regardless of their validity) and to evaluate them," and (3) "to reconstruct non-M hyparchetypes, which in practice means proto-G and, to a lesser extent, proto-S."[3] This is a more complicated goal than the BHQ edition and makes for a more ramified and historicized concept of the book of Proverbs. MT is recognized as a reflex of a very old hyparchetype, but the book continued to evolve in each of its Hebrew branches. After the OG translation, the book continued to evolve in Greek. As Fox says, this kind of textual growth is natural for a book of proverbial literature, which by its generic nature is modular and expandable.

Fox's edition captures these different layers of textual growth and change with impeccable scholarship. The textual commentary is the heart of the edition, taking up 315 pages of the nearly 500-page volume. In contrast, the BHQ edition has a "Commentary on the Critical Apparatus" of 26 pages. Once again, this is a reflex of the different genres: the HBCE is an *editio critica maior*, whereas the BHQ is designed to be an *editio critica*

---

3. Michael V. Fox, *Proverbs: An Eclectic Edition with Introduction and Textual Commentary*, HBCE 1 (Atlanta: SBL Press, 2015), 3.

minor. The BHQ is primarily interested in the background of MT, whereas the HBCE is interested in the whole array of the textual tradition.

De Waard's BHQ edition is a fine work of scholarship and serves its series well. I mean no criticism of his work to point out these differences of genre and concept. But it seems to me that the BHQ's representation of the biblical books—particular a protean one like Proverbs—is problematic in the light of post-Qumran textual scholarship. As Emanuel Tov once wrote, "M and the biblical text are *not* identical concepts."[4] Even a text-critically annotated MT is not the same as the biblical text, although it is a valuable resource. It is time for critical editions that, like Fox's *Proverbs*, more fully represent the complexity of the biblical text and attempt to recapture, to the extent feasible, its various ancient forms. The goal will change from book to book, but the HBCE attempts to represent for each book either its archetype or (where this is not possible, as in Proverbs) its hyparchetypes, and its variant ancient editions, plus all ancient variant readings, accompanied by extensive text-critical commentary. This is a complicated and innovative project, but, as Fox's volume shows, it yields impressive results.

---

4. Emanuel Tov, *Textual Criticism of the Hebrew Bible*, 1st ed. (Minneapolis: Fortress, 1992), xxxviii, emphasis original.

Bibliography

Adler, Yonatan. "Identifying Sectarian Characteristics in the Phylacteries from Qumran." *RevQ* 23 (2007): 79–92.

Aejmelaeus, Anneli. "Corruption or Correction? Textual Development in the MT of 1 Samuel 1." Pages 1–17 in *Textual Criticism and Dead Sea Scroll Studies in Honour of Julio Trebolle Barrera: Florilegium Complutense*. Edited by Andrés Piquer Otero and Pablo A. Torijano Morales. JSJSup 157. Leiden: Brill, 2012.

———. "How to Reach the Old Greek in 1 Samuel and What to Do with It." Pages 185–205 in *Congress Volume Helsinki 2010*. Edited by Martti Nissinen. VTSup 148. Leiden: Brill, 2012.

———. *On the Trail of the Septuagint Translators: Collected Essays*. 2nd ed. CBET 50. Leuven: Peeters, 2007.

———. "Septuagintal Translation Techniques: A Solution to the Problem of the Tabernacle Account?" Pages 107–21 in *On the Trail of the Septuagint Translators: Collected Essays*. 2nd ed. CBET 50. Leuven: Peeters, 2007.

Aḥituv, Shmuel. *Echoes from the Past: Hebrew and Cognate Inscriptions from the Biblical Period*. Translated by Anson Rainey. Jerusalem: Carta, 2008.

Albrektson, Bertil. "Masoretic or Mixed: On Choosing a Textual Basis for a Translation of the Hebrew Bible." Pages 121–34 in *Text, Translation, Theology: Selected Essays on the Hebrew Bible*. Farnham, UK: Ashgate, 2010.

———. "Reflections on the Emergence of a Standard Text of the Hebrew Bible." Pages 47–62 in *Text, Translation, Theology: Selected Essays on the Hebrew Bible*. Farnham, UK: Ashgate, 2010.

———. "Translation and Emendation." Pages 95–105 in *Text, Translation, Theology: Selected Essays on the Hebrew Bible*. Farnham, UK: Ashgate, 2010.

Albright, William F. "New Light on Early Recensions of the Hebrew Bible." Pages 140–46 in *Qumran and the History of the Biblical Text*. Edited by Frank Moore Cross and Shemaryahu Talmon. Cambridge: Harvard University Press, 1975.

Anderson, Robert T., and Terry Giles. *The Samaritan Pentateuch: An Introduction to Its Origin, History, and Significance for Biblical Studies*. RBS 72. Atlanta: Society of Biblical Literature, 2012.

Asso, Cecilia. "Martin Dorp and Edward Lee." Pages 167–95 in *Biblical Humanism and Scholasticism in the Age of Erasmus*. Edited by Erika Rummel. BCCT 9. Leiden: Brill, 2008.

Avigad, Nahman. *Hebrew Bullae from the Time of Jeremiah: Remnants of a Burnt Archive*. Jerusalem: Israel Exploration Society, 1986.

Baillet, Maurice. "Texts des grottes 2Q, 3Q, 6Q, 7Q à 10Q." Pages 45–168 in *Les "petites grottes" de Qumrân: Exploration de la falaise, les grottes 2Q,3Q,5Q,6Q,7Q a 10Q, le rouleau de cuivre*. Edited by Maurice Baillet, Józef T. Milik, and Roland de Vaux. DJD III. Oxford: Clarendon, 1962.

Bainton, Roland H. "The Bible in the Reformation." Pages 1–37 in *The Cambridge History of the Bible*. Vol. 3, *The West from the Reformation to the Present Day*. Edited by Stanley L. Greenslade. Cambridge: Cambridge University Press, 1963.

———. *Erasmus of Christendom*. New York: Scribner's Sons, 1969.

Bañez, Domingo. *Scholastica Commentaria in Primam Partem Angelici Doctoris D. Thomae*. Venice: Concordiae, 1585.

Bar-Ilan, Meir. "Scribes and Books in the Late Second Commonwealth and Rabbinic Period." Pages 21–38 in *Mikra: Text, Translation, Reading and Interpretation of the Hebrew Bible in Ancient Judaism and Early Christianity*. Edited by Martin J. Mulder and Harry Sysling. CRINT 2.1. Assen: Van Gorcum, 1988.

Barkay, Gabriel, Marilyn J. Lundberg, Andrew G. Vaughn, and Bruce Zuckerman. "The Amulets from Ketef Hinnom: A New Edition and Evaluation." *BASOR* 334 (2004): 41–71.

Baroni, Victor. *La Contre-Réforme devant la Bible: La question biblique*. Lausanne: Concorde, 1943.

Barr, James. *Comparative Philology and the Text of the Old Testament*. Oxford: Oxford University Press, 1968.

———. "'Determination' and the Definite Article in Biblical Hebrew." *JSS* 34 (1989): 307–35.

———. "The Nature of Linguistic Evidence in the Text of the Bible." Pages 35–57 in *Language and Texts: The Nature of Linguistic Evidence*. Edited by H. H. Paper. Ann Arbor: Center for the Coordination of Ancient and Modern Studies, 1975.

———. Review of *Biblia Hebraica Stuttgartensia*, ed. Karl Elliger and Wilhelm Rudolph. *JSS* 25 (1980): 98–105.

———. Review of *Critique textuelle de l'Ancien Testament: Tome 1*, ed. Dominique Barthélemy. *JTS* 37 (1986): 445–50.

———. Review of *Invitation to the Septuagint*, by Karen H. Jobes and Moisés Silva. *RBL* (2002): http://tinyurl.com/SBL7010a.

———. *The Typology of Literalism in Ancient Biblical Translations*. MSU 15. Göttingen: Vandenhoeck & Ruprecht, 1979.

———. *The Variable Spellings of the Hebrew Bible*. Schweich Lectures. Oxford: Oxford University Press, 1989.

Barton, John. "What Is a Book? Modern Exegesis and the Literary Conventions of Ancient Israel." Pages 1–14 in *Intertextuality in Ugarit and Israel: Papers Read at the Tenth Joint Meeting of The Society for Old Testament Study and Het Oudtestamentisch Werkgezelschap in Nederland en België, Held at Oxford, 1997*. Edited by Johannes C. de Moor. OTS 40. Leiden: Brill, 1998.

Barthélemy, Dominique. *Critique textuelle de l'Ancien Testament*. 4 vols. OBO 50. Fribourg: Éditions Universitaires. Göttingen: Vandenhoeck & Ruprecht, 1982–2005.

———. *Studies in the Text of the Old Testament: An Introduction to the Hebrew Old Testament Text Project*. Translated by Stephen Pisano, Peter A. Pettit, Joan E. Cook, and Sarah Lind. TCT 3. Winona Lake, IN: Eisenbrauns, 2012.

Bataillon, Marcel. *Érasme et l'Espagne: Recherches sur l'histoire spirituelle du XVIe siècle*. Geneva: Droz, 1998.

Beit-Arié, Malachi. "The Damascus Pentateuch: MS Jerusalem, Jewish National and University Library Heb. 4° 5702: Orient, ca. 1000." Pages 111–27 in *The Makings of the Medieval Hebrew Book: Studies in Palaeography and Codicology*. Jerusalem: Magnes, 1993.

———. "Transmission of Texts by Scribes and Copyists: Unconscious and Critical Inferences." *BJRL* 75 (1993): 33–51.

Beit-Arié, Marcel, Colette Sirat, and Mordechai Glatzer. *Codices Hebraicis Litteris Exarati quo Tempore Scripti Fuerint Exhibentes*. Vol. 1, *Jusqu'à 1020*. Turnhout: Brepols, 1997.

Bellarmine, Robert. *Disputationes de Controversiis Christianae Fidei Adversus Hujus Temporis Haereticos.* 3 vols. Inglestadt: Sartorius, 1586–1593.

———. *Opera Omnia.* 6 vols. Naples: Giuliano, 1856–1562.

Ben-Dov, Jonathan. "Early Texts of the Torah: Revisiting the Greek Scholarly Context." *JAJ* 4 (2013): 210–34.

Benedict, Philip. *Christ's Churches Purely Reformed: A Social History of Calvinism.* New Haven: Yale University Press, 2002.

Bengel, Johann A. *Novum Testamentum Græcum.* Tübingen: Cotta, 1734.

Benin, Stephen D. *The Footprints of God: Divine Accommodation in Jewish and Christian Thought.* Albany: State University of New York Press, 1993.

Bentley, Jerry H. *Humanists and Holy Writ: New Testament Scholarship in the Renaissance.* Princeton: Princeton University Press, 1983.

Bernstein, Moshe. "What Has Happened to the Laws? The Treatment of Legal Material in 4QReworked Pentateuch." *DSD* 15 (2008): 24–49.

Biblia Polyglotta Complutensis. 6 vols. Alcalá de Henares: Brocar, 1514–1517. Repr. *Biblia Políglota Complutense.* Valencia: Fundación Biblica Española; Universidad Complutense de Madrid, 1987.

Bietenholz, Peter G. *Encounters with a Radical Erasmus: Erasmus' Work as a Source of Radical Thought in Early Modern Europe.* Erasmus Studies. Toronto: University of Toronto Press, 2009.

Blackwell, Richard J. *Galileo, Bellarmine, and the Bible: Including a Translation of Foscarini's Letter on the Motion of the Earth.* Notre Dame: University of Notre Dame Press, 1991.

Bloch, Marc. *The Historian's Craft.* Translated by Peter Putnam. New York: Vintage, 1953.

Boer, P. A. H. de. "Research into the Text of 1 Samuel xviii–xxxi." *OtSt* 6 (1949): 1–100.

———. *Research into the Text of Samuel I–XVI: A Contribution to the Study of the Books of Samuel.* Amsterdam: Paris, 1938.

Borbone, Pier G. *Il libro del profeta Osea: Edizione critica del testo ebraico.* QHenoch 2. Turin: Zamorani, 1990.

Borges, Jorge Luis. "On Exactitude in Science." Page 325 in *Collected Fictions.* Translated by Andrew Hurley. New York: Penguin, 1998.

———. *Selected Non-fictions.* Translated by Eliot Weinberger. New York: Penguin, 1999.

———. *Seven Nights.* Translated by Eliot Weinberger. New York: New Directions, 1984.

Bourdieu, Pierre. *Outline of a Theory of Practice.* Translated by Richard Nice. CSSA 16. Cambridge: Cambridge University Press, 1977.

Bouwsma, William J. *John Calvin: A Sixteenth Century Portrait.* New York: Oxford University Press, 1988.

Bowley, James E., and John C. Reeves. "Rethinking the Concept of 'Bible': Some Theses and Proposals." *Hen* 25 (2003): 3–18.

Boyarin, Daniel. "Patron Saint of the Incongruous: Rabbi Me'ir, the Talmud, and Menippean Satire." *CritInq* 35 (2009): 523–51.

Bravo, Benedetto. "*Critice* in the Sixteenth and Seventeenth Centuries and the Rise of the Notion of Historical Criticism." Pages 135–95 in *History of Scholarship: A Selection of Papers from the Seminar on the History of Scholarship Held Annually at the Warburg Institute.* Edited by Christopher Ligota and Jean-Louis Quantin. Oxford: Oxford University Press, 2006.

Breed, Brennan W. *Nomadic Text: A Theory of Biblical Reception History.* ISBL. Bloomington: Indiana University Press, 2014.

Brighton, Mark A. *The Sicarii in Josephus's Judean War: Rhetorical Analysis and Historical Observations.* EJL 27. Atlanta: Society of Biblical Literature, 2009.

Brock, Sebastian. "Jewish Traditions in Syriac Sources." *JJS* 30 (1979): 212–32.

Brooke, George J. "The Qumran Scrolls and the Demise of the Distinction between Higher and Lower Criticism." Pages 1–17 in *Reading the Dead Sea Scrolls: Essays in Method.* EJL 39. Atlanta: Society of Biblical Literature, 2013.

Browning, Robert. "Recentiores non deteriores." *BICS* 7 (1960): 11–21.

Bruning, Brandon E. "The Making of the Mishkan: The Old Greek Text of Exodus 35–40 and the Literary History of the Pentateuch." PhD diss., University of Notre Dame, 2014.

Burnett, Stephen G. *From Christian Hebraism to Jewish Studies: Johannes Buxtorf (1564–1629) and Hebrew Learning in the Seventeenth Century.* SHCT 68. Leiden: Brill, 1996.

Busby, Keith. *Codex and Context: Reading Old French Verse Narrative in Manuscript.* Amsterdam: Rodopi, 2002.

Buxtorf, Johannes, Jr. *Anticritica: seu Vindiciae Veritatis Hebraicae.* Basel: Regis, 1653.

Calvin, John. "Acts of the Council of Trent: With the Antidote." Pages 17–188 in vol. 3 of *Tracts Relating to the Reformation.* Translated by Henry Beveridge. Edinburgh: Calvin Translation Society, 1849.

————. *Commentaires sur le Nouveau Testament. Tome premier: Sur la concordance ou harmonie composée de trois évangélistes*. Paris: Meyrueis, 1854.

————. *Genesis*. Translated by John King. Edinburgh: Calvin Translation Society, 1847. Repr. 1984.

Campbell, Lyle. *Historical Linguistics: An Introduction*. 2nd ed. Cambridge: MIT Press, 2004.

Camps, Jean-Baptiste. "Copie, authenticité, originalité dans la philologie et son histoire." *Questes* 29 (2015): 35–67.

Canfora, Luciano. *Filologia e libertà: La più eversiva delle discipline, l'indipendenza di pensiero e il diritto alla verità*. Milan: Mondadori, 2008.

Cappel, Louis. *Critica Sacra, sive de Variis quae in Sacris Veteris Testamenti Libris Occurrunt Lectionibus Libri Sex*. Paris: Cramoisy, 1650. Repr., Halle: Hendel, 1775.

Carlebach, Elisheva. *Divided Souls: Converts from Judaism in Germany, 1500–1750*. New Haven: Yale University Press, 2001.

Carr, David M. *The Formation of the Hebrew Bible: A New Reconstruction*. New York: Oxford University Press, 2011.

————. *Writing on the Tablet of the Heart: Origins of Scripture and Literature*. New York: Oxford University Press, 2005.

Catastini, Alessandro. *Storia di Giuseppe (Genesi 37–50)*. Venice: Marsilio, 1994.

Cerquiglini, Bernard. *In Praise of the Variant: A Critical History of Philology*. Translated by Betsy Wing. Parallax. Baltimore: Johns Hopkins University Press, 1999.

Chartier, Roger, and Peter Stallybrass. "What Is a Book?" Pages 188–204 in *The Cambridge Companion to Textual Scholarship*. Edited by Neil Fraistat and Julia Flanders. Cambridge: Cambridge University Press, 2013.

Chiesa, Bruno. *L'Antico Testamento ebraico secondo la tradizione palestinense*. Turin: Erasmo, 1978.

————. *Filologia storica della Bibbia ebraica*. 2 vols. Studi biblici 125, 135. Brescia: Paideia, 2000.

————. "Textual History and Textual Criticism of the Hebrew Old Testament." Pages 257–72 in vol. 1 of *The Madrid Qumran Congress: Proceedings of the International Congress on the Dead Sea Scrolls, Madrid, 18–21 March, 1991*. Edited by Julio Trebolle Barrera and Luis Vegas Montaner. 2 vols. STDJ 11. Leiden: Brill, 1992.

Chrétien, C. Douglas. "Shared Innovations and Subgrouping." *IJAL* 29 (1963): 66–68.

Clines, David J. A. "The Pyramid and the Net: The Postmodern Adventure in Biblical Studies." Pages 138–57 in *On the Way to the Postmodern: Old Testament Essays 1967–1998*. Vol. 1. JSOTSup 292. Sheffield: Sheffield Academic, 1998.

Cohen, Menachem. "The Idea of the Sanctity of the Biblical Text and the Science of Textual Criticism" [Hebrew]. Pages 42–69 in *The Bible and Us*. Edited by Uriel Simon. Tel Aviv: Dvir, 1979. English translation by Ahava Cohen and Isaac B. Gottlieb at http://tinyurl.com/SBL7010c.

———, ed. *Mikra'ot Gedolot Ha-Keter*. Ramat Gan: Bar Ilan University Press, 1992–2013.

Cohen, Shaye J. D. "Parallel Historical Tradition in Josephus and Rabbinic Literature." Pages 154–61 in *The Significance of Yavneh and Other Essays in Jewish Hellenism*. TSAJ 136. Tübingen: Mohr Siebeck, 2010.

———. "The Place of the Rabbi in the Jewish Society of the Second Century." Pages 282–96 in *The Significance of Yavneh and Other Essays in Jewish Hellenism*. TSAJ 136. Tübingen: Mohr Siebeck, 2010.

Collins, Anthony. *A Discourse of Free-Thinking, Occasion'd by the Rise and Growth of a Sect call'd Free-Thinkers*. London: n.p., 1713.

Cornill, Carl Heinrich. *Das Buch des Propheten Ezechiel*. Leipzig: Hinrichs, 1886.

———. *Einleitung in das Alte Testament: Mit einschluss der Apokryphen und Pseudepigraphen*. Freiburg: Mohr, 1891.

———. *Introduction to the Canonical Books of the Old Testament*. Translated by G. H. Box. New York: Putnam's Sons, 1907.

———. "The Polychrome Bible." *The Monist* 10 (1899): 1–21.

Cousturier, Pierre. *De Tralatione Bibliae et Novarum Reprobatione Interpretationum*. Paris: Petit, 1525.

Cox, Christoph. *Nietzsche: Naturalism and Interpretation*. Berkeley: University of California Press, 1999.

Crane, Mark. "A Scholastic Response to Biblical Humanism: Nöel Beda against Lefèvre d'Etaples and Erasmus (1526)." *HumLov* 59 (2010): 55–81.

Crawford, Sidnie White. "4QDeut[n]." Pages 117–28 in *Qumran Cave 4.IX: Deuteronomy to Kings*. By Eugene Ulrich et al. DJD XIV. Oxford: Clarendon, 1995.

———. "4QTemple? (4Q365A) Revisited." Pages 87–96 in *Prayer and Poetry in the Dead Sea Scrolls and Related Literature: Essays in Honor of Eileen Schuller on the Occasion of Her 65th Birthday.* Edited by Jeremy Penner, Ken M. Penner, and Cecilia Wassen. STDJ 98. Leiden: Brill, 2012.

———. "A Response to Elizabeth Owen's '4QDeut[n]: A Pre-Samaritan Text?'" *DSD* 5 (1998): 92–94.

———. *Rewriting Scripture in Second Temple Times.* SDSS. Grand Rapids: Eerdmans, 2008.

———. "The 'Rewritten Bible' at Qumran: A Look at Three Texts." *ErIsr* 26 (1999): 1–8.

———. "Scribal Traditions in the Pentateuch and the History of the Early Second Temple Period." Pages 167–84 in *Congress Volume Helsinki 2010.* Edited by Martti Nissinen. VTSup 148. Leiden: Brill, 2012.

———. "Understanding the Textual History of the Hebrew Bible: A New Proposal." Pages 60–69 in *The Hebrew Bible in Light of the Dead Sea Scrolls.* Edited by Nóra Dávid, Armin Lange, Kristin De Troyer, and Shani Tzoref. FRLANT 239. Göttingen: Vandenhoeck & Ruprecht, 2012.

Crawford, Sidnie White, Jan Joosten, and Eugene Ulrich. "Sample Editions of the Oxford Hebrew Bible: Deuteronomy 32:1–9, 1 Kings 11:1–8, and Jeremiah 27:1–10 (34 G)." *VT* 58 (2008): 352–66.

Cross, Frank Moore. "4QExod[b]." Pages 79–95 in *Qumran Cave 4.VII: Genesis to Numbers.* Edited by Eugene Ulrich and Frank Moore Cross. DJD XII. Oxford: Clarendon, 1994.

———. "4QExod–Lev[f]." Pages 133–44 in *Qumran Cave 4.VII: Genesis to Numbers.* Edited by Eugene Ulrich and Frank Moore Cross. DJD XII. Oxford: Clarendon, 1994.

———. "4QGen–Exod[a]." Pages 7–30 in *Qumran Cave 4.VII: Genesis to Numbers.* Edited by Eugene Ulrich and Frank Moore Cross. DJD XII. Oxford: Clarendon, 1994.

———. *The Ancient Library of Qumran.* 3rd ed. Minneapolis: Fortress, 1995.

———. *The Ancient Library of Qumran and Modern Biblical Studies.* Garden City, NY: Doubleday, 1958.

———. "The Contributions of the Qumran Discoveries to the Study of the Biblical Text." Pages 278–92 in *Qumran and the History of the Biblical Text.* Edited by Frank Moore Cross and Shemaryahu Talmon. Cambridge: Harvard University Press, 1975.

———. "The Evolution of a Theory of Local Texts." Pages 306–20 in *Qumran and the History of the Biblical Text*. Edited by Frank Moore Cross and Shemaryahu Talmon. Cambridge: Harvard University Press, 1975.

———. "The Fixation of the Text of the Hebrew Bible." Pages 205–18 in *From Epic to Canon: History and Literature in Ancient Israel*. Baltimore: Johns Hopkins University Press, 1998.

———. "The History of the Biblical Text in the Light of Discoveries in the Judaean Desert." Pages 177–95 in *Qumran and the History of the Biblical Text*. Edited by Frank Moore Cross and Shemaryahu Talmon. Cambridge: Harvard University Press, 1975.

———. "A New Qumran Biblical Fragment Related to the Original Hebrew Underlying the Septuagint." *BASOR* 132 (1953): 15–26.

———. "Notes on a Generation of Qumrân Studies." Pages 171–91 in *The Ancient Library of Qumran*. 3rd ed. Minneapolis: Fortress, 1995.

———. "Problems of Method in the Textual Criticism of the Hebrew Bible." Pages 31–54 in *The Critical Study of Sacred Texts*. Edited by Wendy Doniger O'Flaherty. BRSS 2. Berkeley: Graduate Theological Union, 1979.

———. "Reminiscences of the Early Days in the Discovery and Study of the Dead Sea Scrolls." Pages 932–43 in *The Dead Sea Scrolls Fifty Years after Their Discovery: Proceedings of the Jerusalem Congress, July 20–25, 1997*. Edited by Lawrence H. Schiffman, Emanuel Tov, and James C. VanderKam. Jerusalem: Israel Exploration Society, 2000.

———. "The Stabilization of the Canon of the Hebrew Bible." Pages 219–29 in *From Epic to Canon: History and Literature in Ancient Israel*. Baltimore: Johns Hopkins University Press, 1998.

Cross, Frank Moore, Donald W. Parry, and Richard J. Saley. "4QSam[a]." Pages 1–216 in *Qumran Cave 4.XII: 1–2 Samuel*. Edited by Frank Moore Cross et al. DJD XVII. Oxford: Clarendon, 2005.

Cross, Frank Moore, and Shemaryahu Talmon, eds. *Qumran and the History of the Biblical Text*. Cambridge: Harvard University Press, 1975.

Culley, Robert C. "Oral Tradition and Biblical Studies." *OrT* 1 (1986): 30–65.

Davidson, Donald. *Inquiries into Truth and Interpretation*. Oxford: Clarendon, 1984.

Davila, James R. "4QGen[b]." Pages 31–38 in *Qumran Cave 4.VII: Genesis to Numbers*. Edited by Eugene Ulrich and Frank Moore Cross. DJD XII. Oxford: Clarendon, 1994.

———. "4QGen[h]." Pages 61–64 in *Qumran Cave 4.VII: Genesis to Numbers*.

Edited by Eugene Ulrich and Frank Moore Cross. DJD XII. Oxford: Clarendon, 1994.

———. "4QGen^k." Pages 75–78 in *Qumran Cave 4.VII: Genesis to Numbers.* Edited by Eugene Ulrich and Frank Moore Cross. DJD XII. Oxford: Clarendon, 1994.

———. "Text-Type and Terminology: Genesis and Exodus as Test Cases." *RevQ* 16 (1993): 3–37.

Debel, Hans. "Greek 'Variant Literary Editions' to the Hebrew Bible?" *JSJ* 41 (2010): 161–90.

———. "Rewritten Bible, Variant Literary Editions and Original Text(s): Exploring the Implications of a Pluriform Outlook on the Scriptural Tradition." Pages 65–91 in *Changes in Scripture: Rewriting and Interpreting Authoritative Traditions in the Second Temple Period.* Edited by Hanne von Weissenberg, Juha Pakkala, and Marko Marttila. BZAW 429. Berlin: de Gruyter, 2011.

Delbrück, Berthold. *Einleitung in das Sprachstudium: Ein Beitrag zur Geschichte und Methodik der vergleichenden Sprachforschung.* Leipzig: Breitkopf & Härtel, 1880.

———. *Introduction to the Study of Language: A Critical Survey of the History and Methods of Comparative Philology of the Indo-European Languages.* Translated by E. Channing. Leipzig: Breitkopf & Härtel, 1882.

Delitzsch, Friedrich. *Die Lese-und Schreibfehler im Alten Testament, nebst den dem Schrifttexte einverleibten Randnoten, klassifiziert.* Berlin: de Gruyter, 1920.

Delph, Ronald K. "Emending and Defending the Vulgate Old Testament: Agostino Steuco's Quarrel with Erasmus." Pages 297–317 in *Biblical Humanism and Scholasticism in the Age of Erasmus.* Edited by Erika Rummel. BCCT 9. Leiden: Brill, 2008.

Díaz-Esteban, Fernando. *Sefer Oklah we-Oklah.* Madrid: Consejo Superior de Investigaciones Científicas, 1975.

Díez Macho, Alejandro. *The Pentateuch with the Masorah Parva and the Masorah Magna and with Targum Onkelos, MS. Vat. Heb. 448.* Jerusalem: Makor, 1977.

Diringer, David. *The Book before Printing: Ancient, Medieval and Oriental.* New York: Dover, 1982.

Dotan, Aron. "Reflections towards a Critical Edition of Pentateuch Codex Or. 4445." Pages 39–50 in *Estudios Masoréticos (X Congreso de la IOMS): En memoria de Harry M. Orlinsky.* Edited by Emilia Fernández Tejero and Maite T. Ortega Monasterio. Madrid: Instituto de Filología, 1993.

Doyle, Arthur Conan. *The Hound of the Baskervilles: Another Adventure of Sherlock Holmes*. New York: Grosset & Dunlap, 1902.

Dukan, Michèle. *La Bible hébraïque: Les codices copiés en Orient et dans la zone séfarade avant 1280*. Turnhout: Brepols, 2006.

Duncan, Julie A. "4QDeut[b]." Pages 9–14 in *Qumran Cave 4.IX: Deuteronomy to Kings*. By Eugene Ulrich et al. DJD XIV. Oxford: Clarendon, 1995.

———. "4QDeut[h]." Pages 61–70 in *Qumran Cave 4.IX: Deuteronomy to Kings*. By Eugene Ulrich et al. DJD XIV. Oxford: Clarendon, 1995.

———. "4QDeut[j]." Pages 75–91 in *Qumran Cave 4.IX: Deuteronomy to Kings*. By Eugene Ulrich et al. DJD XIV. Oxford: Clarendon, 1995.

———. "New Readings for the 'Blessing of Moses' from Qumran." *JBL* 114 (1995): 273–90.

Dunkelgrün, Theodor W. "The Multiplicity of Scripture: The Confluence of Textual Traditions in the Making of the Antwerp Polyglot Bible (1568–1573)." PhD diss., University of Chicago, 2012.

Eco, Umberto. *Interpretation and Overinterpretation*. Cambridge: Cambridge University Press, 1992.

Eggert, Paul. *Securing the Past: Conservation in Art, Architecture and Literature*. Cambridge: Cambridge University Press, 2009.

Eichhorn, Johann Gottfried. *Einleitung in das Alte Testament*. 3 vols. Leipzig: Weidmanns, Erben & Reich, 1780–1783.

———. *Einleitung in das Alte Testament*. 3rd ed. 3 vols. Leipzig: Weidmann, 1803.

———. *Introduction to the Study of the Old Testament*. Partial translation of 3rd ed. by G. T. Gollop. London: Spottiswoode, 1888.

———. Review of *Vetus Testamentum Hebraicum cum Variis Lectionibus*, by Benjamin Kennicott. *Jenaische Zeitungen von Gelehrten Sachen* (1776): 825–32.

Elgvin, Torleif, Michael Langlois, and Kipp Davis, eds. *Gleanings from the Caves: Dead Sea Scrolls and Artefacts from the Schøyen Collection*. LSTS 71. London: T&T Clark, 2016.

Emerton, John A. "Was There an Epicene Pronoun *Hū'* in Early Hebrew?" *JSS* 45 (2000): 267–76.

Engel, Edna, and Mordechay Mishor. "An Ancient Scroll of the Book of Exodus: The Reunion of Two Separate Fragments." *Israel Museum Studies in Archaeology* 7 (2015): 24–60.

Erasmus, Desiderius. *Novum Instrumentum*. Basel, Froben, 1516.

———. *Opera Omnia*. Edited by Jean Le Clerc. Leiden: van der Aa, 1703–1706.

———. *Opus Epistolarum Des. Erasmi Roterodami*. Vol. 2, *1514–1517*. Edited by Percy S. Allen. Oxford: Clarendon, 1910.

Eshel, Esther. "4QDeut[n]—A Text That Has Undergone Harmonistic Editing." *HUCA* 62 (1991): 117–54.

———. "6Q30, a Cursive Šîn, and Proverbs 11." *JBL* 122 (2003): 544–46.

Eshel, Esther, and Hanan Eshel. "Dating the Samaritan Pentateuch's Compilation in Light of the Qumran Biblical Scrolls." Pages 215–40 in *Emanuel: Studies in Hebrew Bible, Septuagint and Dead Sea Scrolls in Honor of Emanuel Tov*. Edited by Shalom M. Paul, Robert A. Kraft, Lawrence H. Schiffman, and Weston W. Fields. VTSup 94. Leiden: Brill, 2003.

———. "New Fragments from Qumran: 4QGen[f], 4QIsa[b], 4Q226, 8QGen, and XQpapEnoch." *DSD* 12 (2005): 134–57.

———. "A Preliminary Report on Seven New Fragments from Qumran." *Meghillot* 5–6 (2007): 271–78.

Falk, Daniel K. *The Parabiblical Texts: Strategies for Extending the Scriptures in the Dead Sea Scrolls*. LSTS 63. London: T&T Clark, 2007.

Farge, James K. "Nöel Beda and the Defense of the Tradition." Pages 143–64 in *Biblical Humanism and Scholasticism in the Age of Erasmus*. Edited by Erika Rummel. BCCT 9. Leiden: Brill, 2008.

Fassberg, Steven E. "The Kethiv/Qere הוא, Diachrony, and Dialectology." Pages 171–80 in *Diachrony in Biblical Hebrew*. Edited by Cynthia L. Miller-Naudé and Ziony Zevit. LSAWS 8. Winona Lake, IN: Eisenbrauns, 2012.

Faulenbach, Heiner. *Die Struktur der Theologie des Amandus Polanus von Polansdorf*. Zurich: EVZ-Verlag, 1967.

Fernández-Armesto, Felipe. "Cardinal Cisneros as a Patron of Printing." Pages 149–68 in *God and Man in Medieval Spain: Essays in Honour of J. R. L. Highfield*. Edited by Derek W. Lomax and David Mackenzie. Warminster: Aris & Phillips, 1989.

Finkelberg, Margalit. "The *Cypria*, the *Iliad*, and the Problem of Multiformity in Oral and Written Tradition." *CP* 95 (2000): 1–11.

———. "The Original Versus the Received Text with Special Emphasis on the Case of the *Comma Johanneum*." *IJCT* 21 (2014): 183–97.

Foucault, Michel. "Nietzsche, Genealogy, History." Pages 76–100 in *The Foucault Reader*. Edited by Paul Rabinow. New York: Pantheon, 1984.

———. "What Is an Author?" Pages 101–20 in *The Foucault Reader*. Edited by Paul Rabinow. New York: Pantheon, 1984.

Fox, Michael V. *Proverbs: An Eclectic Edition with Introduction and Textual Commentary*. HBCE 1. Atlanta: SBL Press, 2015.

Freedman, David Noel. *The Leningrad Codex: A Facsimile Edition*. Grand Rapids: Eerdmans, 1998.

———. "The Massoretic Text and the Qumran Scrolls: A Study in Orthography." Pages 196–211 in *Qumran and the History of the Biblical Text*. Edited by Frank Moore Cross and Shemaryahu Talmon. Cambridge: Harvard University Press, 1975.

———. "Variant Readings in the Leviticus Scroll from Qumran Cave 11." *CBQ* 36 (1974): 525–34.

Freedman, David Noel, and Kenneth A. Matthews. *The Paleo-Hebrew Leviticus Scroll (11QpaleoLev)*. Winona Lake, IN: American Schools of Oriental Research, 1985.

Garbini, Giovanni. *Il Cantico dei Cantici: Testo, traduzione note e commento*. Brescia: Paideia, 1992.

Geddes, Alexander. *The Holy Bible, or the Books Accounted Sacred by Jews and Christians; Otherwise Called the Books of the Old and New Covenants: Faithfully Translated from Corrected Texts of the Originals*. 2 vols. London: Davis, 1792–1797.

Geiger, Abraham. *Urschrift und Uebersetzungen der Bibel in ihrer abhängigkeit von der inner Entwickelung des Judenthums*. Breslau: Hainauer, 1857.

Gelston, Anthony. "Isaiah 52:13–53:12: An Eclectic Text and a Supplementary Note on the Hebrew Manuscript Kennicott 96." *JSS* 35 (1990): 187–211.

Gerrish, Brian A. "The Word of God and the Words of Scripture: Luther and Calvin on Biblical Authority." Pages 51–68 in *The Old Protestantism and the New: Essays on the Reformation Heritage*. Chicago: University of Chicago Press, 1982.

Gibert, Pierre. "The Catholic Counterpart and Response to the Protestant Orthodoxy." Pages 758–73 in vol. 2 of *Hebrew Bible/Old Testament: The History of Its Interpretation*. Edited by Magne Saebø. Göttingen: Vandenhoeck & Ruprecht, 2008.

Ginsberg, H. L. "Studies on the Biblical Hebrew Verb: Masoretically Misconstrued Internal Passives." *AJSL* 46 (1929): 53–56.

Ginsburg, Christian D. *Introduction to the Massoretico-Critical Edition of the Hebrew Bible*. London: Trinitarian Biblical Society, 1897.

———. *The Massoreth Ha-Massoreth of Elias Levita: Being an Exposition of the Massoretic Notes on the Hebrew Bible; or the Ancient Critical Apparatus of the Old Testament in Hebrew.* London: Longmans, 1867.

Ginzburg, Carlo. "Clues: Roots of an Evidential Paradigm." Pages 96–125 in *Clues, Myths, and the Historical Method.* Translated by John and Anne Tedeschi. Baltimore: Johns Hopkins University Press, 1989.

———. "Family Resemblances and Family Trees: Two Cognitive Metaphors." *CritInq* 30 (2004): 537–56.

———. "Spie: Radici di un paradigma indiziario." Pages 59–106 in *Crisi della ragione.* Edited by Aldo Gargani. Turin: Einaudi, 1979.

Goodblatt, David M. *Elements of Ancient Jewish Nationalism.* Cambridge: Cambridge University Press, 2006.

Goodman, Martin. "Texts, Scribes and Power in Roman Judaea." Pages 79–90 in *Judaism in the Roman World: Collected Essays.* AGJU 66. Leiden: Brill, 2007.

Goodman, Nelson. *Languages of Art: An Approach to a Theory of Symbols.* Indianapolis: Bobbs-Merrill, 1968.

Goshen-Gottstein, Moshe H. *Biblia Rabbinica: A Reprint of the 1525 Venice Edition.* 2 vols. Jerusalem: Makor, 1972.

———. *The Book of Isaiah: Sample Edition with Introduction.* Jerusalem: Magnes, 1965.

———. "Editions of the Hebrew Bible: Past and Future." Pages 221–42 in *"Sha'arei Talmon": Studies in the Bible, Qumran, and the Ancient Near East Presented to Shemaryahu Talmon.* Edited by Michael Fishbane and Emanuel Tov. Winona Lake, IN: Eisenbrauns, 1992.

———. "Hebrew Biblical Manuscripts: Their History and Their Place in the HUBP Edition." Pages 42–89 in *Qumran and the History of the Biblical Text.* Edited by Frank Moore Cross and Shemaryahu Talmon. Cambridge: Harvard University Press, 1975.

———. "Die Jesaiah-Rolle und das Problem der hebräischen Bibelhandschriften." *Bib* 35 (1954): 429–42.

———. "The Rise of the Tiberian Bible Text." Pages 79–122 in *Biblical and Other Studies.* Edited by Alexander Altmann. S&T 1. Cambridge: Harvard University Press, 1963.

———. "The Textual Criticism of the Old Testament: Rise, Decline, Rebirth." *JBL* 102 (1983): 365–99.

———. "Theory and Practice of Textual Criticism: The Text-Critical Use of the Septuagint." *Text* 3 (1963): 130–58.

Goshen-Gottstein, Moshe H., Shemaryahu Talmon, and Galen Marquis. *The Book of Ezekiel.* HUBP. Jerusalem: Magnes, 2004.

Gould, Stephen J. "Evolution and the Triumph of Homology, or Why History Matters." *AmSci* 74 (1986): 60–69.

Grafton, Anthony. *Joseph Scaliger: A Study in the History of Classical Scholarship.* Vol. 1, *Textual Criticism and Exegesis.* Oxford: Clarendon, 1993.

———. "The Scholarship of Poliziano and Its Context." Pages 47–75 in *Defenders of the Text: The Traditions of Scholarship in an Age of Science, 1450–1800.* Cambridge: Harvard University Press, 1991.

Grafton, Anthony, and Lisa Jardine. *From Humanism to the Humanities: Education and the Liberal Arts in Fifteenth- and Sixteenth-Century Europe.* Cambridge: Harvard University Press, 1986.

Grafton, Anthony, and Joanna Weinberg. *"I Have Always Loved the Holy Tongue": Isaac Casaubon, the Jews, and a Forgotten Chapter in Renaissance Scholarship.* Cambridge: Harvard University Press, 2011.

Greenblatt, Stephen. "The Dream of the Master Text." Pages 67–75 in *The Norton Shakespeare, Based on the Oxford Edition: Essential Plays/The Sonnets.* Edited by Stephen Greenblatt, Walter Cohen, Jean E. Howard, and Katharine Eisaman Maus. New York: Norton, 1997.

Greenstein, Edward L. "Misquotation of Scripture in the Dead Sea Scrolls." Pages 71–83 in vol. 1 of *The Frank Talmage Memorial Volume.* Edited by Barry Walfish. 2 vols. Haifa: Haifa University Press, 1993.

Greetham, David C. *Theories of the Text.* Oxford: Oxford University Press, 1999.

Greg, W. W. "The Rationale of Copy-Text." *SBib* 3 (1950–1951): 19–36.

Grendler, Paul F. "Italian Biblical Humanism and the Papacy, 1515–1535." Pages 227–76 in *Biblical Humanism and Scholasticism in the Age of Erasmus.* Edited by Erika Rummel. BCCT 9. Leiden: Brill, 2008.

Hadas-Lebel, Mireille. "Le P. Houbigant et la critique textuelle." Pages 103–12 in *Le siècle des Lumières et la Bible.* Edited by Yvon Belavel and Dominique Bourel. BTT 7. Paris: Beauchesne, 1986.

Hall, Basil. "Biblical Scholarship: Editions and Commentaries." Pages 38–93 in *The Cambridge History of the Bible.* Vol. 3, *The West from the Reformation to the Present Day.* Edited by Stanley L. Greenslade. Cambridge: Cambridge University Press, 1963.

Haran, Menahem. "Book-Scrolls at the Beginning of the Second Temple Period: The Transition from Papyrus to Skins." *HUCA* 54 (1983): 111–22.

———. Book-Scrolls in Israel in Pre-exilic Times." *JJS* 33 (1982): 161–73.

Hasan-Rokem, Galit. "Rabbi Meir, the Illuminated and the Illuminating: Interpreting Experience." Pages 227–43 in *Current Trends in the Study of Midrash*. Edited by Carol Bakhos. JSJSup 106. Leiden: Brill, 2006.

Haupt, Paul. *The Sacred Books of the Old Testament: A Critical Edition of the Hebrew Text, Printed in Colors, with Notes, Prepared by Eminent Biblical Scholars of Europe and America Under the Editorial Direction of Paul Haupt*. 16 vols. Baltimore: Johns Hopkins University Press, 1893–1904.

Hayward, C. T. R. *Saint Jerome's Hebrew Questions on Genesis*. OECS. Oxford: Clarendon, 1995.

Helm, Paul. *John Calvin's Ideas*. Oxford: Oxford University Press, 2004.

Hendel, Ronald. *The Epic of the Patriarch: The Jacob Cycle and the Narrative Traditions of Canaan and Israel*. HSM 42. Atlanta: Scholars, 1987.

———. "A Hasmonean Edition of MT Genesis? The Implications of the Editions of the Chronology in Genesis 5." *HBAI* 1 (2012): 1–17.

———. "Mind the Gap: Modern and Postmodern in Biblical Studies." *JBL* 133 (2014): 422–43.

———. "The Oxford Hebrew Bible: Prologue to a New Critical Edition." *VT* 58 (2008): 324–51.

———. "Plural Texts and Literary Criticism: For Instance, 1 Samuel 17." *Text* 23 (2007): 97–114.

———. *The Text of Genesis 1–11: Textual Studies and Critical Edition*. New York: Oxford University Press, 1998.

———. "The Two Editions of the Royal Chronology in Kings." Pages 99–114 in *Textual Criticism and Dead Sea Scroll Studies in Honour of Julio Trebolle Barrera: Florilegium Complutense*. Edited by Andrés Piquer Otero and Pablo A. Torijano Morales. JSJSup 157. Leiden: Brill, 2012.

Hennig, Willi. "Phylogenetic Systematics." *ARevEnt* 10 (1965): 97–116.

———. *Phylogenetic Systematics*. Translated by D. Dwight Davis and Rainer Zangerl. Urbana: University of Illinois Press, 1966.

Hestrin Ruth, and Michal Dayagi-Mendels. *Inscribed Seals: First Temple Period: Hebrew, Ammonite, Moabite, Phoenician and Aramaic*. Jerusalem: Israel Museum, 1979.

Hetzron, Robert. "Two Principles of Genetic Reconstruction." *Lingua* 38 (1976): 89–108.

Hiebert, Robert J. V. "Genesis." Pages 1–42 in *A New English Translation of the Septuagint: And the Other Greek Translations Traditionally Included under That Title.* Edited by Albert Pietersma and Benjamin G. Wright. New York: Oxford University Press, 2007.

Hoenigswald, Henry M. "Language Families and Subgroupings, Tree Model and Wave Theory, and Reconstruction of Protolanguages." Pages 441–54 in *Research Guide on Language Change.* Edited by Edgar C. Polomé. TiLSM 48. Berlin: de Gruyter, 1990.

Hoenigswald, Henry M., and Linda F. Wiener, eds. *Biological Metaphor and Cladistic Classification: An Interdisciplinary Perspective.* Philadelphia: University of Pennsylvania Press, 1987.

Hognesius, Kjell. *The Text of 2 Chronicles 1–16: A Critical Edition with Textual Commentary.* ConBOT 64. Stockholm: Almqvist & Wiksell, 2003.

Holmes, Michael W. "From 'Original Text' to 'Initial Text': The Traditional Goal of New Testament Textual Criticism in Contemporary Discussion." Pages 637–88 in *The Text of the New Testament in Contemporary Research: Essays on the* Status Quaestionis. Edited by Bart D. Ehrman and Michael W. Holmes. 2nd ed. NTTSD 46. Leiden: Brill, 2013.

Horst, Ulrich. *Der Streit um die Autorität der Vulgata: Zur Rezeption des trienter Schriftdekrets in Spanien.* Coimbra: Coimbra Editora, 1983.

Houbigant, Charles François. *Notae Criticae in Universos Veteris Testamenti Libros.* 2 vols. Frankfurt am Main: Varrentrapp & Wenner, 1777.

Housman, A. E. "The Application of Thought to Textual Criticism." *PCA* 18 (1921): 67–84. http://tinyurl.com/SBL7010d.

———. "Preface to Juvenal." Pages 53–62 in *Selected Prose.* Edited by John Carter. Cambridge: Cambridge University Press, 1961.

Huehnergard, John. "What Is Aramaic?" *Aram* 7 (1995): 261–82.

Hughes, Jeremy. "Post-biblical Features of Biblical Hebrew Vocalization." Pages 67–80 in *Language, Theology, and the Bible: Essays in Honour of James Barr.* Edited by Samuel E. Balantine and John Barton. Oxford: Clarendon, 1994.

Hurvitz, Avi. "The Origins and Development of the Expression מגלת ספר: A Study in the History of Writing-Related Terminology in Biblical Times." Pages 37*–46* in *Texts, Temples, and Traditions: A Tribute to Menahem Haran.* Edited by Michael V. Fox et al. Winona Lake, IN: Eisenbrauns, 1996.

Hutzli, Jürg. *Die Erzählung von Hanna und Samuel: Textkritische und literarische Analyse von 1. Samuel 1–2 unter Berücksichtigung des Kontextes.* ATANT 89. Zurich: TVZ, 2007.

Jahn, Johann. *Biblia Hebraica Digessit, et Graviores Lectionum Varietates.* Vienna: Wappler & Beck, 1806.

James, William. *Pragmatism and Other Writings*. Edited by Giles Gunn. New York: Penguin, 2000.

Jastram, Nathan. "4QNum[b]." Pages 205–67 in *Qumran Cave 4.VII: Genesis to Numbers*. Edited by Eugene Ulrich and Frank Moore Cross. DJD XII. Oxford: Clarendon, 1994.

———. "A Comparison of Two 'Proto-Samaritan' Texts from Qumran: 4QpaleoExod[m] and 4QNum[b]." *DSD* 5 (1998): 264–89.

———. "Numbers, Book of." *EDSS* 2:615–19.

———. "The Severus Scroll and Rabbi Meir's Torah." Pages 137–46 in *The Text of the Hebrew Bible: From the Rabbis to the Masoretes*. Edited by Elvira Martín-Contreras and Lorena Miralles-Maciá. JAJSup 13. Göttingen: Vandenhoeck & Ruprecht, 2014.

Jedin, Hubert. *A History of the Council of Trent*. Vol. 2, *The First Sessions at Trent, 1545–1547*. Translated by Ernest Graf. London: Nelson, 1961.

Jenkins, Alan K., and Patrick Preston. *Biblical Scholarship and the Church: A Sixteenth Century Crisis of Authority*. Aldershot: Ashgate, 2007.

Johnson, William A. *Bookrolls and Scribes in Oxyrhynchus*. SBPC. Toronto: University of Toronto Press, 2004.

Joosten, Jan. *Collected Studies on the Septuagint: From Language to Interpretation and Beyond*. FAT 83. Tübingen: Mohr Siebeck, 2012.

———. "Le débat sur la vocalisation massorétique de la Bible d'Élie Levita à Louis Cappel." In *Les hébraïsants français au seizième siècle*. Edited by Annie Noblesse Rocher and Gilbert Dahan. Geneva: Droz, forthcoming.

———. "Is There a Place for Conjectures in a Critical Edition of the Hebrew Bible? Reflections in Preparation of a Critical Text of 1 Kings." Pages 365–75 in *In the Footsteps of Sherlock Holmes: Studies in the Biblical Text in Honour of Anneli Aejmelaeus*. Edited by Kristin De Troyer, Timothy M. Law, and Marketta Liljeström. BETL 72. Leuven: Peeters, 2014.

———. "Language as Symptom: Linguistic Clues to the Social Background of the Seventy." Pages 185–94 in *Collected Studies on the Septuagint: From Language to Interpretation and Beyond*. FAT 83. Tübingen: Mohr Siebeck, 2012.

———. "A Note on the Text of Deuteronomy xxxii 8." *VT* 57 (2007): 548–55.

———. "Textual Developments and Historical Linguistics." Pages 21–31 in *After Qumran: Old and Modern Editions of the Biblical Texts; The*

Historical Books. Edited by Hans Ausloos, Bénédicte Lemmelijn, and Julio Trebolle Barrera. BETL 246. Leuven: Peeters 2012.

——. "The Tiberian Vocalization and the Edition of the Hebrew Bible." Pages 19–32 in *Making the Biblical Text: Textual Studies in the Hebrew and Greek Bible*. Edited by Innocent Himbaza. OBO 275. Fribourg: Academic Press; Göttingen: Vandenhoeck & Ruprecht, 2015.

Kahle, Paul. "Untersuchungen zur Geschichte des Pentateuchtextes." Pages 3–37 in *Opera Minora*. Leiden: Brill, 1956.

Kamesar, Adam. *Jerome, Greek Scholarship, and the Hebrew Bible: A Study of the Quaestiones hebraicae in Genesim*. OCM. Oxford: Clarendon, 1993.

Kant, Immanuel. *Die Metaphysik der Sitten*. 2nd ed. 2 vols. Königsberg: Nicolovius, 1803.

——. *The Metaphysics of Morals*. Edited and translated by Mary Gregor. CTHP. Cambridge: Cambridge University Press, 1996.

Kartveit, Magnar. *The Origin of the Samaritans*. VTSup 128. Leiden: Brill, 2009.

Kawashima, Robert S. *Biblical Narrative and the Death of the Rhapsode*. ISBL. Bloomington: Indiana University Press, 2004.

Kenney, E. J. *The Classical Text: Aspects of Editing in the Age of the Printed Book*. SCL 44. Berkeley: University of California Press, 1974.

——. "Textual Criticism." Pages 189–95 in vol. 18 of *The New Encyclopædia Britannica*. 15th ed. Chicago: Encyclopædia Britannica, 1974. http://tinyurl.com/SBL7010e.

Khan, Geoffrey. "Biblical Hebrew: Pronunciation Traditions." Pages 341–52 in vol. 1 of *Encyclopedia of Hebrew Language and Linguistics*. Edited by Geoffrey Khan. Leiden: Brill, 2013.

——. *A Short Introduction to the Tiberian Masoretic Bible and Its Reading Tradition*. GHand. Piscataway, NJ: Gorgias, 2012.

Kim, Kyungrae. "Studies in the Relationship between the Samaritan Pentateuch and the Septuagint." PhD diss., Hebrew University, 1994.

Kimmel, Seth. *Parables of Coercion: Conversion and Knowledge at the End of Islamic Spain*. Chicago: University of Chicago Press, 2015.

Kister, Menahem. "Textual and Lexical Implications of Phonetic and Orthographic Phenomena" [Hebrew]. *Leshonenu* 78 (2016): 7–20.

Kittel, Rudolf. *The Books of Chronicles: Critical Edition of the Hebrew Text Printed in Colors Exhibiting the Composite Structure of the Book*. SBOT 20. Baltimore: Johns Hopkins University Press, 1895.

———. *Über die Notwendigkeit und Möglichkeit einer neuen Ausgabe der hebräischen Bibel: Studien und Erwägungen.* Leipzig: Deichert, 1902.

Klauber, Martin I. "The Demise of Reformed Scholasticism and the Abrogation of the Helvetic Formula Consensus of 1675." Pages 143–64 in *Between Reformed Scholasticism and Pan-Protestantism: Jean-Alphonse Turretin (1671–1737) and Enlightened Orthodoxy at the Academy of Geneva.* Cranbury, NJ: Associated University Presses, 1994.

———. "The Helvetic Formula Consensus (1675): An Introduction and Translation." *TJ* 11 (1990): 103–23.

Klein, Michael L. *The Fragment-Targums of the Pentateuch: According to Their Extant Sources.* 2 vols. AnBib 76. Rome: Biblical Institute Press, 1980.

Knight, Douglas A. *Rediscovering the Traditions of Israel.* SBLDS 9. Missoula, MT: Scholars Press, 1975.

Knoppers, Gary N. *1 Chronicles 1–9: A New Translation with Introduction and Commentary.* AB 12A. New York: Doubleday, 2003.

———. *Jews and Samaritans: The Origins and History of Their Early Relations.* New York: Oxford University Press, 2013.

Koltun-Fromm, Ken. *Abraham Geiger's Liberal Judaism: Personal Meaning and Religious Authority.* JLC. Bloomington: Indiana University Press, 2006.

Kooij, Arie van der. "Preservation and Promulgation: The Dead Sea Scrolls and the Textual History of the Hebrew Bible." Pages 29–40 in *The Hebrew Bible in Light of the Dead Sea Scrolls.* Edited by Nóra Dávid, Armin Lange, Kristin De Troyer, and Shani Tzoref. FRLANT 239. Göttingen: Vandenhoeck & Ruprecht, 2012.

———. "The Textual Criticism of the Hebrew Bible before and after the Qumran Discoveries." Pages 167–77 in *The Bible as Book: The Hebrew Bible and the Judaean Desert Discoveries.* Edited by Edward D. Herbert and Emanuel Tov. London: British Library, 2002.

Korzybski, Alfred. *Science and Sanity: An Introduction to Non-Aristotelian Systems and General Semantics.* 5th ed. Brooklyn: Institute of General Semantics, 1994.

Kugel, James L. "Early Interpretation: The Common Background of Late Forms of Biblical Exegesis." Pages 9–106 in *Early Biblical Interpretation.* Edited by James L. Kugel and Rowan A. Greer. LEC 3. Philadelphia: Westminster, 1986.

La Servière, Joseph de. *La Théologie de Bellarmin.* Paris: Beauchesne, 1908.

Lachmann, Karl. *Kleinere Schriften: Zur classischen Philologie.* 2 vols. Berlin: Reimer, 1876.

Lagarde, Paul de. *Anmerkungen zur griechischen Übersetzung der Proverbien.* Leipzig: Brockhaus, 1863.

———. *Genesis Graece.* Leipzig: Teubner, 1868.

———. *Materialien zur Kritik und Geschichte des Pentateuchs.* Leipzig: Teubner, 1867.

———, ed. *Hieronymi, Quaestiones hebraicae in libro Geneseos.* Leipzig: Teubner, 1868.

Lake, Peter. *Moderate Puritans and the Elizabethan Church.* Cambridge: Cambridge University Press, 1982.

Lambdin, Thomas O. "Philippi's Law Reconsidered." Pages 135–45 in *Biblical and Related Studies Presented to Samuel Iwry.* Edited by Ann Kort and Scott Morschauser. Winona Lake, IN: Eisenbrauns, 1985.

Lambe, P. J. "Biblical Criticism and Censorship in *Ancien Régime.* France: The Case of Richard Simon." *HTR* 78 (1985): 149–77.

Lange, Armin. *Handbuch der Textfunde vom Toten Meer.* Vol. 1: *Die Handschriften biblischer Bücher von Qumran und den anderen Fundorten.* Tübingen: Mohr Siebeck, 2009.

———. "The Severus Scroll Variant List in Light of the Dead Sea Scrolls." Pages 179–207 in *Tradition, Transmission, and Transformation from Second Temple Literature through Judaism and Christianity in Late Antiquity: Proceedings of the Thirteenth International Symposium of the Orion Center for the Study of the Dead Sea Scrolls and Associated Literature, Jointly Sponsored by the Hebrew University Center for the Study of Christianity, 22–24 February, 2011.* Edited by Menahem Kister, Hillel I. Newman, Michael Segal, and Ruth A. Clements. STDJ 113. Leiden: Brill, 2015.

———. " 'They Confirmed the Reading' (*y. Taʿan.* 4.68a): The Textual Standardization of Jewish Scriptures in the Second Temple Period." Pages 29–80 in *From Qumran to Aleppo: A Discussion with Emanuel Tov about the Textual History of Jewish Scriptures in Honor of His 65th Birthday.* Edited by Armin Lange, Matthias Weigold, and József Zsengellér. FRLANT 230. Göttingen: Vandenhoeck & Ruprecht, 2009.

Laplanche, François. *L'Écriture, le sacré et l'histoire: Érudits et politiques protestants devant la Bible en France au XVIIe siècle.* Amsterdam: Holland University Press, 1986.

Lee, Edward. *Annotationum Libri Duo, Alter in Annotationes Prioris Aeditionis Novi Testamenti Desiderij Erasmi, Alter in Annotationes Posterioris Aeditionis Eiusdem*. Paris: Gourmant, 1520.

Lejay, Paul. Review of *Aeli Donati quod fertur Commentum Terenti*, ed. Paul Wessner. *RCHL* 56 (1903): 168–72.

Levine, Lee I. *The Ancient Synagogue: The First Thousand Years*. New Haven: Yale University Press, 2005.

Levita, Johannes Isaac. *Defensio Veritatis Hebraicae Sacrarum Scripturarum*. Cologne: Soter, 1559.

Lim, Timothy H. "Authoritative Scriptures and the Dead Sea Scrolls." Pages 303–22 in *The Oxford Handbook of the Dead Sea Scrolls*. Edited by John J. Collins and Timothy Lim. Oxford: Oxford University Press, 2010.

———. *Holy Scripture in the Qumran Commentaries and Pauline Letters*. Oxford: Oxford University Press, 1997.

Lindanus, William. *De Optimo Scripturas Interpretandi Genere*. Cologne: Cholinum, 1558.

Lipshütz, Lazar. *Kitāb al-Khilaf: Mishael Ben Uzziel's Treatise on the Differences between Ben Asher and Ben Naphtali*. HUBP. Jerusalem: Magnes, 1965.

Lipton, Peter. *Inference to the Best Explanation*. 2nd ed. ILP. London: Routledge, 2004.

Lloyd, Christopher. *The Structures of History*. SSD. Oxford: Blackwell, 1993.

Loewinger, David S., and Malachi Beit-Arié. *The Damascus Pentateuch*. 2 vols. EHMF 1–2. Copenhagen: Rosenkilde & Bagger, 1978–1982. http://tinyurl.com/SBL7010q.

Locke, John. *An Essay Concerning Human Understanding*. London: Holt, 1690.

Maas, Paul. "Leitfehler und stemmatische Typen." *ByzZ* 37 (1937): 289–94.

———. *Textual Criticism*. Translated by Barbara Flower. Oxford: Clarendon, 1958.

Malcolm, Noel. "Hobbes, Ezra, and the Bible: The History of a Subversive Idea." Pages 383–431 in *Aspects of Hobbes*. Oxford: Oxford University Press, 2002.

Margoliouth, George. *Catalogue of the Hebrew and Samaritan Manuscripts in the British Museum*. Part 1. London: British Museum, 1899.

Martin, Gary D. *Multiple Originals: New Approaches to Hebrew Bible Textual Criticism*. TCSt 7. Atlanta: Society of Biblical Literature, 2010.

Martone, Corrado. "All the Bibles We Need: The Impact of the Qumran Evidence on Biblical Lower Criticism." Pages 47–64 in *The Scrolls and Biblical Traditions: Proceedings of the Seventh Meeting of the IOQS in Helsinki*. Edited by George J. Brooke, Daniel K. Falk, Eibert J. C. Tigchelaar, and Molly M. Zahn. STDJ 103. Leiden: Brill, 2012.

McCarter, P. Kyle, Jr. *1 Samuel: A New Translation with Introduction, Notes, and Commentary*. AB 8. Garden City, NY: Doubleday, 1980.

———. *Textual Criticism: Recovering the Text of the Hebrew Bible*. GBS. Philadelphia: Fortress, 1986.

McGann, Jerome J. *A Critique of Modern Textual Criticism*. Charlottesville: University of Virginia Press, 1992.

McLaverty, James. "The Mode of Existence of Literary Works of Art: The Case of the *Dunciad Variorum*." *SBib* 37 (1984): 82–105.

Meer, Michaël van der. "Joshua." Pages 86–101 in *The T&T Clark Companion to the Septuagint*. Edited by James K. Aitken. T&T Clark Companions. London: Bloomsbury, 2015.

Metso, Sarianna. "Evidence from the Qumran Scrolls for the Scribal Transmission of Leviticus." Pages 67–79 in *Editing the Bible: Assessing the Task Past and Present*. Edited by John S. Kloppenborg and Judith H. Newman. RBS 69. Atlanta: Society of Biblical Literature, 2012.

Metzger, Bruce M., and Bart D. Ehrman. *The Text of the New Testament: Its Transmission, Corruption, and Restoration*. 4th ed. New York: Oxford University Press, 2005.

Michaelis, Johann David. *Deutsche Uebersetzung des Alten Testaments mit Anmerkungen für Ungelehrte*. 13 vols. Göttingen: Dieterich: 1769–1785.

Milik, Józef T. "Textes Hébreux et Araméens." Pages 67–205 in *Les grottes de Murabba'ât*. Edited by Pierre Benoit, Józef T. Milik, and Roland de Vaux. DJD 2. Oxford: Clarendon, 1961.

Montano, Benito Arias. "De Psalterii Anglicani Exemplari Animadversio." In vol. 8 of *Biblia Polyglotta*. Antwerp: Plantin, 1569–1573.

Morin, Jean. *Exercitationes Ecclesiasticae in Utrumque Samaritanorum Pentateuchum*. Paris: Vitray, 1631.

Miller, Peter N. "Making the Paris Polyglot Bible: Humanism and Orientalism in the Early Seventeenth Century." Pages 59–85 in *Die europäische Gelehrtenrepublik im Zeitalter des Konfessionalismus*. Edited by Herbert Jaumann. WF 96. Wiesbaden: Harrassowitz, 2001.

———. "The 'Antiquarianization' of Biblical Scholarship and the London Polyglot Bible (1653–57)." *JHI* 62 (2001): 463–82.

Montaigne, Michel de. *The Complete Essays of Montaigne*. Translated by Donald M. Frame. Stanford: Stanford University Press, 1958.

———. *Les Essais*. Edited by Pierre Villey and Verdun-Louis Saulnier. Paris: Presses universitaires, 1965.

Müller, Reinhard, Juha Pakkala, and Bas ter Haar Romeny. *Evidence of Editing: Growth and Change of Texts in the Hebrew Bible*. RBS 75. Atlanta: Society of Biblical Literature, 2014.

Muller, Richard A. "The Debate over the Vowel Points and the Crisis in Orthodox Hermeneutics." Pages 146–54 in *After Calvin: Studies in the Development of a Theological Tradition*. OSHT. New York: Oxford University Press, 2003.

———. *Post-Reformation Reformed Dogmatics*. Vol. 2, *Holy Scripture: The Cognitive Foundation of Theology*. 2nd ed. Grand Rapids: Baker, 2003.

———. "Scholasticism Protestant and Catholic: Francis Turretin on the Object and Principles of Theology." Pages 137–44 in *After Calvin: Studies in the Development of a Theological Tradition*. OSHT. New York: Oxford University Press, 2003.

Najman, Hindy. "Configuring the Text in Biblical Studies." Pages 3–22 in *A Teacher for All Generations: Essays in Honor of James C. Vanderkam*. Edited by Eric F. Mason. JSJSup 153. Leiden: Brill, 2012.

———. *Seconding Sinai: The Development of Mosaic Discourse in Second Temple Judaism*. JSJSup 77. Leiden: Brill, 2003.

Nelson, Richard D. *Joshua: A Commentary*. OTL. Louisville: Westminster John Knox, 1997.

Neubauer, Adolf. "Alfonso de Zamora." *JQR* 7 (1895): 398–417.

Newsom, Carol A. "'Sectually Explicit' Literature from Qumran." Pages 167–87 in *The Hebrew Bible and Its Interpreters*. Edited by William H. Propp, Baruch Halpern, and David Noel Freedman. BJSUCSD 1. Winona Lake, IN: Eisenbrauns, 1990.

Nichols, Aidan. *The Shape of Catholic Theology: An Introduction to Its Sources, Principles, and History*. Collegeville, MN: Liturgical Press, 1991.

Niditch, Susan. *Oral World and the Written Word: Ancient Israelite Literature*. LAI. Louisville: Westminster John Knox, 1996.

Nietzsche, Friedrich. *Digitale Kritische Gesamtausgabe: Werke und Briefe*. http://tinyurl.com/SBL7010f.

———. *On the Advantage and Disadvantage of History for Life*. Translated by Peter Preus. Indianapolis: Hackett, 1980.

———. *The Portable Nietzsche*. Edited and Translated by Walter Kaufmann. New York: Viking Press, 1968.

———. *Unmodern Observations*. Translated by William Arrowsmith. New Haven: Yale University Press, 1990.

———. *Unzeitgemässe Betrachtungen, Zweites Stück: Vom Nutzen und Nachteil der Historie für das Leben*. Leipzig: Fritzsch, 1874.

Niles, John D. "Orality." Pages 205–23 in *The Cambridge Companion to Textual Scholarship*. Edited by Neil Fraistat and Julia Flanders. Cambridge: Cambridge University Press, 2013.

Nir-El, Yoram, and Magen Broshi. "The Black Ink of the Qumran Scrolls." *DSD* 3 (1996): 157–67.

Nirenberg, David. *Anti-Judaism: The Western Tradition*. New York: Norton, 2013.

Nöldeke, Theodor. Review of *Der Text der Bücher Samuelis untersucht*, by Julius Wellhausen. *ZWT* (1873): 117–22.

Noll, Mark, *The Princeton Theology 1812–1921: Scripture, Science, and Theological Method from Archibald Alexander to Benjamin Breckinridge Warfield*. Grand Rapids: Baker, 1983.

Norton, David. *A Textual History of the King James Bible*. Cambridge: Cambridge University Press, 2005.

Ofer, Yosef, and Alexander Lubotzsky. "The *Masorah* as an Error Correcting Code" [Hebrew]. *Tarbiz* 82 (2013): 89–114.

Olin, John C. *Catholic Reform: From Cardinal Ximenes to the Council of Trent, 1495–1563; An Essay with Illustrative Documents and a Brief Study of St. Ignatius Loyola*. New York: Fordham University Press, 1990.

Outhwaite, Ben. "The Oldest Hebrew Fragment in the Collection? T-S NS 3.21." *Fragment of the Month: November 2010*. http://tinyurl.com/SBL7010g.

Owen, Elizabeth. "4QDeut[n]: A Pre-Samaritan Text?" *DSD* 4 (1997): 162–78.

Owen, John. *Of the Divine Original, Authority, Self-Evidencing Light, and Power of the Scriptures*. Oxford: Hall, 1659. Repr., pages 363–446 in vol. 4 of *The Works of John Owen*. Edited by Thomas Russell. London: Baynes, 1826.

———. *Of the Integrity and Purity of the Hebrew and Greek Text of the Scripture: With Considerations on the Prolegomena and Appendix to the Late Biblia Polyglotta*. Oxford: Hall, 1659. Repr., pages 447–537 in vol. 4 of *Works of John Owen*. Edited by Thomas Russell. London: Baynes, 1826.

Peirce, Charles Sanders. "Abduction and Induction." Pages 150–56 in *Philosophical Writings of Peirce*. Edited by Justus Buchler. New York: Dover, 1955.

———. "Prolegomena to an Apology for Pragmaticism." Pages 530–72 in vol. 4 of *Collected Papers of Charles Sanders Peirce*. Edited by Charles Hartshorne, Paul Weiss, and Arthur W. Burks. Cambridge: Harvard University Press, 1931–1958.

Penkower, Jordan S. "Rabbinic Bible." Pages 361–64 in vol. 2 of *Dictionary of Biblical Interpretation*. Edited by John. H. Hayes. Nashville: Abingdon, 1999.

———. "A Tenth-Century Pentateuchal MS from Jerusalem (MS C3), Corrected by Mishael Ben Uzziel" [Hebrew]. *Tarbiz* 58 (1988): 49–74.

Perani, Mauro. "Il più antico rotolo del Pentateuco ebraico integro: Una scoperta alla Biblioteca Universitaria di Bologna." *TECA* (2013): 87–97.

Person, Raymond F. "The Ancient Israelite Scribe as Performer." *JBL* 117 (1998): 601–9.

Pisano, Stephen. *Additions or Omissions in the Books of Samuel: The Significant Pluses and Minuses in the Massoretic, LXX and Qumran Texts*. OBO 57. Fribourg: Universitätsverlag; Göttingen: Vandenhoeck & Rupprecht, 1984.

Plumed, Jesús de Prado. "The Commission of Targum Manuscripts and the Patronage of Christian Hebraism in Sixteenth-Century Castile." Pages 146–65 in *A Jewish Targum in a Christian World*. Edited by Alberdina Houtman, Eveline van Staalduine-Sulman, and Hans-Martin Kirn. JCPS. Leiden: Brill, 2014.

———. "La enseñanza del hebreo en Alcalá: La búsqueda complutense de Dios/Teaching Hebrew in Alcalá: The Complutense Search for God." Pages 452–86 in *V Centenario de la Bíblia Políglota Complutense*. Edited by José L. G. Sánchez-Molero. Madrid: Universidad Complutense, 2014.

Polak, Frank. "Book, Scribe, and Bard: Oral Discourse and Written Text in Recent Biblical Scholarship." *Prooftexts* 31 (2011): 118–40.

———. "Style Is More Than the Person: Sociolinguistics, Literary Culture and the Distinction between Written and Oral Narrative." Pages 38–103 in *Biblical Hebrew: Studies in Chronology and Typology*. Edited by Ian Young. JSOTSup 369. London: T&T Clark, 2003.

Polanus, Amandus. *Syntagma Theologiae Christianae*. Hanover: Aubrius, 1615.

Pollack, Sheldon. "Future Philology: The Fate of a Soft Science in a Hard World." *CritInq* 35 (2009): 931–61.

Popkin, Richard H. "Jewish Christians and Christian Jews in Spain, 1492 and After." *Judaism* 41 (1992): 247–67.

Porter, James I. *Nietzsche and the Philology of the Future*. Stanford: Stanford University Press, 2000.

Propp, William H. C. *Exodus: A New Translation with Introduction and Commentary*. AB 2. 2 vols. New York: Doubleday, 1999–2006.

Pugliatti, Paola. "Textual Perspectives in Italy: From Pasquali's Historicism to the Challenge of 'Variantistica' (and Beyond)." *Text* 11 (1998): 155–88.

Qimron, Elisha. *The Hebrew of the Dead Sea Scrolls*. HSS 29. Atlanta: Scholars Press, 1986.

Quine, W. V. *Quiddities: An Intermittently Philosophical Dictionary*. Cambridge: Harvard University Press, 1987.

———. *Word and Object*. Studies in Communication. Cambridge: MIT Press, 1960.

Reeve, Michael D. "Archetypes." Pages 107–17 in *Manuscripts and Methods: Essays on Editing and Transmission*. Rome: Edizioni di storia e letteratura, 2011.

———. Foreword to *Everything You Always Wanted to Know about Lachmann's Method: A Non-standard Handbook of Genealogical Textual Criticism in the Age of Post-structuralism, Cladistics, and Copy-Text*. By Paolo Trovato. Storie e linguaggi 7. Padua: Libreriauniversitaria, 2014.

———. "Shared Innovations, Dichotomies, and Evolution." Pages 55–103 in *Manuscripts and Methods: Essays on Editing and Transmission*. Rome: Edizioni di storia e letteratura, 2011.

Reich, Ronny, Eli Shukron, and Omri Lernau. "Recent Discoveries in the City of David, Jerusalem." *IEJ* 57 (2007): 153–69.

Resnick, Irven M. "The Falsification of Scripture and Medieval Christian and Jewish Polemics." *MedEnc* 2 (1996): 344–80.

Rodríguez, Carlos del Valle. "Antonio Nebrija's Biblical Scholarship." Pages 57–72 in *Biblical Humanism and Scholasticism in the Age of Erasmus*. Edited by Erika Rummel. BCCT 9. Leiden: Brill, 2008.

Rofé, Alexander. "4QMidrash Samuel? Observations Concerning the Character of 4QSam^a." *Text* 19 (1998): 63–74.

———. "The Acts of Nahash according to 4QSam^a." *IEJ* 32 (1982): 129–33.

———. "Digesting DJD 12: Its Contribution to the Textual Criticism of the Pentateuch." *DSD* 23 (2016): 97–104.

———. "Emendation by Conjecture of the Masoretic Text" [Hebrew]. *Tarbiz* (forthcoming).

———. "The End of the Book of Joshua According to the Septuagint." *Hen* 4 (1982): 17–36.

———. "The End of the Song of Moses (Deuteronomy 32:43)." Pages 47–54 in *Deuteronomy: Issues and Interpretation*. OTS. London: T&T Clark, 2002.

———. "The Historical Significance of Secondary Readings." Pages 393–402 in *The Quest for Context and Meaning: Studies in Biblical Intertextuality in Honor of James A. Sanders*. Edited by Craig A. Evans and Shemaryahu Talmon. BibInt 28. Leiden: Brill, 1997.

———. "The Methods of Late Biblical Scribes as Evidenced by the Septuagint Compared with the Other Textual Witnesses." Pages 259–70 in *Tehillah le-Moshe: Biblical and Judaic Studies in Honor of Moshe Greenberg*. Edited by Mordechai Cogan, Barry L. Eichler, and Jeffrey H. Tigay. Winona Lake, IN: Eisenbrauns, 1997.

———. "The Nomistic Correction in Biblical Manuscripts and Its Occurrence in 4QSam^a." *RevQ* 14 (1989): 247–54.

Rogerson, John. "Charles-François Houbigant: His Background, Work and Importance for Lowth." Pages 83–92 in *Sacred Conjectures: The Context and Legacy of Robert Lowth and Jean Astruc*. Edited by John Jarick. LHBOTS 457. London: T&T Clark, 2007.

Rösel, Martin. "The Septuagint-Version of the Book of Joshua." *SJOT* 16 (2002): 5–23.

Rosenmüller, E. F. K. *Handbuch für die Literatur der biblischen Kritik und Exegese*. 4 vols. Göttingen: Vandenhoeck & Ruprecht, 1797–1800.

Rummel, Erika. *Erasmus and His Catholic Critics*. 2 vols. BHRef 45. Nieuwkoop: de Graaf, 1989.

———. *The Humanist-Scholastic Debate in the Renaissance and Reformation*. HHS 120. Cambridge: Harvard University Press, 1995.

———, ed. *Biblical Humanism and Scholasticism in the Age of Erasmus*. BCCT 9. Leiden: Brill, 2008.

Sanders, James A. "Stability and Fluidity in Text and Canon." Pages 203–17 in *Tradition of the Text: Studies Offered to Dominique Barthélemy in Celebration of His 70th Birthday*. Edited by Gerard J. Norton and Stephen Pisano. OBO 109. Fribourg: Universitätsverlag; Göttingen: Vandenhoeck & Ruprecht, 1991.

------. "The Task of Text Criticism." Pages 315–27 in *Problems in Biblical Theology: Essays in Honor of Rolf Knierim*. Edited by H. T. C. Sun and Keith L. Eades. Grand Rapids: Eerdmans, 1997.

Sanders, Paul. "The Ashkar-Gilson Manuscript: Remnant of a Proto-Masoretic Model Scroll of the Torah." *JHS* 14 (2014): art. 7. http://tinyurl.com/SBL7010h.

Sanderson, Judith E. "4QExod^c." Pages 97–125 in *Qumran Cave 4.VII: Genesis to Numbers*. Edited by Eugene Ulrich and Frank Moore Cross. DJD XII. Oxford: Clarendon, 1994.

------. "4QExod^j." Pages 149–50 in *Qumran Cave 4.VII: Genesis to Numbers*. Edited by Eugene Ulrich and Frank Moore Cross. DJD XII. Oxford: Clarendon, 1994.

------. *An Exodus Scroll from Qumran: 4QpaleoExod^m and the Samaritan Tradition*. HSS 30. Atlanta: Scholars Press, 1986.

Sandys-Wunsch, John. *What Have They Done to the Bible? A History of Modern Biblical Interpretation*. Collegeville, MN: Liturgical Press, 2005.

Schenker, Adrian. "The Edition Biblia Hebraica Quinta (BHQ)." *HBAI* 2 (2013): 6–16.

------. "Eine Neuausgabe der Biblia Hebraica." *ZAH* 9 (1996): 58–61.

------. "The Polyglot Bible of Alcalá 1514–17." Pages 286–91 in vol. 2 of *Hebrew Bible/Old Testament: The History of Its Interpretation*. Edited by Magne Saebø. Göttingen: Vandenhoeck & Ruprecht, 2008.

------. "The Polyglot Bibles of Antwerp, Paris and London: 1568–1658." Pages 774–84 in vol. 2 of *Hebrew Bible/Old Testament: The History of Its Interpretation*. Edited by Magne Saebø. Göttingen: Vandenhoeck & Ruprecht, 2008.

------, ed. *The Earliest Text of the Hebrew Bible: The Relationship between the Masoretic Text and the Hebrew Base of the Septuagint Reconsidered*. SCS 52. Atlanta: Society of Biblical Literature, 2003.

------, et al., eds. *General Introduction and Megilloth*. BHQ 18. Stuttgart: Deutsche Bibelgesellschaft, 2004.

Schenker, Adrian, and Philippe Hugo. "Histoire de texte et critique textuelle de l'Ancien Testament dans la recherche récente." Pages 11–33 in *L'enfance de la Bible hébraïque: L'histoire du texte de l'Ancien Testament à la lumière de recherches récente*. Edited by Adrian Schenker and Philippe Hugo. MdB 52. Geneva: Labor et Fides, 2005.

Schökel, Luis Alonso, et al. *Anejo a la edición facsimile de la Biblia Polí-*

glota Complutense. Valencia: Fundación Biblica Española/Universidad Complutense de Madrid, 1987.

Schorch, Stefan. "The Libraries in 2 Macc 2:13–15, and the Torah as a Public Document in Second Century BC Judaism." Pages 169–80 in *The Books of the Maccabees: History, Theology, Ideology; Papers of the Second International Conference on the Deuteronomical Books, Pápa, Hungary, 9–11 June, 2005*. Edited by Géza G. Xeravits and József Zsengellér. JSJSup 118. Leiden: Brill, 2007.

———. "The Samaritan Version of Deuteronomy and the Origin of Deuteronomy." Pages 23–37 in *Samaria, Samarians, Samaritans: Studies on Bible, History and Linguistics*. Edited by József Zsengellér. SJ 66. Berlin: de Gruyter, 2011.

———. "Which Kind of Authority? The Authority of the Torah during the Hellenistic and Roman Periods." Pages 1–15 in *Scriptural Authority in Early Judaism and Ancient Christianity*. Edited by Géza G. Xeravits, Tobias Nicklas, and Isaac Kalimi. DCLS 16. Berlin: de Gruyter, 2013.

Schreckenberg, Heinz. "Text, Überlieferung und Textkritik von *Contra Apionem*." Pages 49–82 in *Josephus' Contra Apionem: Studies in Its Character and Context with a Latin Concordance to the Portion Missing in Greek*. Edited by Louis H. Feldman and John R. Levison. AGJU 34. Leiden: Brill, 1996.

Schwartz, Daniel R. " 'Scribes and Pharisees, Hypocrites': Who are the 'Scribes' in the New Testament?" Pages 89–101 in *Studies in the Jewish Background of Christianity*. WUNT 60. Tübingen: Mohr Siebeck, 1992.

Seeligman, Isaac L. "Problems and Perspectives in Modern Septuagint Research." *Text* 15 (1990): 169–232.

Segal, Michael. "4QReworked Pentateuch or 4QPentateuch?" Pages 391–99 in *The Dead Sea Scrolls: Fifty Years after Their Discovery: Proceedings of the Jerusalem Congress, July 20–25, 1997*. Edited by Lawrence H. Schiffman, Emanuel Tov, and James C. VanderKam. Jerusalem: Israel Exploration Society, 2000.

———. "Biblical Interpretation: Yes and No." Pages 63–80 in *What Is Bible?* Edited by Karin Finsterbusch and Armin Lange. CBET 67. Leuven: Peeters, 2012.

———. "The Hebrew University Bible Project." *HBAI* 2 (2013): 38–62.

———. "The Text of the Hebrew Bible in Light of the Dead Sea Scrolls." *MG* 12 (2007): 5–20.

Segal, Michael, Emanuel Tov, William B. Seales, Clifford S. Parker, Pnina Shor, Yosef Porath, with an appendix by Ada Yardeni. "An Early Leviticus Scroll from En-Gedi: Preliminary Publication." *Textus* 26 (2016): 1–20.

Segal, Moshe H. *The Books of Samuel* [Hebrew]. Jerusalem: Kiryat Sefer, 1964.

Segre, Cesare. "Critique textuelle, théorie des ensembles et diasystème." *BCLSB* 62 (1976): 279–92.

———. "Problemi teorici e pratici della critica testuale." Pages 356–73 in *Opera Critica*. Edited by Alberto Conte and Andrea Mirabile. Milan: Mondadori, 2014.

Shalev, Zur. "The Antwerp Polyglot Bible: Maps, Scholarship, and Exegesis." Pages 23–71 in *Sacred Words and Worlds: Geography, Religion, and Scholarship, 1550–1700*. SLCTI 2. Leiden: Brill, 2012.

Sheehan, Jonathan. *The Enlightenment Bible: Translation, Scholarship, Culture*. Princeton: Princeton University Press, 2005.

Shillingsburg, Peter L. "Text as Matter, Concept, and Action." *SBib* 44 (1991): 31–82.

———. *Resisting Texts: Authority and Submission in Constructions of Meaning*. ETLC. Ann Arbor: University of Michigan Press, 1997.

Shoham, Yair. "Hebrew Bullae." Pages 29–57 in *Excavations at the City of David 1978–1985 Directed by Yigal Shiloh*. Vol. 6, *Inscriptions*. Edited by Donald T. Ariel. Qedem 41. Jerusalem: Hebrew University Institute of Archaeology, 2000.

Shuger, Debora K. *The Renaissance Bible: Scholarship, Sacrifice, and Subjectivity*. New Historicism 29. Berkeley: University of California Press, 1994.

Sieg, Ulrich. *Germany's Prophet: Paul de Lagarde and the Origins of Modern Antisemitism*. TISEJ. Hanover, NH: Brandeis University Press, 2012.

Siegel, Jonathan P. *The Severus Scroll and 1QIsaᵃ*. MasS 2. Missoula, MT: Scholars Press, 1975.

Simon, Richard. *A Critical History of the Old Testament*. London: Davis, 1682.

———. *Histoire critique du Vieux Testament*. 2nd ed. Rotterdam: Leers, 1685.

Sirat, Colette. *Hebrew Manuscripts of the Middle Ages*. Cambridge: Cambridge University Press, 2002.

———. *Les papyrus en caractères hébraïques trouvés en Égypte*. MMCH. Paris: Centre National de la Recherche Scientifique, 1985.

Sirat, Colette, Michèle Dukan, and Ada Yardeni. "Rouleaux de la Tora antérieurs à l'an mille." *CRAI* 138 (1994): 861–87.

Skehan, Patrick W. "Exodus in the Samaritan Recension from Qumran." *JBL* 74 (1955): 182–87.

Skehan, Patrick W., Eugene Ulrich, and Judith E. Sanderson. "4Qpaleo-Genesis–Exodus^l." Pages 17–52 in *Qumran Cave 4.IV: Palaeo-Hebrew and Greek Biblical Manuscripts*. Edited by Patrick W. Skehan, Eugene Ulrich, and Judith E. Sanderson. DJD IX. Oxford: Clarendon, 1992.

———. "4QpaleoExodus^m." Pages 53–130 in *Qumran Cave 4.IV: Palaeo-Hebrew and Greek Biblical Manuscripts*. Edited by Patrick W. Skehan, Eugene Ulrich, and Judith E. Sanderson. DJD IX. Oxford: Clarendon, 1992.

Skehan, Patrick W., and Eugene Ulrich. "4QDeut^q." Pages 137–42 in *Qumran Cave 4.IX: Deuteronomy to Kings*. Edited by Eugene Ulrich et al. DJD XIV. Oxford: Clarendon, 1995.

Skinner, John. *A Critical and Exegetical Commentary on Genesis*. 2nd ed. ICC. Edinburgh: T&T Clark, 1930.

Sommer, Benjamin D. "The Scroll of Isaiah as Jewish Scripture, or, Why Jews Don't Read Books." Pages 225–42 *Society of Biblical Literature 1996 Seminar Papers*. Atlanta: Scholars Press, 1996.

Steuco, Agostino. *Veteris Testamenti ad Veritatem Hebraicam Recognitio*. 2nd ed. Lyons: Gryphium, 1531.

Stevens, Wallace. *The Palm at the End of the Mind: Selected Poems and a Play*. Edited by Holly Stevens. New York: Vintage, 1972.

Strawn, Brent A. "Excerpted Manuscripts at Qumran: Their Significance for the Textual History of the Hebrew Bible and the Socio-religious History of the Qumran Community and Its Literature." Pages 107–67 in *The Dead Sea Scrolls and the Qumran Community*. Vol. 2 of *The Bible and the Dead Sea Scrolls*. Edited by James H. Charlesworth. Waco, TX: Baylor University Press, 2006.

Swift, Jonathan. *An Argument to Prove That the Abolishing of Christianity in England May, as Things Now Stand, Be Attended with Some Inconveniences, and Perhaps Not Produce Those Many Good Effects Proposed Thereby*. Pages 225–41 in vol. 1 of *The Works of Dr. Jonathan Swift*. Edinburgh: Donaldson, 1774.

Ta-Shma, Israel M. "The 'Open' Book in Medieval Hebrew Literature: The Problem of Authorized Editions." *BJRL* 75 (1993): 17–24.

Talmon, Shemaryahu. "Double Readings in the Masoretic Text." Pages

217–66 in *Text and Canon of the Hebrew Bible: Collected Studies.* Winona Lake, IN: Eisenbrauns, 2010.

———. "Hebrew Fragments from Masada." Pages 1–149 in *Masada VI: The Yigael Yadin Excavations 1963–1965 Final Report.* Masada Reports. Edited by Shemaryahu Talmon and Yigael Yadin. Jerusalem: Israel Exploration Society, 1999.

———. "The Old Testament Text." Pages 1–41 in *Qumran and the History of the Biblical Text.* Edited by Frank Moore Cross and Shemaryahu Talmon. Cambridge: Harvard University Press, 1975.

———. "Synonymous Readings in the Masoretic Text." Pages 171–216 in *Text and Canon of the Hebrew Bible: Collected Studies.* Winona Lake, IN: Eisenbrauns, 2010.

———. "Textual Criticism: The Ancient Versions." Pages 383–418 in *Text and Canon of the Hebrew Bible: Collected Studies.* Winona Lake, IN: Eisenbrauns, 2010.

———. "The Textual Study of the Bible: A New Outlook." Pages 321–400 in *Qumran and the History of the Biblical Text.* Edited by Frank Moore Cross and Shemaryahu Talmon. Cambridge: Harvard University Press, 1975.

———. "The Three Scrolls of the Law That Were Found in the Temple Court." Pages 329–46 in *Text and Canon of the Hebrew Bible: Collected Studies.* Winona Lake, IN: Eisenbrauns, 2010.

———. "The Transmission History of the Text of the Hebrew Bible in the Light of Biblical Manuscripts from Qumran and Other Sites in the Judean Desert." Pages 40–50 in *The Dead Sea Scrolls: Fifty Years after their Discovery.* Edited by Lawrence H. Schiffman, Emanuel Tov, and James C. VanderKam. Jerusalem: Israel Exploration Society, 2000.

Talshir, Zipora. "The Relationship between Sam-MT, 4QSam^a, and Chr and the Case of 2 Sam 24." Pages 273–98 in *In the Footsteps of Sherlock Holmes: Studies in the Biblical Text in Honour of Anneli Aejmelaeus.* Edited by Kristin De Troyer, Timothy M. Law, and Marketta Liljeström. CBET 72. Leuven, Peeters, 2014.

———. "Textual Criticism at the Service of Literary Criticism and the Question of an Eclectic Edition of the Hebrew Bible." Pages 33–60 in *After Qumran: Old and Modern Editions of the Biblical Texts; The Historical Books.* Edited by Hans Ausloos, Bénédicte Lemmelijn, and Julio Trebolle Barrera. BETL 246. Leuven, Peeters 2012.

———. "Texts, Text-Forms, Editions, New Composition and the Final

Products of Biblical Literature." Pages 40–66 in *Congress Volume Munich 2013*. Edited by Christl M. Maier. VTSup 163. Leiden: Brill, 2014.

Tanselle, G. Thomas. "Editing without a Copy-Text." *SBib* 47 (1994): 1–22.

———. *A Rationale of Textual Criticism*. Philadelphia: University of Pennsylvania Press, 1989.

Teeter, David Andrew. *Scribal Laws: Exegetical Variation in the Textual Transmission of Biblical Law in the Late Second Temple Period*. FAT 92. Tübingen: Mohr Siebeck, 2014.

Thenius, Otto. *Die Bücher Samuelis erklärt*. 2nd ed. Leipzig: Hirzel, 1864.

Tigay, Jeffrey H. "Conflation as a Redactional Technique." Pages 53–95 in *Empirical Models for Biblical Criticism*. Edited by Jeffrey H. Tigay. Philadelphia: University of Pennsylvania Press, 1985.

Tigchelaar, Eibert. "Assessing Emanuel Tov's 'Qumran Scribal Practice.'" Pages 173–207 in *The Dead Sea Scrolls: Transmission of Traditions and Production of Texts*. Edited by Sarianna Metso, Hindy Najman, and Eileen Schuller. STDJ 92. Leiden: Brill, 2010.

———. "Editing the Hebrew Bible: An Overview of Some Problems." Pages 41–65 in *Editing the Bible: Assessing the Task Past and Present*. Edited by John S. Kloppenborg and Judith H. Newman. RBS 69. Atlanta: Society of Biblical Literature, 2012.

———. "In Search of the Scribe of 1QS." Pages 439–52 in *Emanuel: Studies in Hebrew Bible, Septuagint and Dead Sea Scrolls in Honor of Emanuel Tov*. Edited by Shalom M. Paul, Robert A. Kraft, Lawrence H. Schiffman, and Weston W. Fields. VTSup 94. Leiden: Brill, 2003.

———. "Notes on Three Qumran-Type Yadin Fragments Leading to a Discussion of Identification, Attribution, Provenance, and Names." *DSD* 19 (2012): 198–214.

Timpanaro, Sebastiano. *The Freudian Slip: Psychoanalysis and Textual Criticism*. Translated by Kate Soper. London: NLB, 1976.

———. *The Genesis of Lachmann's Method*. Translated by Glenn W. Most. Chicago: University of Chicago Press, 2005.

Toorn, Karel van der. *Scribal Culture and the Making of the Hebrew Bible*. Cambridge: Harvard University Press, 2007.

Tov, Emanuel. "4QLev^d." Pages 193–95 in *Qumran Cave 4.VII: Genesis to Numbers*. Edited by Eugene Ulrich and Frank Moore Cross. DJD XII. Oxford: Clarendon, 1994.

———. "*Biblia Hebraica Quinta*: An Important Step Forward." Pages 189–98 in *Hebrew Bible, Greek Bible, and Qumran: Collected Essays*. TSAJ 121. Tübingen: Mohr Siebeck, 2008.

———. "The Biblical Texts from the Judean Desert: An Overview and Analysis." Pages 128–54 in *Hebrew Bible, Greek Bible, and Qumran: Collected Essays*. TSAJ 121. Tübingen: Mohr Siebeck, 2008.

———. "The Contribution of the Qumran Scrolls to the Understanding of the Septuagint." Pages 285–300 in *The Greek and Hebrew Bible: Collected Essays on the Septuagint*. VTSup 72. Leiden: Brill, 1999. Repr., Atlanta: Society of Biblical Literature, 2006.

———. "Criteria for Evaluating Textual Readings: The Limitations of Textual Rules." *HTR* 75 (1982): 429–48.

———. "Eclectic Text Editions of Hebrew Scripture." Pages 121–31 in *Textual Criticism of the Hebrew Bible, Qumran, Septuagint: Collected Essays*. VTSup 167. Leiden: Brill, 2015. Leiden: Brill, 2015.

———. "Excerpted and Abbreviated Biblical Texts from Qumran." Pages 27–41 in *Hebrew Bible, Greek Bible, and Qumran: Collected Essays*. TSAJ 121. Tübingen: Mohr Siebeck, 2008.

———. "Foreword." Pages xi–xii in *Qumran Cave 4.XII: 1–2 Samuel*. Edited by Frank Moore Cross et al. DJD XVII. Oxford: Clarendon, 2005.

———. "From 4QReworked Pentateuch to 4QPentateuch (?)." Pages 45–59 in *Textual Criticism of the Hebrew Bible, Qumran, Septuagint: Collected Essays*. VTSup 167. Leiden: Brill, 2015.

———. "The Genealogical Lists in Genesis 5 and 11 in Three Different Versions." Pages 221–38 in *Textual Criticism of the Hebrew Bible, Qumran, Septuagint: Collected Essays*. VTSup 167. Leiden: Brill, 2015.

———. "Groups of Biblical Texts Found at Qumran." Pages 85–102 in *Time to Prepare the Way in the Wilderness: Papers on the Qumran Scrolls*. Edited by Devorah Dimant and Lawrence H. Schiffman. STDJ 16. Leiden: Brill, 1995.

———. "The Growth of the Book of Joshua in Light of the Evidence of the Septuagint." Pages 385–96 in *The Greek and Hebrew Bible: Collected Essays on the Septuagint*. VTSup 72. Leiden: Brill, 1999. Repr., Atlanta: Society of Biblical Literature, 2006.

———. "The Hebrew Qumran Texts and the Septuagint: An Overview." Pages 353–67 in *Textual Criticism of the Hebrew Bible, Qumran, Septuagint: Collected Essays*. VTSup 167. Leiden: Brill, 2015.

————. "Hebrew Scripture Editions: Philosophy and Praxis." Pages 247–70 in *Hebrew Bible, Greek Bible, and Qumran: Collected Essays.* TSAJ 121. Tübingen: Mohr Siebeck, 2008.

————. "The History and Significance of a Standard Text of the Hebrew Bible." Pages 49–66 in vol. 1.1 of *Hebrew Bible/Old Testament: The History of Its Interpretation.* Edited by Magne Saebø. Göttingen: Vandenhoeck & Ruprecht, 1996.

————. "A Modern Textual Outlook Based on the Qumran Scrolls." *HUCA* 53 (1982): 11–27.

————. "The Nature and Background of Harmonizations in Biblical Manuscripts." *JSOT* 31 (1985): 3–29.

————. "A Qumran Origin for the Masada Non-Biblical Texts?" *DSD* 7 (2000): 57–73.

————. "Reflections on the Many Forms of Scripture in Light of the LXX and 4QReworked Pentateuch." Pages 3–19 in *Textual Criticism of the Hebrew Bible, Qumran, Septuagint: Collected Essays.* VTSup 167. Leiden: Brill, 2015.

————. "The Relevance of Textual Theories for the Praxis of Textual Criticism." Pages 23–35 in *A Teacher for All Generations: Essays in Honor of James C. Vanderkam.* Edited by Eric F. Mason. JSJSup 153. Leiden: Brill, 2012.

————. "Rewritten Bible Compositions and Biblical Manuscripts, with Special Attention Paid to the Samaritan Pentateuch." Pages 57–70 in *Hebrew Bible, Greek Bible, and Qumran: Collected Essays.* TSAJ 121. Tübingen: Mohr Siebeck, 2008.

————. "The Samaritan Pentateuch and the Dead Sea Scrolls: The Proximity of the Pre-Samaritan Qumran Scrolls to the SP." Pages 387–410 in *Textual Criticism of the Hebrew Bible, Qumran, Septuagint: Collected Essays.* VTSup 167. Leiden: Brill, 2015.

————. *Scribal Practices and Approaches Reflected in the Texts Found in the Judean Desert.* STDJ 54. Leiden: Brill, 2004.

————. "Some Sequence Differences between the Masoretic Text and the Septuagint and Their Ramifications for Literary Criticism." Pages 411–18 in *The Greek and Hebrew Bible: Collected Essays on the Septuagint.* VTSup 72. Leiden: Brill, 1999. Repr., Atlanta: Society of Biblical Literature, 2006.

————. "The Status of the Masoretic Text in Modern Text Editions of the Hebrew Bible: The Relevance of Canon." Pages 234–51 in *The Canon*

Debate. Edited by Lee M. McDonald and James A. Sanders. Peabody, MA: Hendrickson, 2002.

———. *The Text-Critical Use of the Septuagint in Biblical Research.* 2nd ed. Jerusalem: Simor, 1997.

———. *The Text-Critical Use of the Septuagint in Biblical Research.* 3rd ed. Winona Lake, IN: Eisenbrauns, 2015.

———. "The Text of the Hebrew/Aramaic and Greek Bible Used in the Ancient Synagogues." Pages 171–88 in *Hebrew Bible, Greek Bible, and Qumran: Collected Essays.* TSAJ 121. Tübingen: Mohr Siebeck, 2008.

———. "The Textual Basis of Modern Translations of the Hebrew Bible." Pages 92–106 in *Hebrew Bible, Greek Bible, and Qumran: Collected Essays.* TSAJ 121. Tübingen: Mohr Siebeck, 2008.

———. "The Textual Character of 11QpaleoLev" [Hebrew]. *Shnaton* 3 (1978–1979): 238–44.

———. *Textual Criticism of the Hebrew Bible.* Minneapolis: Fortress, 1992.

———. *Textual Criticism of the Hebrew Bible.* 3rd ed. Minneapolis: Fortress, 2012.

———. "Textual Criticism of the Hebrew Bible 1947–1997." Pages 61–81 in *Perspectives in the Study of the Old Testament and Early Judaism: A Symposium on Honour of Adam S. van der Woude on the Occasion of His 70th Birthday.* Edited by Florentino García Martínez and Ed Noort. VTSup 73. Leiden: Brill, 1998.

———. "The Textual Development of the Torah." Pages 239–49 in *Textual Criticism of the Hebrew Bible, Qumran, Septuagint: Collected Essays.* VTSup 167. Leiden: Brill, 2015.

———. "Textual Harmonization in the Stories of the Patriarchs." Pages 166–88 in *Textual Criticism of the Hebrew Bible, Qumran, Septuagint: Collected Essays.* VTSup 167. Leiden: Brill, 2015.

———. "Textual Harmonizations in the Ancient Texts of Deuteronomy." Pages 271–82 in *Hebrew Bible, Greek Bible, and Qumran: Collected Essays.* TSAJ 121. Tübingen: Mohr Siebeck, 2008.

Tov, Emanuel, Kipp Davis, and Robert Duke, eds. *Dead Sea Scrolls Fragments in the Museum Collection.* Leiden: Brill, 2016.

Tov, Emanuel, and Sidnie White (Crawford). "Reworked Pentateuch." Pages 187–351 in *Qumran Cave 4.VIII: Parabiblical Texts, Part I.* Edited by Harold W. Attridge et al. DJD XIII. Oxford: Clarendon, 1994.

Trebolle Barrera, Julio. "Qumran Evidence for a Biblical Standard Text and for Non-standard and Parabiblical Texts." Pages 89–106 in *The Dead*

Sea Scrolls in Their Historical Context. Edited by Timothy H. Lim. Edinburgh: T&T Clark, 2000.

Trovato, Paolo. *Everything You Always Wanted to Know about Lachmann's Method: A Non-standard Handbook of Genealogical Textual Criticism in the Age of Post-structuralism, Cladistics, and Copy-Text*. Storie e linguaggi 7. Padua: Libreriauniversitaria, 2014.

Troxel, Ronald L. "What Is the 'Text' in Textual Criticism?" *VT* 66 (2016): 603–26.

Tucker, Aviezer. *Our Knowledge of the Past: A Philosophy of Historiography*. Cambridge: Cambridge University Press, 2004.

Turretin, Francis. *The Doctrine of Scripture: Locus 2 of Institutio Theologiae Elencticae*. Edited and translated by John W. Beardslee. Grand Rapids: Baker, 1981.

———. *Institutio Theologiae Elencticae*. 3 vols. Geneva: Tournes, 1679–1685.

Ulrich, Eugene. "4QLev–Numᵃ." Pages 153–76 in *Qumran Cave 4.VII: Genesis to Numbers*. Edited by Eugene Ulrich and Frank Moore Cross. DJD XII. Oxford: Clarendon, 1994.

———. "The Canonical Process, Textual Criticism, and the Latter Stages in the Composition of the Bible." Pages 51–78 in *The Dead Sea Scrolls and the Origins of the Bible*. SDSS. Grand Rapids: Eerdmans, 1999.

———. *The Dead Sea Scrolls and the Developmental Composition of the Bible*. VTSup 169. Leiden: Brill, 2015.

———. *The Dead Sea Scrolls and the Origins of the Bible*. SDSS. Grand Rapids: Eerdmans, 1999.

———. "The Developmental Growth of the Pentateuch in the Second Temple Period." Pages 29–46 in *The Dead Sea Scrolls and the Developmental Composition of the Bible*. VTSup 169. Leiden: Brill, 2015.

———. "Double Literary Editions of Biblical Narratives and Reflection on Determining the Form to Be Translated." Pages 34–50 in *The Dead Sea Scrolls and the Origins of the Bible*. SDSS. Grand Rapids: Eerdmans, 1999.

———. "Joshua's First Altar in the Promised Land." Pages 47–65 in *The Dead Sea Scrolls and the Developmental Composition of the Bible*. VTSup 169. Leiden: Brill, 2015.

———. "The Masada Scrolls." Pages 251–63 in *The Dead Sea Scrolls and the Developmental Composition of the Bible*. VTSup 169. Leiden: Brill, 2015.

———. "Multiple Literary Editions: Reflections toward a Theory of the

History of the Biblical Text." Pages 99–120 in *The Dead Sea Scrolls and the Origins of the Bible*. SDSS. Grand Rapids: Eerdmans, 1999.

———. "'Nonbiblical' Scrolls Now Recognized as Scriptural." Pages 187–200 in *The Dead Sea Scrolls and the Developmental Composition of the Bible*. VTSup 169. Leiden: Brill, 2015.

———. "The Notion and Definition of Canon." Pages 265–79 in *The Dead Sea Scrolls and the Developmental Composition of the Bible*. VTSup 169. Leiden: Brill, 2015.

———. "The Palaeo-Hebrew Biblical Manuscripts from Qumran Cave 4." Pages 121–47 in *The Dead Sea Scrolls and the Origins of the Bible*. SDSS. Grand Rapids: Eerdmans, 1999.

———. "Pluriformity in the Biblical Text, Text Groups, and Questions of Canon." Pages 79–98 in *The Dead Sea Scrolls and the Origins of the Bible*. SDSS. Grand Rapids: Eerdmans, 1999.

———. *The Qumran Text of Samuel and Josephus*. HSM 19. Chico, CA: Scholars Press, 1978.

———. "The Samuel Scrolls." Pages 73–108 in *The Dead Sea Scrolls and the Developmental Composition of the Bible*. VTSup 169. Leiden: Brill, 2015.

———. "The Septuagint Scrolls." Pages 151–67 in *The Dead Sea Scrolls and the Developmental Composition of the Bible*. VTSup 169. Leiden: Brill, 2015.

———. "Two Perspectives on Two Pentateuchal Manuscripts from Masada." Pages 453–64 in *Emanuel: Studies in Hebrew Bible, Septuagint and Dead Sea Scrolls in Honor of Emanuel Tov*. Edited by Shalom M. Paul, Robert A. Kraft, Lawrence H. Schiffman, and Weston W. Fields. VTSup 94. Leiden: Brill, 2003.

Ulrich, Eugene, and Frank Moore Cross. *Qumran Cave 4.VII: Genesis to Numbers*. DJD XII. Oxford: Clarendon, 1994.

Ulrich, Eugene, et al. *Qumran Cave 4.IX: Deuteronomy to Kings*. DJD XIV. Oxford: Clarendon, 1995.

Valle, Carlos del. "Un poema hebreo de Alfonso de Zamora en alabanza de la versión latina bíblica de Pedro Ciruelo." *Sefarad* 59 (1999): 419–37.

Van Rooden, Peter T. *Theology, Biblical Scholarship, and Rabbinical Studies in the Seventeenth Century: Constantijn L'Empereur (1591–1648), Professor of Hebrew and Theology at Leiden*. Leiden: Brill, 1989.

Vanderjagt, Arjo. "*Ad fontes!* The Early Humanist Concern for the *Hebraica veritas*." Pages 154–89 in vol. 2 of *Hebrew Bible/Old Testament: The*

History of Its Interpretation. Edited by Magne Saebø. Göttingen: Vandenhoeck & Ruprecht, 2008.

VanderKam, James C., and Peter Flint. *The Meaning of the Dead Sea Scrolls: Their Significance for Understanding the Bible, Judaism, Jesus, and Christianity.* San Francisco: Harper, 2002.

Vinaver, Eugène. "Principles of Textual Emendation." Pages 351–69 in *Studies in French Language and Mediaeval Literature Presented to Professor Mildred K. Pope.* Manchester: Manchester University Press, 1939.

Waard, Jan de. *Proverbs.* BHQ 17. Stuttgart: Deutsche Bibelgesellschaft, 2008.

Walton, Brian. *A Brief Description of an Edition of the Bible, in the Original Hebr. Samar. and Greek, with the Most Ancient Translations of the Jewish and Christian Churches, viz. The Sept. Greek, Chaldee, Syriack, Aethiopick, Arabick, Persian, etc., and the Latine Versions of Them All, A New Apparatus, etc.* London: Norton, 1653.

———. *The Considerator Considered: Or, a Brief View of Certain Considerations upon the Biblia Polyglotta, the Prolegomena, and Appendix Thereof* (London: Roycroft, 1659). Repr., vol. 2 of *Memoirs of the Life and Writings of the Right Rev. Brian Walton.* Edited by H. J. Todd. London: Rivington, 1821.

Wegner, Paul A. *A Student's Guide to Textual Criticism of the Bible: Its History, Methods, and Results.* Downers Grove, IL: IVP Academic, 2006.

Weis, Richard D. "*Biblia Hebraica Quinta* and the Making of Critical Editions of the Hebrew Bible." *TC* 7 (2002). http://tinyurl.com/SBL7010i.

———. "'Lower Criticism': Studies in the Masoretic Text and the Ancient Versions of the Old Testament as Means of Textual Criticism." Pages 346–92 in vol. 3.1 of *Hebrew Bible/Old Testament: A History of Its Interpretation.* Edited by Magne Saebø. Göttingen: Vandenhoeck & Ruprecht, 2013.

Weitzman, Michael P. "The Analysis of Open Traditions." *SBib* 38 (1985): 82–120.

———. *The Syriac Version of the Old Testament: An Introduction.* Cambridge: Cambridge University Press, 1999.

Wellhausen, Julius. *Der Text der Bücher Samuelis untersucht.* Göttingen: Vandenhoeck & Ruprecht, 1871.

Wetzel, Linda. *Types and Tokens: On Abstract Objects.* Cambridge: MIT Press, 2009.

———. "Types and Tokens." In *The Stanford Encyclopedia of Philosophy*. http://tinyurl.com/SBL7010j.

Whitaker, William. *Disputatio de Sacra Scriptura; Contra Huius Temporis Papistas*. Cambridge: Thomas, 1588.

———. *Disputation on Holy Scripture, against the Papists, Especially Bellarmine and Stapleton*. Translated by William Fitzgerald. Cambridge: Cambridge University Press, 1849.

Whitman, Walt. *Leaves of Grass: A Textual Variorum of the Printed Poems*. Edited by Sculley Bradley et al. New York: New York University Press, 1980.

Wilamowitz-Moellendorff, Ulrich von. "Future Philology!" Translated by Gertrude Postl, Babette Babich, and Holger Schmid. *New Nietzsche Studies* 4 (2000): 1–33.

Williamson, H. G. M. "Do We Need a New Bible? Reflections on the Proposed Oxford Hebrew Bible." *Biblica* 90 (2009): 153–75.

Wilsmore, Susan. "The Literary Work Is Not Its Text." *Ph&Lit* 11 (1987): 307–16.

Wilson, Adrian. "What Is a Text?" *Studies in History and Philosophy of Science* 43 (2012): 341–58.

Wistenetzki, J., ed. *Das Buch der Frommen*. Berlin: Nirdamim, 1891.

Wittgenstein, Ludwig. *Philosophical Investigations*. Translated by G. E. M. Anscombe. 3rd ed. New York: Macmillan, 1968.

Wollheim, Richard. *Art and Its Objects: An Introduction to Aesthetics*. New York: Harper & Row, 1971.

———. *On Art and the Mind*. Cambridge: Harvard University Press, 1974.

Wolterstorff, Nicholas. *Works and Worlds of Art*. Oxford: Clarendon, 1980.

Woodbridge, John D. *Biblical Authority: A Critique of the Rogers/McKim Proposal*. Grand Rapids: Zondervan, 1982.

Worthington, Martin. *Principles of Akkadian Textual Criticism*. SANER 1. Berlin: de Gruyter, 2012.

Würthwein, Ernst. *The Text of the Old Testament: An Introduction to the Biblia Hebraica*. Translated by Erroll R. Rhodes. 2nd ed. Grand Rapids: Eerdmans, 1995.

Würthwein, Ernst, and Alexander A. Fischer. *The Text of the Old Testament: An Introduction to the Biblia Hebraica*. Translated by Erroll R. Rhodes. 3rd ed. Grand Rapids: Eerdmans, 2014.

Yardeni, Ada. *The Book of Hebrew Script: History, Palaeography, Script Styles, Calligraphy and Design*. London: British Library, 2002.

Yeivin, Israel. *Introduction to the Tiberian Masorah*. Edited and translated by E. J. Revell. MasS 5. Missoula, MT: Scholars Press, 1980.

Young, Ian. "The Stabilization of the Biblical Text in the Light of Qumran and Masada: A Challenge for Conventional Qumran Chronology?" *DSD* 9 (2002): 364–90.

Zahn, Molly M. "The Problem of Characterizing the 4QReworked Pentateuch Manuscripts: Bible, Rewritten Bible, or None of the Above?" *DSD* 15 (2008): 315–39.

———. *Rethinking Rewritten Scripture: Composition and Exegesis in the 4QReworked Pentateuch Manuscripts*. STDJ 95. Leiden: Brill, 2011.

———. "Talking about Rewritten Texts: Some Reflections on Terminology." Pages 93–119 in *Changes in Scripture: Rewriting and Interpreting Authoritative Traditions in the Second Temple Period*. Edited by Hanne von Weissenberg, Juha Pakkala, and Marko Marttila. BZAW 419. Berlin: de Gruyter, 2011.

Zeller, Hans. "A New Approach to the Critical Constitution of Literary Texts." *SBib* 28 (1975): 231–64.

CITATIONS INDEX

MODERN AUTHORS INDEX

CPSIA information can be obtained
at www.ICGtesting.com
Printed in the USA
BVOW03s2233021116
466784BV00001B/1/P